New Scientist   505/N43

A goar of pod health 6/N/05

D0592167

A BIBLIOGRAPHY
ON
ANIMAL RIGHTS
AND
RELATED MATTERS

Charles R. Magel

University Press
of America™

HV
4708
M35

TABLE OF CONTENTS

PREFACE

First, a comment on the title "A Bibliography on Animal Rights and Related Matters." Although humans are animals, most of the entries in this bibliography presuppose the non-technical use of "animal," excluding humans (there are instances when the context will indicate that humans are included). There is no need to attempt a precise definition of "animal;" it will suffice to state that insects and birds and oysters and catfish and dolphins and baboons are included.

By "rights" I do not intend a restriction to technical concepts such as "natural rights" or "moral rights" or "legal rights," although these are included. Rather, the term "right" is used to refer to animals counting for something morally. The title "Bibliography on Animals and Ethics" would have been appropriate. Hence, this broad concept of animal rights includes obligations and duties to animals, the moral status of animals, just treatment, and any kind of moral constraints in human treatment of animals. Although the title seems to pre-suppose that animals have rights in this broad interpretation, the bibliography includes entries which deny animals moral status.

Still more vague is the concept "related matters." A study of the literature reveals a wide diversity of opinion on what factors are related to the moral status of animals. No doubt, there are entries which I would find difficult to defend as related to animal rights. My final defense would be: "They were too interesting to exclude."

The bibliography is restricted (with three exceptions) to literature in the English language, and also confined (again with several exceptions) to the thought and practices of the Western world.

It is my conviction that there can
be no complete bibliography on animal rights.
Certainly this bibliography has no pretense
to completeness: it is the result of a two-
year search. And with the literature mush-
rooming in 1980, it is not only impossible
to keep up but it is horribly frustrating to
cut off the search, for publication.

Possibilities for error in an extensive
bibliography seem infinite. I apologize in
advance for those of commission and omission.
It is my plan to continue updating the bibliographic pool for possible revisions of the
bibliography, should reader-interest warrant.
I would welcome readers' comments: weaknesses,
errors, suggestions for improvement, what was
left out that should be in, what is in that
should have been omitted, organization, etc.

I find it impossible to express adequately
my gratitude to all those who were so helpful.
But try I must.

My thanks to the citizens of Minnesota for
the privilege of teaching at Moorhead State
University in a context permitting and encourag-
ing a study of animal rights. In addition to
granting a sabbatical, the University (again,
my gratitude to Minnesota citizens) has provided
a first-rate library, superbly administered,
with excellent library materials, considering
the nature and size of the institution. Especially valuable is the Minnesota Inter-library
Telecommunications Exchange (MINITEX), which
facilitates cooperative sharing of library
resources not only in Minnesota (especially
the University of Minnesota) but also in
Wisconsin, North Dakota, and South Dakota, as
well as referral service to the Center for
Research Libraries, the Midwest Health Science
Library Network, the Library of Congress,
National Library of Medicine, National Agricultural Library and the British Library Lending

Division. Ten years ago the principal jus-
tification for granting sabbaticals at Moorhead
State University was to enable faculty members
to travel to a quality library; today, with
important exceptions of course, faculty who leave
the State of Minnesota miss many of the library
services provided "at home."

As much as I dislike drawing distinctions
between persons who have been so helpful, I
should especially like to express my gratitude
to:

Helen Jones, President of Society for
Animal Rights, Inc. (See 3096). It was
Helen who first suggested the publication of a bibliography on animal rights.
In addition to providing extensive professional and clerical services from the
very beginning through the preparation of
the final manuscript, she negotiated the
publishing contract with University Press
of America. I would also like to thank
the other officers and directors of the
Society for Animal Rights, Inc.

Tom Regan, whose "The Moral Basis of
Vegetarianism" (1771) has had a profound
influence on my life and thought. It
was a privilege to work with Tom on "A
Select Bibliography on Animal Rights and
Human Obligations," Inquiry, Summer 1979
(2234). Tom has been especially support-
ive, keeping me well informed on not only
his own work, but on publications and
conferences, national and international.

Peter Singer, whose Animal Liberation
(1272) has had a profound influence on
my life and thought. Peter's stimulat-
ing visit to Moorhead State University in
March, 1979, has provided a constant source
of motivation. And his keeping me well
informed of publications by himself and

xiii

others, as well as his constructive suggestions, have been most helpful.

Joyce Lambert, informational correspondent _extraordinaire_, who kept me well informed not only on activities in Canada, but also in the United States, and internationally. Author of How To Be Kind (2751) and the illustrated booklets "Rights for Animals?" and "Science, Health and Fair Play" (2745 and 2739), Joyce is indeed a friend of animals and of all friends of animals.

Clive Hollands, author of Compassion is the Bugler--The Struggle for Animal Rights (2183) and Director of Scottish Society for the Prevention of Vivisection (2914). Clive has been a most cooperative and efficient source of information on the animal welfare movement in the United Kingdom. And two days with Clive in London provided insights which months of study could not have enabled.

Richard Ryder, author of Victims of Science-- The Use of Animals in Research (1613), unfortunately now out of print. A day in Richard's personal library--with Richard the guide--is a rare, strenuous, educational treat especially when punctuated by a Ploughman's Lunch in an authentic, ancient pub in Oxfordshire.

Mary Struck, former student, and friend, whose superb bibliographical assistance kept the project going, whose suggestions resulted in significant improvements, and whose persistence and diligence finally persuaded me that we must stop adding entries and submit the manuscript for publication.

Susan Dapsis, who conscientiously and tirelessly and efficiently prepared the final manuscript for publication.

To colleagues and staff members in the
Moorhead State University Library, my apprecia-
tion for most generous assistance: Elsie Berge,
Shirley Brattland, Kay Ann Erickson, Rodney
Erickson, Bernard Gill, Wilbert Harri, Marguerite
Hubbard, Karen Kivi, Theresa Kroke, Grace
Lafayette, Elsie Lee, Darrel Meinke, Marjorie
Moen, Sandra Paulsen, Lawrence Reed, Carol
Saastad, and Evelyn Swenson.

Also, an expression of appreciation to
the staffs of the libraries at the University
of Minnesota, University of Wisconsin, Yale
University, Princeton University, University
of Texas, North Dakota State University (especially Karen Petersen Vogel) and Concordia
College.

At the risk of missing someone, and with
regret that I cannot provide detailed information
on the manner in which each of the following
provided kind assistance, I would like to list
the following:

David Anderson, Ralph Anslow, Thomas Bahr,
George Boas, Colin Booty, Alan Bowd, Wayne
Buck, Marianna Burt, Edward Carpenter, Mark
Chekola, John Close, Patricia Curtis, Ruth
Dahlke, Dianna Daniels, Roland Dille, Jon
Evans, Michael W. Fox, R.G. Frey, Sidney
Gendin, John Gibbs, Dudley Giehl, Lee
Grugel, Brian Gunn, W. Ferron Halverson,
Judith Hampson, Emily Hahn, Mark Hansel,
Patricia Angvik Herje, Raymond Herje, Earl
Herring, Alice Herrington, Paul Holmer,
Dennis Hamilton, J. Robert Hanson, Mark
Holzer, Dale Jamieson, Arnold Johanson,
Simon Jones, William Jones, Ben Judd, James
Kaplan, Rebecca Knittle, Gill Langley,
Hugh Lehman, Andrew Linzey, Lord Houghton
of Sowerby, Ceil Lundstrom, Jolene Marion,
Jim Mason, Steele Mattingly, Harlan Miller,
Joseph Miller, Victoria Moran, Richard Morgan,

Muriel the Lady Dowding, David Myers,
F. Barbara Orlans, Bill Parker, Nancy
Parlin, David Paterson, Thomas Rickart,
Bernard Rollin, Christine Rosner, Kathy
Roth, Nicholas Rowan, Swaran Sandhu,
Richard Sayer, Thomas Sebeok, Eleanor
Seiling, Ken Shapiro, Brigid Shea, John
Sherman, Colin Smith, Henry Spira, Kathy
Squadrito, Roy Stahl, Jean Stewart, David
Strauss, James Swenson, George Trapp,
Marcello Truzzi, Mark Vinz, Paul Vodden,
Jane Wixon.

Nor should I forget the inspiration from
the birds and rabbits and squirrels in the back
yard, especially Little Red, who shared the
organic garden (and all the peas). Nor should
I forget Lady's patience in sacrificing joyful
walks along the Red River; had the topic been
less momentous for Dachshunds she would have
justifiably protested.

Nor should I forget the animals in laboratories, in factory farms, in slaughter houses,
in traps, in cages, in breeding colonies, in
pounds, in trucks, in airplanes, in films, in
television, in circuses, in rodeos, in bull
fights, in dog fights, in cock fights, in euthanasia chambers, in burned out or gassed out
lairs, in pet shops, in races, on hooks or string-
ers, and in shrinking habitats. Nor the aban-
doned, the clubbed, the netted, the harpooned
and....

Will there by any animals in 2084?

Nor should I forget the inspiration from
Albert Schweitzer.

Charles R. Magel
Moorhead State University
Moorhead, Minnesota 5656(

BRIEF COMMENTS ON SECTIONS I THROUGH X

I. Literature on Animals, Categorized Temp-
    orally

        Entries are listed by century, from the
    time of the Old Testament to August 31, 1980.
    In the Nineteenth Century there is a sig-
    nificant increase in works on animals, espe-
    cially in the United Kingdom; entries are
    classified by subject (the subject heading
    and century are indicated at the top of each
    page). The organization for the Twentieth
    Century is more complex. Three of the cate-
    ories (Animal and Human Nature, Animals and
    Ethics, and Animal Experimentation) are sub-
    divided into two time spans: 1901-50 and
    1951-80. Entries under "Animal and Human
    Nature" are mainly factual, providing answers
    to the questions "What are animals?" and
    "What are humans?" The "Animals and Ethics"
    entries are mainly concerned with the moral
    status of animals and with how humans ought
    to treat animals. The number of 1901-50
    "Animals and Ethics" entries is amazingly
    small; the number in 1951-80 (especially
    1970-80) is amazingly large. I have made no
    attempt to cull the inferior from the superior
    (what is garbage for some organisms is some-
    times food for others).

II. Animals and Law

        During the bibliographic search it be-
    came increasingly evident that the subject
    of animals and law is sufficiently rich to
    justify a separate bibliography. The entries
    listed, mainly on British and American Law,
    constitute a slight beginning. See 2269 for
    information on the new Animal Rights Law
    Reporter, edited by Henry M. Holzer. Also

see 2987 and 2988 for addresses of two newly-established "Attorneys for Animals Rights" organizations.

III. Animals and Literature and Art and Music

Having neither sufficient background nor time to explore the role of animals in literature and art and music, I set up this section as an introduction to a fascinating project for the future. Included are several of the older, more famous, children's stories (for a detailed study of animals as portrayed in children's books see Margaret Blount's Animal Land (2367)).

IV. Conferences and Symposia and Meetings

A growing interest in ethics and animals is evidenced by the number of conferences held, especially in the United States and the United Kingdom. Although proceedings of some will eventually be published, the programs of several organized during the past two years may be of interest.

V. University and College Courses

The entries are suggestive of the growing number of courses, partly or completely on animals and ethics, offered at the university level. Ethics courses in philosophy departments occasionally include sections on animals and ethics. The Scientists' Center for Animal Welfare (see 3090) has been collecting and publishing data on such courses.

VI. Government Documents

Although often boring, government documents are valuable sources of information on the role of governments in activities involving animals. Hearings and inquiries and commissions conducted by governmental bodies

reveal the complexity and controversial
nature of legislative proposals affecting
animals. It is often illuminating to learn
which organizations and persons testify at
hearings having to do with animals. For
example, I was a bit surprised (but should
not have been, had I been more knowledgeable
about the manufacture and marketing of soap)
that the Soap and Detergent Industry Association testified before the Select Committee
on the Laboratory Animals Protection Bill,
House of Lords, 1980 (see 2626).

VII.   Films

        Listed are only a few of the many
films available having to do with animals.
See Films for Humane Education (2688), ed.
by Ronald Scott and Jean Stewart, for
detailed information on over 100 films.

VIII. Organizations Interested in Animals

        A comprehensive knowledge of orga-
nizations interested in animals would reveal
the extent to which modern Western culture--
especially the economy--is animal-based. I
have listed all of the organizations which
I know about--both those interested in
using animals for various purposes and those
critical of various uses. Originally, I had
intended two lists of organizations: those
in some sense "for animals" and those in some
sense "against animals". It became obvious,
however, that the situation is much too complex
to warrant so simple a classification. Only in
those cases where I have accurate information
from the organizations themselves do I indicate the nature of the organization. Also,
when known, relevant literature published
and/or available is indicated (the reader
should not assume that the literature lists
are complete, or that all of the items
listed are available; and those available
often must be purchased), in order to give

an indication of the interests and concerns of the respective organizations. The reader is also advised that addresses change rapidly and that organizations have a habit of popping in and out of existence (currently, the trend seems to be toward popping into existence).

IX. <u>Magazines and Journals</u>

Trade, technical, professional and even popular journals and magazines are a helpful source of information on projects and activities affecting animals. In addition to articles, editorials and advertisements and illustrations are illuminating.

X. <u>Easy-on-Animals Cookbooks</u>

Like cooks, cookbooks vary tremendously in quality and type. I have listed all those with which I am familiar. Regardless of the various motives for vegetarianism and veganism, there are implications for animals. (I would like to thank the Vegetarian Centre and Bookshop (2929), London, for the privilege of spending an afternoon going through its book inventory.)

1. Aristotle, The Basic Works of Aristotle,
ed. by Richard McKeon, Random House,
New York, 1941. Aristotle's analysis
of three types of soul (the nutritive,
the sensitive, and the rational), the
higher types of soul presupposing the
lower, and the lower types for the purpose of the higher, has had an important influence on Western man's views
on animals--and women. St. Thomas
Aquinas and Catholicism were especially influenced.

2. Aristotle, "Animals and Slavery,"
Politics, Book I, Chaps. 5 and 8
Reproduced in Animal Rights and Human
Obligations, ed. by Tom Regan and
Peter Singer (1253).

3. Aristotle, "How Humans Differ from
Other Creatures," On the Soul, Book
II, Chap. 3, 414 a (28) - 415a (10)
and
The Parts of Animals, Book I, Chap. I,
641a (35) - 641b (10).
Reproduced in Animal Rights and Human
Obligations, ed. by Tom Regan and
Peter Singer (1253).

4. Aristotle, De Motu Animalium, text with
translation, commentary, and inter-
pretive essays by Martha C. Nussbaum,
Princeton University Press, Princeton,
N.J., 1978.

5. Aristotle, Generation of Animals, trans.
by A.L. Peck, Loeb Classical Library,
Heinemann, London, 1965.

6. Aristotle, Historia Animalium, with an English translation by A.L. Peck, Harvard University Press, Cambridge, 1965.

7. Lucretius, Of the Nature of Things, E.P. Dutton, New York, 1943.
   Book V:
   769-921: Origins of Vegetable and Animal Life
   922-1008: Origins and Savage Period of Mankind
   1009-1455: Beginnings of Civilization

8. The Old Testament, Genesis 1:20-31, and 9:1-3.

9. Plato, The Collected Dialogues of Plato, ed. by Edith Hamilton and Huntington Cairns, Bollingen Foundation, New York, 1961.
   (Plato's analysis of the tri-part soul (appetitive, spirited, and rational), animals having mainly the appetitive and none of the rational played a significant role in Western man's sharp, qualitative distinction between animals and man (Republic IV, 435a-442e). It is the natural role of the superior rational to rule the inferior appetitive; humans are rational and animals are appetitive; hence inferior animals are to be ruled by superior humans (Statesman, 271e). When the appetitive part of the human soul becomes completely out of control, outside the rule by reason, the human being becomes beastly: shameless, sexually wanton, lawless, murderous, warlike; this characterization of animal existence as beastly in this

2

negative sense has had profound influence on Western human views of animals (Republic IX, 571a-577e).)

10. Pythagoras and Pythagoreanism
    Since Pythagoras (sixth and fifth centuries B.C.) left no writings, and since Pythagoreanism was partially a secret religious society, there is no certainty of Pythagoras' own views. The basic view was that since animals also have souls, and since there is transmigration of souls, flesh should not be eaten because to do so is a form of cannibalism. See W.K.C. Guthrie's "Outline of the Pythagorean Philosophy" in his History of Greek Philosophy, Vol. 1, pp. 181-195, University Press, Cambridge, 1962. Also see DeVogel, C.J., Pythagoras and Early Pythagoreanism, P. 150, 152, 181, 186, 271, VanGorcum Ltd., Assen, Netherlands, 1966.

A.D. Centuries
1: Century

11. Plinius Secundus, Gaius, Natural
    History, ed. by H. Rackham, Loeb
    Classical Library, Heinemann,
    London, 1938.

12. Plutarch, "The Cleverness of Animals,"
    "Beasts Are Rational" (A dialogue
    between Odysseus, Circe, and Gryllus),
    "On the Eating of Flesh" in Plutarch's
    Moralia, trans. by Harold Cherniss and
    William Helmbold, Harvard University
    Press, Cambridge, Mass., 1957. Vol. 12,
    Secs. 959-999.

3: Century

13. Aelian on the Characteristics of Animals,
    trans. by A.F. Scholfield, Harvard
    University Press, Cambridge, Mass., 1958.

14. Boyd, M.J., "Porphyry, De Abstinentia
    I 7-12," Classical Quarterly, Vol. 30,
    July, 1936, pp. 188-91.

15. Porphyry, On Abstinence from Animal Food,
    trans. by T. Taylor, ed. by Esme
    Wynne-Tyson, Centaur Press, 1965.

4: Century

16. Ambrose, Saint, Hexameron: The Six Days
    of Creation, trans. by John J. Savage,
    in The Fathers of the Church, Vol. 42,
    Fathers of the Church, Inc., New York,
    1961.

5: Century

17. Bodenheimer, Friedrich S., On Animals,
    Fragments of a Byzantine Parapharase
    of an Animal Book of the 5th Century

<u>5: Century</u>

> A.D., Academie Internationale
> d'Histoire des Sciences, Paris, 1949.

<u>10: Century</u>

18. Goodman, Lenn E., trans., <u>The Case of</u>
    <u>the Animals Versus Man Before the</u>
    <u>King of the Jinn</u>, Twayne, Boston, 1978.
    (A Tenth-Century Arabic ecological
    fable, accompanied by a discussion by
    Goodman, comparing the fable with the
    views of Western philosophers and
    scientists: Kant, Darwin, Maimonides,
    Spinoza, Plutarch, Descartes, Plato,
    Mary Midgley, Peter Singer, etc.)

<u>13: Century</u>

19. Sherley-Price, Leo, trans., <u>St. Francis</u>
    <u>of Assisi: His Life and Writings As</u>
    <u>Recorded by His Contemporaries</u>, Harper,
    New York, 1959.

20. Thomas Aquinas, Saint, "Differences
    Between Rational and Other Creatures,"
    in his <u>Summa Contra Gentiles,</u> Third
    Book, Part II, Chap. CXII.
    Reproduced in <u>Animal Rights and Human</u>
    <u>Obligations,</u> ed. by Tom Regan and
    Peter Singer (1253).

21. Thomas Aquinas, Saint, "On Killing Living
    Things and the Duty to Love Irrational
    Creatures," from <u>Summa Theologica,</u>
    Part II, Question 64, Art. 1 and
    Question 25, Art. 3
    Reproduced in <u>Animal Rights and Human</u>
    <u>Obligations,</u> ed. by Tom Regan and
    Peter Singer (1253).

22. Montaigne, Michel de, "Man is no Better than the Animals," in Apology for Raymond Sebond, in The Complete Works of Montaigne, trans. by Donald M. Frame, Stanford University Press. Stanford, Cal., 1958 (pp. 330-358). Also, see pp. 306-318. "Of Cruelty."

23. Bayle, Pierre, "Rorarius," "Pereira,"
    "Sennertus" in Bayle's Historical
    and Critical Dictionary; selections,
    ed. by Richard H. Popkin, Bobbs-
    Merrill, Indianapolis, 1965. (These
    articles contain comments on animals.)

24. Descartes, Rene, The Philosophical
    Works of Descartes, rendered into
    English by Elizabeth S. Haldane and
    G.R.T. Ross, Vols. 1 & 2, Dover,
    New York, 1955. (Although it is
    controversial whether Descartes had
    one consistent view of animals, the
    Cartesian view of animals as finite
    extended substances, as non-aware
    automatons, has had a profound in-
    fluence on the modern Western attitude
    toward animals and animal experimen-
    tation.)
    See pp. 115-188, Vol. 1 (from Discourse
    on Method), which are reproduced in
    Animal Rights and Human Obligations,
    ed. by Regan and Singer, under the
    heading "Animals are Machines" (1253.)
    Also see Descartes: Philosophical
    Letters, ed. by Anthony Kenny,
    Clarendon Press, Oxford, 1970:
    > To the Marquess of Newcastle, Nov-
    > ember 26, 1646.
    > To Henry More, February 5, 1649
    > (The above mentioned letters
    > are reproduced in Animal Rights
    > and Human Obligations, ed. by
    > Regan and Singer.) (1253)
    > To Plempius for Fromondus, Oc-
    > tober 3, 1637.

25. Field, John, The Absurdity and False-
    ness of Thomas Trion's Doctrine
    Manifested: In Forbidding to Eat

Flesh Contrary to the Command of God, the Example of Angels, Christ Jesus, and the Holy Apostles, Tho. Howkins, London, 1685. (There is a copy of this at the Earlham College Library, Richmond, Indiana.)

26. Hobbes, Thomas, Body, Man and Citizen, ed. by Richard S. Peters, Collier, New York, 1962.
    Part 3: "Sense, Animal Motion, and Human Behavior"

27. Locke, John. There are no extended discussions of animals by Locke; however, there are important passages:
    An Essay Concerning Human Understanding, edited by Peter H. Nidditch, Clarendon Press, Oxford, 1975:

Book 2,	Chapter 1,	Paragraph	19
" 2,	" 10,	"	10
" 2,	" 11,	"	7
" 2,	" 11,	"	10
" 2,	" 11,	"	11
" 4,	" 3,	"	6
" 4,	" 17,	"	1

    The above passages deal with the questions whether animals have ideas, have minds, can think, can reason, etc.
    Two treatises of Government, edited by Peter Laslett, Cambridge University Press, New York, 1963:

Treatise 1,	Chapter 4,	Paragraphs	21-43
" 2,	" 2,	Paragraphs	4
" 2,	" 5,	Paragraphs	25-51

The above passages discuss human
dominion over and property in
animals.
*The Educational Writings of John
Locke*, edited by James Axfell,
Cambridge University Press,
Cambridge, 1968.
Section 116
Locke urges that children be
taught not to be cruel to animals because cruelty to animals
will harden children's minds
towards humans.

28.   Spinoza, Benedict de, *Ethics*, E.P.
Dutton, New York, 1948. Part IV,
Proposition 37, Note I (Spinoza
argues that since the emotions of
humans are different in nature from
the emotions of animals, humans can
use animals as they will.)
Also see Part III, Proposition 57,
Note.

29.   Topsell, Edward, *The Historie of Foure-
footed Beasts*, Describing the True
and Lively Figure of Every Beast, with
a Discourse of Their Several Names,
Conditions, Kindes, Vertues (both
natural and medicinall), Countries
of Their Breed, Their Love and Hate
to Mankind, and the Wonderful Works
of God in Their Creation, Preservation, and Destruction. Necessary
for all Divines and Students, because
the story of every Beast is amplified
with Narrations out of Scriptures,
Fathers, Philosophers, Physitians, and
Poets; wherein are declared divers
Hyerogliphicks, Emblems, Epigrams,
and other good Histories, Collected

out of all the volumes of Conradus
Gesner, and all other Writers to this
present day, Printed by William
Iaggard, London, 1607.

30. Topsell, Edward, The Historie of
Serpents, or the Second Booke of
Living Creatures, London, 1608.

31. Bentham, Jeremy, The Works of Jeremy
    Bentham, ed. by John Bowring, Russell
    and Russell, New York, 1962, 11
    Volumes.
    See Principles of the Civil Code,
    Part II, Chap. 1, 4, for discussion
    of the origin of animals as property
    of humans (Vol. I, p. 328.)
    See Principles of Penal Law, Part III,
    Chap. 16, for discussion of cruel-
    ty to animals and humane treatment
    of animals (Vol. I, p. 562.)
    See Memoirs of Bentham, Chap. 1, for
    discussion of Bentham's humanity
    to animals (Vol. X, p. 17.)
    See Bentham's Correspondence, Chap. 21,
    for Bentham's letter on humanity to
    animals (Vol. X, p. 549.)
    See Principles of Morals and Legis-
    lation, Chap. 19, 4, footnote, for
    Bentham's inclusion of animals with-
    in the utility principle of morals.
    It is in this footnote that appears
    the sentence "...the question is not,
    Can they reason? nor, Can they talk?
    but Can they suffer?" (Vol. I,
    pp. 142-143.)
    See Memoirs of Bentham, Chap. 26,
    on Bentham's fondness of animals
    (cats, mice, asses) (Vol. XI,
    pp. 80-81.)

32. Clemency for Brutes, the substance of
    two sermons preached on a Shrove Sun-
    day with a particular view to dis-
    suade from that species of cruelty
    practiced in England--the throwing at
    cocks, printed for R. and J. Dodsley,
    London, 1761. (In Yale University
    Library.)

33. Cocchi, Antonio, The Pythagorean Diet
    of Vegetables Only, R. Dodsley,
    London, 1745. (There is a copy of
    this at the Vanderbilt Medical Center,
    Nashville, Tenn.)

34. Daggett, Herman, The Rights of Animals,
    An oration delivered at the commence-
    ment of Providence College, September
    7, 1791, American Society for the
    Prevention of Cruelty to Animals,
    New York, 1926. (In Yale University
    Library.)

35. Hildrop, John, Free Thoughts upon the
    Brute Creation, Printed for R. Minors,
    London, 1742. (There is a copy of
    this in the University of Arizona
    Library.)

36. Hume, David, Essays: Moral, Political and
    Literary, ed. by T.H. Green and T.H.
    Grose, 2 vols., Scientia Verlag, Aalen,
    1964 (1882)
    See: "Dignity or Meanness of Human
    Nature," Vol. I, Part I, Essay XI,
    p. 152. "Of the Reason of Animals,"
    in An Enquiry Concerning Human Under-
    standing, Sec. IX, in Vol. II.

37. Hume, David, A Treatise of Human Nature,
    ed. by L.A. Selby-Bigge, Clarendon
    Press, Oxford, 1960.
    See:
    "Of the Reason of Animals," Book I,
    Part III, Sec. XVI
    "Of the Pride and Humility of Animals,"
    Book II, Part I, Sec. XII
    "Of the Love and Hatred of Animals,"
    Book II, Part II Sec. XII
    "Of Natural Abilities," Book III,
    Part III, Sec. IV, p. 610

14

"Of Personal Identity," Book I, Part
IV, Sec. VI, pp. 253f.
"Of Our Esteem for the Rich and Power-
ful," Book II, Part II, Sec. V, p. 363.
"Of the Direct Passions," Book II,
Part III, Sec. IX, p. 448.
"Moral Distinctions Not Derived From
Reason," Book III, Part I, Sec. I,
p. 468.

38. Jenyns, Soame, "Cruelty to Inferior
Animals," in this author's Disquisi-
tions on Several Subjects, printed
for J. Dodsley, London, 1789. Also
micro-opaque, Lost Cause Press,
Louisville, Ky., 1964, 3 cards.

39. Johnson, Samuel, The Idler, No. 17,
Saturday, August 5, 1758 (attack on
vivisection), in The Yale Edition of
the Works of Samuel Johnson, Vol. II,
ed. by W.J. Bate and John M. Bullitt
and L.F. Powell, Yale University Press,
New Haven, 1963. Also see Johnson's
The Plays of William Shakespeare, Vol.
7, 1765, p. 279.

40. Kant, Immanuel, "Duties to Animals and
Spirits," in his Lectures on Ethics,
trans. Louis Infield, Harper & Row,
New York, 1963. Partially reproduced
in Animal Rights and Human Obligations,
ed. by Tom Regan and Peter Singer
(1253).

41. LaMettrie, Julien Offray de, Man a
Machine, trans. by G.C. Bussey,
Open Court, La Salle, Ill., 1912.

42. Lawrence, John, "The Rights of Beasts,"
in Lawrence's A Philosophical and
Practical Treatise on Horses, and
on the Moral Duties of Man towards

the Brute Creation, printed for
T.N. Longman, London, 1796-98,
Vol. 1, Chap. 3. Also see "The
Philosophy of Sports," in Vol. 2,
Chap. 1.

43. Leibniz, Gottfried Wilhelm, Monadology and Other Philosophical Essays,
trans. by Paul Schrecker and Anne
Schrecker, Bobbs-Merrill, Indianapolis,
1965. (Leibniz held that animals and
humans are collections of monads
(active, perceiving entities). An
animal has a dominant "soul" monad
which has distinct perceptions
accompanied by memory. A human has
a dominant "spirit" monad, which, in
addition to having distinct perceptions accompanied by memory, has
knowledge of necessary and eternal
truths. There is no absolute, qualitative difference between animals
and humans; the difference is one
of degree of perception. The following paragraphs in the Monadology are
suggestive:
19 through 28
66 through 84.)

44. Mandeville, Bernard, The Fable of the
Bees, Clarendon Press, Oxford, 1957,
2 volumes. See Volume 1, pp. 172-
181, on eating flesh for food, cruelty, and feeling in animals.

45. Nicholson, George, On the Conduct of
Man to Inferior Animals, printed and
sold at the office of G. Nicholson,
Manchester, England, 1797. (There is
a copy of this at the University of
Connecticut Library.)

46. Pope, Alexander, "Of Cruelty to Animals,"

in Vallance, Rosalind, ed., Hundred
English Essays, pp. 159-65, (Also in
Carver, George, ed., Periodical
Essays of the Eighteenth Century,
Books for Libraries Press, Essay Index
Reprint Series, Freeport, N.Y., 1970.)

47. Primatt, Humphrey, A Dissertation on the
Duty of Mercy, and Sin of Cruelty to
Brute Animals, T. Constable, London,
1776.

48. Swift, Jonathan, "A Modest Proposal for
Preventing the Children of Poor People
from Being A Burthen to Their Parents
or Country and for Making Them Beneficial to the Public," 1792.
Reproduced in Animal Rights and Human
Obligations, ed. by Tom Regan and Peter
Singer (1253). (Satiric argument that
roast pork is no more defensible than
roast children.)

49. Taylor, Thomas, A Vindication of the
Rights of Brutes (1792), Scholars
Facsimiles and Reprints, Gainesville,
FL., 1966.
(A satirical work by the Cambridge
Platonist, arguing against rights of
women, stressing that equality for
women would also lead to equality for
animals, which of course would be
absurd.)

50. Voltaire, Francois M.A. de, "Beasts,"
in Voltaire's Philosophical Dictionary,
trans. by Peter Gay, Basic Book,
New York, 1962.
Reproduced in Animal Rights and Human
Obligations, ed. by Tom Regan and Peter
Singer (1253).

51. "Affections of Animals," Chamber's
     Edinburgh Journal, Vol. 1, N.S.,
     April 27, 1844, pp. 267-71.

52. "Alarming Increase of Depravity among
     Animals," Blackwood's Edinburgh
     Magazine, Vol. 2, October, 1817, pp.
     82-6.

53. "Animal Depravity," Journal of Science,
     Vol. 6, N.S., October, 1875, pp.
     415-31. Also in Popular Science
     Monthly Supplement, Vol. 7-12, 1878,
     pp. 184-91.

54. "The Animal Dislike of Solitude," The
     Spectator, Vol. 67, September 5, 1891,
     pp. 317-18.

55. "Animal Humanity," Chamber's Edinburgh
     Journal, Vol. 5, N.S., March 21, 1846.
     pp. 177-80.

56. "Animal Intelligence," All the Year
     Round, Vol. 20, July 11, 1868, pp.
     113-5.

57. "Animal Intelligence," Chamber's
     Edinburgh Journal, Vol. 40, December
     12, 1863, pp. 380-2.

58. "Animal Intelligence," The Spectator,
     ⁄Vol. 55, September 9, 1882, pp.
     1170-1172.

59. "Animal Intelligence," Westminster
     Review, Vol. 13, April, 1880, pp.
     216-31.

60. "Animal Language," Chamber's Edinburgh

Journal, Vol. 5, N.S., May 2, 1846, pp. 276-8.

61. "Animal Language," Southern Literary Messenger, Vol. 35, November and December, 1863, pp. 737-41.

62. "Animal Language," The Spectator, Vol. 77, October 24, 1896, pp. 550-1.

63. "Animal Mind," The Spectator, Vol. 75, October 19, 1895, pp. 514-15.

64. "Animal Psychology," British Quarterly Review, Vol. 7, 1848, pp. 347-78.

65. "The Animal Sense of Humor," The Spectator, Vol. 69, October 1, 1892, pp. 444-5.

66. "Animals at Play," The Spectator, Vol. 66, March 14, 1891, pp. 377-8.

67. "Animals' Toilettes," The Spectator, Vol. 65, September 27, 1890, p. 404.

68. "Are Animals Happy?" The Spectator, Vol. 59, August 14, 1886, pp. 1081-82.

69. Arnold, Edwin, "Are Animals Moral?" Idler, Vol. 9, 1896, pp. 516-24.

70. Ballou, William H., "Are the Lower Animals Approaching Man?" North American Review, Vol. 145, November, 1887, pp. 516-23.

71. "Benevolence in Animals," The Spectator, Vol. 81, October 15, 1898, pp. 520-1.

72. Bowen, Francis, "The Human and the Brute Mind," Princeton Review, New Series,

Series 4, Vol. 5, 1878-81, pp. 321-43.

73. Butler, Samuel, "Thought and Language," in Butler, Samuel, The Humor of Homer and Other Essays, Books for Libraries Press, Essay Index Reprint Series, Freeport, N.Y. 1967. (About thought and language in animals and humans.)

74. "Can Animals Reason?" The Spectator, Vol. 68, May 14, 1892, pp. 683-4.

75. Carlill, Briggs, "Are Animals Happy?" Nineteenth Century, Vol. 20, August, 1886, pp. 255-269.

76. Carlill, Briggs, "Are Animals Mentally Happy?" Nineteenth Century, Vol. 21, June, 1887, pp. 804-24.

77. Cary, George L., "The Mental Faculties of Brutes," North American Review, Vol. 108, January, 1869, pp. 37-57.

78. "Church-going Animals," All the Year Round, Vol. 28, January 7, 1882, pp. 424-7.

79. Clarke, James F., "Have Animals Souls?" Atlantic Monthly, Vol. 34, October, 1874, pp. 412-22.

80. Collier, W., "The Comparative Insensibility of Animals to Pain," Nineteenth Century, Vol. 26, October, 1889, pp. 622-7.

81. Cornish, C.J., Animals at Work and Play, Seeley, London, 1896.

82. "Criminal Animals," The Spectator, Vol.69,

September 10, 1892.

83. Darwin, Charles, "Comparison of the
     Mental Powers of Man and the Lower
     Animals," From The Descent of Man,
     Chaps. III and IV, Appleton, New
     York, 1909.
     Reproduced in part in Animal Rights
     and Human Obligations, ed. by Tom
     Regan and Peter Singer (1253).

84. Darwin, Charles, The Expression of
     the Emotions in Man and Animals,
     Philosophical Library, New York,
     1955.

85. Darwin, Charles, On The Origin of
     Species by Means of Natural Selection,
     or the Preservation of Favoured Races
     in the Struggle for Life, A.L. Burt,
     New York, 1881.

86. Delboeuf, M.J., "What May Animals Be
     Taught?" Popular Science Monthly,
     Vol. 29, June 1886, pp. 168-179.

87. "The Depreciation of Animal Character,"
     The Spectator, Vol. 61, September 8,
     1888, pp. 1218-19.

88. "Do Animals Talk?" The Spectator, Vol.
     80, March 5, 1898, pp. 337-8.

89. "Do the Lower Animals Reason?" National
     Quarterly Review, Vol. 9, September
     1864, pp. 286-301.

90. Duthiers, M.D., "New Observations on
     the Language of Animals," Popular
     Science Monthly, Vol. 40, February,
     1892, pp. 528-39.

91. "The Emotion of Grief in Animals," The

Spectator, Vol. 74, June 15, 1895, pp. 817-18.

92. Evans, E.P., "The Aesthetic Sense and Religious Sentiment in Animals," Popular Science Monthly, Vol. 42, February, 1893, pp. 472-481.

93. Evans, E.P., "Ethical Relations Between Man and Beast," Popular Science Monthly, Vol. 45, September, 1894, pp. 634-646.

94. Evans, Edward P., Evolutional Ethics and Animal Psychology, Appleton, New York, 1898.

95. Evans, E.P., "Mind in Man and Brute," Unitarian Review, Vol. 36, November, 1891, pp. 342-65.

96. Evans, E.P., "The Nearness of Animals to Men," The Atlantic Monthly, Vol. 69, February, 1892, pp. 171-184.

97. Evans, E.P., "Progress and Perfectibility in the Lower Animals," Popular Science Monthly, Vol. 40, December, 1891, pp. 170-179.

98. Fernald, F.A., "How Much Animals Know," Popular Science Monthly, Vol. 23, May, 1883, pp. 39-46.

99. Ferrero, William, "Crime among Animals," Forum, Vol. 20, December, 1895, pp. 92-8.

100. Goulding, F.R., "Brute Language," Appleton's Journal, Vol. 10, September 13, 1873, pp. 332-35.

101. Harington, Arthur, "Animal Automatism

and Consciousness, Monist, Vol. 7,
July, 1897, pp. 611-16.

102. "Have Animals Souls?" Putnam's Monthly,
Vol. 7, April, 1856, pp. 361-71.

103. "Have the Lower Animals Souls, or
Reason?" National Quarterly Review,
Vol. 15, September, 1867, pp. 242-62.

104. Hazard, Rowland G., "Animals Not
Automata," Popular Science Monthly,
Vol. 6, February, 1875, pp. 405-20.

105. Hibberd, Shirley, "The Moral Faculties
of Brutes," Intellectual Observer,
Vol. 4, 1863, pp. 211-6.

106. Hieover, Harry, Bipeds and Quadrupeds,
T.C. Newby, London, 1853.

107. Houssay, Frederic, The Industries of
Animals, Walter Scott, London, 1893.

108. Howland, Edward, "The Language of
Animals," Penn Monthly Magazine,
Vol. 10, July, 1879, pp. 509-29.

109. Huxley, T.H., "Are Animals Automatons?"
Popular Science Monthly, Vol. 5
October, 1874, pp. 724-34.

110. Huxley, T.H., "On the Hypothesis that
Animals Are Automata, and Its
History," Fortnightly Review, Vol.
22, November 1, 1874, p. 555.

110. Huxley, Thomas H., "On the Relations
a   of Man to the Lower Animals," in
Adam, or Ape, ed. by L.S.B. Leakey,
and Jack and Stephanie Prost,
Schenkman, Cambridge, Mass. 1971.

111. "Illustrations of Instinct," Christian Remembrancer, Vol. 14, 1847, pp. 436-48.

112. "The Intellect of Animals," London Society, Vol. 15, 1869, pp. 43-7.

113. "The Intellectuality of Animals," Dublin University Magazine, Vol. 15, May, 1840, pp. 495-515.

114. "Intelligence in Animals," Knowledge, Vol. 1, November 11, 1881, pp. 28-9.

115. "The Interpretation of Animal Character," The Spectator, Vol. 60, February 12, 1887, pp. 221-2.

116. James, Joseph F., "The Reasoning Capacity of Animals," American Naturalist, Vol. 15, August, 1881, pp. 604-15.

117. Jones, Leonard A., "The Language of Brutes," Old and New, Vol. 4, 1871, pp. 531-41 and 650-56.

118. Jordan, David S., "Studies in Animal Intelligence," Dial, Vol. 4, 1883-4, pp. 12-14.

119. Kipling, John L., Beast and Man in India, A Popular Sketch of Indian Animals in Their Relations with the People, Macmillan, London and New York, 1891.

120. Kirke, Edmund, "Reasoning Power of Animals," North American Review, Vol. 146, March, 1888, pp. 280-6.

121. Klein, Martial L., "Animal Intelligence," Month, Vol. 47, March, 1883, pp. 376-91.

122. Knauer, Fr., "The Social Life of Animals," Cosmopolitan, Vol. 1, 1886, pp. 283-90.

123. Kropotkin, P., "Mutual Aid Among Animals," Nineteenth Century, Vol. 28, September, 1890, pp. 337-54. Continued in November, 1890, pp. 699-719.

124. Lacassagne, A., "Criminality in Animals," Popular Science Monthly, Vol. 22, December, 1882, pp. 244-255.

125. "The Language of Animals," All the Year Round, Vol. 19, January 25, 1868, pp. 152-6.

126. "Language of Animals," Chambers Edinburgh Review, Vol. 1, New Series, February 17, 1844, pp. 99-101.

127. Lawrence, John, A General Treatise On Cattle, The Ox, the Sheep, and the Swine, Sherwood, Neely and Jones, London, 1809.

128. Le Conte, Joseph, "From Animal to Man," Monist, Vol. 6, April, 1896, pp. 356-381.

129. Le Conte, Joseph, "The Psychical Relation of Man to Animals," Princeton Review, Vol. 13, January-June, 1884, pp. 236-61.

130. Lewis, W.S., "Animal 'Manners'," Leisure Hour, Vol. 39, 1890, pp. 134-6.

131. Lindsay, W. Lauder, Mind in the Lower Animals in Health and Disease, 2 Vols.,

Appleton, New York, 1880.

132. Lindsay, W. Lauder, "The Moral Sense in the Lower Animals," Popular Science Monthly, Vol. 16, January, 1880, pp. 346-53.

133. Lockwood, Samuel, "Animal Humor," American Naturalist, Vol. 10, May, 1876, pp. 257-70.

134. Lubbock, John, On the Senses, Instincts, and Intelligence of Animals, with Special Reference to Insects, D. Appleton and Co., New York, 1888.

135. Marsh, G.P., Man and Nature, Scribner, New York, 1864.

136. Menault, Ernest, The Intelligence of Animals, Charles Scribner, New York, 1871.

137. Mills, Wesley, The Nature and Development of Animal Intelligence, T. Fisher Unwin, London, 1898.

138. Mills, Wesley, "The Nature of Animal Intelligence and the Methods of Investigating It," Psychological Review, Vol. 6, May, 1899, pp. 262-74.

139. "Mind in the Lower Animals," Edinburgh Review, Vol. 152, July, 1880, pp. 19-36.

140. "Mind in the Lower Animals," Living Age, Vol. 146, 1880, pp. 707-25.

141. "Mind in the Lower Animals," The Nation, Vol. 30, April 8, 1880,

pp. 270-1.

142. Morgan, C. Lloyd, "Animal Automatism and Consciousness," Monist, Vol. 7, October, 1896, pp. 1-18.

143. Morgan, C. Lloyd, "Animal Intelligence," Nature, Vol. 26, September 28, 1882, pp. 523-4.

144. Morgan, C. Lloyd, "Animal Intelligence as an Experimental Study," Natural Science, Vol. 13, October, 1898, pp. 265-72.

145. Morgan, C. Lloyd, Animal Life and Intelligence, Arnold Publishing, London, 1890.

146. Morgan, C. Lloyd, "The Limits of Animal Intelligence," Fortnightly Review, Vol. 60, August, 1, 1893, pp. 223-239.

147. Morgan, C. Lloyd, "The Morality of Animals," National Review, London, Vol. 18, 1891-2, pp. 336-46.

148. Morgan, C. Lloyd, "On the Study of Animal Intelligence," Mind, Vol. 11, April, 1886, pp. 174-185.

149. Muller, Max, "The Difference Between Man and Animal," Open Court, Vol. 3, 1889-90, pp. 1980-3.

150. Muller, M., "The Impassable Barrier Between Brutes and Man," in Classics in Biology, ed. by S. Zuckerman, Philosophical Lib., New York, 1960.

151. Newbold, William R., "Will and Reason in Animals," American Naturalist, Vol. 29, October 1895, pp. 948-51.

152. Nutting C.C., "The Mental Processes of Animals," Dial, Vol. 29, September 16, 1900, pp. 169-170.

153. "On the Study of Mind in Animals," Church Quarterly Review, Vol. 18, July, 1884, pp. 283-300.

154. Pearson, Norman, "Animal Immortality," Nineteenth Century, Vol. 29, January, 1891, pp. 154-66.

155. Pringle, Allen, "Reasoning Animals," Popular Science Monthly, Vol. 42, November, 1892, pp.71-5.

156. "Reason in Animals," Once a Week, June 6, 1868, pp. 490-4.

157. Reed, James, "Difference between Men and Animals," New-Church Review, April, 1899, pp. 181-91.

158. Review and discussion of P. Flourens' On the Instinct and Intelligence of Animals, Librairie de L. Hachette et Cie, Paris, 1851, in Eclectic Review, Vol. 6, n.s., December, 1853, pp. 649-65.

159. Ribot, Th., "The Intelligence of Animals," Open Court, Vol. 13, 1899, pp. 85-97.

160. Romanes, George J., Animal Intelligence, D. Appleton & Co., New York, 1883.

161. Romanes, George J., "Animal Intelligence," Popular Science Monthly, Vol. 14, December, 1878, pp. 214-31.

162. Romanes, George, J., "Can an Animal Count?" Nature, Vol. 33, November 26,

19. Animal and Human Nature

1885, p. 80.

163. Romanes, G.J., "Conscience in Animals,"
Journal of Science, April, 1876,
pp. 145-157.

164. Romanes, George J., Critical notice on
Animal Life and Intelligence by C.
Lloyd Morgan, Edward Arnold, London,
1890-91, Mind, Vol. 16, April 1891,
pp. 262-7.

165. Romanes, George J., "Fetichism in
Animals," Living Age, Vol. 136, 1878,
pp. 254-6.

166. Romanes, George J., Mental Evolution in
Animals, Trench & Co., London, 1883.

167. Royer, Clemence, "Animal Arithmetic,"
Popular Science Monthly, Vol. 34,
December, 1888, pp. 252-62.

168. "Speech in Animals," Journal of Science,
Vol. 20, (Vol. 5, Third Series),
January, 1883, pp. 1-7.

169. "The Spiritual in Animals," Journal of
Science, Vol. 16, Vol. 1, in Series 3,
May, 1879, pp. 333-7.

170. "Strange Animal Friendships," Chamber's
Journal, Vol. 55, October 12, 1878,
pp. 654-656.

171. "Studies in Animal Life: Honesty,"
Chamber's Journal, Vol. 61, December
27, 1884, pp. 822-4.

172. "Studies in Animal Life: Maternal
Affection," Chamber's Journal, Vol.
62, September 5, 1885, pp. 573-576.

173. "Studies in Animal Life: Revenge,"
     Chamber's Journal, Vol. 60, Jan-
     uary 13, 1883, pp. 29-91.

174. Sully, James, "Is Man the Only Reasoner?"
     Popular Science Monthly, Vol. 42,
     February, 1892, pp. 506-517.

175. Sutton, W.A., "Animal Intelligence:
     A Reply to M. Romanes," Monthly,
     Vol. 35, January, 1879, pp. 1-21.

176. "The Temper of Animals," The Spectator,
     Vol. 67, December 12, 1891, pp. 840-1.

177. Thorndike, Edward, "Do Animals Reason?"
     Popular Science Monthly, Vol. 55,
     August, 1899, pp. 480-90.

178. Thorndike, Edward, " A Reply to 'The
     Nature of Animal Intelligence and the
     Methods of Investigating It',"
     Psychological Review, Vol. 6, July,
     1899, pp. 412-20.

179. Thorndike, Edward, "Some Experiments
     on Animal Intelligence," Science,
     N.S. Vol. 7, June 17, 1898, pp.
     818-24.

180. Thurston, Robert H., "The Animal as a
     Machine," North American Review, Vol.
     163, No. 480, November 1896, pp. 607-
     19.

181. "Unknown Tongues," Putnam's Monthly, Vol.
     6, August, 1855, pp. 130-8.

182. Van Beneden, P.J., "The Social Life of
     the Lower Animals," American Naturalist,
     Vol. 8, 1874, pp. 521-30.

183. "A Vision of Animal Existences," Cornhill

19. Animal and Human Nature

Magazine, Vol. 5, March, 1862,
pp. 311-18.

184. Weinland, D.F., "Some Principles of
Animal Psychology," American Journal
of Science, Vol. 27, May, 1859, pp.
1-5.

185. Weir, James, Jr., "Animal Intelligence,"
American Naturalist, November, 1893,
pp. 933-43.

186, Weir, James, The Dawn of Reason, or
Mental Traits in the Lower Animals,
Macmillan, London, 1899.

187. Weld, A., "Our Despised Relatives,"
Month, Vol. 19, 1873, pp. 67-93.

188. Wood, John G., Man and Beast, Here and
Hereafter, Daldy, Isbister, London,
1874.

189. Wundt, Wilhelm, Lectures on Human and
Animal Psychology, Trans. by J.E.
Creighton and E.B. Titchener, Swan
Sonnenschein, London, 1894.

190. Young, Egerton R., "Do Animals Reason?"
Popular Science Monthly, Vol. 56,
November, 1899, pp. 105-16.

19: Dogs

(For additional entry related to this topic
see 2566)

191. Cobbe, F.P., "The Consciousness of
Dogs," Quarterly Review, Vol. 133,
1872, pp. 419-51.

192. Cobbe, Frances P., "Dogs Whom I Have
Met," in Cobbe's False Beasts and
True, Ward, Lock and Tyler, London,
1875.

19: Horses

193. Youatt, William, "Early History of
the Horse," "History of the English
Horse," and "A Treatise of Draught,"
in Youatt's The Horse, Charles Knight,
London, 1846.

19: Humans

194. Darwin, Charles, The Descent of Man,
D. Appleton and Co., New York, 1872.

195. Huxley, Thomas H., Man's Place in
Nature, D. Appleton, New York, 1896.

19: Insects

196. Jordan, David S., "Studies of Insect
Life," Dial, Vol. 9, 1888-9 pp.
283-4.

19: Attitudes toward Animals (and Nature)

197. "Animals I Have Known and Loved,"
     Chamber's Journal, Vol. 57, Jan-
     uary 17, 1880, pp. 45-7 and 272.

198. Blakeman, Rufus, "A Philosophical
     Essay on Credulity and Superstition;
     and also on Animal Fascination, or
     Charming," D. Appleton, New York,
     1849.

199. Cobbe, Frances P., "The Fauna of
     Fancy," in Cobbe's False Beasts
     and True, Ward, Lock and Tyler,
     London, 1875.

200. Curtis, Mattoon M., "Sympathy with
     the Lower Animals," Bibliotheca
     Sacra, Vol. 54, 1897, pp. 38-49.

201. "Moral Value of Natural History,"
     Student and Intellectual Observer,
     Vol. 4, 1870, pp. 195-9.

202. Morgan, C. Lloyd, Animal Sketches,
     Edward Arnold, London, 1891.

203. Nietzsche, Friedrich, The Complete
     Works of Friedrich Nietzsche, ed.
     by Oscar Levy, Russell and Russell
     N. Y., 1964.
     Vol. 5: Schopenhauer as Educator,
        No. 5, pp. 147-155 (Human pity for
        animals, the lot of the wild
        beasts).
     Vol. 7: Human, All-Too-Human,
        Part II, "The Wanderer and His
        Shadow," No. 57, "Intercourse
        with Animals," pp. 225-227.
     Vol. 9: The Dawn of Day, No. 286
        "Domestic Animals, Pets and the
        Like," p. 258.

Vol. 10: The Joyful Wisdom, No. 224, "Animal Criticism," p. 100.

204. Thoreau, Henry David, Walden, C.N. Potter, distributed by Crown Publishers, New York, 1970.

204. a "True and False Sentiment about Animals," The Spectator, Vol. 55, March 11, 1882, pp. 323-324.

19: Animals and Religion
(For additional entries related to this topic
see 359, 404, 435.)

205. Austin, P., Our Duty to Animals,
     London, 1885. (Catholic Church's
     view of animals.)

206. Brown, Abbie F., The Book of Saints
     and Friendly Beasts, Houghton
     Mifflin, Boston, 1900.

207. "The Clergy and Vivisection," The
     Spectator, Vol. 57, February 9,
     1884, pp. 191-2.

208. Cobbe, F. P., "The Clergy and Vivi-
     section," The Spectator, Vol. 57,
     1884, p. 517.

209. Cooper, William Earnshaw, The Blood-
     Guiltiness of Christendom, The
     Order of the Golden Age, London, n.d.

210. "The Future State of Animals," The
     Spectator, Vol. 72, March 3, 1894,
     pp. 295-96.

211. "Love for Animals," Catholic World,
     Vol. 13, July, 1871, pp 545-553.

212. Martinengo-Cesaresco, E., "The Friend
     of the Creature," Contemporary Review,
     Vol. 77, June, 1900, pp. 835-44.

213. Márvin, Frederic R., Christ Among the
     Cattle, A Sermon Preached in The
     First Congregational Church, Portland,
     Oregon, J.O. Wright, New York, 1899.
     (In Yale University Library.)

214. Review of "A Sermon on the Sin of
     Cruelty towards the Brute Creation,"

preached in the Abbey Church at
Bath on February 15, 1801, by the
Rev. Legh Richmond, Christian
Observer, Vol. 1, July, 1802, p. 452.

215.   Richmond, Rev. Legh, "A Sermon on the
Sin of Cruelty towards the Brute
Creation," preached in the Abbey
Church at Bath on Feb. 15, 1801,
Rivingtons and Hatchard, London,
1802, p. 28.

216.   Rickaby, Father Joseph, "Of the So-
Called Rights of Animals," from his
Moral Philosophy, London, 1892.
Reproduced in Animal Rights and Human
Obligations, ed. by Tom Regan and
Peter Singer (1253). (View of
Catholicism on animal rights.)

217.   "The Souls of Animals," Catholic World,
Vol. 5, July, 1867, pp. 510-21.

218.   Tyrrell, G., "Jesuit Zoophily: A Reply,"
Contemporary Review, Vol. 68, 1895,
pp. 708-715.

219.   Wood, John G., The Dominion of Man
Bentley, London, 1889.

220. "The Animal Declaration of Independence," Harper's New Monthly Magazine, Vol. 14, January, 1857, pp. 145-63.

221. Carlisle, Harvey, "On Moral Duty Towards Animals," Macmillan's Magazine, Vol. 45, 1881-2, pp. 462-8.

222. Cobbe, Frances P., "The Claims of Brutes," in Cobbe's Life of Frances Power Cobbe, Richard Bentley, London, 1894, Vol. 2, pp. 241-316.

223. Cobbe, F.P., "The Ethics of Zoophily: A Reply," Contemporary Review, Vol. 68, 1897, pp. 497-508.

224. Cobbe, Frances P., "The Rights of Man and the Claims of Brutes," Fraser's Magazine, Vol. 68, November, 1863, pp. 586-602. Also in Cobbe's Christian Ethics and the Ethics of Christ, Trubner, London, 1865.

225. "Dr. Styles on the Claims of the Animal Creation," Christian Observer, Vol. 45, November, 1845, pp. 670-91. A review of "The Animal Creation: Its Claims on Our Humanity Stated and Enforced." A prize essay. By the Rev. John Styles, D.D.

226. Drummond, W. H., Rights of Animals and Man's Obligation to Treat Them with Humanity, London, 1838. (There is a copy of this in the University of Texas Library and also one in the University of Wisconsin Library.)

227. Gompertz, Lewis, Fragments in Defense

of Animals, London, 1852.

228. Gompertz, Lewis, Moral Inquiries On the Situation of Man and of Brutes, London, 1824.

229. Green, Thomas H., The Principles of Political Obligation, University of Michigan Press, Ann Arbor, 1967. (See page 207 on question whether animals can have rights.)

230. "Have Animals Rights?" The Spectator, Vol. 72, March 17, 1894, pp. 367-8.

231. Laws, Thomas C., "The Rights of Animals," Open Court, Vol. 7, September 7, 1893, p. 3791.

232. Lecky, William E.H., History of European Morals, Longmans, Green, London, 1911. (See pp. 171-77 Vol. 2, on Christianity and animals. See pp. 47-9 on Utilitarianism and animals.)

233. Leffingwell, Albert, "An Ethical Basis for Humanity to Animals," Arena, Vol. 10, 1894, pp. 474-82.

234. Mill, John Stuart, Collected Works, ed. by F.E.L. Priestley and Others, University of Toronto Press, Toronto, 1962-1977, 19 Volumes. See Whewell on Moral Philosophy, where Mill defends Bentham's application of Utilitarianism to animals, which was criticized by Whewell. (Vol. 10, pp. 185-187) See Utilitarianism, where Mill argues that the standard of Utilitarianism takes into consideration the pleasures and pains of all sentient beings.

Mill also discusses the pleasures
and pains experienced by animals
compared to those experienced by
humans. (Vol. 10, pp. 212-214)
See Three Essays on Religion, where
Mill argues that predation in nature
is inconsistent with the perfection
of an omnipotent Creator. (Vol. 10,
pp. 398-9)

235. Nicholson, Edward B., The Rights of
an Animal, A New Essay in Ethics,
with a reprint of parts of John
Lawrence's "On the Rights of Beasts,"
"On the Philosophy of Sports," and
"The Animal-Question," Kegan Paul,
London, 1879. (In Yale University
Library.)

236. Powell, E.P., "Animal Rights of
Property," Open Court, Vol. 9,
January 31, 1895, pp. 4375-7.

237. A review and discussion of Reply to
Dr. Style's Prize Essay on the
Claims of the Animal Creation to
the Humanity of Man, by G.F. Berkeley,
Ridgway, London, 1839, in Monthly
Review, London, Vol. 42, Series 4,
1839, pp. 77-92.

238. Ritchie, D.G., "The Rights of Animals,"
International Journal of Ethics, Vol.
10, 1899-1900, pp. 387-9.

239. Ritchie, D.G., "Why Animals Do Not Have
Rights," from his Natural Rights,
Allen and Unwin, London, 1894. Repro-
duced in Animal Rights and Human
Obligations, ed. by Tom Regan and
Peter Singer (1253).

240. Salt, Henry S., "A Reply to Professor

Ritchie," International Journal
of Ethics, Vol. 10, 1899-1900,
pp. 389-390.

241.   Salt, Henry S., "The Rights of
Animals," Ethics, Vol. 10, No. 2,
January, 1900, pp. 206-222.

242.   Schopenhauer, Arthur, On the Basis of
Morality, trans. by E.F.J. Payne,
Bobbs-Merrill, Indianapolis, Ind.,
1965.
See pp. 94-96 for Schopenhauer's
criticism of Kant's view on human
duty towards animals. See pp. 175-
187 for Schopenhauer's view on morals
and animals. Influenced by Hinduism
and Buddhism, Schopenhauer was critical of the Judaic-Christian view of
animals; he also criticized Western
rationalistic philosophies which
drew a sharp dichotomy between rational humans and non-rational animals.

19: Treatment and Uses of Animals (Including Ethics of)

243. Angell, George T., "The Protection of Animals," Journal of Social Science, Vol. 6, 1874, pp. 164-80.

244. Averv, B.P., "Our Speechless Friends," Overland Monthly, Vol. 1, September, 1868, pp. 234-40.

245. Bergh, Henry, "The Cost of Cruelty," North American Review, Vol. 133, July, 1881, pp. 74-81.

246. Carter, Sarah N., For Pity's Sake, DeWolfe, Fiske and Co., Boston, Ma., 1897. (In Yale University Library.)

247. Clarke, R.F., "On Cruelty to Animals in Its Moral Aspect," Month, Vol. 25, December, 1875, pp. 393-406.

248. Craik, James, Cruelty to the Inferior Animals, Opposed to the Design of God Under the Present Dispensation, Alexander Colston, Edinburgh, 1842.

249. Crowe, Henry, Zoophilos, or Considerations on the Moral Treatment of Inferior Animals, London, 1819.

250. "Cruelty to Animals," Cornhill Magazine, Vol. 29, February, 1874, pp. 213-26.

251. "Cruelty to Animals in Italy," Chambers Journal, Vol. 51, January 24, 1874, pp. 62-3.

252. "Cruelties to Brute Animals," Methodist Magazine, London, Vol. 30, 1807, pp. 547-52.

253. De La Ramee, Louise (Ouida), "The Quality of Mercy," Nineteenth Century, Vol. 40, August, 1896, pp. 293-305.

254. Erskine, Thomas, The Speech of Lord Erskine in the House of Peers, on the second reading of the Bill for preventing malicious and wanton cruelty to animals, printed for Richard Phillips, London, 1809. (In Yale University Library.)

255. Fleming, George, "The Wanton Mutilation of Animals," The Nineteenth Century, Vol. 37, March, 1895, pp. 440-461.

256. Hamley, Edward B. Our Poor Relations, A Philozoic Essay, J.E. Tilton and Co., Boston, 1872.

257. Hutchinson, Jonathan, "On Cruelty to Animals," Fortnightly Review, Vol. 26, September 1, 1876, pp. 307-20.

258. Jevons, William S., "Cruelty to Animals: A Study in Sociology," in Jevons' Methods of Social Reform and Other Papers, A.M. Kelley, New York, 1965. Also in Fortnightly Review, Vol. 25, May 1, 1876, pp. 670-84.

259. Macaulay, James, Plea for Mercy to Animals, Partridge, London, 1875(?).

260. Maxwell, Herbert, "Our Obligations to Wild Animals," Blackwood's Edinburgh Magazine, Vol. 166, August, 1899, pp. 224-37.

261. Mushet, David, The Wrongs of the Animal

World, to which is subjoined the
1809 speech of Lord Erskine on the
same subject, Hatchard, London,
1839. (In Yale University Library.)

262. Newman, F.W., "On Cruelty," Fraser's
Magazine, n.s., Vol. 13, 1876, pp.
533-536.

263. "Our Poor Relations," Blackwood's
Edinburgh Magazine, Vol. 107, May,
1870, pp. 531-553.

264. Rhodes, G.M., comp., The Nine Circles
of the Hell of the Innocent, Swan
Sonnenschein, London, 1892.

265. Smith, Abraham, Catechism of Cruelty,
Davis and Porter, London, 1833.
(In Yale University Library.)

266. "The Speech of Lord Erskine, in the
House of Peers, on the Second Reading of the Bill for Preventing Malicious and Wanton Cruelty to Animals,"
Eclectic Review, Vol. 10, 1809, pp.
1150-3.

267. "Speech of the Right Hon. W. Windham
in the House of Commons, June 13,
1809, on Lord Erskine's Bill for
the More Effectual Prevention of
Cruelty Towards Animals," Eclectic
Review, Vol. 12, 1810, pp. 975-97.

268. Trail, H.D., "The Brutes on their
Master," Nineteenth Century, Vol.
15, March, 1884, pp. 435-44.

269. "Treatment of Animals," Chamber's
Journal, Vol. 54, September 1,
1877, pp. 545-8.

270. Young, Thomas, An Essay on Humanity
to Animals, J. Booth, London, 1822.

19: Animal Experimentation

271. Abbott, Rosa G., "The Higher Civilization versus Vivisection," _Arena_ (Boston), Vol. 19, 1898, pp. 127-30.

272. Adams, Charles, _The Coward Science_, Our Answer to Prof. Owen, Hatchards, London, 1882.

273. Aldrich, Thomas B., "The Cruelty of Science," in Aldrich, Thomas B., _Ponkapog Papers_, Books for Library Press, Essay Index Reprint Series, Freeport, N.Y., 1969.

274. Armitt, A., "Man and His Relatives: A Question of Morality," _Modern Review_ (London), Vol. 4, 1883, pp. 368-79.

275. Arnold, F.S., "Do the Interests of Humanity Require Experiments on Living Animals?" in _The Antivivisection Question_, Victoria Street Society for the Protection of Animals from Vivisection, London, 1896.

276. Barry, Alfred, "Do the Interests of Mankind Require Experiments on Living Animals?" in _The Antivivisection Question_, Victoria Street Society for the Protection of Animals from Vivisection, London, 1896.

277. Bell, Ernest, "The Morality of Vivisection," _Contemporary Review_, Vol. 62, December 1892, pp. 849-54.

278. Bell-Taylor, Charles, "For Pity's Sake," in _The Antivivisection_

Question, Victoria Street Society for the Protection of Animals from Vivisection, London, 1896.

279. Bell-Taylor, Charles, "Vivisection: Is It Justifiable?" in The Antivivisection Question, Victoria Street Society for the Protection of Animals from Vivisection, London, 1896.

280. Berdoe, Edward, "The Futility of Experiments with Drugs on Animals," in The Antivivisection Question, Victoria Street Society for the Protection of Animals from Vivisection, London, 1896.

281. Bernard, Claude, An Introduction to the Study of Experimental Medicine, trans. by Henry Copley Green, Schuman, New York, 1949.

282. "Bestiarianism v. Common Sense," Journal of Science, Vol. 19, 1882, pp. 454-60 and 512-19.

283. Bridges, J.H., "Harvey and Vivisection," Fortnightly Review, Vol. 26, July 1, 1876, pp. 1-17.

284. Brunton, T. Lander, "Vivisection and the Use of Remedies," Nineteenth Century, Vol. 11, March, 1882, pp. 479-487.

285. Bryan, Benjamin, ed., Anti-Vivisection Evidences, A Collection of Authentic Statements by Competent Witnesses as to the Immorality, Cruelty, and Futility of Experiments on Living Animals, Society for the Protection of Animals from Vivisection, London, 1895.

286. Carpenter, William B., "The Ethics of Vivisection," _Fortnightly Review_, Vol. 37, February 1, 1882, pp. 237-246.

287. Carroll, Lewis, "Some Popular Falfacies About Vivisection," and "Vivisection As a Sign of the Times," in _The Works of Lewis Carroll_, Hamlyn Publishing, Middlesex, 1965, pp. 1089-1100.

288. Carus, Paul, "The Immorality of the Anti-Vivisection Movement," _The Open Court_, Vol. 11, 1897, pp. 370-76.

289. Clarke, Robert F., "The Vivisection Controversy," _Dublin Review_, Vol. 15, July-October, 1894, pp. 96-121.

290. Cobbe, Frances P., _Bernard's Martyrs_, A Comment on Claude Bernard's Lecons de Physiologic Operatoire, Office of the Society for Protection of Animals from Vivisection, Westminster, 1879.

291. Cobbe, Frances P., "The Fallacy of Restriction Applied to Vivisection," in _The Antivivisection Question_, Victoria Street Society for the Protection of Animals from Vivisection, London, 1896.

292. Cobbe, Frances P., "Light in Dark Places," in _The Antivivisection Question_, Victoria Street Society for the Protection of Animals from Vivisection, London, 1896. (Illustrations of Claude Bernard's experiments on animals.)

293. Cobbe, Frances P., "Mr. Lowe and the

Vivisection Act," Contemporary Review, Vol. 29, February, 1877, pp. 335-47.

294. Cobbe, Frances P., "The Moral Aspects of Vivisection," in The Antivivisection Question, Victoria Street Society for the Protection of Animals from Vivisection, London, 1896.

295. Cobbe, Frances P., "The Recent Debate on Vivisection," The Spectator, Vol. 62, June 1, 1889, pp. 758-59.

296. Cobbe, Frances P., "The Right of Tormenting," in The Antivivisection Question, Victoria Street Society for the Protection of Animals from Vivisection, London, 1896.

297. Cobbe, Frances P., "An Unscientific View of Vivisection," National Review, London, Vol. 19, 1891-2, pp. 144-5.

298. Cobbe, Frances P., "Vivisection: Four Replies," Fortnightly Review, Vol. 37, January 1, 1882, pp. 88-104.

299. Cobbe, Frances P., "Vivisection and Its Two-Faced Advocates," Contemporary Review, Vol. 41, April, 1882, pp. 610-26.

300. Cobbe, Frances P., "Zoophily," Cornhill Magazine, Vol. 45, March, 1882, pp. 279-88.

301. Cobbe, Frances P. and Bryan, Benjamin, Vivisection in America, How It Is Taught and How It Is Practiced, Swan and Sonnenschein, London, 1890.

302. Coleridge, Lord, "Commentary on the Cruelty to Animals Act, 1876," in The Antivivisection Question, Victoria Street Society for the Protection of Animals from Vivisection, 1896.

303. Coleridge, Lord, "The Nineteenth Century Defenders of Vivisection," Fortnightly Review, Vol. 37, February 1, 1882, pp. 225-36.

304. Coleridge, Stephen, "Some London Hospitals and their Audited Accounts," Contemporary Review, Vol. 77, 1900, pp. 343-50.

305. Congreve, Richard, and Bridges, J.H., "Vivisection," Fortnightly Review, Vol. 23, March 1, 1875, pp. 435-7.

306. Dalton, John C., "Magendie as a Physiologist," International Review, Vol. 8, 1880, pp. 120-25.

307. Davis, Noah K., "The Moral Aspects of Vivisection," North American Review, Vol. 140, March, 1885, pp. 203-20.

308. de Cyon, E., "The Anti-Vivisection Agitation," Contemporary Review, Vol. 43, April, 1883, pp. 488-510.

309. De La Ramee, Louise (Ouida), "The Future of Vivisection," Gentleman's Magazine, Vol. 28, April, 1882, pp. 412-23.

310. De La Ramee, Louise (Ouida), "The New Priesthood: A Protest Against Vivisection," New Review, London, Vol. 8, 1893, pp. 151-64.

311. "The Debate on Vivisection at Oxford,"

Nature, Vol. 31, March 19, 1885, pp. 453-4.

312. "Dr. Ferrier and Vivisection, "Knowledge, Vol. 1, November 18, 1881, pp. 58-9.

313. "The Ethics of Vivisection," Cornhill Magazine, Vol. 33, April, 1876, pp. 468-478.

314. "The Ethics of Vivisection," Edinburgh Review, Vol. 190, July, 1899, pp. 147-169.

315. "The Ethics of Vivisection," Public Opinion, Vol. 20, January, 23, 1896, pp. 110-12.

316. Fleming, George, "Vivisection and Diseases of Animals," Nineteenth Century, Vol. 11, March, 1882, pp. 468-78.

317. Foster, Michael, "Vivisection," Popular Science Monthly, Vol. 4, April, 1874.

318. Foster, R.N., "Vivisection and Morality," Open Court, Vol. 11, 1897, pp. 689-93.

319. Freeman, Edward A., "Field Sports and Vivisection," Canadian Monthly and National Review, Vol. 5, 1874, pp. 543-9.

320. Freeman, Edward A., "Field Sports and Vivisection," Fortnightly Review, Vol. 21, May 1, 1874, pp. 618-629.

321. Gaertner, Frederick, "Vivisection," American Naturalist, Vol. 25, 1891, pp. 864-9.

322. Gordon, C.A., The Vivisection

Controversy in Parliament, An
Answer to a Speech Delivered
by Sir Lyon Playfair in the House
of Commons, April 4, 1883, Williams
and Norgate, London, 1888.

323. Grant, Brewin, "Vivisection, or
Painful Experiments on Living
Animals Scientifically and Ethical-
ly Considered," in Vivisection,
Scientifically and Ethically Con-
sidered in Prize Essays, Marshall
Japp, London, 1881.

324. Gray, E. Conder, "Scientific Cruelty,"
Good Words, Vol. 17, 1876, pp. 241-3.

325. Greenwood, George, "Vivisection,"
Macmillan's Magazine, Vol. 40, 1879,
pp. 523-30.

326. Gull, William W., "The Ethics of Vivisection," Nineteenth Century, Vol. 11,
March, 1882, pp. 456-467.

327. Gurney, Edmund, "A Chapter in the Ethics
of Pain," Fortnightly Review, Vol. 36,
December 1,1881, pp. 778-96.

328. Gurney, Edmund, "An Epilogue on Vivisection," Cornhill Magazine, Vol. 45,
February, 1882, pp. 191-9.

329. Hart, Ernest, "Women, Clergymen, and
Doctors," New Review, London, Vol. 7,
1892, pp. 708-18.

330. Hodge, C.F., "The Vivisection Question,"
Popular Science Monthly, Vol. 49,
1896, pp. 614-24. Continued pp. 771-
85.

331. Hoggan, George, Letter on Vivisection,
Morning Post, February 2, 1875,

reproduced in Richard D. French's
Antivivisection and Medical Science
in Victorian Society, pp. 414-5
(1490).

332. Hoggan, George, "Vivisection,"
Fraser's Magazine, Vol. 91 (n.s.11),
April, 1875, pp. 521-9.

333. Horsley, Victor, "The Morality of
Vivisection," The Nineteenth Century,
Vol. 32, November, 1892, pp. 804-11.

334. Hutton, Richard H., "The Anti-Vivisection Agitation," Contemporary
Review, Vol. 43, April, 1883, pp.
510-516.

335. Hutton, Richard H., "The Biologists
on Vivisection," Nineteenth Century,
Vol. 11, January, 1882, pp. 29-39.

336. "Inhumane Humanity," All the Year
Round, Vol. 15, March 17, 1866,
238-40.

337. Jesse, George R., Evidence Given Before
the Royal Commission on Vivisection,
Basil Montagu Pickering, London, 1875.

338. Jones, A. Coppen, "The Benefits of
Vivisection," Fortnightly Review,
Vol. 59, January 1, 1893, pp. 112-15.

339. Keen, William W., "Our Recent Debts
to Vivisection," Popular Science
Monthly, Vol. 27, May, 1885, pp.
1-15.

340. Keen, W.W., "Vivisection and Brain
Surgery, " Harper's New Monthly
Magazine, Vol. 87, June, 1893, pp.
128-39.

19. Animal Experimentation

341. Kingsford, Anna, "The Uselessness of Vivisection," _Nineteenth Century_, Vol. 11, February, 1882, pp. 171-83.

342. Lawson, Henry, "The Vivisection Clamour," _Popular Science Review_, Vol. 15, 1876, pp. 398-405.

343. Lee, Vernon, "Vivisection: An Evolutionist to Evolutionists," _Contemporary Review_, Vol. 41, May, 1882, pp. 788-811.

344. Leffingwell, Albert, "Does Vivisection Pay?" _Scribner's Monthly_, Vol. 20, July, 1880, pp. 391-399.

345. Leffingwell, Albert, _Vivisection_, John Lovell Co., New York, 1889.

346. Leffingwell, Albert, "Vivisection," _Lippincott's Monthly Magazine_, Vol. 34, August, 1884, pp. 126-32.

347. Leffingwell, Albert, "Vivisection in America," and "Vivisection in Amercan Colleges," essays included in Henry S. Salt's _Animals' Rights_, Macmillan, New York, 1894, pp. 133-74.

348. Lewes, George H., "Vivisection," _Nature_, Vol. 9, December 25, 1873, pp. 144-5.

349. Macaulay, James, "Vivisection: Is It Scientifically Useful or Morally Justifiable?" An Essay Addressed Specially to the Medical Profession, in _Vivisection, Scientifically and Ethically Considered in Prize Essays_, Marshall Japp, London, 1881.

350. Macilwain, George, Vivisection,
Being Short Comments on Certain
Parts of the Evidence Given Be-
fore the Royal Commission, Hatchards,
London, 1877.

351. McLean, J. Emery, "Vivisection," New
Science Review, Vol. 2, 1896, pp.
220-8.

352. Manchester, J., "The Morality of
Vivisection: A Reply," The Nineteenth Century, Vol. 32, December,
1892, pp. 980-3.

353. Mercer, Henry C., "Men of Science and
Vivisection," Science, N.S. Vol. 9,
February 10, 1899, pp. 221-3.

354. "Miss Cobbe's 'Modern Rack'," The
Spectator, Vol. 63, August 17,
1889, pp. 213-14.

355. Morison, J.C., "Scientific versus
Bucolic Vivisection," Fortnightly
Review, Vol. 43, 1885, pp. 249-252.

356. Oldfield, Josiah, "The Limits of
Experimentation," Westminster
Review, Vol. 154, August, 1900,
pp. 190-3.

357. Owen, Richard, Experimental Physiology:
Its Benefits to Mankind, Longmans,
Green, London, 1882.

358. Owen, Richard, "Vivisection: Its
Pains and Uses," The Nineteenth
Century, Vol. 10, December, 1881,
pp. 931-5.

359. Oxenham, H.N., "Moral and Religious
Estimate of Vivisection," Gentleman's Magazine, Vol. 21, December,

1878, pp. 713-36.

360. Paget, James, "Vivisection: Its Pains and Uses," The Nineteenth Century, Vol. 10, December 1881, pp. 920-30.

361. "Physiological Experiments: Vivisection," Westminster Review, Vol. 85, January, 1866, pp. 60-70.

362. "The Present State of the Vivisection Question," Journal of Science, Vol. 17, August, 1880, pp. 501-9.

363. "Professor Owen on Vivisection," Knowledge, Vol. 2, 1882, p. 147.

364. Quiddam, Roger, "Vivisection," St. James Magazine, Vol. 38, 1876, pp. 277-86.

365. "The Recent 'Vivisection' Case," Journal of Science, Vol. 18, December, 1881, pp. 727-34.

366. Richet, Charles, "Man's Right over Animals," Popular Science Monthly, Vol. 25, October, 1884, pp. 759-66.

367. Royal Society for the Prevention of Cruelty to Animals, Vivisection, Evidence Presented to the Royal Commission, Smith, Elder, London, 1876.

368. Ruffer, M. Armand, "The Morality of Vivisection," The Nineteenth Century Vol. 32, November, 1892, pp. 812-17.

369. Sanderson, J. Burdon, Ed., Handbook for the Physiological Laboratory, 2 Volumes, London, 1873. (The first manual for the physiological laboratory published in the English language. Witnesses before the Royal

Commission on the Practice of Subjecting Live Animals To Experiments for Scientific Purposes (1876) were heavily questioned in regard to this manual. This book was very important in the antivivisectionist movement in 19th Century England.)

370. Scoffern, J., "Vivisection," Belgravia, A London Magazine, Vol. 2, 1867, pp. 101-9, 216-22.

371. Searle, George M., "Murder in the Name of Science," Catholic World, Vol. 70, January, 1900, pp. 493-504.

372, Shaftesbury, The Earl of, "The Total Prohibition of Vivisection," Substance of a speech in the House of Lords, July 15, 1879, Society for the Protection of Animals from Vivisection, London, 1879.

373. Smith, Stephen, Scientific Research, A View from Within, Elliot Stock, London, 1900.

374. Sordello, "The Ethics of Vivisection," Canadian Monthly, Vol. 12, 1877, pp. 72-6.

375. Tait, Lawson, "The Uselessness of Vivisection," in The Antivivisection Question, Victoria Street Society for the Protection of Animals from Vivisection, London, 1896.

376. Tait, Lawson, The Uselessness of Vivisection upon Animals as a Method of Scientific Research, Herald Press, Birmingham, 18--?

377. Thompson, Ralph, "Mr. Coleridge and the

Middlesex Hospital," _Contemporary Review_, Vol. 77, 1900, pp. 606-8.

378. Thornhill, Mark, _The Case Against Vivisection_, Hatchards, London, 1889.

379. "Vivisection," _Journal of Science_, Vol. 13, July, 1876, pp. 317-36.

380. "Vivisection," _Leisure Hour,_ Vol. 24, 1857, pp. 515-18.

381. "Vivisection," _The Nation_, Vol. 20, February 25, 1875, pp. 128-9.

382. "Vivisection: Its Claims and Results," _Leisure Hour_, Vol. 25, 1876, pp. 554-5.

383. "Vivisection: or Cruelty as an Exact Science," _National Quarterly Review_, Vol. 31, September, 1875, pp. 253-81.

384. "The Vivisection Controversy," _The American_, Philadelphia, Vol. 4, May 13, 1882, pp. 71-2.

385. "Vivisection Question in Germany," _The Nation_, Vol. 28, June 19, 1879, pp. 417-18. Also _The Nation_, Vol. 30, February 5, 1880. pp. 94-5.

386. Wagner, Richard, "Against Vivisection," in Wagner, Richard, _Richard Wagner's Prose Works_, Vol. 6, pp. 195-210, trans. by William A. Ellis, Broude Brothers, N.Y., 1966.

387. Wall, Abiathar, "Painful Experiments on Living Animals, Scientifically and Ethically Considered," in _Vivisection, Scientifically and Ethically Considered in Prize Essays,_ Marshall Japp, London, 1881.

388. Wallace, Lionel J., "Vivisection," Westminster Review, Vol. 137, 1892, pp. 245-260.

389. Waters, Amos, "The Ethics of Anti-Vivisection: A Reply to Dr. Carus," Open Court, Vol. 11, 1897, pp. 686-689.

390. Watson, Thomas, "Vivisection," Contemporary Review, Vol. 25, May, 1875, pp. 867-870.

391. Welch, William H., "Argument against Senate Bill 34, Fifty-Sixth Congress, First Session, Generally Known as the 'Antivivisection Bill'," Journal of the American Medical Association, Vol. 34, May 19, 1900, pp. 1242-48, pp. 1322-1327.

392. Welch, William H., "Objections to the Antivivisection Bill Now before the Senate of the United States," Journal of the American Medical Association, Vol. 30, No. 6, February 5, 1898, pp. 285-290.

393. White, Caroline E., "The Practice of Vivisection," The Forum, Vol. 9, March, 1890, pp. 106-16.

394. Wilberforce, Basil, " 'Women, Clergymen, and Doctors,' : A Reply," New Review, London, Vol. 8, 1893, pp. 85-95.

395. Wilder, Burt G., "Vivisection in the State of New York," Popular Science Monthly, Vol. 23, June, 1883, pp. 169-180.

396. Wilks, Samuel, "The Ethics of Vivisection," Contemporary Review, Vol. 41, May, 1882, pp. 812-818.

19: Animal Experimentation

397. Wilks, Samuel, "Vivisection: Its Pains and Its Uses," Nineteenth Century, Vol. 10, December, 1881, pp. 936-48.

398. Wood, H.C., "The Value of Vivisection," Scribner's Monthly, Vol. 20, September, 1880, pp. 766-70.

399. Yeo, Gerald F., "The Practice of Vivisection in England," Fortnightly Review, Vol. 37, March 1, 1882, pp. 352-69.

400. Yeo, Gerald F., "Vivisection and Practical Medicine," Popular Science Monthly, Vol. 22, March, 1883, pp. 615-21.

19: Eating Animals

401. "Of Animal Food in General," New Monthly Magazine, Vol. 5, 1822, pp. 563-70.

402. Paley, William, "A Right to the Fruits or Vegetable Products of the Earth," and "A Right to the Flesh of Animals," in Paley's Principles of Moral and Political Philosophy, Vol. 1, pp. 100-108, R. Faulder, London, 1803.

403. Wilde, J.R., "Animal Food in Early Times in Ireland," Dublin University Magazine, March, 1854, pp. 317-33.

19: Vegetarianism

404. Abhendenada, Swami, Why a Hindu Is a Vegetarian, Vedanta Society, New York, 1898.

405. Alcott, William A., Vegetable Diet as

Sanctioned by Medical Men and by Experience in All Ages, Marsh, Capen, and Lyon, 1838. (Copy in University of Wisconsin Library.)

406. Axon, William E.A., "Shelley's Vegetarianism," Haskell House, New York, 1971, 13 pp. (First published in 1890.)

407. Carus, Paul, "Vegetarianism," Open Court, Vol. 12, 1898, pp. 565-70.

408. de Neuville, A., "Vegetarianism," Public Opinion, May 27, 1893, p. 181.

409. "Dietetic Charlatanry, or New Ethics of Eating," New York Review, Vol. 1, October, 1837, pp. 336-51.

410. Forward, Charles W., Fifty Years of Food Reform: A History of the Vegetarian Movement in England, 1847-1897, Ideal Publishing Union, 1898.

411. Lankester, Sir Edwin R., "Vegetarians and Their Teeth," in Lankester, Sir Edwin R., Science from an Easy Chair: A Second Series, Books for Libraries Press, Essay Index Reprint Series, Freeport, N.Y., 1971.

412. Napier, C.O. Groom, "Autobiography of a Vegetarian," Eclectic Magazine, Vol. 87, September, 1876, pp. 292-300.

413. Newman, Francis W., "Vegetarianism," Fraser's Magazine, February, 1875, pp. 156-72.

414. Newton, John F., "The Return to Nature

or, A Defence of the Vegetable Regimen, with some Account of an Experiment Made During the Last Three or Four Years in the Author's Family," Pamphleteer, Vol. 19, 1821-2, pp. 497-530. Continued in Vol. 20, 1822, pp. 97-118 and pp. 411-29. (There is a copy of this article in the University of Arizona Library.)

415. Oldfield, Josiah, "Vegetarian Still: A Reply to Sir Henry Thompson," Nineteenth Century, Vol. 44, August, 1898, pp. 246-52.

416. "Physical Puritanism" (vegetarianism), Westminster Review, London, Vol. 57, 1852, pp. 405-42.

417. Power, J.W., "An Answer to 'A Plea for Vegetarianism'," Time (London), Vol. 8, 1892-3, pp. 390-3.

418. "Pythagorean Objections Against Animal Food," London Magazine, Vol. 13, November, 1825, pp. 380-3.

419. Ritson, Joseph, An Essay on Abstinence from Animal Food as a Moral Duty, R. Phillips, London, 1802. (There are copies of this at the libraries of Emory University, Michigan State University, and University of Arizona.)

420. "Ritson on Abstinence from Animal Food," Edinburgh Review, Vol. 2, April, 1803, pp. 128-136.

421. Salt, Henry S., "A Plea for Vegetarianism," Time, A Monthly Magazine (London), Vol. 8, Series 2, 1892-3,

pp. 144-9.

422. Salt, Henry S., "A Word More on Vegetarianism," Time, A Monthly Magazine
(London), Vol. 8, Series 2, 1892-3,
pp. 698-701.

423. Shelley, Percy B., "Essay on the Veg-
etable System of Diet," and "Vin-
dication of Natural Diet," in
Shelley's Prose; or The Trumpet of a
Prophecy, ed. by David Lee Clark,
University of New Mexico Press,
Alburquerque, NM, 1954.

424. "Shelley and Vegetarianism," Book-Lore,
Vol. 3, 1885-6, pp. 121-132.

425. Shrubsole, O.A., "The Practicability
of Vegetarianism," Westminster Review,
Vol. 145, 1896, pp. 312-320.

426. Smith, John, Fruits and Farinacea the
Proper Food of Man: Being an Attempt
to Prove, from History, Anatomy,
Physiology, and Chemistry, that the
Original, Natural, and Best Diet of
Man Is Derived from the Vegetable
Kingdom, Fowler and Wells, New York,
1854.

427. Smith, T.P., "Vegetarianism," Fortnightly Review, Vol. 64, November 1,
1895, pp. 753-764.

428. Thompson, Henry, "Why 'Vegetarian'?"
Nineteenth Century, Vol. 43, April,
1898, pp. 556-569.

429. Thompson, Henry, "Why 'Vegetarian'?
A Reply to critics," Nineteenth
Century, Vol. 43, June, 1898, pp.

966-76.

430. Tolstoy, Leo, "The First Step," in
     Tolstoy, Leo, Recollections and
     Essays, Oxford University Press,
     London, 1961. (This essay, written
     in 1892, was a preface to a Russian
     translation of Howard Williams' The
     Ethics of Diet. It includes de-
     scriptions of his visits to slaughter
     houses and stresses the immorality of
     animal food.)

431. "The Vegetarian Creed," Living Age,
     Vol. 216, January 8, 1898, pp.
     126-8.

432. "The Vegetarian Triumph," Spectator,
     Vol. 70, June 10, 1893, pp. 767-8.

433. "Vegetarianism: The Great Dietetic
     Reform," Journal of Science, Vol.
     13, January, 1876, pp. 14-30.

434. West, Kenyon, "Shelley and Vegetar-
     ianism," Writer, Vol. 7, 1894,
     pp. 34-38.

435. White, Anna, "Vegetarianism among
     Shakers," Mount Lebanon, New York,
     18--?, Western Reserve Historical
     Society Shaker Collection, No. 504,
     microfiche.

436. Williams, Howard, The Ethics of Diet,
     F. Pitman, London, 1883. (History
     of vegetarianism.)

19: Domestication

437. Galton, Francis, "The First Steps
      towards the Domestication of Ani-
      mals," Transactions of the Ethnolog-
      ical Society of London, N.S. Vol. 3,
      1865, pp. 122-38.

19: Hunting

(For additional entry related to this topic
see 320.)

438. "The Cruelty of Sportsmen," Temple
      Bar, Vol. 28, 1869-70, pp. 359-70.

439. Lawrence, John (Scott, William Henry:
      Pseudonym), British Field Sports,
      Embracing Practical Instructions in
      Shooting, Hunting, Coursing, Racing,
      Cocking, Fishing, Breaking and Train-
      ing of Dogs and Horses, Sherwood,
      Neely, and Jones, London, 1818.

440. Stillman, W.J., "A Plea for Wild
      Animals," Contemporary Review,
      Vol. 75, 1899, pp. 667-76.

19: Circuses

441. Aflalo, F. G., "The Ethics of Perform-
      ing Animals," Fortnightly Review,
      Vol. 73, March 1, 1900, pp. 382-91.

442. Bensusan, S.L., "The Torture of Train-
      ed Animals," English Illustrated
      Magazine, Vol. 15, 1896, pp. 25-30.

19: Zoos

443. "Orpheus at the Zoo," The Spectator,
      Vol. 67, October 3, 1891, pp. 445-6.
      Also The Spectator, Vol. 67, 1891,
      pp. 491-2.

19: Work

444. Shaler, N.S., "Beasts of Burden," *Scribner's Magazine*, Vol. 16, July, 1894, pp. 82-100.

445. Buel, C.C., "Henry Bergh and His
      Work," Scribner's Monthly, Vol.
      17, April, 1879, pp. 872-884.

446. Dalton, J.C., "Mr. Bergh as a Com-
      mentator," The Nation, Vol. 29,
      October 16, 1879, pp. 256-7. Also
      November 6, 1879, pp. 309-10. Also
      November 20, 1879, pp. 346-7.

447. "Disunion in the Camp," Journal of
      Science, Vol. 19, January, 1882,
      pp. 8-16.

448. Japp, A.H., "For Bird and Beast,"
      Good Words, Vol. 15, 1874, pp. 531-
      6.

449. LeFann, Emma, "On the Ameliorating
      Influence of the Humane Principles
      Advocated by the Royal Society for
      the Prevention of Cruelty to Animals
      on Society and on Individuals,"
      Sharpe's London Magazine, Vol. 13,
      1851, pp. 188-91.

450. "The Other S.P.C.A." (Society for the
      Promotion of Cruelty to Animals),
      Penn Monthly Magazine, Vol. 12, Jan-
      uary, 1881, pp. 53-71. (A satiric
      criticism of some of the basic prin-
      ciples used by the American Society
      for the Prevention of Cruelty to
      Animals.)

451. Records of Proceedings in Parliament,
      Letters and Articles in the "Times"
      and Other Publications and of the
      General Progress of Public Opinion,
      with Reference to the Prevention of
      Cruelty to Animals and the Promotion
      of Their Proper Care and Treatment,

1800-1895, Royal Society for the
Prevention of Cruelty to Animals,
London.

452. Royal Society for the Prevention of
Cruelty to Animals, <u>Tracts</u>, London,
1860's:
"On Cruelty"
"On Cruelty to Horses"
"On Cruelty to Brutes"
"Humanity to Animals Recommended"
"Birds' Nesting"
"To Drovers"
"A short Essay on Cruelty to Animals"
"The History of William Brown or
Cruelty to Animals Punished"
"The Inculcation of Humanity to
Animals, Essential to Enlight-
ened and Christian Education,"
by The Lord Bishop of St. Davids
"Cruelty Exposed and Humanity
Pleaded"
"An Address to Omnibus Drivers,
Cabmen, Etc."
"An Address to Donkey Drivers and
Others"
"Against Cruelty to Animals, Ad-
dressed to Young Children"
"A Few Words to Drovers and Butchers"
"Cruelty and Humanity"

453. Adams, Donald K., "The Inference of
      Mind," Psychological Review, Vol.
      35, May, 1928, pp. 235-52.

454. Alverdes, F., The Psychology of Ani-
      mals, In Relation to Human Psychol-
      ogy, Harcourt, Brace, London, 1932.

455. Alverdes, F., Social Life in the
      Animal World, trans. by K.C. Creasy,
      Kegan Paul, Trench, Trubner, New
      York, 1927.

456. Balfour-Murphy, K., "Reason in Ani-
      mals," Chamber's Journal, Vol. 78,
      October 12, 1901, pp. 734-6.

457. Bierens de Haan, J.A., Animal
      Psychology, Its Nature and Its
      Problems, Hutchinsons, London, 1946.

458. Buckner, E. D., The Immortality of
      Animals, George W. Jacobs, Phila-
      delphia, 1903.

459. Burroughs, John, "Animal Individual-
      ity," Independent, Vol. 56, 1904,
      pp. 85-7.

460. Burroughs, John, "The Animal Mind,"
      in Burroughs, John, The Writings
      of John Burroughs: The Summit of
      the Years, Houghton Mifflin Co.,
      Boston, 1913.

461. Burroughs, John, "Current Misconcep-
      tions in Natural History," Century
      Illustrated Monthly Magazine, Vol.
      67, February, 1904, pp. 509-517.

462.   Burroughs, John, "Do Animals Reason?"
      Outing Magazine, Vol. 45, 1904-5,
      pp. 758-9.

463.   Burroughs, John, "Do Animals Think?"
      Harper's Monthly Magazine, Vol.
      110, February, 1905, pp. 354-358.

464.   Burroughs, John, "Do Animals Think?"
      Outing Magazine, Vol. 45, 1904-5,
      pp. 379-80.

465.   Burroughs, John, "Human Traits in
      the Animals," Outing Magazine,
      Vol. 49, 1906, pp. 297-304.

466.   Burroughs, John, "On Humanizing the
      Animals," Century Illustrated
      Monthly Magazine, Vol. 67, March,
      1904, pp. 773-780.

467.   Burroughs, John, "What Do Animals
      Know?" "Do Animals Think and Re-
      flect?" in Burroughs, John, Ways
      of Nature, Books for Libraries
      Press, Essay Index Reprint Series,
      Freeport, N.Y., 1971.

468.   Burroughs, John, The Writings of
      John Burroughs, 23 Volumes,
      Houghton Mifflin, Boston, 1923.

469.   Burton, M., "Commentary: An Evalu-
      ation of Animal and Human Mentality,"
      Research, Vol. 3, July, 1950, pp.
      293-7.

470.   Carr, Harvey, "The Interpretation
      of the Animal Mind," Psychological
      Review, Vol. 34, March, 1927, pp.
      87-106.

1901-50: Animal and Human Nature

471. Claparede, Edouard, "Consciousness
of Animals," International Quarterly, Vol. 8, 1903, pp. 296-315.

472. Coleridge, Gilbert, "Collective Action
in Animals," English Review, Vol. 62,
March, 1936, pp. 278-81.

473. Craig, Wallace, "Why Do Animals Fight?"
International Journal of Ethics, Vol.
31, April, 1921, pp. 264-78.

474. Deacon, C.F., "Do Animals Reason?"
Outing Magazine, Vol. 45, 1904-5,
pp. 760-1.

475. "Do Animals Reason?" Spectator, Vol.
102, June 5, 1909, pp. 888-9.

476. Douglas, Gordon, "Some Peculiarities
of the Animal Mind," Cornhill
Magazine, Vol. 67, September, 1929,
pp. 353-64.

477. Douglas, J.W.B. and Whitty, C.W.M.,
"An Investigation of Number Appreciation in Some Sub-Human Primates," Journal of Comparative
Psychology, Vol. 31, February,
1941, pp. 129-43.

478. Drury, Samuel H., "Man and Beast,"
The Atlantic Monthly, Vol. 97,
March, 1906, pp. 420-423.

479. Ealand, C.A., Animal Ingenuity of
Today, A Description of the Skill,
Clever Devices and Stratagems of
Birds, Reptiles, Insects and other
Forms of Animal Life, and Their
Means of Subsistence and Protection,
Seeley, London, 1921.

1901-50: Animal and Human Nature

480. Fraser-Harris, D.F., "The Problem of
      Pain in Animals," Discovery, Vol.
      11, August, 1930, pp. 273-6.

481. Frazer, Sir James G., "Language of
      Animals," in Frazer, Sir James G.,
      Garnered Sheaves, Books for Li-
      braries Press, Freeport, N.Y. 1967.

482. Fuller, B.A.G., "The Messes Animals
      Make in Metaphysics," The Journal of
      Philosophy, Vol. 46, December
      22, 1949, pp. 829-38.

483. Gooch, G.B., "Curiosity in Wild
      Animals," in Essays of the Year:
      1929-1930, Argonaut Press, London,
      1930.

484. Gordon, Douglas, "The Family Life
      of Animals," Quarterly Review,
      Vol. 280, January, 1943, pp. 40-51.

485. Hebb. D. O., "Emotion in Man and
      Animal," Psychological Review, Vol.
      53, March, 1946, pp. 88-106.

486. Hornaday, William T., The Mind and
      Manners of Wild Animals, Charles
      Scribner's, New York, 1922.

487. Huxley, Thomas H., Collected Essays,
      Vol. 2, Darwiniana, D. Appleton
      and Co., New York, 1912. (19th
      Century.)

488. Jenkins, Finley D., "The Problem of
      Mental Evolution," Princeton
      Theological Review, Vol. 22, Jan-
      uary-April, 1924, pp. 46-71 and
      277-302.

489. Jennings, H.S., "Mind in Animals,"

American Naturalist, Vol. 42, November 1908, pp. 754-60.

490. Littman, Richard A., "A Reply to Professor Mandelbaum's Note," Journal of Philosophy, Vol. 40, July 8, 1943, pp. 374-7. (Rejection of anthropomorphism in psychology.)

491. Long, William J., "Animal Individuality," Independent, Vol. 56, 1904, pp. 1242-48.

491. Long, William J., "Do Animals Reason?"
a   Independent, Vol. 59, 1905, pp. 481-5.

492. Long, William J., "The Question of Animal Reason," Harper's Monthly Magazine, Vol. 111, September, 1905, pp. 588-594.

493. Lovejoy, Arthur O., "The Chain of Being in Eighteenth-Century Thought, and Man's Place and Role in Nature," in Lovejoy's The Great Chain of Being, Harper and Row, New York, 1936, pp. 183-207.

494. McCabe, Joseph, "Instinct and Intelligence in the Insect," and "Mind in the Bird," in McCabe's The Evolution of Mind, Adam and Charles Black, London, 1910.

495. MacDougall, Helena, The Larger Social Contract, Essays on Humanity and Sub-Humanity, Essendon Gazette, Victoria, Australia, 1947.

496. McDougall, Kenneth D. and McDougall, William, "Insight and Foresight in

Various Animals--Monkey, Racoon, Rat and Wasp," Journal of Compara‑ tive Psychology, Vol. 11, February, 1931, pp. 237-73.

497. Mach, Ernst, "Some Sketches in Com‑ parative Animal and Human Psychol‑ ogy," Open Court, Vol, 32, June. 1918, pp. 363-76.

498. Mandelbaum, Maurice, "A Note on 'An‑ thropomorphism' in Psychology," Journal of Philosophy, Vol. 40, April 29, 1943, pp. 246-8.

499. Maxwell, Herbert, "Animal Intel‑ ligence," Littell's Living Age, Vol. 238, 1903, pp. 471-83.

500. Mellersh, H.E., "Animals' Play," New Statesman and Nation, Vol. 7, March 24, 1934, pp. 445-6.

501. "The Moral Sense in Animals," The Spectator, Vol, 95, December 30, 1905, pp. 1115-16.

502. Noble, Ruth R., The Nature of the Beast, A Popular Account of Animal Psychology from the Point of View of a Naturalist, Doubleday, Garden City, New York, 1945.

503. Packard, Vance, Animal IQ: The Human Side of Animals, Dial Press, New York, 1950.

504. Pitt, Frances, "Humour in Animals," Spectator, Vol. 140, March 24, 1928, pp. 449-50.

505. Pycraft, W.P., The Courtship of

Animals, Hutchinson, London, 1913.

506. Rabbit, Peter, "Animal Immortality," Harper's Monthly Magazine, Vol. 111, November, 1905, pp. 873-8.

507. Revesz, G., "The Language of Animals," Journal of General Psychology, Vol. 30, April, 1944, pp. 117-47.

508. Rutledge, Archibald, "Feminine Traits in Wild Things," Virginia Quarterly Review, Vol. 3, April, 1927, pp. 201 ll.

509. Schmid, Bastian, Interviewing Animals, trans. by Bernard Miall, Houghton Mifflin, Boston, 1937.

510. Smith, E.M., The Investigation of Mind in Animals, Cambridge University Press, Cambridge, 1915.

511. Spiller, G., "Characters Common to Animals and Man," and "Man's Place Among Living Beings," in Spiller's The Origin and Nature of Man, Williams and Morgate, London, 1935, pp. 37-101, 148-84.

512. Sprague, Lynn T., "Do Animals Think?" Outing Magazine, Vol. 39, 1901-02, pp. 427-31.

513. Thomson, Sir John A., "Do Animals Think?" in Thomson, Sir John A., Riddles of Science, Books for Libraries Press, Essay Index Reprint Series, Freeport, N.Y., 1971.

514. Tolman, Edward C., Purposive Behavior in Animals and Men, Century, New York, 1932.

515. Washburn, Margaret Floy, The Animal Mind, A Textbook of Comparative Psychology, Macmillan, 1908.

516. Watson, John B., Behavior: An Introduction to Comparative Psychology, Holt, New York, 1914.

517. Watson, John B., Psychology: From the Standpoint of a Behaviorist, Lippincott, Philadelphia, 1919.

518. Wilson, J. Stitt, "The Christ-Spirit in the Animal World," Methodist Review, Vol. 106, July and September and November, 1923, pp. 574-9, 768-80, 874-87.

1951-80: Animal and Human Nature
(For additional entries related to this topic
see 2693, 2713, 2600, 2606.)

519. Akmajian, A., Demers, R.A., and Harnish,
     R.M., "Animal Communication Systems,"
     in Linguistics: An Introduction to
     Language and Communication, by A.
     Akmajian, R.A. Demers, and R.M.
     Harnish, MIT Press, Cambridge, 1979,
     pp. 7-66.

520. Allee, Warden C., Cooperation Among
     Animals, with Human Implications,
     Abelard-Schuman, New York, 1951.

521. "Animal Behavior," Special Issue of
     International Wildlife, September-
     October, 1979.

522. Appleton, Tim, "Consciousness in
     Animals," Zygon, Vol. 11, December,
     1976.

523. Archer, John, Animals Under Stress,
     University Park Press, Baltimore,
     1979.

524. Armstrong, David M., "Belief and
     Language," in Armstrong, David M.,
     Belief, Truth and Knowledge, Uni-
     versity Press, Cambridge, 1973.
     (Discussion of whether animals have
     beliefs.) pp. 24-37.

525. Atherton, Margaret and Schwartz, Robert,
     "Linguistic Innateness and Its
     Evidence," Journal of Philosophy, Vol.
     71, No. 6, March 28, 1974, pp. 155-
     168.

526. Balz, Albert G.A., "Cartesian Doc-
     trine and the Animal Soul," in
     Balz, Albert G.A., Cartesian Studies,

Columbia University Press, New York, 1951.

527. Banks, Edwin M., ed., Vertebrate Social Organization, Dowden, Hutchinson and Ross, Stroudesberg, PA, 1977.

528. Barber, Carolyn, Animals at War, Harper and Row, New York, 1971.

529. Bateson, P.P.G., and Klopfer, Peter H., eds., Perspectives in Ethology, 3 Volumes, Plenum Press, New York-London, 1973, 1976, 1978.

530. Bayless, Raymond, Animal Ghosts, University Books, New York, 1970. (On animals and ESP and survival of death.)

531. Beck, Benjamin B., Animal Tool Behavior, The Use and Manufacture of Tools by Animals, Garland STPM Press, New York, 1980.

532. Becker, Earnest, "Toward the Merger of Animal and Human Studies," Philosophy of the Social Sciences, Vol. 4, June-September, 1974, pp. 235-54.

533. Bennett, Jonathan F., Rationality, Humanities Press, New York, 1964. (Includes an analysis of the behavior of honey bees and other animals in relation to language, intelligence and rationality.)

534. Beston, Henry, The Outermost House: A Year of Life on the Great Beach of Cape Cod, Viking Press, New York, 1971. See page 25 for a frequently quoted paragraph:

We need another and a wiser
and perhaps a more mystical concept of animals. Remote from
universal nature, and living by
complicated artifice, man in civilization surveys the creature
through the glass of his knowledge and sees thereby a feather
magnified and the whole image in
distortion. We patronize them
for their incompleteness, for
their tragic fate of having taken
form so far below ourselves.
And therein we err, and greatly
err. For the animal shall not
be measured by man. In a world
older and more complete than ours
they move finished and complete,
gifted with extensions of the
senses we have lost or never
attained, living by voices we
shall never hear. They are not
brethren, they are not underlings;
they are other nations, caught
with ourselves in the net of life
and time, fellow prisoners of the
splendour and travail of the earth.

535. Blyth, Edward, "Psychological Dis-
      tinctions between Man and Other
      Animals," in Loren Eiseley's
      Darwin and the Mysterious Mr. X,
      Dutton, New York, 1979.

536. Bonner, John T., The Evolution of
      Culture in Animals, Princeton Uni-
      versity Press, Princeton, 1980.

537. Boone, J. Allen, Kinship with All
      Life, Harper & Row, New York, 1976.

538. Boone, J.Allen, The Language of
      Silence, Harper & Row, 1970.

539. Borgese, Elizabeth M., The Language Barrier: Beasts and Men, Rinehart and Winston, New York, 1968.

540. Bromfield, Louis, Animals and Other People, Harper, New York, 1955.

541. Brophy, Brigid, "The Darwinist's Dilemma," in Animals' Rights--A Symposium, ed. by David Paterson and Richard D. Ryder (1231)

542. Burton, Maurice, "Can Animals Show Compassion?" Illustrated London News, Vol. 239, December 30, 1961, p. 1156.

543. Burton, Maurice, Infancy in Animals, Hutchinson, London, 1956.

544. Burton, Maurice, Just Like An Animal, Dent, London, 1978.

545. Burton, Maurice, The Sixth Sense of Animals, Taplinger, New York, 1972.

546. Butler, S.T., and Raymond, Robert, Secrets of Animal Behavior, Doubleday, Garden City, New York, 1975. (In comic book style.)

547. Callahan, Philip S., Tuning in to Nature, Solar Energy, Infrared Radiation, and the Insect Communication System, Devin-Adair, Old Greenwich, Conn. 1975.

548. Cansdale, George, Animals and Man, White Lion Publishers, New York, 1953.

549. Carrier, L.S., "Perception and

Animal Belief," Philosophy, Vol.
55, April, 1980, pp. 193-209.

550. Carrighar, Sally, "How Red the Tooth
and Claw?" and "Animals and Men:
The Blurred Borderline," in Carrighar's
Wild Heritage, Houghton Mifflin,
Boston, 1965.

551. Chauvin, Remy, Animal Societies, From
the Bee to the Gorilla, trans. by
George Ordish, Hill and Wang, New
York, 1968.

552. Chesterman, J., Marten, M., May, J.,
and Torrey, L., The Book of Beasts,
Hamlyns, Feltham, Middx., U.K., 1980.

553. Clarke, James F., Man Is the Prey,
Stein and Day, New York, 1969.

554. Cloudsley-Thompson, John, Animal
Migration, ORBIS Publications,
London, 1978.

555. Cohen, Daniel, Watchers in the Wild;
the New Science of Ethology, Little,
Brown, Boston, 1971.

556. Cousteau, Jacques-Y., Invisible Mes-
sages, Angus and Robertson, London,
1974.

557. Cranach, Mario von, "Inference from
Animal to Human Behaviour: Con-
clusions," in Methods of Inference
from Animal to Human Behaviour, ed.
by Mario von Cranach, Aldine, Chicago,
1976, pp. 355-89.

558. Crawford, F.T. and Prestrude, A.M.,
eds., "Animal Hypnosis: Research
and Theory," Psychological Record,

Vol. 27, 1977, pp. 1-218, special issue.

559. Dallery, Carleton, "Thinking and Being with Beasts," in On the Fifth Day, ed. by Morris and Fox (1219). (From the perspective of Phenomenology: Husserl and Merleau-Ponty.)

560. Davis, Flora, Eloquent Animals: A Study in Animal Communication, How Chimps Lie, Whales Sing, and Slime Molds Pass the Message Along, Coward, McCann, and Geoghegan, New York, 1978.

561. Dawkins, Richard, The Selfish Gene, Oxford University Press, London, 1976.

562. Deely, John N., "Animal Intelligence and Concept-Formation," Thomist, Vol. 35, pp. 43-93, January, 1971. (The Thomistic view, in opposition to the view of Peter Geach.)

563. Dembeck, Hermann, Animals and Men, Natural History Press, New York, 1965.

564. Desmond, Adrian, The New Reformation: Darwin and the Reign of Law, Blond and Briggs, London, forthcoming.

565. Droscher, Vitus B., The Friendly Beast; Latest Discoveries in Animal Behavior, trans. by Richard and Clara Winston, Dutton, New York, 1971.

566. Droscher, Vitus B., They Love and Kill, Sex, Sympathy and Aggression in

Courtship and Mating, trans. by
Jan van Heurck, Dutton, New York,
1976.

567. Durrell, Gerald, Encounters with
Animals, Avon, New York, 1970.

568. Eibl-Eibesfeldt, Irenaus, The Biology
of Peace and War, Men, Animals, and
Aggression, trans. by Eric Mosbacher,
Viking, New York, 1979.

569. Eibl-Eibesfeldt, Irenaus, Ethology,
The Biology of Behavior, trans.
by Erich Klinghammer, Holt, Rinehart
and Winston, New York, 1975.

570. Eibl-Eibesfeldt, Irenaus, Love and
Hate: The Natural History of Be-
havior Patterns, trans. Geoffrey
Strachan, Methuen, London, 1971.

571. Eisenberg, John F., and Dillon, Wilton
S., eds., Man and Beast: Comparative
Social Behavior, Smithsonian Insti-
tution Press, Washington, D.C., 1971.

572. Eiseley, Loren, Darwin's Century,
Doubleday, New York, 1955.

573. Eisner, Thomas, and Wilson, Edward O.,
eds., Animal Behavior--Readings from
Scientific American, W.H. Freeman,
San Francisco, 1975.

574. Ekman, Paul, ed., Darwin and Facial
Expression, Academic Press, New
York, 1974.

575. Etkin, William, Social Behavior from
Fish to Man, University of Chicago
Press, Chicago, 1967.

576. Evans, William F., Communication in
the Animal World, Thomas Y. Crowell,
New York, 1968.

577. Filloux, Jean-Claude, The Psychology
of Animals, trans. by James J.
Walling, Walker, New York, 1963.

578. Fink, Harold K., Mind and Performance,
A Comparative Study of Learning in
Mammals, Birds and Reptiles, Vantage,
New York, 1954.

579. Fox, Michael W., ed., Abnormal Behavior
in Animals, W.B. Saunders, Philadelphia, 1968.

580. Fox, Michael W., Between Animal and
Man, Coward, McCann & Geoghegan,
New York, 1976.

581. Fox, Michael W., Concepts in Ethology:
Animal and Human Behavior, University
of Minnesota Press, Minneapolis, 1974.

582. Fox, Michael W., "Man and Nature;
Biological Perspectives," in On the
Fifth Day, ed. by Morris and Fox
(1219).

583. Friedrich, Heinz, comp., Man and
Animal: Studies in Behavior, trans.
by Mechthild Nawiasky, St. Martin's
Press, New York, 1972.

584. Gardner, R. Allen and Beatrice T.,
"Comparative Psychology and Language
Acquisition," in Psychology: The
State of the Art, ed. by Kurt
Salzinger and Florence L. Denmark,
New York Academy of Sciences, New
York, 1978, pp. 37-76.

1951-80: Animal and Human Nature

585. Graven, Jacques, Non-Human Thought,
     The Mysteries of the Animal Psyche,
     trans. by Harold J. Salemson, Stein
     and Day, New York, 1967.

586. Gilbert, Bil, "A Longing to Know
     Other Bloods,: International Wildlife,
     September-October, 1979.

587. Gould, Stephen J., Ever Since Darwin,
     W.W. Norton, New York, 1977.

588. Gould, Stephen J., "Man and Other
     Animals," Natural History, Vol. 84,
     August-September, 1975, pp. 24-30.

589. Graham, Michael, "Crowds and the Like in
     Vertebrates," Human Relations,
     Vol. 17, November, 1964, pp. 377-90.

590. Greene, John C., The Death of Adam;
     Evolution and Its Impact on Western
     Thought, New American Library, New
     York, 1961.

591. Griffin, Donald R., "A Possible Window
     on the Minds of Animals," American
     Scientist, Vol. 64, September-Oc-
     tober, 1976, pp. 530-35.

592. Griffin, Donald R., The Question of
     Animal Awareness, Rockefeller
     University Press, New York, 1976.

593. Gunderson, Keith, "Descartes, LaMettrie,
     Language and Machines," Philosophy,
     Vol. 39, July, 1964, pp. 193-222.

594. Hahn, Emily, "Getting Thru to the
     Others: Animal Communication,"
     Part I: New Yorker, April 17, 1978.
     Part II: New Yorker, April 24, 1978.

595. Hall, Elton A., and King-Farlow, John, "Man, Beast, and Philosophical Psychology," The British Journal for the Philosophy of Science, Vol. 16, August, 1965, pp. 81-101.

596. Hall, Rebecca, Animals Are Equal, An Exploration of Animal Consciousness, Wildwood House, London, 1980.

597. Hartshorne, Charles, "Foundations for Human Ethics: What Human Beings Have in Common with Other Higher Animals," in On the Fifth Day, ed. by Morris and Fox (1219).

598. Hartshorne, Charles, "The Unity of Man and the Unity of Nature," in The Logic of Perfection, Open Court, La Salle, Illinois, 1973.

599. Hawkins, T.S., The Soul of an Animal, George Allen and Unwin, London, not dated.

600. Hays, H.R., Birds, Beasts, and Men, Dent, London, 1973.

601. Heim, Alice, Intelligence and Personality, Pelican Books, Harmondsworth, Middlesex, 1970. See p. 148.

602. Hill, Jane H., "Possible Continuity Theories of Language," Language, Vol. 50, No. 1, March, 1974, pp. 134-150.

603. Hinde, Robert A., Instinct and Intelligence, Oxford Biology Readers: 63, Oxford University Press, London, 1976. (Discusses animal intelligence.)

1951-80: Animal and Human Nature

604. Hinde, R.A., ed., *Non-Verbal Communication*, Cambridge University Press, Cambridge, 1972.

605. Hopson, Janet, "Growl, Bark, Whine and Hiss," *Science 80*, May/June 1980, pp. 80-4. (On animal communication)

606. Hume, C.W., *Man and Beast*, Universities Federation for Animal Welfare, London, 1962.

607. Hunt, Morton, "Man and Beast," in Montague, Ashley, ed., *Man and Aggression*, Oxford University Press, New York, 1973.

609. Irvine, William, *Apes, Angels and Victorians*, McGraw Hill, New York, 1955.

610. Johnson, Sally P., ed., *Everyman's Ark*, A Collection of True First-Person Accounts of Relationships between Animals and Men, Hamish Hamilton, London, 1962.

611. Jonas, Hans, *The Phenomenon of Life*, Harper & Row, New York, 1966.

612. Jones, R.K., "The Ethological Fallacy; A Note in Reply to Mr. Meynell," *Philosophy*, Vol. 47, January, 1972, pp. 71-73.

613. Jordan, W.S., "Altruism and Aggression in Animals," in *Animals' Rights--A Symposium*, ed. by David Paterson and Richard D. Ryder (1231).

614. Katz, David, Animals and Men,
Penguin, Baltimore, 1953.

615. Keehn, J.D. ed., Psychopathology
in Animals, Research and Clinical
Implications, Academic Press, New
York, 1979.

616. Kerr, Richard A. "Quake Prediction
by Animals Gaining Respect," Science,
Vol. 208, May 16, 1980, pp. 695-6.

617. Kiley-Worthington, M., Behavioural
Problems of Animals, Oriel Press,
Newcastle-upon-Tyne, 1977.

618. Klopfer, P.H., McGeorge, L., and
Barnett, R.J., Maternal Care in
Mammals, Addison-Wesley Module
in Biology, No. 4, Addison-Wesley,
Reading, MA, 1973.

619. Kmetz, John M., "A Study of Primary
Perception in Plant and Animal Life,"
American Society for Psychical
Research Journal, Vol. 71, April,
1977, pp. 157-69.

620. Knight, Maxwell, Animals and Ourselves,
Hodder and Stoughton, London, 1962.

621. Koehler, Otto, "Animal Languages and
Human Speech," in The Human Creature,
ed. by Gunter Altner, Anchor Press,
Garden City, N.Y., 1969.

622. Krutch, Joseph Wood, "Undeveloped
Potentialities," (of animals) in
Krutch's The Great Chain of Life,
Houghton Mifflin, Boston, 1977.

623. Landmann, Michael, "Man's Place in

the Animal Kingdom," in his
Philosophical Anthropology, trans.
by D.J. Parent, Westminster Press,
Philadelphia, 1974.

624. Langer, Susanne K., "Man and Animal:
The City and the Hive," in Langer,
Susanne K., Philosophical Sketches,
Johns Hopkins Press, Baltimore, 1962.

625. Leakey, Richard E., and Lewin, Roger,
"Is It Our Culture, Not Our Genes,
That Makes Us Killers?" Smithsonian,
November, 1977.

626. Leakey, Richard E. and Lewin, Roger,
Origins (of man in relation to
primates), Dutton, New York, 1977.

627. Leakey, Richard E. and Lewin, Roger,
People of the Lake, Mankind and Its
Beginnings, Doubleday, Garden City,
N.Y., 1978.

628. Lee, Donald C., "On the Marxian View
of the Relationship between Man and
Nature," Environmental Ethics, Vol.
2, No. 1, Spring, 1980, pp. 3-16.

629. Linden, Eugene, "Darwin in the Temple
of Plato," in the author's Apes,
Men and Language, Saturday Review
Press, New York, 1974. Also Pelican,
Baltimore, 1976.

630. Linzey, Andrew, "Man, Nature and
Animals," Church Times, October
31, 1975.

631. Lipman, Matthew, "Difference between
Animals and Humans," in Lipman's
Harry Stottlemeier's Discovery,

Chapter 7, pp. 31-34, Institute
for the Advancement of Philosophy
for Children, Montclair State College,
Upper Montclair, N.J., 1977. (For
grades 5 and 6).

633. Lockard, Robert B., "Reflections on
the Fall of Comparative Psychology,"
American Psychologist, Vol. 26, February, 1971, pp. 168-179.

634. Lorenz, Konrad, "Ecce Homo! Fish,
Birds, Rats and Men (II)," Encounter,
Vol. 27, September, 1966, pp. 25-39.

635. Lorenz, Konrad, On Aggression, trans.
by Marjorie Kerr Wilson, Harcourt,
Brace, New York, 1963.

636. Lorenz, Konrad, "On Aggression: Fish,
Birds, Rats, and Men (I)," Encounter,
Vol. 27, August, 1966, pp. 29-40.

637. Lorenz, Konrad, "Pitying Animals" and
"The Languages of Animals," in Lorenz'
King Solomon's Ring, trans. by
Marjorie Kerr Wilson, Crowell, New
York, 1952.

638. Lorenz, Konrad, "Rats, Apes, Naked
Apes, Kipling, Instincts, Guilt,
the Generations and Instant Cop-
ulation--A Talk with Konrad Lorenz,"
New York Times Sunday Magazine
Section, July 5, 1970, pp. 4-5, 27,
29-30.

639. Lorenz, Konrad, Studies in Animal and
Human Behavior, trans. by Robert
Martin, 2 Vols., Harvard University
Press, Cambridge, 1970.

1951-80: Animal and Human Nature

640. Maddock, Alison, Animals at Peace, Harper and Row, New York, 1971.

641. Malcolm, Norman, "Thoughtless Brutes," Proceedings of American Philosophical Association, Vol. 46, 1972-73, pp. 5-20. Also in Malcolm's Thought and Knowledge, Cornell University Press, Ithaca, 1977.

642. Marchant, R.A., Man and Beast, Macmillan, New York, 1968.

643. Markowitz, H. and Stevens, V.J., eds., Behavior of Captive Wild Animals, Nelson Hall, Chicago, 1978.

644. Matthews, Gareth B., "Animals and the Unity of Psychology," Philosophy, Vol. 53, October, 1978, pp. 437-54.

645. Matthews, Leonard H., and Knight, Maxwell, The Senses of Animals, Museum Press, London, 1963.

646. Medin, Douglas L., Roberts, William A., and Davis, Roger T., Processes of Animal Memory, Lawrence Erlbaum Associates, Hillsdale, New Jersey, 1976.

647. Mery, Fernand, Animal Languages, trans. by Michael Ross, Saxon House, Farnborough, Hampshire, U.K., 1975.

648. Meynell, Hugo, "Ethology and Ethics," Philosophy, Vol. 45, October, 1970, pp. 290-306.

649. Meynell, Hugo, "On Geese and R.K. Jones," Philosophy, Vol. 50, January, 1975, pp. 104-5.

1951-80: Animal and Human Nature

650. Midgley, Mary, Beast and Man, The
      Roots of Human Nature, Cornell
      University Press, Ithaca, N.Y., 1978.

651. Midgley, Mary, "The Concept of Beast-
      liness: Philosophy, Ethics and Animal
      Behavior," Philosophy, Vol. 48, April,
      1973, pp. 111-35.

652. Midgley, Mary, "Gene-Juggling," Phi-
      losophy, Vol. 54, October, 1979,
      pp. 439-458.

653. Midgley, Mary, "Rational and Animal,"
      New Scientist, Vol. 81, March 15,
      1979, pp. 861-63.

654. Milne, Lorus and Margery, The Senses
      of Animals and Men, Atheneum, New
      York, 1962.

655. Milne, Lorus J. and Margery, and
      Russell, Franklin, The Secret Life
      of Animals, Pioneering Discoveries
      in Animal Behavior, Dutton, New
      York, 1975 (?).

656. Montague, Ashley, ed., Man and
      Aggression, Oxford University Press,
      New York, 1968.

657. Montefiore, Hugh, ed., Man and Nature,
      Collins, London, 1975.

658. Morris, Desmond, Patterns of Repro-
      ductive Behaviour, McGraw Hill,
      New York, 1970.

659. Morris, Robert L., "Parapsychology,
      Biology, and ANPSI," in Handbook
      of Parapsychology, ed. by Benjamin
      B. Wolman, Van Nostrand Reinhold,

1951-80:   Animal and Human Nature

New York, 1977, pp. 687-715.

660.   Muckler, F.A., "On The Reason Of
        Animals: Historical Antecedents
        To The Logic of Modern Behaviorism,"
        Psychological Reports, Vol. 12, 1963,
        p. 863.

661.   Muller-Schwarze, Dietland, Evolution
        of Play Behavior, Dowden, Hutchinson
        and Ross, Stroudsburg, Pennsylvania,
        1978.

662.   Munn, Norman L., "The Rise of Animal
        Intelligence," in Munn's The Evolution
        of the Human Mind, Houghton Mifflin,
        Boston, 1971, pp. 116-60.

663.   Peters, Michael, "Nature and Culture,"
        in Animals, Men and Morals, ed. by
        Godlovitch and Harris (1172).

664.   Premack, D., "On Animal Intelligence,"
        in Jerison, H., ed., Perspectives on
        Intelligence, Appleton-Century-Croft,
        New York, forthcoming.

665.   Premack, David, "On the Assessment of
        Language Competence in the Chimpanzee,"
        in Behavior of Nonhuman Primates, Vol.
        4, ed. by A.M. Schrier and F. Stollnitz,
        Academic Press, New York, 1971, pp.
        185-228.

666.   Premack, David, and Woodruff, Guy,
        "Chimpanzee Problem-Solving: A
        Test for Comprehension," Science,
        Vol. 202, November 3, 1978, pp.
        532-535.

667.   Prince, Jack H., Animals in the Night,
        Senses in Action after Dark, Angus

and Robertson, Sydney, 1968.

668. Prince, Jack H., Languages of the
     Animal World, T. Nelson, Nashville,
     1975.

669. Portmann, Adolf, Animal Forms and
     Patterns, A Study of the Appearance
     of Animals, trans. by Hella Czech,
     Schocken, New York, 1967.

670. Portmann, Adolf, Animals as Social
     Beings, trans. by Oliver Coburn,
     Hutchinson, London, 1961.

671. Ratner, Stanley C., "Comparative
     Aspects of Hypnosis," in Handbook
     of Clinical and Experimental
     Hypnosis, ed. by Jesse E. Gordon,
     Macmillan, New York, 1967.

672. Rees, R.J.W., "Aspects of Stress in
     Man and Animals," Proceedings of
     Royal Society of Medicine, Section
     of Comparative Medicine, Vol. 68,
     1975, pp. 423 ff.

673. Revesz, Geza, "Is There an Animal
     Language?" Hibbert Journal, Vol.
     52, January, 1954, pp. 141-3.

674. Rheingold, Harriet L., Maternal Be-
     havior in Mammals, John Wiley,
     New York, 1963.

675. Rhine, J.B., "The Present Outlook
     on the Question of Psi in Animals,"
     Journal of Parapsychology, Vol. 15,
     1951, pp. 230-51.

676. Rhine, J.B., and Feather, S.R., "The
     Study of Cases of 'Psi-Trailing'

in Animals," Journal of Parapsychology, Vol. 26, 1962, pp.
1-22.

677. Ricard, Matthieu, The Mystery of
Animal Migration, trans. by Peter
J. Whitehead, Hill and Wang, New
York, 1969.

678. Riopelle, A.J., ed., Animal Problem
Solving, Penguin Books, Baltimore,
MD, 1967.

679. Ritchie, A.M., "Can Animals See? A
Cartesian Query," Proceedings of
the Aristotelian Society, Vol. 64,
1963-64, pp. 201-42.

680. Roberts, Catherine, Science, Animals
and Evolution, Reflections on Some
Unrealized Potentials of Biology
and Medicine, Greenwood Press,
Westport, Connecticut, 1980.

681. Roots, Clive, Animals of the Dark,
Praeger, New York, 1974.

682. Ruse, Michael, The Darwinian Rev-
olution, Science Red in Tooth and
Claw, University of Chicago Press,
Chicago, 1979.

683. Sagan, Carl, "The Abstractions of
Beasts," in Sagan's The Dragons
of Eden, Random House, New York,
1977.

684. Sales, Gillian, and Pye, David,
Ultrasonic Communication by Animals, Chapman and Hall, London, 1975.

685. Scheler, Max, "The Stages of Psycho-

physical Life in Plant, Animal and Man," in Scheler's Man's Place in Nature, trans. by Hans Meyerhoff, Beacon Press, Boston, 1961.

686. Schmidt, H., "PK Experiments with Animals as Subjects," Journal of Parapsychology, Vol. 34, 1970, pp. 255-61.

687. Sebeok, Thomas A., "Animal Communication," International Social Science Journal, Vol. 19, 1967, pp. 88-95.

688. Sebeok, Thomas A., ed., Animal Communication, Techniques of Study and Results of Research, Indiana University Press, Bloomington, 1968.

689. Sebeok, Thomas, "Between Animal and Animal," Times Literary Supplement, Vol. 72, October 5, 1973, pp. 1187-9.

690. Sebeok, Thomas A., ed., How Animals Communicate, Indiana University Press, Bloomington, Ind., 1977.

691. Sebeok, Thomas A., "Looking in the Destination for What Should Have Been Sought in the Source," Diogenes, Vol. 104, Winter, 1978, pp. 112-37.

692. Sebeok, Thomas A., Perspectives in Zoosemiotics, Mouton, The Hague, 1972.

693. Sebeok, Thomas A.,"'Talking' with Animals," Animals, Massachussets Society for the Prevention of Cruelty to Animals, December, 1978.

694. Sebeok, Thomas A., "Zoosemiotics: At the Intersection of Nature and Culture," in The Tell-Tale Sign, ed. by Thomas A. Sebeok, Peter de Ridder Press, Lisse, 1975.

695. Sebeok, Thomas A., "Zoosemiotics: Ethology and the Theory of Signs," in Current Trends in Linguistics, ed. by Sebeok, Mouton, The Hague, 1974.

696. Sebeok, Thomas A., and Ramsay, Alexandra, eds., Approaches to Animal Communication, Mouton, The Hague, 1969.

697. Seidler, Michael J., "Hume and the Animals," Southern Journal of Philosophy, Vol. 15, Fall, 1977, pp. 361-72.

698. Selye, H., "The Evolution of the Stress Concept," American Scientist, Vol. 61, 1973, pp. 692-9.

699. Shepard, Paul, Thinking Animals, Animals and the Development of Human Intelligence, Viking, New York, 1978.

700. Singh, Joseph A., and Zingg, Robert M., Wolf Children and Feral Man, Shoe String Press, Hamden, Conn., 1966.

701. Sire, Marcel, Social Life of Animals, trans. by Constance D. Sherman, Studio Vista, London, 1965.

702. Sluckin, Wladyslaw, Early Learning in Man and Animal, Schenkman,

Cambridge, Mass., 1972.

703. Sluckin, Wladyslaw, Fear in Animals and Man, Van Nostrand Reinhold, New York, 1979.

704. Smith, F.V., Attachment of the Young, Imprinting and Other Developments, Oliver and Boyd, Edinburgh, 1969.

705. Smith, F.V., Purpose in Animal Behavior, Hutchinson University Library, London, 1971.

706. Squadrito, Kathleen, "Descartes, Locke and the Soul of Animals," forthcoming, Philosophy Research Archives, a Bilingual Microfilm Journal of Philosophy, published by Philosophy Documentation Center, Bowling Green, Ohio.

707. Stade, George, "K. Lorenz and the Dog Beneath the Skin," Hudson Review, Vol. 26, Spring, 1973, pp. 60-86.

708. Stich, Stephen P., "Do Animals Have Beliefs?" Australasian Journal of Philosophy, Vol. 57, March, 1979, pp. 15-28.

709. Street, Philip, Animal Weapons, Taplinger, New York, 1971.

710. Syme, G.J., and Syme, L.A., Social Structure in Farm Animals, Elsevier, Amsterdam, 1979.

711. Thorpe, W.H., "Animal Communication and Language" and "Animal and Human Nature" in Thorpe's Science, Man and Morals, Cornell University

Press, Ithaca, N.Y., 1966, pp. 93-
11 and 62-92.

712. Thorpe, W.H., Animal Nature and Human
Nature, Methuen, London, 1974, also
Doubleday, New York, 1974.

713. Thorpe, W.H., "The Appearance of
Purposiveness in Animals," "Methods
of Communication between Animals,"
"Bird Voices," "Animal Linguistics,"
"'Speech' by Chimpanzees," "Syntax
in Animal Communication" and "The
Problem of Abstraction in Animals,"
in Thorpe's Purpose in a World of
Chance, A Biologist's View, Oxford
University Press, Oxford, 1978.

714. Thorpe, William H., Learning and
Instinct in Animals, Harvard University Press, Cambridge, 1963.

715. Thorpe, William H., The Origins and
Rise of Ethology, Praeger, New York,
1979.

716. Tinbergen, Nikolaas, The Animal in
Its World, Harvard University
Press, Cambridge, Mass., 1973.

717. Tinbergen, Nikolaas, "On War and
Peace in Animals and Man," Science,
Vol. 160, 1968, p. 1411.

718. Tinbergen, Nikolaas, Social Behaviour
in Animals, With Special Reference
to Vertebrates, Methuen, London, 1965.

719. Tinbergen, Nikolaas, The Study of
Instinct, Oxford University Press,
New York, 1958.

1951-80: Animal and Human Nature

720. Tinbergen, Nikolaas, and Falkus,
      Hugh, Signals for Survival, with
      drawings by Eric Ennion, Clarendon
      Press, Oxford, 1970.

721. Tranoy, Knut Erik, "Hume on Morals,
      Animals, and Men,' Journal of
      Philosophy, Vol, 56, January 29,
      1959, pp. 94-103.

722. Van Hooff, Jan, "The Comparison of
      Facial Expression in Man and Higher
      Primates," in Methods of Inference
      from Animal to Human Behaviour, ed.
      by Mario von Cranach, Aldine, Chicago,
      1976, pp. 165-96.

723. Veselovsky, Z., Are Animals Different?,
      Methuen, London, 1973.

724. Washburn, S.L., "Human Behavior and
      the Behavior of Other Animals,"
      American Psychologist, Vol. 33,
      May, 1978, pp. 405-18.

725. Weiss, Donald, "Professor Malcolm
      on Animal Intelligence," Philosoph-
      ical Review, Vol. 84, January, 1975,
      pp. 88-95.

726. Whitfield, Philip, The Hunters, Hamlyn
      Group, Astronaut House, Feltham,
      Middlesex, 1978. (On predation)

727. Wickler, Wolfgang, "Analogous Moral
      Behavior in Men and Animals," in
      Wickler's The Biology of the Ten
      Commandments, trans. by David Smith,
      McGraw-Hill, New York, 1972, pp. 48-62.

728. Wickler, Wolfgang, "Group Ties in

Animals and Man," in The Human
Creature, ed. by Gunter Altner,
Anchor Press, Garden City, N.Y.,
1969.

729. Wilson, Edward O., Sociobiology,
Harvard University Press, Cambridge,
Mass., 1975.

730. Winograd, Eugene, "Some Issues Re-
lating Animal Memory to Human
Memory," in Animal Memory, ed. by
Werner K. Honig and P.H.R. James,
Academic Press, New York, 1971,
pp. 258-78.

731. Wittgenstein, Ludwig, Philosophical
Investigations, trans. by G.E.M.
Anscombe, Macmillan, New York, 1958.
Passages on animals include:
I:25 (mental capacity of animals;
animals do not talk)
I:495 (animal reacting to signs)
I:647 (natural expression of
intentions in animals)
II: p. 174 (animals and anger,
fright, happiness, unhappiness,
hopefulness, belief, language)
II: p. 184 (evolution of con-
sciousness in animals and
humans)
II: p. 223 (humans could not
understand lions if lions
could talk)

732. Buyukmihci, Hope, Hour of the Beaver, Rand McNally, New York, 1971.

733. Grey Owl, A Book of Grey Owl, Pages from the Writing of Wa-sha-quon-asin (Archibald Stansfeld Belaney), ed. by E.E. Reynolds, Macmillan of Canada, Toronto, 1938.

734. Grey Owl (Wa-sha-quon-asin), (Archibald Stansfeld Belaney), Pilgrims of the Wild, Charles Scribner's, New York, 1971. (Grey Owl, a heavy trapper of beavers in his early life, later lived with pet beavers and stopped trapping.)

20: Birds

(For additional entries related to this topic see 2713, 2340, 2436, 2442, 2455, 1429, 713.)

735. Armstrong, E.A., Bird Display, An Introduction to the Study of Bird Psychology, Cambridge University Press, Cambridge, 1942.

736. Armstrong, Edward A., A Study of Bird Song, Dover, New York, 1973.

737. Collias, N.E., "The Development of Social Behavior in Birds," Auk, Vol. 69, April, 1952, pp. 127-59.

738. Douglis, Marjorie B., "Social Factors Influencing the Hierarchies of Small Flocks of the Domestic Hen," Physiological Zoology, April, 1948, pp. 147-82.

739. Fisher, Allen C., Jr., "Mysteries of Bird Migration," National Geographic, No. 2, August, 1979.

740. Gordon, Douglas, "Memory in Birds

and Beasts," Quarterly Review, Vol. 276, January, 1941, pp. 42-54.

741. Harris, James T., The Peregrine Falcon in Greenland, Observing an Endangered Species, University of Missouri Press, Columbia, MO, 1979.

742. Hinde, R.A., ed., Bird Vocalizations, Cambridge University Press, Cambridge, 1969.

743. Howard, Len, Living with Birds, Collins, London, 1956.

744. Jellis, Rosemary, Bird Sounds and Their Meaning, British Broadcasting Corporation, London, 1977.

745. Key, Alexander, The Strange White Doves, True Mysteries of Nature, Westminster Press, Philadelphia, 1972.

746. Kipps, Clare, Sold for a Farthing, Biography of a Common Sparrow, with a Foreword by Julian Huxley, Frederick Muller, London, 1955.

747. Lorenz, Konrad, The Year of the Greylag Goose, trans. by Robert Martin, Photographs by Sybille and Klaus Kalas, Harcourt Brace Jovanovich, New York, 1979. (Heavily illustrated.)

748. McCoy, J.J., The Hunt for the Whooping Cranes, Lothrop, Lee and Shepard, New York, 1966.

749. Masure, Ralph H. and Allee, W.C.,

"The Social Order in Flocks of the Common Chicken and the Pigeon." Auk, Vol. 51, July, 1934, pp. 306-27.

750. Murton, R.K., Man and Birds, Collins, London, 1971.

751. Nottebohm, Fernando, "Ontogeny of Bird Song," Science, Vol. 167, February 13, 1970, pp. 950-956.

752. Silver, Rae, Ed., Parental Behavior in Birds, Dowden, Hutchinson and Ross, Stroudsburg, Pennsylvania, 1977.

753. Simon, Hilda, The Courtship of Birds, Dodd, Mead, New York, 1977.

754. Skutch, Alexander F., Parent Birds and Their Young, University of Texas Press, Austin, 1976.

755. Smith, Susan T., Communication and other Social Behavior in the Carolina Chickadee, Publication No. 11, Nuttall Ornithological Club, Cambridge, Mass. 1972.

756. Thorpe, William H., Bird Song, Cambridge University Press, Cambridge, 1961.

757. Verhave, T., "The Pigeon as a Quality Control Inspector," American Psychologist, Vol. 21, February, 1966, pp. 109-15.

20: Canids

(For additional entries related to this topic
see 3071, 3129, 2352, 2574, 2049, 2067, 1100,
1424, 1504, 1526, 1558, 1618, 794, 991.)

758. Alexander, Samuel, "Mind of a Dog,"
in Alexander, Samuel, Philosophical
and Literary Pieces, pp. 97-115,
Macmillan, London, 1939. Also University Microfilms, Ann Arbor, Mich.,
1969.

759. Allen, Durward L., Wolves of Minong,
Their Vital Role in a Wild Community, Houghton Mifflin, Boston,
1979.

760. Bain, Read, "The Culture of Canines,"
Sociology and Social Research, Vol.
13, July, 1929, pp. 545-56.

761. Clarkson, Ewan, Wolf Country: A Wilderness Pilgrimage, Dutton, New York,
1975.

762. Colbert, Edwin H., The Origin of the
Dog, American Museum of Natural
History, New York, 1929.

763. Fiennes, R. and Fiennes, A., The
Natural History of the Dog,
Weidenfeld and Nicolson, London,
1968.

764. Fox, Michael W., Behavior of Wolves,
Dogs and Related Canids, Harper,
New York, 1973.

765. Fox, Michael W., The Dog: Its Domestication and Behavior, Garland
STPM Press, New York, 1978.

766. Fox, Michael W., The Soul of the Wolf,
Little, Brown, Boston, 1980.

767. Fox, Michael W., Understanding Your Dog, Coward, McCann & Geoghegan, New York, 1972.

768. Fox, Michael W., ed., The Wild Canids, Van Nostrand Reinhold, New York, 1975.

769. Heimann, Marcel, "The Relationship between Man and Dog," Psychoanalytical Quarterly, Vol. 25, 1956, pp. 568-85.

770. Kinderman, Henny, Lola, or the Thought and Speech of Animals, trans. by Agnes Blake, Dutton, New York, 1923.

771 Lopez, Barry H., Of Wolves and Men, Scribner, New York, 1978.

772. Lorenz, Konrad, Man Meets Dog, trans. by Marjorie Kerr Wilson, Viking Penguin, New York, 1965.

773. Mowat, Farley, Never Cry Wolf, Atlantic Monthly Press, Dell, New York, 1963.

774. Riddle, Maxwell, The Wild Dogs in Life and Legend, Howell Book House, New York, 1979.

775. Ross, Estelle, The Book of Noble Dogs, Thornton Butterworth, London, 1924.

776. Rutter, Russell J. and Pimlott, Douglas H., The World of the Wolf, Lippincott, New York, 1968.

777. Ryden, Hope, God's Dog, A Celebration of the North American Coyote, Penguin, London, 1979.

778. Sebeok, Thomas A., "Talking Dogs: Close

Encounters with Canid Communication of the Third Kind," _Animals_, Massachusetts Society for the Prevention of Cruelty to Animals, February, 1980.

779. Vesey-Fitzgerald, Brian, _Town Fox, Country Fox_, Corgi, London, 1973.

780. Whitney, Leon F., _Dog Psychology: The Basis of Dog Training_, Thomas, Springfield, Illinois, 1964.

781. Wood, G.H. and Cadoret, R.J., "Tests of Clairvoyance in a Man-Dog Relationship," _Journal of Parapsychology_, Vol. 22, 1958, pp. 29-39.

20: Cattle

(For additional entries related to this topic see 995, 1616.)

782. Burton, Maurice, "Analysis of Play in Cattle," Illustrated London News, Vol. 224, June 19, 1954, p. 1054.

20: Elephants

(For additional entries related to this topic see 2063, 2072, 2077, 2079, 1039.)

783. Blond, Georges, The Elephants, trans. by Frances Frenaye, Macmillan, New York, 1961.

784. Carrington, R., Elephants, A Short Account of Their Natural History, Evolution and Influence on Mankind, Penguin, London, 1958.

785. Douglas-Hamilton, Iain and Oria, Among the Elephants, Viking Press, New York, 1975.

786. Rensch, B., "The Intelligence of Elephants," Scientific American, Vol. 196, 1957, pp. 44-9.

20: Felines

(For additional entries related to this topic see 2498, 2065, 1426, 1645.)

787. Adamson, Joy, Born Free, Pantheon Books, New York, 1960.

788. Adamson, Joy, Forever Free, Harcourt, Brace and World, New York, 1962.

789. Adamson, Joy, Living Free, The Story of Elsa and Her Cubs, Collins and Harvill, London, 1961.

790. Brown, C.E. and Hall, G.S., "The Cat

and the Child," Journal of Genetic Psychology, Vol. 11, March, 1904, pp. 3-29.

791. Crawford, Nelson A., "Cats Holy and Profane," Psychoanalytic Review, Vol. 21, April, 1934.

792. Fox, Michael W., Understanding Your Cat, Coward, McCann & Geoghegan, 1977, New York.

793. Gates, Georgina S., The Modern Cat; Her Mind and Manners, An Introduction to Comparative Psychology, Macmillan, New York, 1928.

794. Inge, William R., "Cat and Dog," in Inge's Rustic Moralist, pp. 318-22, Putnam, London, 1937.

795. Mery, Fernand, The Life, History and Magic of the Cat, Grosset and Dunlap, New York, 1968.

796. Osis, K. and Foster, E.B., "A Test of ESP in Cats," Journal of Parapsychology, Vol. 17, 1953, pp. 168-86.

20: Horses

(For additional entries related to this topic see 2741, 3130, 2434, 2542, 2569, 2572, 2594, 1105.)

797. Blake, Henry N., _Talking with Horses_, E.P. Dutton, New York, 1975.

798. Dent, Anthony A., _The Horse Through Fifty Centuries of Civilization_, Holt, Rinehart and Winston, 1974. (Heavily illustrated.)

799. Haines, Francis, _Horses in America_, Thomas Y. Crowell, New York, 1971.

800. Parsons, Denys, "Horse-Sense or Nonsense?" _Hibbert Journal_, Vol. 50, October, 1951, pp. 63-9.

801. Pfungst, Oscar, _Clever Hans: The Horse of Mr. Von Osten_, A Contribution to Experimental and Human Psychology, trans. from the German by Carl L. Rahn, Henry Holt, New York, 1911.

802. Rhine, J.B. and Rhine, Louisa E., "An Investigation of a 'Mind-Reading' Horse," _Journal of Abnormal and Social Psychology_, Vol. 23, January, 1929, pp. 449-66.

803. Rhine, J.B. and Rhine, Louisa E., "Second Report on Lady, the 'Mind-Reading' Horse," _Journal of Abnormal and Social Psychology_, Vol. 24, October, 1929, pp. 287-92.

804. Ryden, Hope, _America's Last Wild Horses_, Dutton, New York, 1978.

805. Ryden, Hope, _Mustangs, A Return to the Wild_, Viking, New York, 1972. (Heavily illustrated.)

20: Horses

806. Sanford, Edmund C., "Der Kluge Hans and the Elberfeld Horses," a review of Oscar Pfungst's Clever Hans: The Horse of Mr. Von Osten, Henry Holt, New York, 1911, and also reviews of five other books (in French and German) on the same topic, American Journal of Psychology, Vol. 25, January, 1914, pp. 131-6.

807. Sanford, Edmund C., "Psychic Research in the Animal Field: Der Kluge Hans and the Elberfeld Horses," American Journal of Psychology, Vol. 25, January, 1914, pp. 1-31.

20: Humans

808. Ardrey, Robert, African Genesis, A Personal Investigation into the Animal Origins and Nature of Man, Collins, London, 1961.

809. Bryant, Clifton D., "The Zoological Connection: Animal-Related Human Behavior," Social Forces, Vol. 58, December, 1979, pp. 399-421.

810. Dubos, Rene, Man Adapting, Yale University Press, New Haven, 1965.

811. Gregory, Michael S., Silvers, Anita, and Sutch, Diane, eds., Sociobiology and Human Nature, Jossey-Bass, San Francisco, 1978.

812. Hinde, R.A., Biological Bases of Human Social Behaviour, McGraw-Hill, New York, 1974.

813. Leakey, Richard E. and Lewin, Roger, "Is It Our Culture, Not Our Genes,

That Makes Us Killers?" Smithsonian,
November, 1977.

814. Milne, Lorus J. and Margery, The
Animal in Man, McGraw-Hill, New
York, 1973.

815. Montagu, Ashley, "Is Man Innately
Aggressive?" in On the Fifth Day,
ed. by Morris and Fox (1219).

816. Morris, Desmond, The Human Zoo, McGraw-
Hill, New York, 1969.

817. Thorpe, W.H., Biology and the Nature
of Man, Oxford University Press,
London, 1962.

818. Twain, Mark, "Man's Place in the Ani-
mal World," in The Works of Mark Twain,
Vol. 19, What Is Man? And Other
Philosophical Writings, ed. by Paul
Baender, pp. 80-89, University of
California Press, Berkeley, 1973.

819. Wilson, Edward O., On Human Nature,
Harvard University Press, Cambridge,
1978.

20: Insects

(For additional entries related to this topic see 2713, 2519, 533, 551.)

819. Collins, Arthur W., "How One Could
a   Tell Were a Bee to Guide His Be-
     haviour by a Rule," Mind, Vol. 77,
     October, 1968, pp. 556-60.

820. Forel, Auguste, The Senses of Insects,
     trans. by Macleod Yearsley, Methuen,
     London, 1908.

821. Gould, J.L., "Do Honeybees Know What
     They Are Doing?" Natural History,
     Vol. 88, June-July, 1979, pp. 66-75.

822. Gould, J.L., Henerey, M., and Macleod,
     M.C., "Communication of Direction by
     the Honey-bee," Science, Vol. 169,
     1970, pp. 544-54.

823. Hapgood, Fred, "Free Bees," Harper's,
     February, 1980, pp. 81-83. (Review
     of Bernd Heinrich's Bumblebee
     Economics, Harvard University Press,
     Cambridge, 1979.)

824. Heinrich, Bernd, Bumblebee Economics,
     Harvard University Press, Cambridge,
     1979.

825. Huxley, Julian, "Are Ants Like Men?"
     Discovery, Vol. 11, March 1930, pp.
     71-4.

826. Kroeber, A.L., "Sign and Symbol in
     Bee Communications," National
     Academy of Sciences Proceedings,
     Vol. 38, September 15, 1952, pp.
     753-7.

827. Lindauer, Martin, Communication
     Among Social Bees, Harvard

University Press, Cambridge, 1971.

828. Nielson, Lewis T., "Mosquitoes, the Mighty Killer," National Geographic, September, 1979.

829. Ritchie, Carson I.A., Insects: The Creeping Conquerors and Human History, Elsevier/Nelson Books, Nashville, Tenn., 1979.

830. Von Frisch, Karl, Bees: Their Vision, Chemical Senses and Language, Cornell University Press, Ithaca, 1971.

831. Von Frisch, Karl, The Dance and Orientation of Bees, Trans. by Leigh E. Chadwick, Belknap Press of Harvard University, Cambridge, 1967.

832. Von Frisch, K., "Honey Bees: Do They Use the Information as to Direction and Distance Provided by Their Dances?" Science, Vol. 158, 1967, pp. 1072-5.

833. Von Frisch, K., "The Language of Bees," Science Progress, Vol. 32, July, 1937, pp. 29-37.

834. Wasmann, Eric, Psychology of Ants and of Higher Animals, B. Herder, St. Louis, Missouri, 1905.

835. Waterston, James, Fleas as a Menace to Man and Domestic Animals, The Trustees of the British Museum, London, 1916.

836. Wenner, Adrian M., The Bee Language

Controversy, An Experience in Science,
Educational Improvement Corporation,
1971.

837. Wilson, Edward O., The Insect Societies,
Harvard University Press, Cambridge,
1974.

20: Marine Mammals

(For additional entries related to this topic
see 3017, 2708, 2709, 2623, 2648, 2649, 2599,
2396, 2494, 2556, 2053, 2061, 1531, 560.)

838. Alpers, Antony, A Book of Dolphins,
John Murray, London, 1965.

839. Brower, Kenneth (text) and Curtsinger,
William R. (photographs), Wake of
the Whale, Friends of the Earth, New
York, 1979.

840. Brown, Robin, The Lure of the Dolphins,
Avon, New York, 1979.

841. Bruemmer, F., The Life of the Harp
Seal, Optimum Publishing, Montreal,
1977.

842. Caldwell, M.C., and Caldwell, D.K.,
"Communication in Atlantic Bottle-
nosed Dolphins," Sea Frontiers,
Vol. 25, May, 1979, pp. 130-9.

843. Cousteau, Jacques-Yves and Diole,
Philippe, Dolphins, trans. by
J.F. Bernard, Doubleday, Garden
City, N.Y., 1975.

844. Cousteau, Jacques-Yves and Diole,
Philippe, The Whale: Mighty Monarch
of the Sea, trans. by J.F. Bernard,
Doubleday & Co., New York, 1972.

845. Dobbs, Horace E., Follow a Wild
Dolphin, The Story of an Extraor-
dinary Friendship, Souvenir Press,
London, 1977.

846. Fichtelius, K., and Sjolander, S.,
Man's Place: Intelligence in Dolphins,
Whales and Humans, Gollancz, London,
1973.

847. Fichtelius, Karl-Erich, Smarter Than
      Man? (whales, dolphins, humans),
      Pantheon Books, New York, 1972.

848. Griffin, E.I., "Making Friends with
      a Killer Whale," National Geographic,
      Vol. 129, 1966, pp. 418-46.

849. Haley, Delphine, ed., Marine Mammals,
      Pacific Search Press, Seattle,
      Washington, 1978. (Heavily il-
      lustrated.)

850. Kellogg, R., "The History of Whales--
      Their Adaptations to Life in the
      Water," Quarterly Review of Biology,
      Vol. 3, 1928, pp. 29-76, 174-208.

851. Lilly, John, Communication Between Man
      and Dolphin, The Possibilities of
      Talking with Other Species, Crown
      Publishers, New York, 1977.

852. Lilly, John C., Lilly on Dolphins,
      Humans of the Sea, Doubleday &
      Co., New York, 1975.

853. Lilly, John, Man and Dolphin, Doubleday
      and Co., New York, 1961.

854. Lilly, John, The Mind of the Dolphin:
      A Non-human Intelligence, Doubleday,
      New York, 1967.

855. Linehan, Edward J., "The Trouble with
      Dolphins," National Geographic
      Magazine, Vol. 155, No.4, April,
      1979.

856. Lister-Kaye, John, The Grey Seal
      Controversy, Penguin, London, 1979.

857. Lopez, Barry, "A Presentation of Whales," Harper's, March, 1980, pp. 68-79.

858. McIntyre, Joan, compiler, Mind in the Waters; a Book to Celebrate the Consciousness of Whales and Dolphins, Scribner, New York, 1974.

859. McNulty, Faith, The Great Whales, Doubleday, New York, 1974.

860. Matthews, Leonard H., The Whale, George Allen and Unwin, London, 1968. (Heavily illustrated.)

861. Montagu, Ashley, and Lilly, John C., The Dolphin in History (Two lectures for the Clark Library Series), William Andrews Clark Memorial Library, Los Angeles, 1963.

862. Mowat, Farley, A Whale for the Killing, Little, Brown, Boston, 1972.

863. Reiger, G., "The Whale-Watchers," Audubon, Vol. 79, 1978, pp. 74-101.

864. Robertson, Robert B., Of Whales and Men, Knopf, New York, 1954.

865. Robson, Frank, Thinking Dolphins, Talking Whales, A.H. & A.W. Reed, London, 1976.

866. Scheffer, Victor B., "Exploring the Lives of Whales," National Geographic, Vol. 150, 1976, pp. 752-67.

867. Scheffer, Victor B., A Natural History of Marine Mammals, Scribner,

New York, 1976.

868. Scheffer, Victor B., The Year of the Seal, Scribner, New York, 1970.

869. Scheffer, Victor B., The Year of the Whale, Decorations by Leonard Everett Fisher, Scribner, New York, 1969.

870. Slijper, E.J., Whales, trans. by A.J. Pomerans, with concluding chapter on whales and whaling by Richard J. Harrison, Cornell University Press, Ithaca, New York, 1979.

871. Small, George L., The Blue Whale, Columbia University Press, New York, 1971.

872. Stenuit, Robert, The Dolphin, Cousin to Man, Sterling, New York, 1969.

20: Pigs
(For additional entry related to this topic see 1565.)

873. Britt, Kent, and Mobley, George F., "The Joy of Pigs," National Geographic, Vol. 154, September, 1978.

20: Primates (non-human)
(For additional entries related to this topic
see 3023, 3037, 3038, 2695, 2700, 2704, 2711,
2713, 2600, 2604, 2500, 2050, 1007, 1019,
1428, 1434, 1438, 1440, 1441, 1453, 1481,
1488,1503, 1511, 713, 551, 1512, 1513, 1519,
722, 560, 1545, 1549, 1556, 665, 1566, 1597,
1634, 1635, 666, 1646, 1648.)

874. Altman, Stuart A., Social Communication
Among Primates, University of Chicago
Press, Chicago, 1967.

875. "Are Those Apes Really Talking?" Time,
March 10, 1980, pp. 50-7.

876. Bourne, Geoffrey H., ed., The Chimpanzee, 6 Vols., S. Karger, White
Plains, New York, 1977.

877. Bourne, Geoffrey H., Primate Odyssey,
Putnam's, New York, 1974.

878. Bourne, Geoffrey H. and Cohen, Maury,
The Gentle Giants: The Gorilla Story,
Putnam's, New York, 1975.

879. Carpenter, C.R., "Behavior and Social
Relations of the Gibbon," Compara-
tive Psychology Monographs, Vol. 16,
No. 5, December, 1940, pp. 1-212.

880. D'Aulaire, Emily and Ola, "The Ape
that 'Talks' with People," The
Reader's Digest, Vol. 107, October,
1975, pp. 94-98.

881. Davenport, R.K., and Rogers, C.M.,
"Perception of Photographs by Apes,"
Behavior, Vol. 39, 1971, pp. 320 ff.

882. Desmond, Adrian J., The Ape's Re-
flexion, Dial Press, New York, 1979.

883. Fleischmann, Mark L., "Vocalization of Chimpanzees in Non-caged Captivity," _Primates_, Vol. 9, pp. 273-282.

884. Foley, John P., Jr., "Judgment of Facial Expression of Emotion in the Chimpanzee," _Journal of Social Psychology_, Vol. 6, February, 1935, pp. 31-67.

885. Fossey, Dian, "Making Friends with Mountain Gorillas," _National Geographic_, Vol. 137, January, 1970. pp. 48-67.

886. Fossey, Dian, "More Years with Mountain Gorillas," _National Geographic_,Vol. 140, October, 1971, pp. 574-85.

887. Fouts, R.S., "Acquisition and Testing of Gestural Signs in Four Young Chimpanzees," _Science_, Vol. 180, 1973, pp. 978-980.

888. Fouts, R.S., "Capacities for Language in the Great Apes," in _Proceedings of the 18th International Congress of Anthropological and Ethnological Sciences_, Mouton, The Hague, 1974.

889. Fouts, R.S., "The Use of Guidance in Teaching Sign Language to a Chimpanzee," _Journal of Comparative and Physiological Psychology_, Vol. 80, pp. 515-22.

890. Fouts, R.S., and Chowin, W., and Goodin, L., "Transfer of Signed Responses in American Sign Language from Vocal English Stimuli

to Physical Object Stimuli by a
Chimpanzee," Learning and Motivation,
Vol. 7, August, 1976, pp. 458-75.

891. Fouts, R.S. and Mellgren, R.L., "Language, Signs, and Cognition in the
Chimpanzees," Sign Language Studies,
Vol. 13, Winter, 1976, pp. 319-46.

892. Freeman, Dan, The Great Apes, Putnams,
New York, 1979.

893. Galdikas, Birute, "Indonesia's
Orangutans: Living with the Great
Orange Apes," National Geographic,
Vol. 157, June, 1980, pp. 830-53.

894. Galdikas, Birute, "Orangutans, Indonesia's 'People of the Forest',"
National Geographic, Vol. 148, October, 1975, pp. 444-72.

895. Gallup, Gordon G., Jr., "Self-Awareness
in Primates," American Scientist,
Vol. 67, July-August, 1979, pp.
417-421.

896. Gallup, Gordon G., Boren, James L.,
Gagliardi, Gregg J., and Wallnau,
Larry B., "A Mirror for the Mind
of Man, or Will the Chimpanzee Create
an Identity Crisis for Homo-
sapiens?" Journal of Human Evolution,
Vol. 6, 1977, pp. 311 ff.

897. Gardner, Beatrice T. and Gardner, R.
Allen, "Comparing the Early Utterances
of Child and Chimpanzee," in Minnesota Symposium on Child Psychology,
Vol. 8, ed. by A. Pick, University
of Minnesota Press, Minneapolis,
1974, pp. 3-23.

898. Gardner, Beatrice T., and Gardner, R. Allen, "Evidence for Sentence Constituents in the Early Utterances of Child and Chimpanzee," Journal of Experimental Psychology, Vol. 104, No. 3, September, 1975, pp. 244-276.

899. Gardner, Beatrice T., and Gardner, R. Allen, "Two-Way Communication with an Infant Chimpanzee," in Behavior of Nonhuman Primates, ed. by A.M. Schrier and F. Stollnitz, Academic Press, New York, 1971.

900. Gardner, R. Allen, and Gardner, Beatrice T., "Teaching Sign Language to a Chimpanzee," Science, Vol. 165, August 15, 1969, pp. 664-672.

901. Gardner, Martin, "Monkey Business," A review of Herbert S. Terrace's Nim: A Chimpanzee Who Learned Sign Language, Knopf, New York, 1979, and of Thomas A. Sebeok's and Donna Jean Umiker-Sebeok's (eds.) Speaking of Apes: A Critical Anthology of Two-Way Communication with Man, Plenum, New York, 1980, in New York Review of Books, Vol. 27, March 20, 1980, pp. 3-6.

902. Gwynne, Peter, et al., "Almost Human," Newsweek, Vol. 89, March 7, 1977, pp. 70-73.

903. Hahn, Emily, Look Who's Talking, Crowell, New York, 1978.

904. Hahn, Emily, "A Reporter at Large: Chimpanzees and Language," The New Yorker, December 11, 1971, pp. 45-98.

905. Hayes, Harold T.P., "The Pursuit of
     Reason," New York Times Magazine,
     June 12, 1977, pp. 21-23 and 73-5.

906. Hayes, Keith J., and Hayes, Catherine,
     "The Intellectual Development of a
     Home-Raised Chimpanzee," American
     Philosophical Society Proceedings,
     Vol. 95, April, 1951, pp. 105-9.

907. Hewes, Gordon, "Primate Communication
     and the Gestural Origin of Language,"
     Current Anthropology, Vol. 14, Feb-
     ruary-April, 1973, pp. 5-24.

908. Hill, J.H., "Apes and Language,"
     Annual Review of Anthropology,
     Vol. 7, pp. 89-112.

909. Hooton, Earnest A., Why Men Behave
     Like Apes and Vice Versa, Princeton
     University Press, Princeton, 1940.

910. Jay, Phillis C., ed., Primates, Holt,
     Rinehart and Winston, New York, 1968.

911. Jenkins, Peter, "Teaching Chimpanzees
     to Communicate," from "Ask No Ques-
     tions," The Guardian, London, July
     10, 1973. Reproduced in Animal
     Rights and Human Obligations, ed.
     by Tom Regan and Peter Singer (1253).

912. Kellogg, W.N., "Humanizing the Ape,"
     Psychological Review, Vol. 38, March,
     1931, pp. 160-76.

913. Kellogg, W.N., and Kellogg, L.A.,
     The Ape and the Child, A Study of
     Environmental Influence upon Early
     Behavior, Hafner, New York, 1967.
     (Facsimile of 1933 edition.)

914. Kevles, Bettyann, Watching the Wild
     Apes, The Primate Studies of Goodall,
     Fossey, and Galdikas, Dutton, New
     York, 1976. (Juvenile literature.)

915. Kohler, Wolfgang, The Mentality of
     Apes, trans. by Ella Winter, Harcourt,
     Brace, New York, 1927.

916. Kohler, Wolfgang, "Intelligence in
     Apes," Journal of Genetic Psychology,
     Vol. 32, December, 1925, pp. 674-90.

917. Kuroda, Ryo, "On the Counting Ability
     of a Monkey (Macacus cynomolgus),"
     Journal of Comparative Psychology,
     Vol. 12, August, 1931, pp. 171-80.

918. Laidler, K., "Language in the Orangutan,"
     in Action, Gesture, and Symbol: The
     Emergence of Language, ed. by A.
     Lock, Academic Press, New York, 1978.

919. Lancaster, Jane B., "Communication
     Systems of Old World Monkeys and
     Apes," International Social Science
     Journal, Vol. 19, 1967, pp. 28-35.

920. Lawick, Hugo, and Lawick-Goodall,
     Jane, Innocent Killers, Ballantine,
     New York, 1973.

921. Lawick-Goodall, Jane, In the Shadow
     of Man, Houghton-Mifflin, Boston,
     1971.

922. Lawick-Goodall, Jane, My Friends,
     the Wild Chimpanzees, National
     Geographic Society, Washington,
     D.C., 1967.

923. Lawick-Goodall, Jane, "A Preliminary

Report on Expressive Movement and Communication in the Gombe Stream Chimpanzees," in Primates, ed. by Phillis C. Jay, Holt, Rinehart and Winston, New York, 1968, pp. 313-74.

924. Lenneberg, E.H., "Of Language, Knowledge, Apes and Brains," Journal of Psycholinguistic Research, Vol. 1, pp. 1-29.

925. Limber, John, "Language in Child and Chimp?" American Psychologist, Vol. 32, April, 1977, pp. 280-95.

926. Lindburg, Donald G., The Macaques, Studies in Ecology, Behavior and Evolution, Van Nostrand Reinhold, New York, 1980.

927. Linden, Eugene, Apes, Men and Language, Dutton, New York, 1974.

928. Marais, Eugene, The Soul of the Ape, with an Introduction by Robert Ardrey, Atheneum, New York, 1969.

929. Marx, Jean L., "Ape-Language Controversy Flares Up," Science, Vol. 207, March 21, 1980, pp. 1330-3.

930. Mason, W.A., "Determinants of Social Behavior in Young Chimpanzees," in Behavior of Non-Human Primates, Vol. 2, Schrier, A.M., Harlow, H.F., and Stollnitz, F., eds., Academic Press, New York, 1965.

931. Meddin, J., "Chimpanzees, Symbols and the Reflective Self," Social Psychology, Vol. 42, pp. 99-109.

932. Menzel, Emil, "Natural Language of Young Chimpanzees," New Scientist, January 16, 1975, pp. 127-30.

933. Morris, Desmond, ed., Primate Ethology, Aldine Pub. Co., Chicago, 1967.

934. Mounin, Georges, "Language, Communication, Chimpanzees," Current Anthropology, Vol. 17, March, 1976, pp. 1-21.

935. Napier, Prue, Monkeys and Apes, Hamlyn, London, 1970.

936. Patterson, Francine G., "The Gestures of a Gorilla: Sign Language Acquisition in Another Pongid Species," Brain and Language, Vol. 5, January, 1978, pp. 72-97.

937. Patterson, Francine, and Cohn, Ronald H., "Conversations with a Gorilla," National Geographic, Vol. 154, October, 1978.

938. Premack, Ann J., Why Chimps Can Read, Harper and Row, New York, 1976.

939. Premack, Ann J., and Premack, David, "Teaching Language to an Ape," Scientific American, Vol. 227, October, 1972, pp. 92-99.

940. Premack, David, Intelligence in Ape and Man, I. Erlbaum Associates, Hillsdale, N.J., 1976. (Distributed by Halsted Press, New York.)

941. Premack, David, "Language and Intelligence in Ape and Man," American Scientist, Vol. 64, November-December, 1976, pp. 674-683.

20: Primates (non-human)

942. Premack, David, "Language in Chimpanzee?" Science, Vol. 172, May 22, 1971, pp. 808-822.

943. Reynolds, Vernon, The Apes, The Gorilla, Chimpanzee, Orangutan and Gibbon: Their History and Their World, E.P. Dutton & Co., New York, 1967.

944. Rock, M.A., "Keyboard Symbols Enable Children to 'Speak'," Smithsonian, Vol. 10, April, 1979, pp. 90-6.

945. Rumbaugh, Duane M., ed., Language Learning by a Chimpanzee: The Lana Project, Academic Press, New York, 1977.

946. Rumbaugh, D.M., Gill, T.V., and Glaserfeld, E., "Conversation with a Chimpanzee in a Computer-Controlled Environment," Biological Psychiatry, Vol. 10, 1975, pp. 627-41.

947. Sarles, Harvey B., "The Study of Language and Communication across Species," Current Anthropology, Vol. 10, April-June, 1969, pp. 211-21.

948. Savage-Rumbaugh, E.S., "Symbolic Communication: Its Origins and Early Development in the Chimpanzee," in New Directions in Child Development, ed. by H. Gardner and D. Wolf, Jossey-Bass San Francisco, 1979, pp. 1-16.

949. Savage-Rumbaugh, E.S. and Rumbaugh,
     D.M., "Symbolization, Language,
     and Chimpanzees: A Theoretical
     Re-evaluation Based On Initial
     Language Acquisition Process in
     Four Young Pan troglodytes,"
     Brain and Language, Vol. 6, No-
     vember, 1978, pp. 265-300.

950. Savage-Rumbaugh, E.S., Rumbaugh, D.
     M., and Boysen, S., "Linguistically
     Mediated Tool Use and Exchange by
     Chimpanzees," The Behavioral and
     Brain Sciences, Vol. 1, 1978, pp.
     539-54.

951. Savage-Rumbaugh, E.S. and Rumbaugh,
     D.M. and Boysen, S., "Symbolic
     Communication in Apes: A Critique
     of the State of the Art," in Lan-
     guage, Mind and Brain, ed. by T.W.
     Simon and R.J. Scholes, Lawrence
     Erlbaum Inc., in press.

952. Savage-Rumbaugh, E. Sue, Rumbaugh,
     Duane M., and Boysen, Sarah, "Do
     Apes Use Language?" American
     Scientist, Vol. 68, January-
     February, 1980, pp. 49-61.

953. Savage-Rumbaugh, E. Sue, Rumbaugh,
     Duane M., and Boysen, Sally,
     "Symbolic Communication between
     Two Chimpanzees," Science, Vol.
     201, August 18, 1978, pp. 641-44.

954. Schiefelbusch, R. and Hollis, J.,
     eds., Language and Communication:
     Primate to Child, University Park
     Press, Baltimore, 1979.

955. Sebeok, Thomas A., and Umiker-Sebeok,

Jean, "Performing Animals: Secrets of the Trade," Psychology Today, Vol. 13, November 1979.

956. Sebeok, Thomas A., and Umiker-Sebeok, Donna J., eds., Speaking of Apes, A Critical Anthology of Two-Way Communications with Man, Plenum, New York, 1980.

957. Seidenberg, M.S., and Petitto, L.A., "Signing Behavior in Apes: A Critical Review," Cognition, Vol. 7, 1978, pp. 177-215.

958. Teas, Jane, "Temple Monkeys of Nepal," National Geographic, Vol. 157, April, 1980, pp. 575-84.

959. Temerlin, Maurice K., Lucy: Growing Up Human, a Chimpanzee Daughter in a Psychotherapist's Family, Science and Behavior Books, Palo Alto, California, 1975.

960. Terrace, H.S., "How Nim Chimpsky Changed My Mind," Psychology Today, Vol. 13, November, 1979.

961. Terrace,H.S.,Nim, Knopf, New York, 1979. (Chimpanzee and language.)

962. Terrace, H.S., (interviewed by S. Duncan), "Nim Chimpsky and How He Grew," New York, Vol. 12, December 3, 1979, pp. 78-86.

963. Tuttle, Russell H., ed., Socioecology and Psychology of Primates, Mouton, The Hague, 1975.

964. Willhoite, Fred H.,Jr., "Primates and

137

Political Authority: A Biobehavioral Perspective," American Political Science Review, Vol. 70, December, 1976, pp. 1110-1126.

965. Yerkes, Robert M., The Great Apes: A Study of Anthropoid Life, Johnson Reprint, New York, 1970.

966. Yerkes, Robert M., Almost Human, Century, New York, 1925.

967. Yerkes, Robert M., The Mental Life of Monkeys and Apes (1916), A Facsimile Reproduction, Scholars' Facsimiles and Reprints, Delmar, New York, 1979.

968. Yerkes, Robert M., The Mind of a Gorilla, Clark University, Worcester, MA, 1926.

969. Yerkes, Robert M., "The Mind of a Gorilla."
Part I: Genetic Psychology Monographs, Vol. 2, 1927, pp. 1-193.
Part II: Genetic Psychology Monographs, Vol. 2, 1927, pp. 375-551.
Part III: Comparative Psychology Monographs, Vol. 5, December, 1928, pp. 1-92.

970. Yerkes, Robert M., Modes of Behavioral Adaptation in Chimpanzee to Multiple-Choice Problems, Johns Hopkins Press, Baltimore, 1934.

971. Yerkes, Robert M., "Primate Cooperation and Intelligence," American Journal of Psychology, Vol. 50, November, 1937, pp. 254-70.

20: Primates (non-human)

972. Yerkes, Robert M., and Ada, W., The Great Apes: A Study of Anthropoid Life, Johnson Reprint, New York, 1971.

973. Yerkes, Robert M., and Learned, B.W., Chimpanzee Intelligence and Its Vocal Expression, Williams & Wilkins, Baltimore, 1925.

974. Yerkes, Robert M., and Tomilin, Michael I., "Mother-Infant Relations in Chimpanzee," Journal of Comparative Psychology, Vol. 20, December, 1935, 321-59.

975. Zuckerman, S., The Social Life of Monkeys and Apes, Kegan Paul, London, 1932.

20: Rodents
(For additional entries related to this topic see 2468, 1435, 1467.)

976. Candy, Thomas Y., and Stanfield, James L., "The Incredible Rat," National Geographic, Vol. 152, July, 1977.

977. Einon, Dorothy, "Rats at Play," New Scientist, Vol. 85, March 20, 1980, pp. 934-6.

978. Eysenck, H.J., "Precognition in Rats," Journal of Parapsychology, Vol. 39, 1975, pp. 222-7.

979. Hall, Calvin S., "Emotional Behavior in the Rat," Journal of Comparative Psychology, Vol. 18, December, 1934, pp. 385-403; Vol. 22, August, 1936, pp. 61-8, and December, 1936, pp. 345-52.

980. Henney, Peter W., Rodents; Their Lives and Habits, Taplinger, New York, 1975.

981. Maier, Norman R.F., "In Defense of Reasoning in Rats: A Reply," Journal of Comparative Psychology, Vol. 19, April, 1935, pp. 197-206.

982. Maier, Norman R.F., "Reasoning in Rats and Human Beings," Psychological Review, Vol. 44, September, 1937, pp. 365-78.

983. Maier, Norman R.F., "Reasoning in White Rats," Comparative Psychology Monographs, Vol. 6, July, 1929, pp. 1-93.

984. Rodham, C., "Cultures, Rats and Men," American Journal of Psychology, Vol.

58, April, 1945, pp. 262-6.

985. Schouten, S., "Psi in Mice: Positive Reinforcement," Journal of Parapsychology, Vol. 36, 1972, pp. 261-82.

986. Wolfe, John B., and Spragg, S.D. Shirley, "Some Experimental Tests of 'Reasoning' in White Rats," Journal of Comparative Psychology, Vol. 18, December, 1934.

987. Yerkes, Robert M., The Dancing Mouse, A Study in Animal Behavior, Macmillan, New York, 1907.

20: Turtles

988. Rudloe, Jack, Time of the Turtle, Knopf, New York, 1979.

20: Attitudes toward and Views of Animals
(For additional entries related to this topic
see 2980, 2633, 2638, 2597, 2356.)

989. Adams, Richard, "Animals and Our
      Inner Voices," Christian Science
      Monitor, January 28, 1980, Midwest-
      ern Edition, pp. 20-21.

990. Boas, George, "Theriophily," Dic-
      tionary of the History of Ideas,
      ed. by Philip P. Wiener, Charles
      Scribner's, New York, 1973, Vol. 4.

991. Brown, Larry T., Shaw, Terry G.,
      and Kirkland, Karen D., "Affection
      for People as a Function of Affec-
      tion for Dogs," Psychological Reports,
      Vol. 31, 1972, pp. 957-8.

992. Burton, Richard, "Our Elder Brothers,"
      in Burton, Richard, Little Essays
      in Literature and Life, Century Co.,
      New York, 1914.

993. Clark, Kenneth, "Animals and Men:
      Love, Admiration and Outright War,"
      Smithsonian, September, 1977.

994. Collins, June M., "The Mythological
      Basis for Attitudes Toward Animals
      Among Salish-Speaking Indians,"
      Journal of American Folklore, Vol.
      65, October 1952, pp. 353-9.

995. Conrad, Jack R., The Horn and the
      Sword: The History of the Bull
      as Symbol of Power and Fertility,
      Dutton, New York, 1957.

996. Durkheim, Emile, "Totemic Beliefs,"
      in Durkheim's The Elementary Forms
      of the Religious Life, trans. by
      Joseph A. Swain, Collier, New York,
      1961, pp. 121-93.

997. Ehrenfeld, David W., The Arrogance
      of Humanism, Oxford University
      Press, New York, 1978.

998. Emeneau, M.B., "Taboos on Animal
      Names," Language, Vol. 24, January,
      1948, pp. 56-63.

999. Frazer, James, Totemism and Exogamy,
      4 Vols., Macmillan, London, 1910.

1000. Freud, Sigmund, Totem and Taboo,
      trans. by James Strachey, Norton,
      New York, 1950.

1001. Gandhi, M.K., How to Serve the Cow,
      ed. by Bharatan Kumarappa, Navajivan
      Pub. House, Ahmedabad, 1959.

1002. Gill, James E., "Theriophily in
      Antiquity: A supplementary
      Account," Journal of History of
      Ideas, Vol. 30, July-Sept., 1969.

1003. Goldfarb, William, "The Animal
      Symbol in the Rorschach Test and
      an Animal Association Test,"
      Rorschach Research Exchange, Vol.
      9, 1945, pp. 8-22.

1004. Gwynne, Peter, "Man's View of the
      Other Animals," International
      Wildlife, September-October, 1979.

1005. Halverson, John, "Animal Categories
      and Terms of Abuse," Man, Vol. 11,
      December, 1976, pp. 505-16.

1006. Harwood, Dix, Love for Animals, and
      How It Developed in Great Britain,

Columbia University Dissertation, New York, 1928.

1007. Janson, H.W., *Apes and Ape Lore in the Middle Ages and Renaissance*, Warburg Institute, London, 1952.

1008. Kellert, Stephen R., "American Attitudes Toward and Knowledge of Animals: An Update," *Inter-National Journal for the Study of Animal Problems*, Vol. 1, March/April, 1980, pp. 87-119.

1009. Kellert, Stephen R., "Perceptions of Animals in American Society," *Humane Education*, Spring, 1977, National Association for the Advancement of Humane Education, Washington, D.C.

1010. Kellert, Stephen R., *Policy Implications of a National Study of American Attitudes and Behavioral Relations to Animals*, September, 1978. For sale by Superintendent of Documents, U.S. Government Printing Office, Washington, D.C. Stock Number 024-010-00482-7. (Working papers presented to the U.S. Fish and Wildlife Service.) (Considers attitudes and behavioral relations of hunters, anti-hunters, various social demographical groups, backpackers, birdwatchers, zoo enthusiasts, trappers, financial contributors to animal welfare causes, animal raisers, pet owners, rodeo enthusiasts.)

1011. Klausner, Samuel Z., "Interspecies Relations and Technological Development: A Call for Research," *Human*

Organization, Vol. 24, Summer, 1965, pp. III-5.

1012. Krutch, Joseph Wood, "Reverence for Life," in Krutch's The Great Chain of Life, Houghton Mifflin, Boston, 1977.

1013. Leach, Edmund, "Animal Categories and Verbal Abuse," New Directions in the Study of Language, ed. by Eric Lenneberg, MIT Press, Cambridge, 1964.

1014. Lehman, Harvey C., "The Child's Attitude Toward the Dog Versus the Cat," Journal of Genetic Psychology, Vol. 35, March, 1928, pp. 62-72.

1015. Levi-Strauss, Claude, The Savage Mind, University of Chicago Press, Chicago, 1966.

1016. Levi-Strauss, Claude, Totemism, Beacon Press, Boston, 1962, trans. by Rodney Needham.

1017. Lonsdale, S.H., "Attitudes Towards Animals in Ancient Greece," Greece and Rome, Vol. 26, 1979, pp. 146-59.

1018. Lovejoy, A.O., and Boas, George, "The Superiority of the Animals," in the authors' Primitivism and Related Ideas in Antiquity, Octagon Books, Farrar, Straus and Giroux, New York, 1965.

1019. McDermott, William C., The Ape in Antiquity, Johns Hopkins, Baltimore, 1938.

20: Attitudes toward and Views of Animals

1020. Marsh, Mabel A., "Children and Animals," in Earl Barnes, Studies in Education, Vol. 2, G.E. Stechert, New York, 1902, pp. 83-99.

1021. Martinengo-Cesaresco, E., "Animals at Rome," Contemporary Review, Vol, 86 August, 1904, pp. 225-34.

1022. Martinengo-Cesaresco, E., "The Greek Conception of Animals," Contemporary Review, Vol, 85, March, 1904, pp. 430-9.

1023. Martinengo-Cesaresco, E., The Place of Animals in Human Thought, T.F. Unwin, London, 1909.

1024. Means, Richard L., "Man and Nature," in Means' The Ethical Imperative, Doubleday, Garden City, N.Y., 1970, pp. 109-39.

1025. Menninger, Karl A., "Totemic Aspects of Contemporary Attitudes toward Animals," in Wilbur, George B., and Muensterberger, Warner, eds., Psychoanalysis and Culture, Int. Univs. Press, New York, 1951.

1026. Montague, Ashley, "The Myth of the Beast," in Mantagu, Ashley, The Humanization of Man, World Pub., Cleveland, 1962.

1027. Moore, J. Howard, The Universal Kinship, C.H. Kerr, Chicago, 1906.

1028. Morris, Richard K., "Man and Animals: Some Contemporary Problems," in On the Fifth Day, ed. by Morris and Fox (1219).

147

1030. Passmore, John, "Attitudes to Nature," in R.S. Peters, ed., Nature and Conduct, Macmillan, London, 1975.

1031. Paton, David, Animals of Ancient Egypt, Princeton University Press, Princeton, 1925.

1032. Quarelli, Ecena, Socrates and the Animals, trans. by Kathleen Speight, Hodder and Stoughton, London, 1960.

1033. Reed, T.J., "Nietzsche's Animals: Idea, Image and Influence," in Pasley, J.M.S., ed., Nietzsche: Imagery and Thought, University of California Press, Berkeley, 1978.

1034. Rensberger, Boyce, "Man and Beast," in Rensberger's The Cult of the Wild, Doubleday, Garden City, N.Y., 1977.

1035. Rodman, John, "The Dolphin Papers," The North American Review, Vol. 259, Spring, 1974.

1036. Rood, Ronald, N., Animals Nobody Loves, S. Greene Press, Brattleboro, Vt., 1971.

1037. Salt, Henry S., The Story of My Cousins, Brief Animal Biographies, Watts and Co., London, 1922 and 1935.

1038. Schweitzer, Albert, The Animal World of Albert Schweitzer, trans. and ed. by Charles R. Joy, Beacon Press, Boston, 1950.

1039. Scullard, H.H., _The Elephant in the Greek and Roman World,_ Thames and Hudson, London, 1974.

1040. Toynbee, Jocelyn M.C., _Animals in Roman Life and Art,_ Cornell University Press, Ithaca, 1973.

1041. Westermarck, Edvard A., "Regard for Lower Animals," in Westermarck's _The Origin and Development of Moral Ideas,_ Vol. 2, Macmillan, London, 1926, pp. 490-514.

1042. Willis, Roy G., _Man and Beast,_ Basic Books, New York, 1974.

20: Animals and Religion

(For additional entries related to this topic
see 2084, 2088, 2132, 2133, 2144, 1711, 1712,
1713, 1748, 1863, 2818, 2821, 2897, 2980, 3092,
1631.)

1043. Agius, Dom Ambrose, God's Animals,
       Catholic Study Circle for Animal
       Welfare, London, 1973.

1044. Altmann, A., "Homo Imago Dei in
       Jewish and Christian Theology,"
       Journal of Religion, Vol. 28,
       1968, pp. 235 ff.

1045. "Animals in the Spiritual World,"
       New-Church Review, April, 1904,
       pp. 305-7.

1046. Armstrong, Edward, Saint Francis:
       Nature Mystic, The Derivation
       and Significance of the Nature
       Stories in the Franciscan Legend,
       University of California Press,
       Berkeley, 1973.

1047. Austin, Jack, "Buddhist Attitudes
       Towards Animal Life," in Animals'
       Rights--a Symposium, ed. by David
       Paterson and Richard D. Ryder, (1231).

1048. Baker, J.A., "Biblical Attitudes to
       Nature," in Man and Nature, ed. by
       Hugh Montefiore, Collins, London,
       1975.

1049. Barbour, Ian G., ed., Earth Might Be
       Fair: Reflections on Ethics, Religion
       and Ecology, Prentice Hall, Englewood
       Cliffs, N.J., 1972.

1050. Black, John N., The Dominion of Man,
       Edinburgh University Press, Edinburgh,
       1970.

1051. Board for Social Responsibility of the Church of England, "Man and Animals," in Man in His Living Environment, An Ethical Assessment, Church Information Office, Church House, Westminster, 1970, pp. 18-25.

1052. Brinton, Howard H., "Quakers and Animals," in Then and Now, ed. by Anna Brinton, University of Pennsylvania Press, Philadelphia, 1960.

1053. Brown, W. Norman, "The Sanctity of the Cow in Hinduism," Economic Weekly (Calcutta), Vol. 16, 1964, pp. 245-55.

1054. Catholic Dictionary, by William E. Addis and Thomas Arnold, B. Herder, St. Louis, Mo., 1960. See "Animals, Lower" (p. 29) for Catholic view on nature of animals and how they are to be treated.

1055. Cobb, John B., Jr., "Beyond Anthropocentrism in Ethics and Religion," in On the Fifth Day, ed. by Morris and Fox (1219).

1056. Cobb, John B., Jr., "Ecology, Ethics, and Theology," in Herman Daly, ed., Toward a Steady-State Economy, Freeman, San Francisco, 1973.

1057. Cobb, John B., Jr., Is It Too Late? A Theology of Ecology, Bruce, Beverly Hills, Ca., 1972.

1058. Cobb, John B., Jr., A review of Andrew Linzey's Animal Rights: A Christian Assessment of Man's Treatment of

Animals, SCM Press, London, 1976,
in Environmental Ethics, Vol. 2,
Spring, 1980, pp. 89-90.

1059. Cohen, A., "Duty to Animals," in
Cohen's Everyman's Talmud, E.P.
Dutton, New York, 1949, pp. 235-7.

1060. Duncan, R., "Adam and the Ark,"
Encounter (Christian Theological
Seminary), Vol. 37, Spring, 1976,
pp. 189-97.

1061. Dunstan, G.R., "A Limited Dominion,"
Conquest, The Journal of the Research
Defence Society, No. 170, March,
1980, pp. 1-8.

1062. Farbridge, Maurice H., "The Animal
Kingdom," in Farbridge's Study in
Biblical and Semitic Symbolism,
Kegan Paul, Trench, Trubner, London,
1923, pp. 53-84.

1063. Ganzfried, Solomon, and Goldin, Hyman
E., Code of Jewish Law, Hebrew
Publishing, New York, 1963.
  Chapter 186: "The Muzzling of
  Animals"
  Chapter 191: "Cruelty to Animals"

1064. Geach, Peter, "Animal Pain," in Geach's
Providence and Evil, Cambridge University Press, Cambridge, 1977.

1065. Ginzberg, Louis, "Jewish Sympathy
for Animals," Nation, Vol. 83,
August 9, 1906, p. 116.

1066. Glacken, Clarence J., "Interpreting
Man's Dominion over Nature," in
Glacken's Traces on the Rhodian

Shore: Nature and Culture in Western
Thought from Ancient Times to the End
of the Eighteenth Century, University
of California Press, Berkeley, 1967,
pp. 295-302.

1067. Hasker, William, "The Souls of Beasts
and Men," Religious Studies, Vol. 10,
September, 1974, pp. 265-77.

1068. Holmes-Gore, Vincent A., These We Have
Not Loved, A Treatise on the Christian
Attitude to the Creatures, C.W. Daniel
Co., Ltd., Ashingdon, Rochford, Essex,
U.K., 1946.

1069. Hume, C.W., "The Religious Attitude
Toward Animals," Hibbert Journal,
Vol. 51, April, 1953, pp. 262-8.

1070. Hume, C.W., The Status of Animals in
the Christian Religion, Universities
Federation for Animal Welfare, London,
1957.

1071. Kingston, A. Richard, "Theodicy and
Animal Welfare," Theology, November,
1967, pp. 482-8.

1072. Lewis, C.S., "Animal Pain," in Lewis'
The Problem of Pain, Macmillan, New
York, 1962.

1073. Lewis, C.S., and Joad, C.E.M., "The
Pains of Animals," in God in the
Dock, Eerdmans Publishing, Grand
Rapids, Mich., 1970.
"The Inquiry," by C.E.M. Joad.
"The Reply," by C.S. Lewis.

1074. Limburg, James, "What Does It Mean to
'Have Dominion over the Earth'?"

Dialog, Summer, 1971, pp. 221-223.

1075. Lind-af-Hageby, L., "St. Francis and the Universal Kinship," Animal Defence Society, London, 1935.

1076. Linzey, Andrew, Animal Rights: A Christian Assessment of Man's Treatment of Animals, SCM Press, London, 1976.

1077. Linzey, Andrew, "Animals and Moral Theology," in Animals' Rights--a Symposium, ed. by David Paterson and Richard D. Ryder (1231).

1078. Linzey, Andrew, "Christian Responsibility to Animals," Oxford Diocesan Magazine, September, 1970.

1079. Linzey, Andrew, "Christian/Theological Basis of Animal Welfare," R.S.P.C.A., London, 1974.

1080. Lowenberg, Miriam E. and others, "Food, Man and Religion," in the authors' Food and Man, Wiley, New York, 1974.

1081. Lynd, Robert, "Saint of the Animals," New Statesman, Vol. 27, October 9, 1926, pp. 734-5. (St. Francis)

1082. Martinengo-Cesaresco, E., "The Hebrew Conception of Animals," Open Court, Vol. 15, 1901, pp. 110-14.

1083. Montefiore, C.G., and Loewe, H., eds., A Rabbinic Anthology, Schocken Books, New York, 1974. (See "Animals" in "General Index," p. 777.)

1084. Moule, Charles F.D., Man and Nature in

the New Testament, Fortess Press, Philadelphia, 1967.

1085. Northrup, F.S.C., "Naturalistic Realism and Animate Compassion," in On the Fifth Day, ed. by Morris and Fox (1219). (Buddhism on Animals)

1086. "Our Relationship with Animals," Awake, Watchtower Bible and Tract Society, New York and Toronto, June 22, 1980, pp. 5-15.

1087. Sherley-Price, Leo, trans., St. Francis of Assisi: His Life and Writings As Recorded by His Contemporaries, Harper, New York, 1959.

1088. Shoshan, A., "Jewish Attitudes toward Animals," Michigan State University Veterinarian, Vol, 21, 1960, pp. 30-1.

1089. Singer, Jacob, "Taboos of Food and Drink," in Singer's Taboo in the Hebrew Scriptures, Open Court, Chicago, 1928, pp. 3-17.

1090. Squadrito, Kathy, "Locke's View of Dominion," Environmental Ethics, Vol. 1, Fall, 1979, pp. 255-62.

1091. Taylor, Edward B., Religion in Primitive Culture, Part II, Harper Torchbooks, New York, 1958, pp. 320 ff.

1092. Thomas, Ruth Edith, The Sacred Meal in the Older Roman Religion, Private Edition, University of Chicago Libraries, Chicago, 1937.

1093. Turnbull, Eric, "Animals and Moral Theology," in Animals' Rights--a

Symposium, ed. by David Paterson and Richard D. Ryder, pp. 43-7 (1231).

1094. Waddell, Helen, trans., Beasts and Saints, Constable, London, 1946.

1095. Wallace-Hadrill, D.S., The Greek Patristic View of Nature, Manchester University Press, Manchester, 1968.

1096. Wellbourn, F.B., "Man's Dominion," Theology, Vol. 78, 1975, pp. 561 ff.

1097. Westermarck, Edvard A., "Christianity and the Regard for the Lower Animals," in Westermarck's Christianity and Morals, Macmillan, New York, 1939, pp. 379-93.

1098. White, Andrew D., "Theological Teachings Regarding the Animals and Men," in White's A History of the Warfare of Science with Theology, Vol. 1, pp. 24-49, Appleton, New York, 1907.

1099. Wong, Yuk, "Attitude of Chinese Religions and Christianity towards the Animal Kingdom," Journal of Dharma, Vol. 4, January-March, 1979, pp. 47-55.

20: Animals and Civilization and Culture

1100. Jordan, J.W., "An Ambivalent Relationship: Dog and Human in the Folk Culture of the Rural South," Appalachian Journal, Vol. 2, Spring, 1975, pp. 238-48.

1101, Klaits, Joseph and Barrie, eds., Animals and Man in Historical

Perspective, Harper & Row, N.Y., 1974.

1102. Leeds, Anthony, and Vayda, Andrew P.,
eds., Man, Culture, and Animals,
The Role of Animals in Human
Ecological Adjustments, American
Association for the Advancement
of Science, Washington, D.C., 1965.

1103. Lewinsohn, Richard, Animals, Men and
Myths, A History of the Influence
of Animals on Civilization and
Culture, Harper, New York, 1954.

1104. Webster, Gary (Webb Black Garrison),
Codfish, Cats, and Civilization,
Kennikat Press, Port Washington,
NY, 1959.

1105. Wissler, Clark, "The Influence of
the Horse in the Development of
Plains Culture," American Anthro-
pologist, Vol. 16, January-March,
1914, pp. 1-25.

1106. Zinsser, Hans, Rats, Lice, and History,
Bantam Books, New York, 1935.

20: Animals and Ethics (Includes Animal Rights, Animal Liberation, Speciesism, Obligations to Animals)

1901-50: Animals and Ethics

1107. Bradford, Nettie, "Property Rights of Animals," Bulletin of University of Utah, Vol. 37, No. 9, Salt Lake City, 1946.

1108. Bradley, F.H., Ethical Studies, Clarendon Press, Oxford, 1927. (See pp. 31-2, footnote 2, where Bradley suggests that "a time would seem coming when we shall hear of the 'rights of the beast.' Why not, in Heaven's name?")

1109. Harwood, Dix, "The Rights of Animals," in Harwood's Love for Animals, And How It Developed in Great Britain, Ph. D. Dissertation, Philosophy, Columbia University, New York, 1928. (Copy in University of Wisconsin Library), pp. 160-71.

1110. Hornaday, William T., "The Rights of Wild Animals," in Hornaday's The Mind and Manners of Wild Animals, Scribner's, New York, 1922, pp. 49-53. (26 articles.)

1111. Hughes, Rupert, "Animal and Vegetable Rights," Harper's Monthly Magazine, Vol. 103, November, 1901, pp. 852-3.

1112. Inge, William R., "Rights of Animals," in Inge, William R., Wit and Wisdom of Dean Inge, Books for Libraries Press, Essay Index Reprint Series, Freeport, N.Y., 1968.

1901-50: Animals and Ethics

1113. MacIver, A.M., "Ethics and the Beetle," Analysis, Vol 8, April, 1948, pp. 65-70. Also in Ethics, ed. by Judith J. Thomson and Gerald Dworkin, Harper & Row, New York, 1968.

1114. Moore, J. Howard, The New Ethics (The Golden Rule applicable to humans and animals), Samuel Bloch, Chicago, 1901.

1115. Salt, Henry S., Animals' Rights, G. Bell and Sons, London, 1922. A new edition published by Society for Animal Rights. Clarks Summit, Pa., 1980.

1116. Salt, Henry S., "Animals' Rights," in Salt's Animals' Rights, reproduced in Animal Rights and Human Obligations, ed. by Tom Regan and Peter Singer (1253).

1117. Salt, Henry S., The Creed of Kinship, Dutton, New York, 1935.

1118. Salt, Henry S., "The Rights of Animals," in The Animals' Cause, ed. by L. Lind-af-Hageby, The Animal Defence and Anti-Vivisection Society, London, 1909, pp. 311-15.

1119. Schweitzer, Albert, "The Ethic of Reverence for Life," from Civilization and Ethics (Part II of The Philosophy of Civilization). Reproduced in Animal Rights and Human Obligations, ed. by Tom Regan and Peter Singer (1253).

1120. Schweitzer, Albert, "The Sacredness of All That Lives," in Albert Schweitzer, An Anthology, Harper & Bros., New York, 1947.

1951-80:   Animals and Ethics
(For additional entries related to this topic
see 2739, 3139, 2767, 2826, 2907, 2930, 2979,
2996, 3013, 3026, 3029, 3045, 3056, 3096,
3098, 3132, 2624, 2614, 2616, 2617, 2619,
2622, 2596, 2597, 2598, 2599, 2600, 2601,
2602, 2603, 2604, 2605, 2606, 2607, 2287.)

1121.   Aiken, William, "Animals and Rights:
        A Reply to Regan," Etyka (Poland),
        Vol. 18, 1980.

1122.   Armstrong, Susan B., The Rights of
        Nonhuman Beings: A Whiteheadian
        Study, Ph.D. Dissertation, Bryn
        Mawr College, Pennsylvania, 1976,
        160 pp. Available from University
        Microfilms International, Ann
        Arbor, Michigan, under Number
        HGK77-06512.

1123.   Benn, Stanley, "Egalitarianism and
        the Equal Consideration of Inter-
        ests," in Equality, ed. by James
        R. Pennock and John W. Chapman.
        Nomos: Yearbook of the American
        Society for Political and Legal
        Philosophy, No. 9, Atherton
        Press, New York, 1967.

1124.   Benson, John, "Duty and the Beast,"
        Philosophy, Vol. 53, October,
        1978, pp. 529-49.

1125.   Benson, John, "Hog in Sloth, Fox in
        Stealth: Man and Beast in Moral
        Thinking," Royal Institute of
        Philosophy Lectures, Vol. 8,
        Nature and Conduct, Macmillan,
        London, 1975.

1126.   Broadie, Alexander and Pybus, Elizabeth,
        "Kant's Treatment of Animals,"
        Philosophy, Vol. 49, October, 1974,

163

pp. 375-83.

1127. Brophy, Brigid, "The Rights of Animals," Sunday Times, London (October 10, 1965.) Reprinted by The Vegetarian Society (U.K.) Limited, Parkdale, Dunham Road, Altrincham, Cheshire, United Kingdom. Also in Brophy's Don't Never Forget, Holt, Rinehart and Winston, New York, 1966.

1128. Brophy, Brigid, "The Zoophile Case," The Listener, June 30, 1977.

1129. Brumbaugh, Robert S., "Of Man, Animals, and Morals: A Brief History," in On the Fifth Day, ed. by Morris and Fox (1219).

1130. Burch, Robert W., "Animals, Rights and Claims," Southwestern Journal of Philosophy, Vol. 8, Summer, 1977, pp. 53-9.

1131. Caplan, Arthur L., "Rights Language and the Ethical Treatment of Animals," in Implications of History and Ethics to Medicine--Veterinary and Human, ed. by Laurence B. McCullough and James P. Morris III, Centennial Academic Assembly, Texas A and M University, College Station, 1978.

1132. Carpenter, Edward, Chairman, Animals and Ethics, A Report of the Working Party, Watkins, London, 1980. (Other members of the Working Party are Angela Bates, Trevor Beeson, David Coffey, Ruth Harrison, Sydney Jennings, Andrew Linzey, Hugh Montefiore, and W.H. Thorpe.)

1951-80: Animals and Ethics

1133. Carter, W.R., "Once and Future Persons," American Philosophical Quarterly, Vol. 17, January, 1980, pp. 61-6.

1134. Clark, Stephen R.L., "Animal Wrongs," Analysis, Vol. 38, June, 1978, pp. 147-9.

1135. Clark, Stephen R.L., "How to Calculate the Greater Good," in Animals'Rights-- a Symposium, ed. by David Paterson and Richard D. Ryder (1231).

1136. Clark, Stephen R.L., The Moral Status of Animals, Oxford University Press, New York, 1977.

1137. Clark, Stephen R.L., "The Rights of Animals," Etyka (Poland), Vol. 18, 1980.

1138. Clark, Stephen R.L., "The Rights of Wild Things," Inquiry, Vol. 22, Spring-Summer, 1979, pp. 171-88.

1139. Cottingham, John, "'A Brute to the Brutes?': Descartes' Treatment of Animals," Philosophy, Vol. 53, October, 1978, pp. 551-9.

1140. Curtis, Patricia, "Animal Rights," in Curtis's Animal Rights, Stories of People Who Defend the Rights of Animals, Four Winds Press, New York, 1980, pp. 129-39.

1141. Donaghy, Kevin, "Singer on Speciesism," Philosophic Exchange, Vol. 1, Summer, 1974, pp. 125-7.

1142. Dooley-Clarke, Dolores, Review of Stephen R.L. Clark's The Moral

Status of Animals, Clarendon Press, Oxford, 1977, *Philosophical Studies* (Ireland), Vol. 26, 1979, pp. 341-2.

1143. Duffy, Maureen, "Life, Liberty and Pursuit of Happiness," in *Animals' Rights--a Symposium*, ed. by David Paterson and Richard D. Ryder, pp. 112-14. (1231)

1144. Dworkin, Ronald, *Taking Rights Seriously*, Harvard University Press, Cambridge, 1977. (Does not discuss animals, but there are implications for animal rights.)

1145. Elliot, Robert, "Regan on the Sorts of Beings That Can Have Rights," *Southern Journal of Philosophy*, Vol. 16, Spring, 1978, pp. 701-5.

1146. Feinberg, Joel, "Can Animals Have Rights?" in *Animal Rights and Human Obligations*, ed. by Tom Regan and Peter Singer (1253).

1147. Feinberg, Joel, "Human Duties and Animal Rights," in *On the Fifth Day*, ed. by Morris and Fox. Also in *Etyka* (Poland), Vol. 18, 1980.

1148. Feinberg, Joel, "The Rights of Animals and Unborn Generations," in *Philosophy and Environmental Crisis*, ed. by W. Blackstone, University of Georgia Press, Athens, Ga., 1974.

1149. Feinberg, Joel, "What Kinds of Beings Can Have Rights?" in David Sidorsky, ed., *Social and Political Philosophy*, Harper and Row, New York, 1974.

1951-80: Animals and Ethics

1150. Foot, Philippa, _Virtues and Vices and Other Essays in Moral Philosophy_, University of California Press, Berkeley and Los Angeles, 1978, pp. 38-47. (Discussion of what is beneficial to plants, humans and animals)

1151. Fowler, Corbin, and Manig, Thomas, "Freedom: Animal Rights, Human Rights, and Super-human Rights," _Auslegung_, Vol. 4, November, 1976, pp. 52-63.

1152. Fox, Michael A., " 'Animal Liberation': A Critique," _Ethics_, Vol. 88, January, 1978, pp. 106-18.

1153. Fox, Michael A., "Animal Rights: Misconceived Humaneness," _Dalhousie Review_, Vol. 58, June, 1978.

1154. Fox, Michael A., "Animal Suffering and Rights," _Ethics_, Vol. 88 January, 1978, pp. 134-8.

1155. Fox, Michael W., _Animal Rights and Human Liberation_, Viking Press, New York, 1980.

1156. Fox, Michael W., "Animal Rights and Nature Liberation," in _Animals' Rights--a Symposium_, ed., by David Paterson and Richard D. Ryder (1231).

1157. Fox, Michael W., "From Animal Science to Animal Rights," in _Proceedings of First World Congress on Ethology Applied to Zootechnics_, Madrid, 1978.

1951-80: Animals and Ethics

1158. Fox, Michael W., _Animal Rights and Human Liberation_, Viking, New York, 1980.

1159. Francis, Leslie Pickering, and Norman, Richard, "Some Animals Are More Equal than Others," _Philosophy_, Vol. 53, October, 1978, pp. 507-27.

1160. Frankena, William K., "The Ethics of Respect for Life," in Barker, Stephen F., ed., _Respect for Life in Medicine, Philosophy, and the Law_, Johns Hopkins University Press, Baltimore, 1976.

1161. Fraser, A., "Ethology and Ethics," _Applied Animal Ethology_, Vol. 1, 1975, pp. 211-12.

1162. Frey, R.G., "Animal Rights," _Analysis_, Vol. 37, June, 1977, pp. 186-9.

1163. Frey, R.G., "Interests and Animal Rights," _Philosophical Quarterly_, Vol. 27, July, 1977, pp. 254-9.

1164. Frey, R.G., _Interests and Rights_, The Case Against Animals, Clarendon Press, Oxford, 1980.

1165. Frey, R.G., A review of Peter Singer's _Practical Ethics_, Cambridge University Press, London, 1979, _Mind_, forthcoming.

1166. Frey, R.G., "Rights, Interests, Desires and Beliefs," _American Philosophical Quarterly_, Vol. 16, July, 1979, pp. 233-9.

1167. Frey, R.G., "What Has Sentiency to Do

with the Possession of Rights?"
in Animals' Rights--a Symposium,
ed. by David Paterson and Richard
D. Ryder, (1231).

1168. Godfrey, Peter, "The R.S.P.C.A. Gives
Animals Charter of Rights," Times,
August 20, 1977.

1169. Godfrey-Smith, William, "The Rights
of Non-Humans and Intrinsic Values,"
in M.A. McRobbie, D. Mannison and
R. Routley,   eds.,   Environmental
Philosophy, Australian National
University Research School of
Social Sciences, Canberra, forth-
coming.

1170. Godlovitch, Roslind, "Animals and
Morals," in Animals, Men and Morals,
ed. by Godlovitch and Harris (1172).

11/1. Godlovitch, Roslind, "Animals and
Morals," Philosophy, Vol. 46,
January, 1971, pp. 23-33.

1172. Godlovitch, Stanley and Roslind, and
Harris, John, eds., Animals, Men
and Morals, Gollancz, London, 1971;
and Taplinger, New York, 1971.

1173. Goodpaster, Kenneth, "On Being Morally
Considerable," Journal of Philosophy,
Vol. 75, June, 1978, pp. 308-25.

1174. Goodrich, T., "The Morality of Killing,"
Philosophy, Vol. 44, April, 1969,
pp. 127-39.

1175. Hampson, Judith, "Animal Liberation--
a Plea for Action," in Animal Welfare,
September/October, 1979, published by
British Union for Abolition of Vivi-

section, London.

1176. Hampson, Judith, "Reviewing Animal
Rights," in Animal Welfare, September/October, 1977, published by
British Union for Abolition of
Vivisection, London.

1177. Hanula, Robert W. and Hill, Peter
Waverly, "Using Metaright Theory
to Ascribe Kantian Rights to
Animals Within Nozick's Minimal
State," Arizona Law Review,
University of Arizona, Vol. 19,
No. 1, 1977.

1178. Harrison, Frank R., "What Kind of
Beings Can Have Rights?" Philosophy
Forum (Dekalb), Vol. 12, September,
1972, pp. 113-28.

1179. Hart, H.L.A., "Are There Any Natural
Rights?" in A. Quinton, ed.,
Political Philosophy, Oxford University Press, London, 1967.

1180. Hart, H.L.A., "Death and Utility," A
review of Peter Singer's Practical
Ethics, Cambridge University Press,
Cambridge, New York Review of Books,
Vol. 27, May 15, 1980, pp. 25-32.

1181. Hartshorne, Charles, "The Rights of
the Subhuman World," Environmental
Ethics, Vol. 1, Spring, 1979, pp.
49-60.

1182. Haworth, Lawrence, "Rights, Wrongs,
and Animals," Ethics, Vol. 88,
January, 1978, pp. 95-105.

1183. Hunt, W. Murray, "Are Mere Things

Morally Considerable?" Environmental Ethics, Vol. 2, Spring, 1980, pp. 59-62.

1184. Jamieson, Dale, "Egoism and Animal Rights," Etyka (Poland), Vol. 18, 1980.

1185. Jamieson, Dale, and Regan, Tom, "Animal Rights: A Reply to Frey's 'Animal Rights'," Analysis, Vol. 38, January, 1978, pp. 32-6.

1186. Johnson, Edward, Species and Morality, Doctoral Dissertation, Princeton University, 1976, available from University International Dissertation Copies, Ann Arbor, Michigan, Order No. 77-2150, 258 pages.

1187. Jones, Hardy, "Reply: Concerning the Moral Status of Animals," Southwestern Journal of Philosophy, Vol. 8, Summer, 1977, pp. 61-3.

1188. Kock, Carl Henrik, "Man's Duties to Animals: A Danish Contribution to the Discussion of Rights of Animals in the Eighteenth Century," Danish Yearbook of Philosophy, Vol. 13, 1976.

1189. Kruzel, Mary K., "The Question of Animal Rights," Equus, February, 1980, pp. 68-71.

1190. Lawler, J.G., "On the Rights of Animals," Anglican Theological Review, April, 1965.

1191. Lehman, Hugh, Review of Stephen R.L. Clark's The Moral Status of Animals,

Clarendon Press, Oxford, 1977,
Social Indicators Research, Vol.
8, March, 1980, pp. 117-8.

1192. Levin, Michael, "All In a Stew About
Animals: A Reply to Singer,"
Humanist, Vol. 37, Sept.-Oct., 1977.

1193. Levin, Michael, "Animal Rights
Evaluated," Humanist, Vol. 37,
July-August, 1977.

1194. Linzey, Andrew, "Animal Rights Now,"
Christian Action Journal, July,
1971.

1195. Linzey, Andrew, Animal Rights: A
Christian Assessment of Man's
Treatment of Animals, SCM Press,
London, 1979.

1196. Linzey, Andrew, "Animals, Men and
Morals," Peace News, October 29,
1971.

1197. Linzey, Andrew, "Animals' Moral Rights,"
Animal Welfare, British Union for
Abolition of Vivisection, May, 1976.

1198. Linzey, Andrew, "Animals' Rights,"
Crucible, October/December, 1976.

1199. Linzey, Andrew, "The Rights of
Animals," New Fire, Winter, 1971.

1200. Lipman, Matthew, "Animal Rights:
Reasoning about Views," in Lipman's
Lisa, Chapter 1, pp. 1-8, Institute
for the Advancement of Philosophy
for Children, Montclair State College,
Upper Montclair, N.J., 1976. (For
grades 7,8, and 9).

1951-80: Animals and Ethics

1201. Lockwood, Michael, "Singer on Killing and the Preference for Life," Inquiry, Vol. 22, Spring-Summer, 1979, pp. 157-70.

1202. Lowry, Jon, "Natural Rights: Men and Animals," Southwestern Journal of Philosophy, Vol. 6, Summer, 1975, pp. 109-22.

1203. McCloskey, H.J., "Moral Rights and Animals," Inquiry, Vol. 22, Spring-Summer, 1979, pp. 23-54.

1204. McCloskey, H.J., "The Right to Life," Mind, Vol. 84, July, 1975, pp. 403-25.

1205. McCloskey, H.J., "Rights," Philosophical Quarterly, Vol. 15, April, 1965, pp. 115-27.

1206. McGinn, Colin, "Evolution, Animals, and the Basis of Morality," Inquiry, Vol. 22, Spring-Summer, 1979, pp. 81-99.

1207. Mackie, J.L., "Can There Be a Right-Based Moral Theory?" Midwest Studies In Philosophy, Vol. 3, 1978, pp. 350-59. (Does not discuss animals but there are implications for animal rights.)

1208. Mackie, J.L., Ethics, Inventing Right and Wrong, Penguin, New York, 1977, pp. 193-5.

1209. Mackinnon, Barbara, "A Review of Animal Liberation: A New Ethics for Our Treatment of Animals," Modern Schoolman, Vol. 54, 420-421, May, 1977, pp. 420-21.

1210.   Magel, Charles R., "A Boundless Ethic
which Includes the Animals Also."
Magel interviewed by John Ydstie,
Producer/Reporter, KCCM, Minnesota
Public Radio, Concordia College,
Moorhead, Minnesota. Available in
the form of an 80 minute cassette
tape; may be purchased from the
Moorhead State University Philosophy
Department, Moorhead, MN 56560.

1211.   Magel, Charles R., Review of Stephen
R.L. Clark's The Moral Status of
Animals, Clarendon Press, Oxford,
1977, Environmental Ethics, Vol.
2, Summer, 1980, pp. 179-85.

1212.   Margolis, Joseph, "Animals Have No
Rights and Are Not the Equal of
Humans," Philosophic Exchange, Vol.
1, Summer, 1974, pp. 119-23.

1213.   Martin, Antonia, "Animal Rights,"
Spectator, September 17, 1977.

1214.   May, William E., "What Makes a Human
Being To Be a Being of Moral Worth?"
Thomist, Vol. 40, July, 1976, pp.
416-43. (Also discusses what makes
other animals not be beings of moral
worth.)

1215.   Melden, A.I., Rights and Persons,
University of California Press,
Berkeley and Los Angeles, 1977.
(On the question of animal rights
see pp. 1, 17, 44, 111, 186, 188-9,
207, 209, 214, 219.)

1216.   Miller, Kim, "Animal Lib: Attack of
the Animal Lovers," This new army
of crusaders isn't marching to save

Bambi, The Province Magazine, June
22, 1980, Vancouver, B.C., pp. 3-6.

1217. Monticone, George T., "Animals and
Morality," Dialogue, Vol. 17, 1978,
683-695,

1218. Morris, Jan, "Views on 'Animal Rights,'"
Encounter, Vol. 53, No. 3, September,
1979, pp. 89-91.

1219. Morris, Richard Knowles and Fox, Michael
W., eds., On the Fifth Day: Animal
Rights and Human Ethics, Acropolis
Press, Washington, D.C., 1978.

1220. Mulder, J.B., "Who Is Right About
Animal Rights?" Laboratory Animal
Science, Vol. 29, 1979, pp. 435-6.

1221. Murphy, Jeffrie G., "Moral Death: A
Kantian Essay on Psychopathy,"
Ethics, Vol. 82, July, 1972. See
pp. 294-295 and footnote 23. (It
is argued that both animal and
psychopaths are morally dead, are
not persons, and do not have any
rights.)

1222. Naess, Arne, "Self-realization in
Mixed Communities of Humans, Bears,
Sheep, and Wolves," Inquiry, Vol.
22, Spring-Summer, 1979, pp. 231-41.

1223. Narveson, Jan, "Animal Rights,"
Canadian Journal of Philosophy,
Vol. 7, March, 1977, pp. 161-78.
Also in Etyka (Poland) Vol. 18,
1980.

1224. Nelson, Leonard, "Duties To Animals,"
in his System of Ethics (pp. 136-

144), Yale University Press, New
Haven, 1956. Also in Animals, Men
and Morals, ed. by Godlovitch and
Harris (1172).

1225. Nevin, David, "Scientist Helps Stir
New Movement for 'Animal Rights',"
Smithsonian, April, 1980, pp. 50-8.

1226. Nielsen, Kai, "Persons, Morals and the
Animal Kingdom," Man and World, Vol.
11, 1978, 231-256.

1227. Nozick, Robert, "Constraints and
Animals," in Nozick, Robert, Anarchy,
State, and Utopia, pp. 35-51, Basic
Books, New York, 1974.

1228. O'Neill, Onora, Review of Stephen
L.R. Clark's The Moral Status of
Animals, Oxford University Press,
1977, Journal of Philosophy, Vol.
77, July, 1980, pp. 440-6.

1229. Ostmann, Robert, Jr., "The Business of
Animals," Minneapolis Star, Saturday
Magazine, March 31, 1979, pp. 8-13.

1230. Passmore, John, "The Treatment of
Animals," Journal of History of
Ideas, Vol. 36, April-June, 1975,
pp. 195-218.

1231. Paterson, David, and Ryder, Richard D.,
Animals' Rights--a Symposium,
Centaur Press, Fontwell, Sussex,
1979.

1232. Pierce, Christine, "Can Animals Be
Liberated?" Philosophical Studies,
Vol. 36, July, 1979, pp. 69-75.

1233. Povilitis, Anthony J., "On Assigning
Rights to Animals and Nature,"
Environmental Ethics, Vol. 2, Spring
1980, pp. 67-71.

1234. Puka, Bill, Review of Animal Liberation
by Peter Singer in Philosophical
Review, Vol. 86, October, 1977,
pp. 557-60.

1235. Pybus, Elizabeth M. and Broadie,
Alexander, "Kant on the Maltreat-
ment of Animals," Philosophy, Vol.
53, October, 1978, pp. 560-1.

1236. Rachels, James, "Do Animals Have a
Right to Liberty?" in Animal Rights
and Human Obligations, ed., by Tom
Regan and Peter Singer (1253).

1237. Rachels, James, "A Reply to VanDeVeer,"
in Animal Rights and Human Obligations,
ed., by Tom Regan and Peter Singer
(1253).

1238. Rawls, John, A Theory of Justice,
Harvard University Press, Cambridge,
1971. (Little discussion of animals
(p. 17, pp. 504-12) but there are
implications for the just treatment
of animals.)

1239. Reeve, E. Gavin, "Speciesism and
Equality," Philosophy, Vol. 53,
October, 1978, pp. 562-3.

1240. Regan, Tom, "Animal Rights, Human
Wrongs," Environmental Ethics,
Vol. 2, Summer, 1980, pp. 99-120.
Also in Etyka (Poland) Vol. 18,
1980.

1241. Regan, Tom, "Broadie and Pybus on Kant," _Philosophy_, Vol. 51, October, 1976, pp. 471-2.

1242. Regan, Tom, "Cruelty, Kindness and Unnecessary Suffering," _Philosophy_, October, 1980.

1243. Regan, Tom, "The Debate over Animal Rights: An Introduction," in _Animals in Education_, Proceedings of the Conference on the Use of Animals in High School Biology Classes and Science Fairs, ed. by H. McGriffin and M. Brownley, Institute for the Study of Animal Problems, Washington, D.C., 1980.

1244. Regan, Tom, "An Examination and Defense of One Argument Concerning Animal Rights," _Inquiry_, Vol. 22, Spring-Summer, 1979, pp. 189-219.

1245. Regan, Tom, "Exploring the Idea of Animal Rights," in _Animals' Rights-- a Symposium_, ed. by David Paterson and Richard D. Ryder, pp. 73-86 (1231).

1246. Regan, Tom, "Feinberg On What Sorts of Beings Can Have Rights," _Southern Journal of Philosophy_, Vol. 14, Winter, 1976, pp. 485-98.

1247. Regan, Tom, "Fox's Critique of Animal Liberation," _Ethics_, Vol. 88, January, 1978, pp. 126-33.

1248. Regan, Tom, "Frey on Interests and Animal Rights," _Philosophical Quarterly_, Vol. 27, October, 1977, pp. 335-7.

1951-80: Animals and Ethics

1249. Regan, Tom, "McCloskey on Why Animals Cannot Have Rights," Philosophical Quarterly, Vol. 26, July, 1976, pp. 251-7.

1250. Regan, Tom, "Narveson on Egoism and the Rights of Animals," The Canadian Journal of Philosophy, Vol. 7, March, 1977, pp. 179-86.

1251. Regan, Tom, "On the Right to be Spared Gratuitous Suffering," Canadian Journal of Philosophy, Vol. 10, No. 3, September, 1980.

1252. Regan, Tom, A Review of The Moral Status of Animals, by Stephen R.L. Clark, in Philosophical Books, Vol. 19, October, 1978.

1253. Regan, Tom, and Singer, Peter, eds., Animal Rights and Human Obligations, Prentice-Hall, Englewood Cliffs, N.J., 1976.

1254. "Rethinking Animal Rights," Futurist, Vol. 13, June, 1979, pp. 238-9

1255. Rodman, John, "The Liberation of Nature?" Inquiry, Vol. 20, Spring, 1977, pp. 83-131. (A discussion of Peter Singer's Animal Liberation and Christopher Stone's Should Trees Have Standing?)

1256. Rollin, Bernard E., "Beasts and Men: The Scope of Moral Concern," Modern Schoolman, Vol. 55, March, 1978, pp. 241-60. Also in Etyka (Poland), Vol. 18, 1980.

1257. Rollin, Bernard E., "Moral Philosophy

and Veterinary Medical Education,"
*Journal of Veterinary Medical
Education*, Fall, 1977.

1258. Rollin, Bernard E., "Updating Veterinary Medical Ethics," *Journal
of the American Veterinary Medical
Association*, Vol. 173, No. 8, 1978.

1259. Ross, W.D., "Rights," in Ross' *The
Right and the Good*, pp. 48-56,
Clarendon Press, Oxford, 1961.
(Includes a discussion of rights
and duties as applied to children
and animals.)

1260. Routley, Richard and Val, "Against
the Inevitability of Human
Chauvinism," in Goodpaster, Kenneth
E., and Sayre, Kenneth M., eds.,
*Ethics and Problems of the 21st
Century*, University of Notre Dame
Press, Notre Dame, 1979.

1261. Ryder, Richard D., "Animal Liberation,"
R.S.P.C.A. Today, Vol. 12, December,
1973.

1262. Ryder, Richard D., "Animals Have
Rights Too," *Observer*, June 26,
1977.

1263. Ryder, Richard D. "A New Beginning
for Animals' Rights," *Oxford Mail*,
June 3, 1976.

1264. Ryder, Richard D., "Speciesism,"
Journal of Medical Ethics, Vol.
2, September, 1976.

1265. Ryder, Richard D., "Speciesism: The
Ethics of Animal Abuse," Royal

Society for the Prevention of
Cruelty to Animals, Horsham,
Sussex, 1979.

1266. Ryder, Richard D., "The Struggle
Against Speciesism," in Animals'
Rights--a Symposium, ed. by David
Paterson and Richard D. Ryder,
Centaur Press, Fontwell, Sussex,
1979, pp. 3-14. (This short article
is a very condensed history of the
struggle against speciesism,
especially in the 17th, 18th, and
19th centuries. See pp. 218-28
for an extensive, detailed
"Bibliography and Principal Notes.")

1267. Sapontzis, S.F., "Are Animals Moral
Beings?" American Philosophical
Quarterly, Vol. 17, January 1980,
pp. 45-52.

1268. Shepard, P., "Animal Rights and Human
Rites," North American Review, Vol.
259, Winter, 1974, pp. 35-42.

1269. Silverstein, Harry S., "Universality
and Treating Persons as Persons,"
Journal of Philosophy, Vol. 71,
February 14, 1974, pp. 57-71.
Especially see pp. 63-8.

1270. Singer, Peter, "All Animals Are
Equal," Philosophic Exchange,
Vol. 2, No. 5, Summer, 1974,
pp. 103-15.

1271. Singer, Peter, "Animal Liberation,"
A review of Animals, Men and Morals,
ed. by Stanley and Roslind Godlovitch
and John Harris (1172), The New York
Review of Books, Vol. 20, April 5, 1973.

1272. Singer, Peter, _Animal Liberation_, A New Ethics for Our Treatment of Animals, A New York Review Book distributed by Random House, New York, 1975; also Avon Books, New York, 1977.

1273. Singer, Peter, "Animals and Humans as Equals," _Etyka_ (Poland) Vol. 18, 1980.

1274. Singer, Peter, "Animals and the Value of Life," in Regan, Tom ed., _Matters of Life and Death_, Random House, New York, 1980.

1275. Singer, Peter, "The Case for Animal Liberation," _The Age_ (Melbourne), March 13, 1976.

1276. Singer, Peter, "Do Animals Have Equal Rights?" _Animal Industry Today_, Vol. 2, July/August, 1979, pp. 4-8.

1277. Singer, Peter, "Equality for Animals," "What's Wrong with Killing?" and "Taking Life: Animals," in Singer's _Practical Ethics_, Cambridge University Press, Cambridge, 1979, pp. 48-105.

1278. Singer, Peter, "The Fable of the Fox and the Unliberated Animals," _Ethics_, Vol. 88, January, 1978, pp. 119-25.

1279. Singer, Peter, "Killing Humans and Killing Animals," _Inquiry_, Vol. 22, Spring-Summer, 1979, pp. 145-56.

1280. Singer, Peter, "A Reply to Professor

Levin's Animal Rights Evaluated',"
Humanist, Vol. 37, July-August, 1977.

1281. Singer, Peter, "Value of Life,"
Encyclopedia of Bioethics, Vol. 2,
The Free Press, A Division of
Macmillan Publishing Co., New York,
1978.

1282. Spira, Henry, "Toward Animal Rights,"
_Agenda: A Journal of Animal Lib-
eration_, No. 2, March, 1980, P.O.
Box 5234, Westport, CT, 06880.

1283. Sprigge, T.L.S., "Metaphysics, Phys-
icalism, and Animal Rights,"
Inquiry, Vol. 22, Spring-Summer,
1979, pp. 101-43.

1284. Squadrito, Kathy, "A Note Concerning
Locke's View of Property Rights
and the Rights of Animals,"
Philosophia (Israel), forthcoming.

1285. Steinbock, Bonnie, "Speciesism and
the Idea of Equality," _Philosophy_,
Vol. 53, April, 1978, pp. 247-56.

1286. Sumner, L.W., "A Matter of Life and
Death," _Nous_, Vol. 10, May, 1976,
pp. 145-71. (See especially pp.
164-5.)

1287. Sumner, L.W., Review of _The Moral
Status of Animals_, by Stephen
R.L. Clark, _Dialogue_ (Canada),
Vol. 17, pp. 570-575, 1978.

1288. Sumner, L.W., Review of Peter Singer's
Animal Liberation, Avon Books, New
York, 1977, and of Tom Regan and
Peter Singer, eds., _Animal Rights_

and Human Obligation, Prentice-
Hall, Englewood Cliffs, 1976,
Environmental Ethics, Vol. 1,
Winter, 1979, pp. 365-70.

1289. Tooley, Michael, "Abortion and
Infanticide," Philosophy and Public
Affairs, Vol. 2, No. 1, Fall, 1972,
pp. 37-65.

1290. Townsend, Aubrey, A Review of The
Moral Status of Animals by Stephen
R.L. Clark, Australasian Journal
of Philosophy, Vol. 57, No. 1,
March, 1979.

1291. VanDeVeer, Donald, "Animal Suffering,"
Canadian Journal of Philosophy, Vol.
10, No. 3, September, 1980.

1292. VanDeVeer, Donald, "Defending Animals
by Appeal to Rights," in Animal
Rights and Human Obligations, ed.
by Tom Regan and Peter Singer (1253).

1293. VanDeVeer, Donald, "Interspecific
Justice," Inquiry, Vol. 22, Spring-
Summer, 1979, pp. 55-79.

1294. VanDeVeer, Donald, "Of Beasts, Persons,
and the Original Position," Monist,
Vol. 62, July, 1979, pp. 368-77.

1295. Vlastos, Gregory, "Justice and
Equality," in Human Rights, ed. by
A.I. Melden, Wadsworth, Belmont,
CA, 1970, pp. 76-95. (Does not
discuss animals but there are im-
plications for animal rights.)

1296. Warnock, Geoffrey J., "Morals and
Rationality," in Warnock's The

Object of Morality, Methuen & Co.,
London, 1971. (See pp. 150-152
for discussion of animals as moral
objects.)

1297.   Watson, Richard A., "Self-Consciousness
and the Rights of Nonhuman Animals
and Nature," Environmental Ethics,
Vol. 1, Summer, 1979, pp. 99-129.

1298.   Weiner, Jonathan, "Animal Liberation,"
Cosmopolitan, June, 1980, pp. 142 ff.

1299.   Wenz, Peter S., "Act-Utilitarianism and
Animal Liberation," Personalist, Vol.
60, October, 1979, pp. 423-8.

1300.   Williams, Meredith, " Rights, Interest,
and Moral Equality," Environmental
Ethics, Vol. 2, Summer, 1980, pp.
149-61.

1301.   Wye, Charles, "Towards a New Ethic:
A Humanitiarian Philosophy with
Special Reference to Man's Relation-
ship to Animals," Philosophical
Society of England, 81 Lavington
Road, London, W 13, 1957.

1302.   Ydstie, John, producer, "The Rights
of Animals," 45 minute taped discussion broadcast July 15, 1978.
Participants:
        Charles Magel, Professor of
        Philosophy, Moorhead State
        University
        Tom Morse, Manager, Fargo Beef
        Industries, West Fargo, N.D.
        William Beatty, Professor of
        Psychology, North Dakota
        State University
        Cassette Tape available from

Minnesota Public Radio, 400 Sibley St., St. Paul, Minn., 55101, Tape No. M-029.

1303. Young, Robert, "What Is So Wrong with Killing People?" Philosophy, Vol. 54, October 1979, pp. 515-528. Especially see pp. 526-8.

20: Treatment and Uses of Animals (Including Ethics of)

(For additional entries related to this topic see 3140, 2925, 2907, 2615, 2550.)

1304. Amory, Cleveland, Man Kind? Our Incredible War on Wildlife, Harper & Row, New York, 1974.

1305. Bell, Ernest, Fair Treatment for Animals, G. Bell and Sons, London, 1927.

1306. Bowman, John C., Animals for Man, E. Arnold, London, 1977.

1307. Caras, Roger, "Are We Right in Demanding an End to Animal Cruelty?" in On the Fifth Day, ed. by Morris and Fox (1219).

1308. Carson, Gerald, Men, Beasts, and Gods: A History of Cruelty and Kindness to Animals, Charles Scribner's Sons, New York, 1972.

1309. Chalmers, Dr., "Cruelty to Animals," Methodist Magazine, Vol. 9, 1926, pp. 259-66.

1310. Coleridge, Stephen, "On Cruelty," in Coleridge's Digressions, Mills and Boon, London, 1925.

1311. Coward, T.A., "Prevention of Cruelty to Wild Animals," Westminster Review, Vol. 157, May, 1902, pp. 546-51.

1312. "Cruelty," New Statesman, Vol. 9, September 1, 1917, pp. 512-3.

1313. Curtis, Patricia, Animal Rights, Stories of People Who Defend the Rights of Animals, Four Winds Press,

187

New York, 1980. (For teenagers
but also useful for adults.)

1314. Diole, Philippe, The Errant Ark: Man's
Relationship with Animals, trans. by
J.F. Bernard, Putnam's, New York, 1974.

1315. Douglas, J.S., "Cruelty to Foxes,"
Spectator, Vol. 156, January 17,
1936, pp. 95-6.

1316. Dreyfus, Marie, compiler, Crimes
against Creation: A Compilation,
Privately printed by Massey and
Co., Trowbridge, Wiltshire, U.K.,
and obtainable through Miss M.
Dreyfus, 101 Hampden Road, Hornsey,
London, N8, 1966.

1317. Fallows, James, "Lo, the Poor Animals!"
Atlantic Monthly, September, 1976.

1318. Fox, Michael A., "The Use and Abuse
of Animals," Queen's Quarterly,
Spring, 1976, Vol. 83, pp. 178-187.

1319. Fox, Robin, and Tiger, Lionel, The
Imperial Animal, Delta, New York,
1972. (Human dominance over other
species.)

1320. Frucht, K., "Animal Protection in the
Year 2000," Animal Regulation Studies,
Vol. 2, June, 1979.

1321. Galsworthy, John, "Animals and Birds:
A Stocktaking," Spectator, Vol. 143,
November 23, 1929, pp. 748-9.

1322. Galsworthy, John, "For Love of Beasts,"
in Galsworthy's A Sheaf, William
Heinemann, London, 1916.

1323. Galsworthy, John, "A Talk on Playing the Game with Animals and Birds." Royal Society for the Prevention of Cruelty to Animals, London, 1926.

1324. Godlovitch, Stanley, "Utilities" (using other beings), in Animals, Men and Morals, ed. by Godlovitch and Harris (1172).

1325. Hughes, John, The Animals Came In, Taplinger, New York, 1971.

1326. Hutchings, Monica M., and Carver, Mavis, Man's Dominion: Our Violation of the Animal World (performing animals, bull fighting, rodeos, pets, zoos, animal traffic, hunting, factory farming, furs, experimenting on animals), Rupert Hart-Davis London, 1970.

1327. Inge, William R., "Our Poor Relations," in Inge's Rustic Moralist, pp. 313-17, Putnam, London, 1937.

1328. Lambert, Joyce, How To Be Kind, The Book of the Kindness Club, Unipress, Fredericton, N.B., Canada, 1975. (Juvenile) (see 2751)

1329. Lee, Amy Freeman, "A Game for All Seasons," in On the Fifth Day, ed. by Morris and Fox (1219). (Violence, hunting, trapping, rodeos, furs.)

1330. Lord of Carnage: A Literary and Sociological Study of the Human Beast's Monstrous Crimes against Other Animal Species, 11 Clematis St., Blackburn (Lancs.), B.B. Books, 1968.

1331. Lorince, Gabriel, "Moscow's Cruelty Charts," New Statesman, Vol. 74, November 24, 1967, pp. 712-3.

1332. McCoy, Joseph J., In Defense of Animals, Seabury Press, New York, 1978.

1333. Midgley, Mary, "Brutality and Sentimentality," Philosophy, Vol. 54, July, 1979, pp. 385-394.

1334. Miles, Mrs. Eustace, The Cry of the Animals and Birds to Their Human Friends, Drane's, London, 1910. (Juvenile) (In Yale University Library.)

1335. Morse, Mel, Ordeal of the Animals, Prentice-Hall, Englewood Cliffs, N.J., 1968.

1336. Mouras, Belton P., I Care about Animals: Moving from Emotion to Action, A.S. Barnes, South Brunswick, N.J., 1977.

1337. Pedlar, Kit, "Urgent Changes Are Necessary to Protect Animals," Guardian Extra, October 8, 1975.

1338. Rolph, C.H., "All Animals are Equal," New Statesman, Vol. 64, July 20, 1962, p. 76.

1339. Ryder, Richard D., "Man's Lopsided Tyranny," Guardian, May 2, 1977.

1340. Salt, Henry S., ed., Cruelties of Civilization, William Reeves, London, (Humanitarian Leagues Publication, Vol. 2; there is a copy of this in the Princeton University Library.)

1341. Salt, Henry S., Seventy Years Among

Savages, G. Allen & Unwin, London,
1921 and Thomas Seltzer, New York,
1921.

1342. Scheffer, Victor B., "Benign Uses
of Wildlife," International Journal
for the Study of Animal Problems,
Vol. 1, January/February, 1980,
pp. 19-32.

1343. Scheffer, Victor B., A Voice for
Wildlife (hunting, killing for
subsistence, killing for the fur
trade, killing for science,
sealing, an ethic toward wildlife,
etc.), Scribner, New York, 1974.

1344. Serjeant, Richard, "Cruelty to
Animals," in Serjeant's The
Spectrum of Pain, Rupert Hart-
Davis, London, 1969, pp. 87-95.

1345. Trevelyan, Helen, Heaven's Rage,
C.W. Daniel, London, 1934.

1346. Trist, Sidney, The Under Dog, A
Series of Papers by Various Authors
on the Wrongs Suffered by Animals
at the Hand of Man, Animals'
Guardian Office, London, 1913.

1347. Turner, Ernest S., All Heaven in a
Rage, Michael Joseph, London, 1964.

1348. Verney, Peter, Animals in Peril: Man's
War Against Wildlife, Bringham Young
University Press, Provo, Utah, 1980.
(Also published under title Homo
Tyrannicus: A History of Man's War
Against Animals, Mills and Boon,
London, 1980.)

1349. Weber, William J., _Wild Orphan Babies,_
      Mammals and Birds; Caring for Them
      and Setting Them Free, Holt, Rinehart
      and Winston, New York, 1975.

1350. White, Elinor, _Lesser Lives_, W.R. Smith
      and Paterson, Brisbane, 1937.

1351. Wood, David, "Strategies," (social and
      individual delusional mechanisms
      used by humans in indefensible
      treatment of animals), in _Animals,_
      Men and Morals, ed. by Godlovitch
      and Harris (1172).

1352. Wynne-Tyson, Jon, "Red in Tooth and
      Claw," in his _The Civilized Alter-_
      native, Centaur, London, 1972, pp.
      89-120.

20: Animal Experimentation (Includes Experimentation on Humans, Alternatives to Animal Experimentation)

1901-50: Animal Experimentation
(For additional entries related to this topic
see 2393, 2433, 2506, 2517, 2525, 2574, 2585.)

1353. Articles on The Royal Commission on
Vivisection, Reprinted from The
Verulam Review, Elliot Stock, London,
1909.

1354. Baillie-Weaver, Mr., "Theosophy and
Vivisection," Theosophical Society,
Oxford, 1912.

1355. Berdoe, Edward, A Catechism of Vivisection, The Whole Controversy
Argued in All Its Details, Swan
Sonnenschein, London, 1903.

1356. Coleridge, Stephen, Evidence to the
Royal Commission on Vivisection,
National Anti-Vivisection Society,
London, 1907.

1357. Coleridge, Stephen, Great Testimony
Against Scientific Cruelty, John
Lane, London, 1918.

1358. Coleridge, Stephen, "An Open Letter
to the Home Secretary," National
Review (London), Vol. 46, 1905-6,
pp. 130-4.

1359. Coleridge, Stephen, "An Open Letter
to the Registrar-General," Contemporary Review, Vol. 82, 1902, pp.
510-15.

1360. Coleridge, Stephen, "An Open Letter
to the Right Hon. The Secretary of

State, Home Office," Fortnightly Review, Vol. 75 (N.S., Vol. 69), 1901, pp. 88-92.

1361. Coleridge, Stephen, "The Royal Commission on Experiments on Live Animals," Contemporary Review, Vol. 90, 1906, pp. 809-12.

1362. Coleridge, Stephen, "Torture Unrestrained by Law," National Anti-Vivisection Society, London, 1927.

1363. Coleridge, Stephen, "Vivisection," Discovery, Vol. 15, January, 1934, p. 15.

1364. Coleridge, Stephen, Vivisection, A Heartless Science, John Lane, London, 1916.

1365. Collingwood, Bertram, "The Task Before the Anti-vivisectionists," Dublin Review, Vol. 140, April, 1907, pp. 334-50.

1366. Davidson, Eugene, The Trial of the Germans: Nuremberg 1945-1946, Macmillan, London, 1966. (Experimentation on humans.)

1367. Dewey, John, "The Ethics of Animal Experimentation," Committee on Experimental Medicine of the Medical Society of the State of New York Series, National Society for Medical Research, Rochester, Minn., 1909.

1368. Dimmick, F.L., Ludlow, N., and Whiteman, A., "A Study of 'Experimental Neurosis' in Cats," Journal of Comparative Psychology, Vol. 28, August, 1939,

pp. 39-43.

1369. Ernst, Harold C., "Animal Experimentation," Journal of Social Science,
Vol. 42, 1904, pp. 98-109.

1370. Farris, E.J., and Griffith, J.Q.,
eds. The Rat in Laboratory Investigation, (2nd ed.), J.P. Lippincott,
Philadelphia, 1949.

1371. Flexner, S., and Flexner, J.T., William
Henry Welch and the Heroic Age of
American Medicine, Viking Press, New
York, 1941, pp. 254-65.

1372. Foley, John P., Jr., "An Apparatus for
Restraining Monkeys and Other Lesser
Primates," American Journal of
Psychology, Vol. 47, April, 1935,
pp. 312-15.

1373. Ford, Edward K., The Brown Dog and
His Memorial, The Animal Defence
and Anti-Vivisection Society, London,
1908.

1374. Foster, Burnside, "Results of Animal
Experimentation," Yale Review, Vol.
2, January, 1913, pp. 301-14.

1375. Galsworthy, John, "Vivisection of
Dogs," in Galsworthy's A Sheaf
(1322).

1376. Hadwen, Walter R., and Paget, Stephen,
"A Debate on: Is Vivisection Immoral,
Cruel, Useless and Unscientific?"
British Union for the Abolition of
Vivisection, London, 1908.

1377.   Haldane, John B.S., "Some Enemies of
        Science," in his Possible Worlds
        and Other Essays, Chatto and Windus,
        London, 1945.

1378.   Henson, Rev. H., "What are the
        Scientist's Moral Obligations?"
        Discovery, Vol. 14, 1933, pp.
        336-8, 368-71.

1379.   Hill, A.V., "Anti-Vivisection,"
        Nation and Athenaeum, London, Vol.
        40, December 18, 1926, pp. 412-14.

1380.   Holmes, Samuel J., "Some Controverted
        Questions of Right and Wrong," in
        Holmes, Samuel J., Life and Morals,
        Macmillan, 1948, pp. 144-75.   (On
        animal experimentation.)

1381.   Hughes, Helen M., "Newspapers and
        the Moral World," Canadian Journal
        of Economics and Political Science,
        Vol. 11, May, 1945, pp. 177-88.
        (On journalism and animal exper-
        imentation.)

1382.   James, William, "A Letter on Vivi-
        section," reproduced in Albert
        Leffingwell's An Ethical Problem,
        G. Bell and Sons, London, 1914,
        pp. 200-202.

1383.   Keen, William W., Animal Experimentation
        and Medical Progress, Houghton
        Mifflin, New York, 1914.

1384.   Kilduffe, Robert A., "What Are the
        Facts? A Discussion of Medical
        Research," American Journal of
        Nursing, Vol. 35, January, 1935,
        pp. 40-4.

1385. Lawrence, William, "Vivisection and a Humane Spirit," Outlook, Vol. 76, April 9, 1904, pp. 873-876.

1386. Leffingwell, Albert, An Ethical Problem, or Sidelights Upon Scientific Experimentation on Man and Animals, G. Bell and Sons, London, 1914.

1387. Leffingwell, Albert, "For Restriction and Limitation of Vivisection," Outlook, Vol. 76, April 9, 1904, pp. 876-879.

1388. Leffingwell, Albert, The Vivisection Controversy, Essays and Criticisms, The London and Provincial Anti-Vivisection Society, London, 1908.

1389. Leffingwell, Albert, "The Vivisection Problem," International Journal of Ethics, Vol. 15, January, 1905, pp. 221-231.

1390. Lind-af-Hageby, L., Ecrasez L'Infame!, An Exposure of the Mind, Methods, Pretences and Failure of the Modern Inquisition, Animal Defence and Anti-Vivisection Society, London, 1929.

1391. Lind-af-Hageby, L., Evidence Submitted to the Royal Commission on Vivisection, May 1 and June 5, 1907, Animal Defence and Anti-Vivisection Society, London, 1907.

1392. Lind-af-Hageby, L., "Vivisection and Medical Students: The Cause of Growing Distrust of the Hospitals and the Remedy," in The Animals'

Cause, ed. by L. Lind-af-Hageby, The Animal Defence and Anti-Vivisection Society, London, 1909, pp. 88-98.

1393. Lind-af-Hageby, L., and Halliburton, W.D., "A Public Debate," Is Vivisection Necessary to the Advancement of Science and Medicine, and Is Its Practice in Accordance with the Claims of Morality and the Further Development of Altruism? May 16, 1907, London, Published by the Organizing Committee for Miss Lind-af-Hageby's Anti-Vivisection Lectures and Debates.

1394. Lind-af-Hageby, L. and Schartau, L.K., The Shambles of Science, Extracts from the Diary of Two Students of Physiology, Ernest Bell, London, 1903.

1395. MacDonald, Greville, "Vivisection and Progress," Contemporary Review, Vol. 87, June, 1905, pp. 790-802.

1396. Merwin, Henry C., "Vivisection," The Atlantic Monthly, Vol. 89, March, 1902, pp. 320-5.

1397. Myers, C.S., "Is Vivisection Justifiable?" International Journal of Ethics, Vol. 14, April, 1904, pp. 312-322.

1398. Munn, Norman, Handbook of Psychological Research on the Rat, Houghton Mifflin, Boston, 1950.

1399. Nolan, Frank R., "Man's Greatest Shame," British Union for the

Abolition of Vivisection, London,
1926.

1400. Ohmsted, J.M.D., Claude Bernard:
Physiologist, Harper, New York,
1938.

1401. Paget, Stephen, "The Case Against
Anti-Vivisection," in Paget's
Experiments on Animals, James
Nisbet, London, 1906.

1402. Paget, Stephen, For and Against
Experiments on Animals, Evidence
Before the Royal Commission on
Vivisection, Paul B. Hoeber, New
York, 1912.

1403. Paget, Stephen, "Mr. Stephen
Coleridge's 'Open Letter to the
Registrar-General'," Contemporary
Review, Vol. 82, 1902, pp. 725-
31.

1404. Pickering, G., "The Place of
Experimental Method in Medicine,"
Proceedings of the Royal Society
of Medicine, Vol. 42, 1949,
p. 229.

1405. Richet, Charles, The Pros and Cons
of Vivisection, Duckworth, London,
1908.

1406. Sackville-West, V., "Vivisection,"
New Statesman and Nation, Vol. 16,
December 3, 1938, pp. 913-4.

1407. Shaw, George Bernard, "Against Vivisection," Sunday Express, August
7, 1927.

1408. Shaw, George Bernard, "Man of Science,"
      in Shaw, George B., Everybody's
      Political What's What, Dodd, Mean
      and Co., New York, 1944. (On
      animal experimentation.)

1409. Shaw, George Bernard, "Preface on
      Doctors," in Shaw's The Doctor's
      Dilemma: A Tragedy, in Bernard
      Shaw, Collected Plays with Their
      Prefaces, The Bodley Head, London,
      1971. (An extended discussion on
      the medical profession and vivi-
      section.)

1410. Shaw, George Bernard, Shaw on Vivi-
      section, ed. by G.H. Bowker, Allen
      and Unwin, London, 1949.

1411. Shaw, George Bernard, "Vivisection,"
      New Statesman and Nation, Vol. 16,
      December 17, 1938, pp. 1047-8; also
      December 31, 1938, p. 1125.

1412. Smith, Stephen, ed., Fruitless
      Experiment, An Examination and
      Critical Analysis of the Claims
      Advanced on Behalf of Vivisection,
      London Anti-Vivisection Society,
      London, 1904.

1413. Spragg, S.D.S., "Morphine Addiction
      in Chimpanzees," Comparative
      Psychology Monographs, Vol. 15,
      April, 1940, pp. 1-132.

1414. Vallery-Radot, R., The Life of
      Pasteur, Doubleday, Page, New York,
      1909.

1415. "Vivisection: A Plain Issue,"
      Spectator, Vol. 108, May 18,

1912, pp. 798-9.

1416. "The Vivisection Report," Spectator, Vol. 108, March 16, 1912, pp. 430-1.

1417. Wells, H.G., "For Vivisection," Sunday Express, July 24, 1927, (Reprinted by British Union for Abolition of Vivisection, London, 1927). (See 1407 for a response by G.B. Shaw.)

1418. Westacott, Evalyn A., Boomerang (some considerations against vivisection), Battley Bros., London, 1950.

1419. Westacott, Evalyn A., A Century of Vivisection and Anti-Vivisection, C.W. Daniel, London, 1949.

1420. Whipple, George H., "Value of Animal Experimentation to Mankind," American Journal of Public Health, Vol. 11, February, 1921, pp. 105-7.

1421. Yerkes, Robert M., Chimpanzees--A Laboratory Colony, Yale University Press, New Haven, 1943.

1422. Yerkes, Robert M., "A Program of Anthropoid Research," American Journal of Psychology, Vol. 39, December, 1927, pp. 181-99.

1951-80:   Animal Experimentation
(For additional entries related to this topic
see 2935, 2943, 2944, 2945, 2951, 1326, 2899,
2907, 2911, 2912, 2914, 2925, 3134, 2737,
2740, 2745, 2763, 2765, 2766, 2783, 2784,
2785, 2786, 2791, 2813, 2815, 2818, 2821,
2822, 2823, 2831, 2847, 2849, 2856, 2860,
2870, 2871, 2872, 2878, 2880, 2883, 2897,
2704, 2963, 2977, 2980, 2983, 2984, 2625,
3000, 3004, 3016, 3026, 3031, 3033, 2627,
3037, 3047, 3049, 3056, 3062, 2629, 3084,
3086, 3096, 3107, 2690, 2692, 2630, 2631,
2632, 2635, 2636, 2637, 2639, 2640, 2641,
2645, 2646, 2647, 2652, 2653, 2656, 2657,
2659, 2661, 2663, 2671, 2680, 2683, 2595,
2597, 2598, 2599, 2601, 2602, 2605, 2606,
2607, 2322, 2364, 2437, 2468, 2497, 2568,
2573, 2248, 2249, 2281, 2288, 2295, 2321,
2206.)

1423.   Adams, Richard, "How to Stop the
        Bloody Massacre," Observer,
        March 18, 1979, London.

1424.   Anderson, Allen C., ed., The
        Beagle as an Experimental Dog,
        Iowa State University Press,
        Ames, 1970.

1425.   "Are Experiments Really Necessary?"
        Sunday Observer, Colour Supplement,
        March 16, 1980.

1426.   Aronson, Lester R., and Cooper,
        Madeline L., Department of Animal
        Behavior, American Museum of
        Natural History, "Animal Welfare
        and Scientific Research," a letter,
        Science, Vol. 194 (Nov. 19, 1976),
        p. 784. (About experiments on cats
        at American Museum of Natural
        History.)

1427.   Arrington, Lewis, R., Introductory

Laboratory Animal Science, The
Breeding, Care, and Management
of Experimental Animals, Interstate
Printers and Publishers, Danville,
IL, 1978.

1428.   Austen, C.R., "The Use of Non-human
Primates as Models for Research
on Human Problems," in Chivers,
D.J., and Ford, E.H.R., eds.,
Recent Advances in Primatology,
Volume 4: Medicine, Academic Press,
London, 1978, pp. 223-7.

1429.   Azrin, N.H., "A Technique for
Delivering Shock to Pigeons,"
Journal of the Experimental
Analysis of Behavior, Vol. 10,
1967, pp. 393 ff.

1430.   Baasch, M.L., Frenkel, I., and
Kramer, G., eds., Bibliography
of Selected Tissue Culture
Experiments under the Aspect of
Replacing Animal Experiments,
Salem Research Institute,
Munich, West Germany, 1976.

1431.   Bachrach, Arthur J., "Ethical Considerations in Animal Research
and Human Research," in Bachrach's
Psychological Research, Random
House, New York, 1965, pp. 100-10.

1432.   Balls, M., "Alternatives to Living
Animals in Medical Experiments:
Towards a Rational View of Current
Status and Future Prospects," ATLA
Abstracts, Vol. 5, No. 1, 10-19,
1977.

1433.   Barber, Bernard, "The Ethics of

Experimentation with Human Subjects,"
Scientific American, Vol. 234, February, 1976, pp. 25-31.

1434. Barnes, Donald, "Psychologist Criticises
Cruelty to Primates at Brooks Air
Force Base," International Primate
Protection League *Newsletter*, Vol. 7,
March, 1980, pp. 6-7.

1435. Barnett, Samuel A., *The Rat: A Study in
Behavior*, Aldine Pub. Co., Chicago,
1963.

1436. Beary, E.G., *Laboratory Animals*, Their
Care and Use in Research: A Checklist.
Bibliography. U.S. Army, Natlick
Laboratories, Natlick, Mass., 1968.

1437. Blackstone, William T., "The American
Psychological Association Code of
Ethics for Research Involving Human
Participants: An Appraisal," *South-
ern Journal of Philosophy*, Vol. 13,
No. 4, Winter, 1975.

1438. Blythe, Jeffrey, "Tortured, Manacled
and Blinded: Horror of the Helpless
Monkeys," illustrated article in
Sunday People, London, June 8, 1980,
p. 25. (Resignation of psychologist
Dr. Donald Barnes at School of
Aerospace Medicine, U.S. Brooks Air
Force Base, San Antonio, Texas.)

1439. Bolles, R.C., "Shock Density and
Effective Shock Intensity, a Comparison of Different Shock Scram-
blers," *Journal of Experimental
Analysis of Behavior*, Vol. 9, 1966,
pp. 553 ff.

1440. Bourne, Geoffrey H., The Ape People, Putnam's, New York, 1971. (About the Yerkes Regional Primate Center, Atlanta, Georgia.)

1441. Bourne, G.H., ed., Progress in Ape Research, Academic Press, New York, 1977.

1442. Bowd, Alan D., "Ethical Reservations about Psychological Research with Animals," Psychological Record, Vol. 30, 1980, pp. 201-10.

1443. Bowd, Alan D., "Ethics and Animal Experimentation," American Psychologist, Vol. 35, February, 1980, pp. 224-5.

1444. Bowd, Alan D., "Reply to Gallup and Suarez," Psychological Record, Vol. 30, 1980, pp. 423-5.

1445. British Psychological Society, "Report of British Psychological Society Working Party on Animal Experimentation," Bulletin of the British Psychological Society, Vol. 32, 1979, pp. 44-52.

1446. Britten, S., "Animal Research: Whose Responsibility?" World Medicine Journal, Vol. 24, 1977, pp. 51-53.

1447. Broad, William J., "Legislating an End to Animals in the Lab," Science, Vol. 208, May 9, 1980, pp. 575-6.

1448. Broadhurst, Peter, The Science of Animal Behavior, Penguin Books, Baltimore, 1963.

1449. Brook, Maurice, "Animal Experiments: A Personal View," Biologist, Vol. 23, February, 1976, pp. 8-11.

1450. Brophy, Brigid, "In Pursuit of a Fantasy," (on vivisection) in Animals, Men and Morals, ed. by Godlovitch and Harris (1172).

1451. Brophy, Brigid, "The Silent Victims," A review of Richard D. Ryder's Victims of Science, Davis Poynter, 1975, New Statesman, February 28, 1975, pp. 278-9.

1452. Browne, Alister, "Morality and Medical Experimentation: Experiments on Human Subjects and Non-human Subjects," in Medical Responsibility, ed. by Wade L. Robison and Michael S. Pritchard, HUMANA Press, Clifton, New Jersey, 1979, pp. 101-112.

1453. Burne, Jerome, "Primate Business," The Beast, October-November, 1979, pp. 22-28.

1454. Burr, Stephen I., "Animal Experimentation: The British Point of View," Animals, Massachussets Society for the Prevention of Cruelty to Animals, August, 1979.

1455. Campbell, B.A. and Masterson, F.A. "Psychophysics of Punishment," in Punishment and Aversive Behavior, ed. by B.A. Campbell and R.M. Church, Appleton-Century-Crofts, New York, 1969.

1456. Campbell, Clare, and Worden, Alastair, and Ryder, Richard D., "Experiments on Animals: With a Review Discussion of *The Plague Dogs* by Richard Adams," *Theoria to Theory*, Vol. 12, April, 1978.

1457. "Can Some Knowledge Simply Cost Too Much?" A discussion generated by Frederick Wiseman's film *Primate*, with participation by:
Graham Shedd   David Baltimore
Frederick Wiseman   Richard Lewontin
Adrian Perachio   Robert Nozick
The Hastings Center Report, Vol. 5, No. 1, February, 1975, pp. 6-8.

1458. Cass, Jules S., ed., *Laboratory Animals*: An Annotated Bibliography of Informational Resources, Covering Medicine-Science-Technology, Hafner, New York, 1971.

1459. Charles River Breeding Laboratories, Inc., Presentation by Henry L. Foster, President, to the New York Society of Security Analysts, April 6, 1979, *The Wall Street Transcript*, May 21, 1979, pp. 54409-54410.

1460. Cherfas, Jeremy, "The Scientist as Good Shepherd," People have the power to use, and abuse, animals in any way they choose, So how are they to make their choices? *New Scientist*, March 27, 1980, pp. 1002-3.

1461. Chesney, W.D., *Inhuman Medical Experiments on Humans and Pets*, Chesney Publishing, Panama City, Florida, 1966.

1462. Clark, Stephen R.L., "Licensed

Torture?" Journal of Medical Ethics,
Vol. 2, September, 1976.

1463.   Coates, M.E., The Germ-free Animal in
Research, Academic Press, New York,
1968.

1464.   Coleman, V., Paper Doctors--A Critical
Assessment of Medical Research,
Transatlantic Arts, Levittown, N.Y.,
1977.

1465.   Cowey, Alan, "The Fate of the Guinea
Pig," A review of Richard D. Ryder's
Victims of Science, Davis Poynter,
1975, Times Literary Supplement,
April 18, 1975. This review re-
sulted in the following letters
published in the Times Literary
Supplement:
  May 2, 1975, Stephen R.L. Clark
  May 16, 1975, Richard D. Ryder
  June 6, 1975, Alan Cowey
  July 4, 1975, Stephen R.L. Clark
  July 11, 1975, Richard D. Ryder
  July 18, 1975, Alan Cowey

1466.   Cranefield, P.F., The Way In and the
Way Out, Francois Magendie, Charles
Bell, and the Roots of the Spinal
Nerves, Futura, New York, 1974.

1467.   Crispens, Charles G., Jr., Handbook
of the Laboratory Mouse, Charles C.
Thomas, Springfield, Ill., 1975.

1468.   Curtis, Patricia, "New Debate Over
Experimenting with Animals," The
New York Times Magazine, December
31, 1978, pp. 18-23. A condensed
version of this article appears in
Reader's Digest, February, 1980,

pp. 181-186.

1469.   Curtis, Patricia, "Of Mice and Men:
        Laboratory Animal Experimentation,"
        in Curtis' Animal Rights (1313), pp.
        1-19.

1470.   Curtis, Patricia, "Skeleton in the
        Laboratory Closet: Animal Experimen-
        tation," Animals, Massachussets
        Society for the Prevention of Cruelty
        to Animals, Boston, 1979.

1471.   DeBoer, J., Archibald, J., and Downie,
        H.G., An Introduction to Experimental
        Surgery: A Guide to Experimenting
        with Laboratory Animals, American
        Elsevier Pub. Co., New York, 1975.

1472.   Demaree, Allan T., "Henry Foster's
        Primately-for-Profit Business,"
        Fortune, Vol. 97, April 10, 1978,
        pp. 70-82.

1473.   Dennehy, Raymond, "The Philosophy of
        Human Experimentation," New
        Scholasticism, Vol. 52, pp. 80-90,
        Winter, 1978.

1474.   Dennis, Clarence, "America's Little-
        wood Crisis: The Sentimental
        Threat to Animal Research," Surgery,
        Vol. 60, pp. 827-839, 1966.

1475.   Diner, Jeff, Physical and Mental
        Suffering of Experimental Animals:
        A Review of Scientific Literature,
        1975-1978, Animal Welfare Institute,
        Washington, D.C., 1978.

1476.   Dixon, Bernard, "Animal Experiments:
        Time for a New Approach," in

Animals' Rights--a Symposium, ed. by David Paterson and Richard D. Ryder, Centaur Press, Fontwell, Sussex, 1979, pp. 178-86.

1477. Dixon, B., "Antivivisection, Constructive Moves," *New Scientist*, Vol. 69, 1976, p. 691.

1478. Dixon, B., "Leave Littlewood on the Shelf," *New Scientist*, Vol. 40, 1968, pp. 552-3.

1479. Dixon, Bernard, "Live Animal Experimentation," Jon Evans Interviewing Dr. Bernard Dixon, *Animals' Defender*, National Anti-Vivisection Society, London, January/February, 1980, pp. 17-20.

1480. Domer, Floyd R., *Animal Experiments in Pharmacological Analysis*, Charles Thomas, Springfield, IL., 1971.

1481. Dost, F.N., Johnson, D.E., and Wang, D.H., "A Restraint System for Squirrel Monkeys," *Laboratory Animal Science*, Vol. 22, 1972, pp. 893 ff.

1482. Dowding, Lord, "Lord Dowding on Vivisection," A speech delivered by Air Chief Marshal Lord Dowding in the House of Lords on Tuesday, 14th October, 1952, printed at the Ditchling Press, Ditchling, Sussex, U.K.

1483. Duffy, Maureen, "Go, Poor Fly," A review of Richard D. Ryder's *Victims of Science*, Davis Poynter,

1975, New Society, February 27,
1975, pp. 535-6.

1484. Eagles, Julie, "Are All Animal
Experiments Necessary?" Nursing
Times, Vol. 75, March 8, 1979,
pp. 398-9.

1485. Edwards, Rem B., and Marsh, Frank H.,
"Reasonableness, Murder and Modern
Science," Phi Kappa Phi Journal,
Vol. 58, No. 1, Winter, 1978, pp.
24-29.

1486. Fallaci, Oriana, "The Dead Body and
the Living Brain," Look, November
28, 1967. (On Robert White's
experiments with monkeys--head
transplants, keeping brain alive
after removal of body.)

1487. Festing, M., "Bad Animals Mean Bad
Science," New Scientist, Vol. 73,
1977, pp. 130-1.

1488. Findley, J.D., Robinson, W.W., and
Gilliam, W., "A Restraint System
for Chronic Study of the Baboon,"
Journal of the Experimental Analysis
of Behavior, Vol. 15, 1971, pp. 69 ff.

1489. French, Richard D., "Animal Experimen-
tation: Historical Aspects,"
Encyclopedia of Bioethics, Vol. 1,
The Free Press, A Division of
Macmillan Publishing Co., New York,
1978.

1490. French, Richard D., Antivivisection
and Medical Science in Victorian
Society, Princeton University Press,
Princeton, 1975. (Extensive,

detailed footnotes to literature
of the Nineteenth Century.)

1491. Freshel, M.R.L., compiler, Selections
from Three Essays by Richard Wagner
with Comment on a Subject of Such
Vital Importance to the Moral Progress of Humanity That It Constitutes
an Issue in Ethics and Religion,
The Millennium Guild, New York, 1933.
(on vivisection) (19th Century.)

1492. Freund, P.A., ed., Experimentation
with Human Subjects, G. Braziller,
New York, 1970.

1493. Gallup, G.G., Jr., and Suarez, S.D.,
"On the Use of Animals in Psychological Research," The Psychological Record, Vol. 30, 1980,
pp. 211-18.

1494. Galton, Lawrence, "Pain is Cruel,
But Disease is Cruel Too," New York
Times Magazine, February 26, 1967,
pp. 30-31.

1495. Garrison, W.B., "Storm Center of
Medical Research," in Garrison,
Webb, B., Codfish, Cats and
Civilization, pp. 80-89, Doubleday,
New York, 1959.

1496. Gay, W.I., ed., Methods of Animal
Experimentation, 5 vols., Academic
Press, New York, 1965-1974.

1497. Geison, Gerald L., "A Scientist's
Dilemma in Historical Perspective:
Pasteur's Work on Rabies: Re-
examining the Ethical Issues,"
Hastings Center Report, Vol. 8,

April, 1978, pp. 26-33.

1498. Goldman, L., "Animal Guinea Pigs, the Permissive Society," World Medicine, Vol. 6, 1970, pp. 17-22.

1499. Goldman, Louis, "Controversial Aspects of Current Animal Experimentation," in Animals' Rights--a Symposium, ed. by David Paterson and Richard D. Ryder, Centaur Press, Fontwell, Sussex, 1979, pp. 187-93.

1500. Goldman, L., "Experiments on Animals-- Another Look," World Medicine, Vol. 7, 1971, pp. 52-61.

1501. Gould, D., "Animal Experiments, the Search for Understanding, World Medicine, Vol. 11, 1976, pp. 17-24.

1502. Gould, D., "In Place of Lab Animals," New Scientist, Vol. 73, 1977, p. 210.

1503. Gould, Donald, "Medical Monkey Business," New Statesman, Vol. 86, December 28, 1973, p. 976.

1504. Gould, Donald, "The Smoking Beagles," New Statesman, March 14, 1975.

1505. Gowans, J.L., "Alternatives to Animal Experiments in Medical Research," British Medical Journal, March 23, 1974, pp. 557-9.

1506. "Guide to Clinical Research--The Declaration of Helsinki," adopted by the World Medical Association, June, 1964. Reproduced in (1638), pp. 101-103. (Experiments on humans)

1951-80: Animal Experimentation

1507. Gwynne, Peter, and Begley, Sharon,
"Animals in the Lab," Newsweek,
March 27, 1978, pp. 84-85.

1508. Hampson, Judith, Animal Experimentation,
1876-1976: Historical and Contemporary Perspectives, An Analysis
of Moves Towards the Reform of
British Legislation Controlling
the Practice of Animal Experimentation and of Contemporary Trends
in the Search for Humane Alternatives,
Ph.D. Thesis, University of Leicester,
1978. (Copies can be ordered through
Dr. Judith Hampson, c/o FRAME, 312A
Worple Road, London, SW 20 8QU,
England.)

1509. Hampson, J.E., "Animal Experiments--
Are They Always Justifiable?"
Kings Magus (King's College, London,
Student Magazine), June 20, 1977.

1510. Hampton, G.R., Sharp, W.V., and Anderson,
G.J., "Long-term Rabbit Restraint--
a Simple Method," Laboratory Animal
Science, Vol. 23, 1973, pp. 500 ff.

1511. Harlow, Harry F., Speaking of Love:
Theory and Therapy, a 2-cassette
Album, produced by Charles C. Wall
and Ronald Kidd, McGraw-Hill, New
York, 1974. (Experiments on
monkeys.)

1512. Harlow, Harry F., and Mears, Clara,
The Human Model: Primate Per-
spectives, V.H. Winston and Sons,
Washington, D.C., 1979.

1513. Harlow, Harry F., and Harlow, Margaret
K., "Psychopathology in Monkeys,"

in Experimental Psychopathology, ed.
by H.D. Kimmel, Academic Press, New
York, 1971.

1514. Hegarty, Terence, "Alternatives"
(to experimenting on animals), in
Animals, Men and Morals, ed. by
Godlovitch and Harris (1172).

1515. Hegarty, T.W., "Comments on the Paper
'The Ethics of Animal Experimentation',
by W. Lane-Petter," Journal of Medical
Ethics, Vol. 2, 1976, pp. 122-4.

1516. Hegarty, Terence, "More about Alternatives," Parenthese, Summer, 1975.

1517. Heim, Alice, "Report of the Working
Party on Animal Experimentation,"
Bulletin of the British Psychological
Society, Vol. 32, 1979, pp. 112-14.

1518. Heim, Alice, "The Use of Animals in
Experimental Psychology," Address
to the International Association
Against Painful Experiments on
Animals, July 12, 1979. Copies
available from the American Fund for
Alternatives to Animal Research, 175
West 12th St., New York, N.Y., 10011.

1519. Henry, K.R., and Bowman, R.E., "A
Long-Term Restraint Device for
Primates," Physiology and Behavior,
Vol. 7, 1971, pp. 271 ff.

1520. Hillman, H., "'Humane' Killing of
Animals for Medical Experiments,"
World Medical Journal, Vol. 25,
September/October, 1978, pp. 68-70.

1521. Hillman, H., "A Programme for

Diminishing the Use of Animals in Teaching and Research," ATLA Abstracts, Vol. 4, December, 1976, pp. 6-9.

1522. Hoff, Christina, "Immoral and Moral Uses of Animals," New England Journal of Medicine, Vol. 302, No. 2, January 10, 1980, pp. 114-118.

1523. Hoff, Christina, "Moral Considerations on Animal Experimentation," Etyka (Poland), Vol. 18, 1980.

1524. Hollands, Clive, "Animals That Suffer," Oxford Times, December 31, 1976.

1525. Hollands, Clive, "Kindness Is Not Enough," The Beast, No. 4, Dec.-Jan., 1980, pp. 20-21.

1526. Horton, M.L., Harris, A M., Van Slee, E.W., and Back, K.C., "Versatile, Protective Jacket for Chronically Instrumented Dogs," Laboratory Animal Science, Vol. 25, 1975, pp. 500 ff.

1527. Houghton of Sowerby, Lord, "Without Pity," A review of Richard D. Ryder's Victims of Science, Davis Poynter, London, 1975, The Spectator, March 1, 1975, pp. 241-2.

1528. Humane Society of the United States, Animals in a Research Laboratory, Washington, D.C., 1961.

1529. Hume, C.W., "The Ethics of Experiments on Animals," Nature, Vol. 424, February 10, 1951, pp. 213-5.

1951-80: Animal Experimentation

1530. Iggo, A., "Experimental Study of Pain in Animals--Ethical Aspect," in Advances in Pain Research and Therapy, Vol. 3, ed. by John J. Bonica et al., Raven Press, New York, 1979, pp. 773-8.

1531. Jamieson, Dale, "Experimenting on Cetaceans: Some Ethical Considerations," A submission to the Conference on Cetacean Behavior and Intelligence and the Ethics of Killing Cetaceans, Washington, D.C., April, 1980.

1532. Jolly, D.W., "The Benefit of Animal Experimentation to Animals," Conquest, Research Defence Society, London, Vol. 169, 1979, pp. 15-16.

1533. Jonas, H., "Philosophical Reflections Upon Human Experimentation," in Experimentation with Human Subjects, ed. by P.A. Freund, G. Braziller, New York, 1970.

1534. Jordan, W.J., "Animals Have Rights," Contemporary Review, Vol. 226, February, 1975, pp. 82-6.

1535. Keehn, J.D., "In Defence of Experiments with Animals," Bulletin of the British Psychological Society, Vol. 30, 1977, pp. 404-5.

1536. Lane-Petter, W., ed., Animals for Research, Principles of Breeding and Management, Academic Press, New York, 1963.

1537. Lane-Petter, W., "The Ethics of Animal Experimentation," Journal of Medical Ethics, Vol. 2, 1976, pp. 122-126.

1538. Lane-Petter, W., "The Place and Importance of the Experimental Animal in Medicine Today," Proceedings of the Royal Society of Medicine, Vol. 65, 1972, pp. 343-53.

1539. Lane-Petter, William, Provision of Laboratory Animals for Research, A Practical Guide, Elsevier, London, 1961.

1540. Lane-Petter, W., "Science, Animals, and Humanity," Nature, Vol. 174, September 18, 1954, pp. 532-4.

1541. Lane-Petter, W., Fell, B., and Mellanby, Kenneth, "Animal Experimentation," Biologist, Vol. 24, 1977, pp. 229-35.

1542. Lane-Petter, W., and Pearson, A.E.G., The Laboratory Animal--Principles and Practice, Academic Press, London and New York, 1971.

1543. LaPage, Geoffrey, Achievement: Some Contributions of Animal Experiments to the Conquest of Disease, W. Heffer, Cambridge, 1960.

1544. Lea, S.E.G., "Alternatives to the Use of Painful Stimuli in Physiological Psychology and the Study of Animal Behavior," ATLA Abstracts, Vol. 7, 1979, No. 1, P. 20.

1545. LeCornu, A., and Rowan, A.N., "The Use of Non-human Primates in the

Development and Production of Poliomyelitis Vaccines," *ATLA Abstracts*, Vol. 7, No.1, 1979, pp. 10-19.

1546. Lee, Ronnie, "How Long Shall These Things Be?" A review of Richard D. Ryder's *Victims of Science*, Davis Poynter, 1975, *Peace News* (London), April 4, 1975, pp. 8-9.

1547. Lewis, C.S., "Vivisection," in *God in the Dock*, Eerdmans Publishing, Grand Rapids, Mich., 1970.

1548. Lewis, Donald J., "Rats and Men," *American Journal of Sociology*, Vol. 59, September, 1953, pp. 131-5.

1549. Lilly, J.C., "Development of a Double-Table-Chair Method of Restraining Monkeys for Physiological and Psychological Research," *Journal of Applied Physiology*, Vol. 12, 1958, pp. 134 ff.

1550. Lindsey, J. Russell, "NSMR: Its Image, Direction and Future," *International Journal for the Study of Animal Problems*, Vol. 1, July/August, 1980, pp. 229-33. (On National Society for Medical Research)

1551. Linzey, Andrew, "Experiments on Animals," *Church Times*, November 3, 1972.

1552. McMillan, Bill, "Vivisection: Do

We Have Double Standards?"
Nursing Times, Vol. 75, March 8,
1979, pp. 397-9.

1553. McPherson, Charles, "Animal Resources Essential to Biomedical
Research," *Research Resources
Reporter*, U.S. National Institutes
of Health, Vol. 3, No. 8, August,
1979.

1554. Magel, Charles R., "Humane Experimentation on Humans and Animals...
or Muddling Through," National
Anti-Vivisection Society, Chicago,
1980. (Copies are available,
without cost, from National
Anti-Vivisection Society. See
3049.)

1555. Marcuse, F.L., and Pear, J.J.,
"Ethics and Animal Experimentation:
Personal Views," in *Psychopathology
in Animals*, ed. by J.D. Keehn,
Academic Press, New York, 1979,
pp. 305-29.

1556. Mason, J.W., "A Restraining Chair
for the Experimental Study of
Primates," *Journal of Applied
Physiology*, Vol. 12, 1958, pp.
130 ff.

1557. Mason, William A., "The Role of
Primates in Research," *Research
Resources Reporter*, May, 1979,
National Institutes of Health,
Bethesda, Maryland. Dr. Mason
is head of the behavior biology
department, California Primate
Research Center, Davis, Cali-
fornia. He is also professor of

psychology at the University of California, also president of the International Primatological Society. Quotation from above article, page 13:

I have never been able to reconcile fully the conflict between my interest in understanding the world as it is--that is to say, in science--and my feelings and moral attitudes toward the animals that I work with. Moreover, I do not expect ever to be able to resolve it completely. On the one hand, I believe implicitly in the value of the scientific approach. It is in many respects the most noble, effective, and progressive institution that man has yet evolved. On the other hand, I believe just as firmly in the inherent value of the animals I work with and their right to a free and independent existence. Even if I were absolutely sure that my particular research would improve the human condition, I would find it very difficult to attach a specific moral value to my findings that could persuade me completely that the end justified the means.

My personal response to the problem has been to muddle through.

1558. Mather, G.W., "Restraint of the Laboratory Dog," _Federation Proceedings_, Vol. 28, 1969, pp. 1423-7.

1559. Mayo, Charles W., "The Paradox of the Well-Intentioned Enemies of Medical Research," President's Address, read before the 71st Annual Session of the Western Surgical Association, Galveston, Texas, Nov. 21-23, 1963, published in _Archives of Surgery_, April, 1964, Copies of this address are available from the American Anti-Vivisection Society, Philadelphia, Pa.

1560. Melby, Edward C., and Altman, Norman H., eds., _CRC Handbook of Laboratory Animal Science_, CRC Press, Cleveland, 1974-1976.

1561. Milgram, Stanley, _Obedience to Authority_, Harper and Row, New York, 1974. (Experiments on humans demonstrating that humans will follow instructions to give painful electric shocks to other humans. Actually there were no electric shocks; the victims were only pretending to be in great pain; but the subjects were not aware of this deception.)

1562. Mitruka, B.M., Rawnsley, H.M., and Vadehra, D.V., _Animals for Medical Research: Models for the Study of Human Disease_, Wiley Medical, New York, 1976.

1563. Mitscherlich, Alexander, and Mielke, F., _The Death Doctors_, trans. by

James Cleugh, Elek Books, London 1962. (Experimentation on humans-- and animals--in German concentration camps.)

1564. Morris, Rosalind, "How Live Animals Suffer Pain for Trivial Research." Observer, March 2, 1975.

1565. Mount, L.E., and Ingram, D.L., The Pig as a Laboratory Animal, Academic Press, New York, 1971.

1566. Mountjoy, D.G. and Baker, M.A., "Limb Immobilization Devices for Chaired Waking Monkeys," Journal of Applied Physiology, Vol. 36, 1974, pp. 385 ff.

1567. Musto, David F., "Freedom of Inquiry and Subjects' Rights: Historical Perspective," American Journal of Psychiatry, Vol. 134, August, 1977, pp. 893-9.

1568. "The Nuremburg Code of Ethics in Medical Research," Report of the National Conference on the Legal Environment of Medical Science sponsored by the National Society for Medical Research and the University of Chicago, May 27-28, 1959, pp. 91-92. Reproduced in (1638) pp. 101-103. (Experiments on humans.)

1569. Nyman, J., "Moral Issues in the Use of Animals in Experimental Research from the Renaissance to the Twentieth Century," Animal Regulation Studies, Vol. 2, June, 1979, pp. 31-6.

1570. Orlans, F. Barbara, Animal Care--From Protozoa to Small Animals, Addison-Wesley, Menlo Park, Ca., 1977.

1571. Otten, Jim, and Russow, Lilly-Marlene, "Forum: Experimentation on Animals," Eros, Department of Philosophy, Purdue University, April, 1977.

1572. Ozer, Mark N., "The British Vivisection Controversy," Bulletin of the History of Medicine, Vol. 40, 1966, pp. 158-67.

1573. Paget, G.E., "Animal Experiment: The Ethical Questions," Biologist, Vol. 25, 1978, pp. 145-7.

1574. Paget, G.E., "The Ethics of Vivisection," Theology, July, 1975.

1575. Pappworth, M.H., Human Guinea Pigs: Experimentation on Man, Beacon Press, Boston, 1968.

1576. Paton, W.D.M., "Animal Experiment and Medical Research: A Study in Evolution," Conquest, The Journal of the Research Defence Society, London, Vol. 169, 1979, pp. 1-14.

1577. Paton, W.D.M., "Animal Experiment: Some Controversial Questions," Biologist, Vol. 25, 1978, pp. 142-4.

1578. Peddie, Fred, "Man-made Hell for Animals," Dogs in Canada, Vol. 71, No. 2.

1579. Porter, George, and Lane-Petter,

W., eds., Notes for Breeders of
Common Laboratory Animals, T.F.H.
Publications, Jersey City, New
Jersey, 1962. Also Academic Press,
London, 1962.

1580.   Pratt, Dallas, Alternatives to Pain
in Experiments on Animals, Argus
Archives, New York, forthcoming.

1581.   Ross, M.W., "The Ethics of Animal
Experimentation: Control in
Practice," Australian Psychologist,
Vol. 13, 1978, pp. 375-8.

1582.   Regan, Tom, "Animal Rights and Animal
Experimentation," in Conference
Proceedings: Fourth and Fifth
Conferences on Ethics, Humanism
and Medicine (at the University
of Michigan), Alan R. Liss, New
York, forthcoming.

1583.   Remfry, J., "The Humane Approach to
Experimental Animals," World
Medicine Journal, Vol. 24, 1977,
p. 54.

1584.   Risdon, Wilfred, "Lawson Tait on
Vivisection," in Risdon's Robert
Lawson Tait, National Anti-Vivisection Society, London, 1967,
pp. 12-50.

1585.   Roberts, Catherine, "The Utilization
of Animals in Medical Research,"
and "Humanism and the Rhesus," in
Roberts' The Scientific Conscience,
George Braziller, New York, 1967.

1586.   Roberts, Catherine, "A New Approach
to Animal Experimentation" and

"A Debate with an Animal Experi-
menter," in Roberts' Science, Animals,
and Evolution, Greenwood Press,
Westport, Conn., 1980, pp. 89-123.
The debate is with Robert J. White.
White's "Antivivisection: The
Relctant Hydra" and "Replies" are
included. (White's Antivivisection:
The Reluctant Hydra" is also re-
produced in Animal Rights and Human
Obligations, ed. by Regan and
Singer (1253), pp. 163-9.)

1587. Rollin, Bernard E., "Definition of
the Concept of 'Humane Treatment'
in Relation to Food and Laboratory
Animals," International Journal
for the Study of Animal Problems,
Vol. 1, July/August, 1980, pp.
234-41.

1588. Rollin, Bernard E., "Moral Concern
and Animal Experimentation,"
Colorado: People and Policy,
University of Denver, Spring, 1979.

1589. Rowan, Andrew N., "Alternatives and
Animals Rights: A Reply to Maurice
Visscher," International Journal
for the Study of Animal Problems,
Vol. 1, July/August, 1980, pp.
210-12.

1590. Rowan, Andrew N., "Alternatives to
Laboratory Animals," The Bart's
Journal, Spring, 1977, pp. 19-20.

1591. Rowan, Andrew N., "Alternative to
Laboratory Animals," in New
Perspectives on Animal Experimen-
tation, ed. by D. Sperlinger, J.
Wiley and Sons, Chichester, Sussex,

forthcoming.

1592. Rowan, Andrew N., "Alternatives to Laboratory Animals in Biomedical Programs," Animal Regulation Studies, Vol. 1, November, 1977, pp. 103-128.

1593. Rowan, Andrew N., "Alternatives to the Use of Animals in Toxicology Testing," Script Pharmaceutical News, April 30, 1977, pp. 20-21.

1594. Rowan, Andrew N., "Animals, Alternatives and Biomedical Research and Testing," World Medicine Journal, Vol. 24, 1977, pp. 55-56.

1595. Rowan, Andrew N., "Are There Feasible Alternatives to Laboratory Animals?" School Science Review, Vol. 58, 1976, pp. 210-16.

1596. Rowan, Andrew N., "Laboratory Animals and Alternatives in the 80's," International Journal for the Study of Animal Problems, Vol. 1, May/June, 1980, pp. 162-9.

1597. Rowan, Andrew N., "Primate Testing: Adequate Alternative," (letter) Science, Vol. 199, 1978, p. 934.

1598. Rowan, A.N., and Stratmann, C.J., eds., The Use of Alternatives in Drug Research, Proceedings of a Symposium at the Royal Society, London, April 11-12, 1978, Macmillans, London, 1980.

1599. Ruesch, Hans, Slaughter of the Innocent, Bantam, New York, 1978.

(A history and critique of animal experimentation in the medical and drug industries, with the thesis that such experimentation is doing more harm--to humans--than good.)

1600. Russell, W.M.S. and Burch, R.L., The Principles of Humane Experimental Technique, Methuen and Co., London, 1959.

1601. Ryder, Richard D., "Animal Experiments-- Realism Must Replace Red Tape," Times, August 14, 1975.

1602. Ryder, Richard D., "Experiments on Animals," in Animal Welfare, published by British Union for Abolition of Vivisection, London, 1976.

1603. Ryder, Richard D., "Experiments on Animals," in Animals, Men and Morals, ed. by Godlovitch and Harris. Also in Animal Rights and Human Obligations, ed. by Tom Regan and Peter Singer (1253).

1604. Ryder, Richard D., "Experiments: Time for Revision," Doctor, June 5, 1975.

1605. Ryder, Richard D., "The Extensive Use of Animals in Non-Medical Research," Scottish Society for the Prevention of Vivisection, Edinburgh, 1975.

1606. Ryder, Richard D., "Laboratory Animals and Politics," copies available from The American Fund for Alternatives to Animal Research,

175 West 12th St., New York, N.Y., 10011.

1607. Ryder, Richard D., "Professor Shuster-- A Reply," New Scientist, Vol, 77, January 12, 1978, pp. 82-3.

1608. Ryder, Richard D., "Scientific Cruelty for Commercial Profit," Scottish Society for the Prevention of Vivisection, Edinburgh, 1976.

1609. Ryder, Richard D., "A Scientist Speaks on the Extensive Use of Animals in Non-Medical Research," Scottish Society for the Prevention of Vivisection, Edinburgh, 1972.

1610. Ryder, Richard D., "Speciesism: The Ethics of Vivisection," Scottish Society for the Prevention of Vivisection, Edinburgh, 1974.

1611. Ryder, Richard D., "Time to Unlock the Laboratories," The Spectator, November 1, 1975.

1612. Ryder, Richard D., "Towards Humane Methods of Identification," in Animal Marking: Recognition Marking of Animals in Research, ed. by Bernard Stonehouse, University Park Press, Baltimore, 1979.

1613. Ryder, Richard D., Victims of Science, The Use of Animals in Research, Davis-Poynter, London, 1975.

1614. Salisbury, David, "Research with Animals," The Christian Science Monitor, Boston, Mass., March 8,

9, 10, 1978.

1615. Schiller, Joseph, "Claude Bernard and Vivisection," Journal of the History of Medicine, Vol. 22, 1967, pp. 246-60.

1616. Schwabe, Calvin W., Cattle, Priests, and Progress in Medicine, University of Minnesota Press, Minneapolis, 1978.

1617. Seligman, Martin E.P., "Learned Helplessness," Cassette Tape, produced by Psychology Today, distributed by Speed Cassette Duplication, 1246 10th St., Manhattan Beach, California.

1618. Seligman, Martin E.P., "Learned Helplessness in the Dog," "Death from Helplessness in Animals" and "Death from Helplessness in Humans," in Seligman's Helplessness, W.H. Freeman, San Francisco, 1975, pp. 23-37, 169-75, 175-88.

1619. Serban, George, and Kling, Arthur, Animal Models in Human Psychobiology, Plenum Press, New York, 1976.

1620. Sharp, John A., An Introduction to Animal Tissue Culture, Edward Arnold, London, 1977.

1621. Short, Douglas J., and Woodnott, Dorothy P., The Institute of Animal Technicians Manual of Laboratory Animal Practice and Techniques, Crosby Lockwood, London, 1971.

1622. Shuster, Sam, "The Anti-Vivisection-
ists--A Critique," New Scientist,
Vol. 77, January 12, 1978, pp.
80-2.

1623. Shuster, Sam, "Why We Need Animal
Research," World Medicine, Vol.
13, November 30, 1977, pp. 19-
37.

1624. Singer, Peter, "Animal Experimentation:
Philosophical Perspectives,"
Encyclopedia of Bioethics, Vol. 1,
The Free Press, Division of Mac-
millan Publishing Co., New York,
1978.

1625. Singer, Peter, "The Morality of
Experimenting with Animals," in
Philosophy and Science: The Wide
Range of Interaction, ed. by
Frederick E. Mosedale, Prentice-
Hall, Englewood Cliffs, NJ, 1979.
(Reprint of sections of "Animal
Liberation," a review of Animals,
Men and Morals, New York Review
of Books, Vol. 20, No. 3, April
5, 1973.)

1626. Singer, Peter, "Tools for Research...
Or What the Public Doesn't know
It Is Paying for," in Singer's
Animal Liberation (1272), pp.
27-91.

1627. Smyth, David H., Alternatives to
Animal Experimentation, Scolar
Press, 39 Great Russell St.,
London, 1978.

1628. Sperlinger, David, "Scientists and
Their Experimental Animals," in

Animals' Rights--a Symposium, ed.
by David Paterson and Richard D.
Ryder, Centaur Press, Fontwell,
Sussex, 1979, pp. 196-200.

1629. Sperlinger, D., "Working Party on
Animal Experimentation," Bulletin
of the British Psychological Society,
Vol. 32, 1979, pp. 291-2.

1630. Sternbach, Richard A., "Ethical
Problems in Human Pain Research,"
in Advances in Pain Research and
Therapy, Vol. 3, ed. by John J.
Bonica et al., Raven Press, New
York, 1979, pp. 837-42.

1631. Stevenson, Lloyd G., "Religious
Elements in the Background of the
British Anti-Vivisection Movement,"
Yale Journal of Biology and Medicine,
Vol. 29, 125-157, 1956.

1632. Stevenson, L.G., "Science Down the
Drain," Bulletin of the History of
Medicine, Vol. 29, 1955, pp. 1-26.

1633. Stonehouse, B., ed., Animal Marking:
Recognition Marking of Animals in
Research, University Park Press,
Baltimore, Md., 1979.

1634. Stretch, R., and Gerber, G.J., "A
Method for Chronic Intravenous
Drug Administration in Squirrel
Monkeys," Canadian Journal of
Physiology and Pharmacology, Vol.
48, 1970, pp. 575 ff.

1635. Travis, C., "Harry, You Are Going
to Go Down in History as the
Father of the Cloth Mother,"

Psychology Today, Vol. 6, No. 11, 1973, pp. 65-77. (About Harry Harlow's experiments on monkeys.)

1636. University of Michigan, "Animals in Science: Laboratory Animal Medicine," Research News, University of Michigan, February-March, 1978.

1637. Visscher, Maurice B., "The Animal Experimentation Control Bills in the United States Congress," The Physiologist, Vol. 6, No. 1, February, 1963, pp. 53-62.

1638. Visscher, Maurice B., Ethical Constraints and Imperatives in Medical Research, Thomas, Springfield, Ill., 1975.

1639. Visscher, Maurice B., "Animal Rights and Alternative Methods," The Pharos, Fall, 1979, pp. 11-19.

1640. Visscher, Maurice B., "Medical Research and Ethics," Journal of the American Medical Association, Vol. 199, No. 9, Feb. 27, 1967.

1641. "Vivisection-Vivistudy: The Facts and the Benefits to Animal and Health," American Journal of Public Health, Vol. 57, 1967, pp. 1597-1626. (Four papers presented at a symposium of medical and veterinary specialists.)

1642. Vyklicky, Ladislav, "Techniques for the Study of Pain in Animals," in Advances in Pain Research and Therapy, Vol. 3, ed. by John J. Bonica et al., Raven Press, New

York, 1979, pp. 727-45.

1643. Vyvyan, John, The Dark Face of Science, Michael Joseph, London, 1971. (Also Transatlantic Arts, Inc., Levittown, New York, 1972.)

1644. Vyvyan, John, In Pity and in Anger: A Study of the Use of Animals in Science, Michael Joseph, London, 1969.

1645. Wade, Nicholas, "Animal Rights: NIH Cat Sex Study Brings Grief to New York Museum," Science, Vol. 194, October 8, 1976.

1646. Wade, N., "New Vaccine May Bring Man and Chimpanzee into Tragic Conflict," Science, Vol. 200, 1978, pp. 1027-30.

1647. Watts, Geoff, "Programming Out the Guinea Pig," World Medicine, Vol. 8, 1973, pp. 17-24.

1648. Whitney, Robert A., Jr., Johnson, Donald J., and Cole, William C., Laboratory Primate Handbook, Academic Press, New York, 1973.

1649. Whittaker, Alan, "The Case Against Vivisection," Nursing Times, Vol. 75, March 8, 1979, pp. 396-9.

1650. Windeatt, Phil, and May, John, "Charles River: The General Motors of Animal Breeding," The Beast, Summer, 1980, pp. 27-31.

1951-80: Factory Farming
(For additional entries related to this topic
see 3133, 2764, 2781, 2807, 2820, 2824, 2837,
2838, 2844, 2849, 2628, 2885, 2887, 2925,
2927, 2597, 2954, 3016, 3028, 3029, 3053,
3055, 3064, 3080, 3081, 3108, 2694, 2605,
2606, 2557, 2247, 2260, 2267, 1326.)

1651. Alrawi, B., and Craig, J.V., "Agonistic
     Behavior of Caged Chickens Related
     to Group Size and Area Per Bird,"
     Applied Animal Ethology, Vol. 2,
     1975, pp. 69 ff.

1652. Anderson, Marilyn, "Animal Farms--
     1980 Style," Toronto Star, July
     20, 1980, pp. B1 and B5.

1653. Bellerby, John R., ed., Factory
     Farming: A Symposium Held on
     August 23, 1968, in Dundee,
     British Association for the
     Advancement of Science, London,
     1970.

1654. Benson, V.W., and Witzig, T.J., The
     Chicken Broiler Industry: Structure,
     Practices, and Costs, U.S. Department
     of Agriculture, Agricultural Eco-
     nomic Report 381, Washington, D.C.,
     August, 1977.

1655. Blount, W.P., ed., Intensive Live-
     stock Farming, Heinemann Medical
     Books, London, 1968.

1656. Bryant, Arthur, "Consideration for
     Animals and Raising Animals to Eat,"
     Illustrated London News, Vol. 237,
     July 30, 1960, p. 174.

1657. Curtis, Patricia, "We Are What We
     Eat: Factory Farming," in Curtis'
     Animal Rights (1313), pp. 73-89.

1658. Dunn, P.G.C., "Intensive Livestock Production: 'Costs Exceed Benefits'," Veterinary Record, Vol. 106, February 9, 1980, pp. 131-2.

1659. Folsch, D.W., ed., The Ethology and Ethics of Farm Animal Production, Proceedings of the 28th Annual Meeting, Commission on Animal Management and Health, Session III, IV, held in Brussels, August 1977, Animal Management Series, Vol. 6, Birkhauser, Verlag, Basel, Stuttgart, 1978.

1660. Fox, Michael W., "Animal Factories," Humane Society News, Vol. 25, Spring, 1980, pp. 4-9. Humane Society of the United States, Washington, D.C.

1661. Fox, Michael W., "Factory Farming," Humane Society of the United States, Washington, D.C., 1980.

1662. Fox, Michael W., "Suffering: The Hidden Cost of Factory Farming," Humane Society News, Vol. 23, Winter, 1978, pp. 15-20. Humane Society of the United States, Washington, D.C.

1663. Fraser, A.F., "Behavior of Livestock under Intensive Conditions of Husbandry," Applied Animal Ethology, Vol. 1, 1975, pp. 111 ff.

1664. Freeman, B.M., "Stress and the Domestic Fowl," World Poultry Science Journal, Vol. 27, 1971, pp. 263 ff.

1665. Gallimore, W.W., and Irwin, R.J.,

1951-80: Factory Farming

The Turkey Industry: Structure, Practices, and Costs, U.S. Department of Agriculture, Marketing Research Report 1000, Washington, D.C., June, 1973.

1666. Gaunt, Stanley N., and Harrington, Roger M., eds., Raising Veal Calves, The Massachusetts Cooperative Extension Service, University of Massachusetts, No. 106, no date.

1667. Grandin, Temple, "Livestock Behavior as Related to Handling Facilities Design," International Journal for the Study of Animal Problems, Vol. 1, January/February, 1980, pp. 33-52.

1668. Halverson, Diane, "A Discussion of Current Methods and Trends in the Rearing of Cattle and Swine," prepared for the Animal Welfare Committee of the U.S. Animal Health Association Annual Meeting, October 30, 1979, Animal Welfare Institute, Washington, D.C.

1669. Harrison, Ruth, Animal Machines: The New Factory Farming Industry, Stuart, London, 1964.

1670. Harrison, Ruth, "Ethical Questions Concerning Livestock Farming," in Animals' Rights--A Symposium, ed. by David Paterson and Richard D. Ryder (1231).

1671. Harrison, Ruth, "On Factory Farming," in Animals, Men and Morals, ed. by Stanley and Roslind Godlovitch and John Harris, Taplinger, New York, 1972.

1951-80: Factory Farming

1672. "Is Pain the Price of Farm Efficiency?"
New Scientist, October 18, 1973.

1673. Jensen, A., et al., Management and
Housing for Confinement Swine
Production, University of Illinois,
College of Agriculture, Cooperative
Extension Service Circular 1064,
Urban-Champaign, IL, November, 1972.

1674. Kiley-Worthington, M., Behavioural
Problems of Farm Animals, Kegan
Paul, Oxford, 1977.

1675. Kingrey, B.W., "Ethical Problems
and Decisions in Food Animal
Medicine," in Implications of
History and Ethics to Medicine--
Veterinary and Human, ed. by
Laurence B. McCullough and James
P. Morris III, Centennial Academic
Assembly, Texas A and M University,
College Station, 1978.

1676. Kramer, Mark, Three Farms; Making
Milk, Meat and Money from the Soil,
Little, Brown, Boston, 1980.

1677. Lambert, C. Roger, "Slaughter of the
Innocents: The Public Protests
AAA Killing of Little Pigs," Midwest Quarterly, Vol. 14, Spring,
1973, pp. 247-54.

1678. Lindgren, N.O., "The Conflict between Technical Advances and Ethics
in Animal Production," World's
Poultry Science Journal, Vol. 32,
1976, pp. 243-8.

1679. Loew, Franklin M., "The Veterinarian
and Intensive Livestock Production:

Humane Considerations," _Veterinarian Journal_, Vol. 13, No. 10, October, 1972.

1680. Mann, C.M., and Harvey, P.N., "Cage Size and Stocking Density for Laying Hens," _World Poultry Science Journal_, Vol. 27, 1971, pp. 350 ff.

1681. Mason, Jim, and Singer, Peter, _Animal Factories_, Crown, New York, 1980.

1682. Proceedings of a Joint Symposium between the RSPCA and the Society for Veterinary Ethology, "Stress in Farm Animals," _British Veterinary Journal_, Vol. 130, 1974, pp. 85 ff.

1683. Roberts, Peter, "The Experts Say This Is Not So Cruel...," in _Animals' Rights--a Symposium_, ed. by David Paterson and Richard D. Ryder, Centaur Press, Fontwell, Sussex, 1979, pp. 131-4.

1684. Schertz, Lyle P. and others, _Another Revolution in U.S. Farming?_ U.S. Department of Agriculture, Agricultural Economic Report No. 441, Washington, D.C., December, 1979.
    "Beef," by J. Rod Martin, pp. 85-118.
    "Dairy," by Robert H. Forste and George Frick, pp. 119-47.
    "Poultry and Eggs," by George B. Rogers, pp. 148-89.
    "Pork," by Roy N. Van Arsdall and Henry C. Gilliam, pp. 190-254.

1685. Singer, Peter, "Down on the Factory Farm," in _Animal Rights and Human_

Obligations, ed. by Tom Regan and Peter Singer (1253).

1686.   Smith, Page, and Daniel, Charles, *The Chicken Book*, Little, Brown, Boston, 1975.

1687.   Smith, W.J., and Robertson, A.M., "Observations on Injuries to Sows Confined in Part Slatted Walls," *Veterinary Record*, Vol. 89, 1971, pp. 531 ff.

1688.   Swan, Christopher, "Factory Farming: Machines with Feeling," *The Christian Science Monitor*, Midwestern Edition, November 8, 1979, pp. B1-B23.

1689.   Wood-Gush, D.G.M., Duncan, I.J.H., and Fraser, D., "Social Stress and Welfare Problems in Agricultural Animals," in *The Behaviour of Domestic Animals*, ed. by E.S.E. Hafez, Bailliere Tindall, London, 1975.

20: Flesh Diet

(For additional entries related to this topic
see 3136, 2959, 2989, 3058, 3092, 2698, 2550,
2557.)

1690. Davis, William H., "Man-Eating Aliens,"
Journal of Value Inquiry, Vol. 10,
Fall, 1976, pp. 178-85.

1691. Diamond, Cora, "Eating Meat and Eating People," Philosophy, Vol. 53,
October, 1978, pp. 465-79.

1692. Frey, R.G., The Ethics of Eating Meat,
(tentative title), B.H. Blackwell,
Oxford, forthcoming.

1693. Leffingwell, Albert, American Meat,
G. Bell and Sons, London, 1910.

1694. McClure, Jon A., Meat Eaters Are
Threatened, Pyramid, New York, 1973.

1695. Romans, John R. and Ziegler, P. Thomas,
The Meat We Eat, Interstate Publishers, Danville, Illinois, 1977.

1696. Scharffenberg, John A., Problems
with Meat, Woodbridge Press,
Santa Barbara, California, 1979.

1697. Schwabe, Calvin W., Unmentionable
Cuisine, University Press of
Virginia, Charlottesville, 1979.

1698. Simoons, Frederick J., Eat Not This
Flesh, Food Avoidances in the Old
World, University of Wisconsin
Press, Madison, 1961.

1699. Wellford, Harrison, "The Politics of
Meat," in Sowing the Wind, by
Harrison Wellford, A Report from
Ralph Nader's Center for Study of

Responsive Law on Food Safety and the Chemical Harvest, Bantam, New York, 1973, pp. 1-186.

20: Slaughter

(For additional entries related to this topic see 2838, 2925, 2980, 3028, 2643, 2644, 2681, 2682, 2416, 2549, 2550, 2243, 1667.)

1700. "An Appeal to British Jews," Spectator, Vol. 139, October 1, 1927, pp. 493-4.

1701. Cockerill, George, "The Old Horse: Exportation for Slaughter," Saturday Review, Vol. 157, June 16, 1934, pp. 699-700.

1702. Coville, Marion E., An Appeal Against Slaughter, Are You Able to Hear?, C.W. Bardeen, Syracuse, NY, 1914.

1703. Duchess of Hamilton and Brandon, "Our Slaughter-houses," English Review, Vol. 36, April, 1923, pp. 372-6.

1704. Emanuel, Charles H.L., "Humane Slaughter of Animals," English Review, Vol. 38, February, 1924, pp. 264-6.

1705. Galsworthy, John, "The Slaughter of Animals for Food," Royal Society for the Prevention of Cruelty to Animals, London, 1912. Also in Galsworthy's A Sheaf (1322).

1706. Grandin, Temple, "Designs and Specifications for Livestock Handling Equipment in Slaughter Plants," International Journal for the Study of Animal Problems, Vol. 1,

May/June, 1980, pp. 178-200.

1707. Grandin, Temple, "Mechanical, Electrical and Anesthetic Stunning Methods for Livestock," International Journal for the Study of Animal Problems, Vol. 1, July/August, 1980, pp. 242-63.

1708. Harrison, Ruth, "Pre-Slaughter Welfare," Animalia, World Federation for the Protection of Animals, Vol. 7, April-June, 1980, pp. 1-3.

1709. Harrison, Ruth, "Pre-Slaughter Welfare," The Ark, Bulletin of the Catholic Study Circle for Animal Welfare, Vol. 47, Christmas, 1979, pp. 15-22.

1710. Leach, T.M. and Miekwitz, G. von, Review of Pre-Slaughter Stunning in the Economic Community, Information on Agriculture, No. 30, Commission of the European Communities, Directorate General for Agriculture, Brussels and Luxembourg, 1977, (Office for Official Publications of the European Communitites, Boite Postale 1003, Luxembourg), English and German.

1711. Levinger, I.M., "Jewish Attitude Toward Slaughter," Animal Regulation Studies, Vol. 2, December, 1979, pp. 103-10.

1712. Levinger, I.M., "Jewish Method of Slaughtering Animals for Food

and Its Influence on Blood Supply
to the Brain and on the Normal
Functioning of the Nervous System,"
Animal Regulation Studies, Vol. 2,
December, 1979, pp. 111-26.

1713. Munk, E., and Munk, M.L., eds.,
Shechita: Religious, Historical
and Scientific Aspects, Gur
Aryeh Publishing, Jerusalem, 1976.

1714. Paget, Major J.B., "Humane Slaughter
of Animals," English Review, Vol.
37, December, 1923, pp. 734-6.

1715. Paget, Major J.B., "The Humane
Slaughter of Animals," English
Review, Vol. 38, February, 1924,
pp. 266-8.

1716. Sabine, Ernest L., "Butchering in
Mediaeval London," Speculum,
Vol. 8, July, 1933, pp. 335-53.

1717. Scott, W.N., "The Slaughter of
Poultry for Human Consumption,"
Animal Regulation Studies, Vol.
1, No. 3, May, 1978.

1718. Strachey, John, "Where Meat Comes
From," Spectator, Vol. 142, May
4, 1929, pp. 679-81.

1719. Train, Arthur, Jr., "The Butchers
of Berlin," The First Modern
Abattoirs, World Today, London,
Vol. 6, August, 1932, pp. 211-17.

20: Vegetarianism

(For additional entries related to this topic see 3141-3210, 3138, 2866, 2868, 2927, 2929, 2930, 2931, 2932, 2970, 2971, 2976, 2989, 3008, 3012, 3047, 3070, 3092, 3096, 3101, 3110-3127, 2605, 2421, 2452, 2487, 2550, 3086.)

1720. Adams, Carol, The Oedible Complex: Feminism and Vegetarianism, To the Lighthouse Press, Provincetown, Mass., 1976.

1721. Allaway, Gertrude E., "How It Strikes a Vegetarian," Spectator, Vol. 118, March 17, 1917, p. 334.

1722. Altman, Nathaniel, Eating for Life, Theosophical Publishing House, Wheaton, Ill., 1977. (On vegetarianism and veganism.)

1723. Altman, Nathaniel, "Food for Health Can be Food for Pleasure," Vegetarian Times, January/February, 1980, pp. 60-61.

1724. The Annual Directory of Vegetarian Restaurants, Daystar Publishing Co., P.O. Box 707, Angwin, CA 94508, 1980.

1725. Auxter, Thomas, "The Right Not To Be Eaten," Inquiry, Vol. 22, Spring-Summer, 1979, pp. 221-30.

1726. Axon, William E.A., "Shelley's Vegetarianism," Haskell House, N.Y., 1971, 13 pp.

1727. Bargen, Richard, The Vegetarian's Self-Defense Manual, Quest Books, Wheaton, Ill., 1979.

1728. Barkas, Janet, The Vegetable Passion,
A History of the Vegetarian State
of Mind, Scribner's, New York, 1975.

1729. Berry, Rynn, Jr., The Vegetarians,
Fourteen famous men and women tell
why they have turned to vegetarianism, Autumn Press, Brookline, Mass.,
1979.

1730. Binding, G.J., About Soya Beans,
Thorsons Publishers, Northants,
England, 1971.

1731. Bolitho, Hector, "A Note on Bernard
Shaw and H.E. Bates," Texas
Quarterly, Vol. 11, Spring, 1968,
pp. 100-12.

1732. Braunstein, Mark M., Radical Veg-
etarianism: A Dialectic of
Diet and Ethic, Panjandrum Books,
San Francisco, CA, 1980.

1733. Brockhaus, Wilhelm, Das Recht der
Tiere in der Zivilisation; das
Grundlagenbuch des Vegetarismus,
Hirthammer Verlag, Munich, West
Germany, 1975.

1734. Brophy, Brigid, "The Way of No
Flesh," in The Genius of Shaw,
ed. by Michael Holroyd, Holt,
Rinehart and Winston, New York,
1979.

1735. Carson, Gerald, Cornflake Crusade,
Rinehart, New York, 1957.

1736. Chesterton, Gilbert K., "Meaning
of Mock Turkey," in Chesterton,
Gilbert K., Man Who Was Chesterton,

comp. and ed. by R.T. Bond,
Dodd, New York, 1937, pp. 71-9.

1737. Clark, David L., " The Date and
Source of Shelley's 'A Vin-
dication of Natural Diet',"
Studies in Philology, Vol. 36,
January, 1939, pp. 70-6.

1738. Clooney, F.X., "Vegetarianism and
Religion," America, Vol. 140,
February 24, 1979, pp. 133-4.

1739. Cox, Michael and Crockett, Desda,
The Subversive Vegetarian,
Thorsons Publishers Limited,
Wellingborough, Northants,
England, 1979.

1740. Devine, Philip E., "The Moral Basis
of Vegetarianism," Philosophy,
Vol. 53, October, 1978, pp. 481-
505.

1741. Doyle, Rodger, The Vegetarian
Handbook: A Guide to Vegetarian
Nutrition, Crown Publisher, New
York, 1979.

1742. Dwyer, J.T., Diet, W.H., Jr., Hass,
G., and Susking, R., "Risk of
Nutritional Rickets Among Veg-
etarian Children," American
Journal of Diseases of Children,
Vol. 133, 1979, pp. 134-40.

1743. Fellows, Alfred, "The Vegetarian
Guest," Living Age, Vol. 250,
1906, pp. 346-53.

1744. Ferrier, J. Todd, On Behalf of the
Creatures, Order of the Cross,

London, 1903. (Argument against
human carnivorism.)

1745. Gandhi, Mohandas K., Diet and Diet
Reform, Navajivan Pub. House,
Ahmedabad, 1949.

1746. Gandhi, Mohandas, The Moral Basis of
Vegetarianism, Navajivan Publishing
House, Ahmedabad, 1959.

1747. Giehl, Dudley, Vegetarianism: A
Way of Life, with Foreward by
Isaac Bashevis Singer, Harper and
Row, New York, 1979.

1748. Groner, Arlene P., "The Greening of
Kashrut," The National Jewish
Monthly, April, 1976, pp. 12-20.

1749. Harris, John, "Killing for Food,"
in Animals, Men and Morals, ed.
by Godlovitch and Harris (1172).

1750. Harris, John, "Killing for Food," in
Animals' Rights--a Symposium, ed. by
David Paterson and Richard D. Ryder.
(This is not identical in content
with 1749 regardless of the identity
of title.)

1751. Haussleiter, Johannes, "Der Vegetarismus in der Antike,"
Religionsgeschichtliche Versuche
und Vorarbeiten, Vol. 22, 1935,
pp. 1-427.

1752. Holzer, Hans, Vegetarian Way of
Life, Pyramid Publications,
Moonachie, N.J., 1973.

1753. Hur, Robin, Food Reform: Our

Desperate Need, Heidelberg Pubs.,
Austin, Texas, 1975.

1754. Hur, Robin, "Vegetarians for a World
of Plenty," Moneysworth, March, 1979.

1755. Jast, L. Stanley, "Why I Am Not a
Vegetarian," in Jast, L. Stanley,
Libraries and Living, Books for
Libraries Press, Essay Index Re-
print Series, Freeport, N.Y., 1969.

1756. Kingsford, Anna β., and Maitland,
Edward, Addresses and Essays on
Vegetarianism, J.M. Watkins,
London, 1908.

1757. Klemesrud, Judy, "Vegetarianism:
Growing Way of Life, Especially
Among the Young," The New York
Times, March 21, 1975, p. 43:1.

1758. Lappe, Frances Moore, Diet for a
Small Planet, Ballantine Books,
New York, 1971.

1759. Lappe, F.M., and Collins, J., and
Fowler, C., Food First, Houghton
Mifflin, Boston, 1977.

1760. Lin, Yu-t'ang, "Confessions of a
Vegetarian," in Lin, Yu-t'ang,
With Love and Irony, p. 99-103,
John Day Co., New York, 1940.

1761. "Look Who's Supporting Vegetarianism
Now!" A statement by Paul Harvey in
Vegetarian Times, Issue 38, June,
1980, p. 6.

1762. Martin, Michael, "A Critique of
Moral Vegetarianism," Reason

Papers, Vol. 3, Fall, 1976, pp. 13-43.

1763. Mason, James, "Vegetarianism Is a Human Rights Struggle," Vegetarian Times, Issue 38, June, 1980, pp. 47-9.

1764. Mendel, Lafayette B., "Some Historical Aspects of Vegetarianism," Popular Science Monthly, Vol. 64, 1903-4, pp. 457-465.

1765. Moran, Victoria, "Compassion, the Ultimate Ethic--an Exploration of Veganism," Richter Fellowship Paper, North Central College, Department of Religious Studies, Naperville, IL, 1980.

1766. Nearing, Helen and Scott, "Eating for Health," in their Living the Good Life, Schocken Books, New York, 1970, pp. 109-41.

1767. Paget, Major J.B., "The Health of the Nation," English Review, Vol. 38, March, 1924, pp. 377-85.

1768. Paget, Ralph S., "Health and Diet," English Review, Vol. 42, March, 1926, pp. 389-95.

1769. Phillips, Davis A., "Man's Vegetarian Heritage," and "The Pythagorean Ideal," in Phillips' From Soil to Psyche, A Total Plan of Natural Living for the New Age, Woodbridge Press, Santa Barbara, California, 1977, pp. 64-103.

1770. Rachels, James, "Vegetarianism and 'The Other Weight Problem'" in Aiken, W. and LaFollette, H., eds., World Hunger and Moral Obligation, Prentice-Hall, Englewood Cliffs, N.J., 1977.

1771. Regan, Tom, "The Moral Basis of Vegetarianism," The Canadian Journal of Philosophy, Vol. 5, October, 1975, pp. 181-214.

1772. Regan, Tom, "Vegetarianism, Utilitarianism and Animal Rights," Philosophy and Public Affairs, Fall, 1980.

1773. Rhodes, Richard, "A Bean to Feed the World?" Atlantic Monthly, January, 1975, pp. 38-43.

1774. Rudd, Geoffrey L., Why Kill for Food?, Indian Vegetarian Congress, Madras, 1973.

1775. Ryder, Richard D., "The Silent Scream," The Vegetarian, April, 1975.

1776. Sale, George, "Eat or Be Eaten," English Review, Vol. 42, June 1926, pp. 830-5.

1777. Salomon, Louis B., "The Least-Remembered Alcott," New England Quarterly, Vol. 34, March 1961, pp. 87-93.

1778. Salt, Henry S., The Humanities of Diet, Some Reasonings and Rymings, The Vegetarian Society, Manchester, 1914.

1779. Salt, Henry S., "Logic of the Larder,"
       and "The Humanities of Diet," from
       Salt's The Humanities of Diet, re-
       produced in Animal Rights and Human
       Obligations, ed. by Tom Regan and
       Peter Singer (1253).

1780. Salt, Henry S., The Logic of Veg-
       etarianism. London Vegetarian
       Society, London, 1933.

1781. Salt, Henry S., "Two Anti-Vegetarian
       Sages," (G.K. Chesterton and Dean
       Inge),"Concerning Cranks" (veg-
       etarians), in Salt's Company I
       Have Kept, George Allen and Unwin,
       London, 1930.

1782. Shaw, George Bernard, "To Tokyo on
       Buttermilk," originally published
       in a Royal Air Force journal in
       1942, reprinted in Bolitho, Hector,
       "A Note on Bernard Shaw and H.E.
       Bates," Texas Quarterly, Vol. 11,
       Spring, 1968, pp. 100-12. (Shaw
       wrote this in response to a request
       from an R.A.F. officer facing the
       problems of persuading flyers to
       eat more vegetables in flight.)

1783. Shaw, George Bernard, "Vegetarian
       Diet," (A printed postcard which
       Shaw used to answer inquiries
       about vegetarianism) in Chappelow,
       Allan, Shaw-"The Chucker-Out,"
       AMS Press, New York, 1971, pp.
       15-16.

1784. Sheldon, Charles M., "The Confes-
       sions of a Vegetarian," Independent,
       Vol. 60, 1906, pp. 1457-8.

1785. Simons, Madeleine A., "Rousseau's Natural Diet," Romantic Review, Vol. 45, February, 1954, pp. 18-28.

1786. Singer, Peter, "Becoming a Vegetarian... Or How to Reduce Animal Suffering and Human Starvation at the Same Time," in Singer's Animal Liberation (1272), pp. 163-91.

1787. Singer, Peter, "Utilitarianism and Vegetarianism," Philosophy and Public Affairs, Fall, 1980.

1788. Sussman, Vic, The Vegetarian Alternative, Rodale Press, Emmaus, Pa. 1978.

1789. "Syndicated Vegetarian News" (SVN), a news service to radio stations, Vegetarian Society of D.C., 1455 Harvard St., N.W., Washington, D.C. 20009.

1790. Treber, Grace J., Why Kill To Eat?, Source Publishers, New York, 1972.

1791. Tyler, Robert L., "Plant Liberation: The Struggle against Fauna Chauvinism," The Humanist, Vol. 38, No. 1, January/February 1978, pp. 30-32.

1792. "Vegetarian 'Meats'," Consumer Reports, Vol. 45, June, 1980, pp. 362-5.

1793. The Vegetarian Times Guide to Dining in the U.S.A., by the editors of Vegetarian Times, compiled by Kathleen Moore, Atheneum/SMI, New York, 1980.

1794.   Weber, Shierry M., "Vegetarianism:
        The Experience of Praxis," in
        Critical Interruptions, ed. by.
        Paul Breines, Herder and Herder,
        New York, 1970, pp. 55-59.

1795.   "WHFS Vegetarian News," weekly radio
        news and information about veg-
        etarians and vegetarianism, WHFS,
        Washington, D.C.

1796.   Wilkinson, Clennell, "The Vegetarian's
        Dilemma," Outlook, Vol. 58, Novem-
        ber 6, 1926, p. 429.

1797.   Wilson, Frank, Food Fit for Humans,
        Daniel, London, 1975.

1798.   Wilson, Frank, Food for the Golden
        Age, Daniel, London, 1954.

1799.   Wynne-Tyson, Jon, "Dietethics: Its
        Influence on Future Farming Patterns,"
        in Animals' Rights--a Symposium, ed.
        by David Paterson and Richard D.
        Ryder (1231).

1800.   Wynne-Tyson, Jon, Food for a Future:
        The Ecological Priority of a
        Humane Diet, Davis-Poynter, London,
        1975.

20: Capture, Restraint, Transportation, Marketing

(For additional entries related to this topic see 2737, 2925, 2980, 3029, 3037, 3057, 3105, 2647, 2655, 2665, 2679, 2685, 2686, 1326.)

1801. Beck, C.C., "Chemical Restraint of Exotic Species," Journal of Zoo Animal Medicine, Vol. 3, 1972, pp. 3-66.

1802. Burton, R.R., and Beljan, J.R., "Animal Restraint Applications in Space (Weightless) Environment," Aerospace Medicine, Vol. 41, 1970, pp. 1060-5.

1803. Domalain, Jean-Yves, The Animal Connection: Confessions of an Ex-Wild Animal Trafficker, trans. by Marguerite Barnett, William Morrow, New York, 1977.

1804. Ewbank, R., "The Behavior of Animals in Restraint," in Abnormal Behavior in Animals, ed. by M.W. Fox, W.B. Saunders, Philadelphia, 1968.

1805. Fowler, Murray E., Restraint and Handling of Wild and Domestic Animals, Iowa State University Press, Ames, 1978. (Heavily illustrated.)

1806. Graham-Jones, O., "Some Aspects of Air Transport of Animals," International Zoo Yearbook, Vol. 14, 1974, pp. 34-7.

1807. Harthoorn, Antonie M., The Chemical Capture of Animals, A guide to the Chemical Restraint of Wild and Captive Animals, Bailliere, Tindall, London, 1976.

20: Capture, Restraint, Transportation, Marketing

1808. Henry, K.R., and Bowman, R.E., "A Long-term Restraint Device for Primates," Physiology and Behavior, Vol. 7, 1971, pp. 271 ff.

1809. IATA Live Animal Manual, 2nd ed., International Air Transport Association, Montreal, Canada, 1970.

1810. Leahy, J.R., and Barrow, P., Restraint of Animals, 2nd ed., Cornell Campus Store, Ithaca, N.Y., 1953.

1811. Sims, John A., Animals in the American Economy, Iowa State University Press, Ames, Iowa, 1972.

1812. Whittingham, R.A., "Trapping and Shipping Baboons," Institute of Animal Technicians Journal, Vol. 22, 1971, pp. 66-82.

1813. Young, E.M., ed., The Capture and Care of Wild Animals, Human and Rousseau, Capetown, South Africa 1973.

1814. Zeehandlelaar, Frederik J., Zeebongo: The Wacky Wild Animal Business, Prentice-Hall, Englewood Cliffs, New Jersey, 1971.

20: Domestication

1815. Angress, Shimon, and Reed, Charles A., "An Annotated Bibliography on the Origin and Descent of Domestic Animals, 1900-1955, "Fieldiana: Anthropology, Volume 54, No. 1, Published by Chicago Natural History Museum, Chicago, October 26, 1962, pp. 5-142.

20: Domestication

1816. Bokonyi, S., _History of Domestic Animals in Central and Eastern Europe_, Akademiai Kiado, Budapest, 1974.

1817. Chenevix-Trench, Charles, _A History of Horsemanship_, Doubleday, New York, 1970. (Heavily illustrated.)

1818. Cockrill, W. Ross, "The Potential and Global Exploitation of Domestic Animals," _Animal Regulation Studies_, Vol. 1, No. 3, May, 1978.

1819. Davis, Patrick D.C., _Animals That Changed the World_, Phoenix House, London, 1966.

1820. Downs, James F., "Domestication: An Examination of the Changing Social Relationships between Man and Animals," _Kroeber Anthropological Society Papers_, No. 22, Spring, 1960, pp. 18-67.

1821. Dyson, Robert H., Jr., "Archeology and the Domestication of Animals in the Old World," _American Anthropologist_, Vol. 55, 1953, pp. 661-73.

1822. Epstein, Hellmut, _Domestic Animals of China_, Holmes and Meier, New York, 1971.

1823. Epstein, Hellmut, _Domestic Animals of Nepal_, Holmes and Meier, New York, 1977.

1824. Epstein, Hellmut, "Domestication Features in Animals as Functions of Human Society," _Agricultural_

History, Vol. 29, 1955, pp. 137-46.

1825. Epstein, Hellmut, Origin of the Domestic Animals of Africa, 2 Vols.,
Africana, New York, 1971.

1826. Glacken, Clarence J., "Count Buffon:
On Domestication," in Glacken's
Traces on the Rhodian Shore: Nature
and Culture in Western Thought from
Ancient Times to the End of the
Eighteenth Century, University of
California Press, Berkeley, 1967,
pp. 672-9.

1827. Hermanns, Matthias, "Were Animals
First Domesticated and Bred in
India?" Journal of the Bombay
Branch of the Royal Asiatic
Society, Vol. 27, Part II, 1952,
pp. 134-73.

1828. Hyams, E., Animals in the Service
of Man: 10000 Years of Domestication, Dent, London, 1972.

1829. Isaac, Erich, "On the Domestication
of Cattle," Science, Vol. 137,
July 20, 1962, pp. 195-204.

1830. Mourant, A.E., and Zeuner, F.E.,
eds., Man and Cattle, Royal
Anthropological Institute of
Great Britain and Ireland,
London, Occassional Paper No.
18, 1963.

1831. Perkins, Dexter, Jr., "The Beginnings of Animal Domestication in
the Near East," American Journal
of Archaeology, Vol. 77, July,
1973, pp. 279-282.

1832.   Reed, Charles A., "Animal Domesti-
        cation in the Prehistoric Near
        East," Science, Vol. 130, Decem-
        ber 11, 1959, pp. 1629-39.

1833.   Sauer, Carl O., Agricultural Origins
        and Dispersals: The Domestication
        of Animals and Foodstuffs, Massa-
        chusetts Institute of Technology
        Press, Cambridge, 1969.

1834.   Simoons, Frederick J., "Notes on the
        Domestication of Common Cattle,"
        in Simoons' A Ceremonial Ox of
        India, University of Wisconsin
        Press, Madison, 1968, pp. 234-58.

1835.   Towne, Charles W., and Wentworth,
        Edward N., Cattle and Men, Uni-
        versity of Oklahoma Press, Norman,
        1955.

1836.   Trench, C.C., A History of Horseman-
        ship, Doubleday, Garden City, N.Y.,
        1970.

1837.   Ucko, P.J., and Dimbleby, G.W., The
        Domestication of Plants and Animals,
        Aldine-Atherton, Chicago, 1969.

1838.   Wilkinson, Paul F. "Oomingmak: A
        Model for Man-Animal Relationships
        in Prehistory," Current Anthro-
        pology, Vol. 13, February, 1972,
        pp. 23-44.

1839.   Zeuner, Frederick E., A History of
        Domesticated Animals, Harper &
        Row, N.Y., 1963.

20: Educational Uses (Including Science Fairs)
(For Additional entries related to this topic see 2847, 2855, 2925, 2956, 2957, 2980, 3029, 3031, 3050, 3062, 3096, 2597, 2607.)

1840. Drewett, R.F., "On the Teaching of Vivisection," New Scientist, November 3, 1977, p. 292.

1841. Henig, R.M., "Animal Welfare Groups Press for Limits on High School Research," Bioscience, Vol. 29, November, 1979, pp. 651-3.

1842. Hillman, H., "A Programme for Diminishing the Use of Animals in Teaching and Research," ATLA Abstracts, Vol. 4, No. 2, 1976, pp. 6-9.

1843. Kelly, P.J., and Wray, J.D., The Educational Use of Living Organisms, The English Universities Press, London, 1975.

1844. Morris, Richard K., "The Misuse of Animals in the Science Classroom," Proceedings, National Leadership Conference, Humane Society of the United States, Hershey, Pa., 1969.

1845. Orlans, F. Barbara, "The Boundaries of Use of Animals in High School Biology," Science Teacher, Vol. 35, No. 7, 1968, p. 44.

1846. Orlans, F. Barbara, "Living Organisms in High School Biology," The American Biology Teacher, Vol. 34, No. 9, September, 1972.

1847. Orlans, F. Barbara, "Painless Animal Experimentation for High School

Students," _Scholastic Teacher_, April 6, 1970.

1848. "Rules of the 32nd International Science and Engineering Fair," Milwaukee, Wisconsin, May 11-16, 1981. Prepared and published by Science Service, 1719 N Street, N.W., Washington, D.C. 20036. (See "Rules for Research Involving Human Subjects," p. 14, and "Rules for Research Involving Vertebrate Animals," pp. 11-13.)

1849. Russell, George K., _Laboratory Investigations in Human Physiology_, Macmillan, New York, 1978. (Alternate method of teaching physiology: instead of using laboratory animals, the students themselves become the subjects of all experiments.)

1850. Russell, George K., "Vivisection and the True Aims of Education in Biology," _American Biology Teacher_, Vol. 34, May, 1972.

1851. Savesky, Kathleen, "Unfair Competition: School Science Fairs," _Animals_, Massachusetts Society for the Prevention of Cruelty to Animals, Boston, April, 1980, pp. 26-31.

1852 Secord, D., and Rowsell, H., "Proper Use of Animals in Schools," Canadian Veterinarian Journal, Vol. 15, 1974, p. 42.

20: Educational Uses

1853. Tamir, Pinchas, and Sever, Efrat,
"Students' Attitudes Toward the
Use of Animals in Biology Teach-
ing," American Biology Teacher,
Vol. 42, February, 1980, pp. 100-
3, 109.

20: Hunting, Fishing

(For additional entries related to this topic
see 3135, 2808, 2833, 2849, 2857, 2874, 2886,
2900, 2907, 2910, 2918, 3006, 3008, 3016,
3019, 3047, 3060, 3061, 3074, 2697, 2699,
2705, 2706, 2718, 2634, 2606, 2512, 1961,
1989, 2000, 1010, 1326, 1329, 1343.)

1854. Barter, Gwendolen, "Children and
Hunting," in Against Hunting, ed.
by Patrick Moore, Victor Gollancz,
London, 1965.

1855. Beaglehood, Ernest, Hopi Hunting
and Hunting Ritual, Yale University Press, New Haven, 1936.

1856. Bell, Clive, "Blood Sports," New
Statesman and Nation, Vol. 38,
1949, pp. 92-3.

1857. Brander, Michael, Hunting and
Shooting, From Earliest Times
to the Present Day, Putnam,
New York, 1971.

1858. Brander, Michael, The Hunting
Instinct, The Development of
Field Sports over the Ages,
Oliver and Boyd, London, 1964.

1859. Brander, Michael, Portrait of a
Hunt, The History of the Puck-
eridge and Newmarket and Thurlow

Combined Hunts, Hutchinson, London, 1976.

1860. Bryant, J.M., "Animal Exploitation in Human Recreation," in Animals' Rights--A Symposium, ed. by David Paterson and Richard D. Ryder (1231).

1861. Bryant, Nelson, "Behold the Hunter," The Atlantic, December, 1977.

1862. Caras, Roger A., Death as a Way of Life, Little, Brown and Co., Boston, 1970.

1863. Carpenter, Edward, "Christian Faith and the Moral Aspect of Hunting," in Against Hunting, ed. by Patrick Moore, Victor Gollancz, 1965.

1864. Carr, Raymond, A History of English Fox Hunting, Weidenfeld and Nicolson, London, 1976.

1865. Chalmers, Patrick, The History of Hunting, Seeley, Service, London, not dated.

1866. "Cruelty in Sport," Spectator, Vol. 132, March 29, 1924, pp. 496-8.

1867. Douglas, Gordon, "Psychology of Sport," Cornhill Magazine, Vol. 56, February, 1924, pp. 191-9.

1868. Galsworthy, John, "Reverie of a Sportsman," in Galsworthy's A Sheaf (1322).

1869. Glacken, Clarence J., "Hunting," in Glacken's Traces on the Rhodian Shore: Nature and Culture in Western Thought

from Ancient Times to the End of
the Eighteenth Century, University
of California Press, Berkeley,
1967, pp. 346-7.

1870. Gwynn, Stephen, "The Case for Certain
Cruelties," Spectator, Vol, 132,
June 7, 1924, pp. 912-3.

1871. Gwynne, Peter, "Hunting Under Fire,"
National Wildlife, Vol. 12, October-
November, 1974, pp. 38-41.

1872. Hewitt, W.I., Hare Hunting, Seeley,
London, 1975.

1873. Higginson, A. Henry, Two Centuries
of Fox Hunting, Collins, London,
1946.

1874. Holliday, Laurel, "Man's Dominion:
The Hunter Today," in Holliday's
The Violent Sex, Male Psychobiology
and the Evolution of Consciousness,
Bluestocking Books, Guerneville,
Ca., 1978.

1875. James, David, and Stephens, Wilson,
eds., In Praise of Hunting, Hollis
and Carter, London, 1960.

1876. Johnson, Paul, "Hunting and Humbug,"
New Statesman, Vol. 66, July 12,
1963, pp. 41-2.

1877. Kimball, David and Jim, "The Future
of Hunting: Philosophies and
Ethics," in the authors' The Market
Hunter, Dillon Press, Minneapolis,
Minn., 1969.

1878. Lee, Richard B., and DeVore, Irven,

20. Hunting, Fishing

eds., Man the Hunter, Aldine, Chicago, 1968.

1879. Lynd, Robert, "The Huntsman," New Statesman, Vol. 28, December 4, 1926, pp. 233-5.

1880. Martin, Ernest W., The Case against Hunting, Dennis Dobson, London, 1959.

1881. Martin, H., Jr., "Plutarch's De Sollertia Animalium 958 B.C.: The Discussion of the Encomium of Hunting," American Journal of Philology, Vol. 100, Spring, 1979, pp. 99-106.

1882. Monk-Jones, Arnold, "Hunting: Past and Present," in Against Hunting, ed. by Patrick Moore, Victor Gollancz, London, 1965.

1883. Moore, Patrick, ed., Against Hunting, Gollancz, London, 1965.

1884. Moore, Patrick, "Fox Hunting and R.S.P.C.A.," in Against Hunting, ed. by Patrick Moore, Victor Gollancz, London, 1965.

1885. O'Connor, John J., "'The Guns of Autumn' hunted and the hunters," New York Times, Sept. 14, 1975, p. D25.

1886. Ortega y Gasset, Meditations on Hunting, trans. by H.B. Wescott, Scribners, New York, 1972.

1887. Page, Robin, Hunter and the Hunted, A Countryman's View of Bloodsports,

Davis-Poynter, London, 1977.

1888. Pine, Leslie G., History of Hunting,
League Against Cruel Sports, London,
1973.

1889. Reiger, G., "Hunting and Trapping in
the New World," in Wildlife and
America, H.P. Brokaw, ed., Council
on Environmental Quality, Washington,
D.C., 1978, p. 42.

1890. Rohlfing, A.H., "Hunter Conduct and
Public Attitudes," Transactions of
the 43rd North American Wildlife
and Natural Resources Conference,
Wildlife Management Institute,
Washington, D.C., 1978, pp. 404-11.

1891. Salt, Henry S., "Fallacies of Sportsmen," in Henry S. Salt, ed., Killing
for Sport, G. Bell, London, 1915.

1892. Salt, Henry S., ed., Killing for
Sport, with a Preface by Bernard
Shaw, G. Bell, London, 1915.

1893. Salt, Henry S., "The Manly Folk"
(hunters) in Salt's Company I Have
Kept, George Allen and Unwin, London,
1930.

1894. Savage, Henry L., "Hunting in the
Middle Ages," Speculum, Vol. 8,
January, 1933, pp. 30-41.

1895. Scott, S.H., "Cruelty in Sport,"
Spectator, Vol. 143, July 6, 1929,
pp. 8-10.

1896. Shaw, G.B., "Killing for Sport," in
Hamalian, L. and Volpe, E.L., eds.,

Great Essays by Nobel Prize Winners,
Noonday, 1960.

1897. Sheppard, Vera, My Head Against the Wall,
A Decade in the Fight Against
Bloodsports, Moonraker Press, Brad-
ford-on-Avon, Wilts, U.K., 1979.

1898. Walton, Izaak, The Complete Angler,
E.P. Dutton, New York, 1906.
(17th Century.)

1899. Watson, J.N.P., Book of Fox Hunting,
Batsford, London, 1977.

1900. Windeatt, Phil, and Marten, Michael,
"HUNT Is a Four Letter Word," The
Beast, October-November, 1979,
Issue No. 3, pp. 16-21. (Discussion
of the Hunt Saboteurs Association.)

1901. Woodcock, N., Fifty Years a Hunter
and Trapper, Fur-Fish-Game,
Columbus, Ohio, 1972.

20: Pets (Including Exotic)
(For additional entries related to this topic
see 3137, 2738, 2849, 2854, 2869, 2907, 2925,
2930, 2956, 2966, 2977, 2980, 2984, 3016,
3019, 3026, 3028, 3029, 3031, 3096, 2689,
2703, 2598, 1326.)

1902. Allen, Robert D., and Westbrook
       William H., eds., The Handbook
       of Animal Welfare, Biomedical, Psy-
       chological and Ecological Aspects
       of Pet Problems and Control, Gar-
       land STPM Press, New York and
       London, 1979.

1903. Anderson, R.S., ed., Pet Animals and
       Society, Williams and Wilkins,
       Baltimore, MD., 1975.

1904. Beck, A.M., "The Dog: America's
       Sacred Cow?" Nation's Cities,
       Vol. 12, February, 1974, pp.
       29-31, 34-5.

1905. Beck, Alan M., The Ecology of Stray
       Dogs; A Study of Free-ranging
       Urban Animals, York Press,
       Baltimore, 1973.

1906. Beck, Alan M., "Ecology of Unwanted
       and Uncontrolled Pets," in Pro-
       ceedings of the National Conference
       on the Ecology of the Surplus Dog
       and Cat Problem, May 21-23, 1974,
       sponsored by American Humane Asso-
       ciation and others, pp. 31-9.

1907. Benning, Lee E., The Pet Profiteers,
       the Exploitation of Pet Owners and
       Pets in America, Quadrangle, New
       York, 1976.

1908. Bucke, W. Fowler, "Children's Thoughts,
       Reactions, and Feelings Toward Pet

271

Dogs," _Journal of Genetic Psychology_, Vol. 10, December, 1903, pp. 459-513.

1909. Curtis, Patricia, "Raining Cats and Dogs: The Treatment of Pets," in Curtis' _Animal Rights_ (1313), pp. 21-33.

1910. Djerassi, Carl, Israel, Andrew, and Jochle, Wolfgang, "Planned Parenthood for Pets?" _Bulletin of the Atomic Scientists_, Vol. 29, January, 1973, pp. 10-19.

1911. Feldman, B.M., "Why People Own Pets," _Animal Regulation Studies_, Vol. 1, August, 1977.

1912. Feldman, B.M., and Carding, T.H., "Free-Roaming Urban Pets," _Health Service Reports_, Vol. 88, 1973, pp. 956-62.

1913. Fox, Michael W., _Understanding Your Pet_, Coward, McCann & Geoghegan, 1978, New York.

1914. Gates, Arthur M., "Greek and Roman Pets," _South Atlantic Quarterly_, Vol. 30, October, 1931, pp. 405-19.

1915. Hopkins, A.F., Jr., "Ethical Implications in Issues and Decisions in Companion Animal Medicine," in _Implications of History and Ethics to Medicine--Veterinary and Human_, ed. by Laurence B. McCullough and James P. Morris III, Centennial Academic Assembly, Texas A and M University, College Station, 1978.

20: Pets

1916. Kaylor, M.A., "Feelings, Thought, and Conduct of Children Toward Animal Pets," Journal of Genetic Psychology, Vol. 16, June, 1909, pp. 205-39.

1917. Leigh, D., "The Psychology of the Pet Owner," Journal of Small Animal Practice, Vol. 7, 1966, pp. 517-21.

1918. Levinson, Boris M., Pets and Human Development, Thomas, Springfield, Ill., 1972.

1919. Levinson, Boris M., "Pets and Personality Development," Psychological Reports, Vol. 42, June, 1978, pp. 1031-8.

1920. Levinson, Boris M., "Psychology of Pet Ownership," in Proceedings of the National Conference on the Ecology of the Surplus Dog and Cat Problem, May 21-23, 1974, sponsored by American Humane Association and others, pp. 18-30.

1921. Mason, Jim, "Dog Days for Pedigrees," Vegetarian Times, July, 1980, pp. 58-60. (Criticism of purebred-dog practices and shows.)

1922. Nilsson, Greta, The Bird Business, Animal Welfare Institute, Washington, D.C., 1980.

1923. Nowell, Iris, The Dog Crisis, McClelland and Stewart, Toronto, 1978.

1924. Phineas, Charles, "Household Pets and Urban Alienation," Journal

of Social History, Vol. 7, Spring,
1974, pp. 338-43.

1925. Reiger, George, "The Scandal of Living
Room Zoos," National Wildlife, Vol.
12, October-November, 1974, pp. 4-
12.

1926. Ryder, Richard D., "Pets Are Good for
People," Pet Food Manufacturers'
Association, London, 1974.

1927. Rynearson, E.K., "Humans and Pets and
Attachment," British Journal of
Psychiatry, Vol. 133, December, 1978,
pp. 550-55.

1928. Sloan, Allyn, Dog and Man: The Story
of a Friendship, Blom, New York,
1971.

1929. Szasz, Kathleen, Petishism?: Pets
and Their People in the Western
World, Holt-Reinhart-Winston,
New York, 1968.

1930. Wylder, Joseph, Psychic Pets, Dent,
London, 1980.

20: Psychotherapy
(For additional entries related to this topic
see 2986, 3039, 2597.)

1931. Levinson, Boris M., "The Dog as a
'Co-Therapist'," Mental Hygiene,
Vol. 46, January, 1972, pp. 59-
65.

1932. Levinson, Boris, Pet Oriented Child
Psychotherapy, (Esp. see "Histor-
ical Background," pp. 3-28),
Thomas, Springfield, Ill., 1969.

1933. Siegel, A., "Reaching the Severely
       Withdrawn Through Pet Therapy,"
       American Journal of Psychiatry,
       Vol. 18, May, 1962, pp. 1045-6.

20. Safety Testing (Including Cosmetics, Draize Test, L.D. 50 Test)

(For additional entries related to this topic
see 2804, 2814, 2822, 2823, 2847, 2880, 2907,
2914, 2923, 2925, 2989, 3005, 3007, 3016,
3026, 3029, 3047, 3066, 3096, 3107, 2717,
2637, 2641, 2652, 2657, 2220, 1992, 1593,
1594, 1597.)

1934. Hampson, Judith, "Beauty and the
       Beasts," Vole, Vol. 6, February,
       1978, pp. 40-4.

1935. Hampson, J.E., and Rowan, A.N.,
       "Alternatives to the Use of Ani-
       mals in Toxicity Testing," SRIP
       Pharmaceutical News, April 30,
       1977, pp. 20-1.

1936. Heneson, Nancy, "Live Animals in
       Car Crash Studies," International
       Journal for the Study of Animal
       Problems, Vol. 1, July/August,
       1980, pp. 224-6.

1937. Lesser, E., "Thalidomide and Phar-
       macologists," New Scientist, Vol.
       62, 1974, pp. 472-3.

1938. Magee, P.N., "Toxicology and Certain-
       ty," New Scientist, Vol. 46, 1970,
       pp. 61-2.

1939. Page, George E., ed., Methods in
       Toxicology, F.A. Davis Co.,
       Philadelphia, 1970.

20: Safety Testing

1940. Singer, Peter, "Advocacy, Objectivity and the Draize Test," *International Journal for the Study of Animal Problems*, Vol. 1, July/August, 1980, pp. 212-13.

1941. Styles, J.A., "The Use of Tissue Culture in Toxicological Testing," in *Current Approaches in Toxicology*, ed. by Bryan Ballentyne, John Wright and Sons, Bristol, 1977, Chap. 3.

1942. Tirbutt, Susan, "The Deadly Side of Cosmetics," *Yorkshire Post*, May 28, 1975.

1943. Wilks, Louis P., "The Meaning of LD 50," *Pesticides Annual*, December, 1971, pp. 86-104.

20: Sexual Use

1944. Dubois-Desaulle, Gaston, *Beastiality: An Historical, Medical, Legal and Literary Study*, trans. by A.F. Niemoeller, Panurge Press, New York, 1933.

1945. Rappaport, E.A., "Zoophily and Zooerasty," *Psychoanalytic Quarterly*, Vol. 37, 1968, pp. 565-87.

20: **Spectator Entertainment (Circuses, Rodeos, Races, Animal Fights, Bull Fights, Motion Pictures, Television, Menageries, Animal Shows, etc.)**
(For additional entries related to this topic see 2862, 2894, 2907, 2956, 3016, 3019, 3028, 3029, 3032, 3082, 3096, 2597, 2263, 2018, 1326, 1329.)

1946. "The Abomination of Performing Animals," The Nation and The Athenaeum, March 1, 1922, pp. 855-6.

1947. Amaral, Anthony A., Movie Horses: Their Treatment and Training, Bobbs-Merrill, Indianapolis, 1967.

1948. Baumann, Charly, Tiger, Tiger, Playboy Press, Chicago, 1975, (About circuses.)

1949. Beatty, Clyde, and Anthony, Edward, The Big Cage, Century, New York, 1933.

1950. Beatty, Clyde, and Wilson, Earl, Jungle Performers, Robert M. McBride, New York, 1941.

1951. Blake, A., "Animal Shows of Bygone Days," Spectator, Vol. 127, September 10, 1921, pp. 326-7.

1952. Bostock, Frank C., The Training of Wild Animals, Appleton-Century New York, 1937.

1953. Burne, Jerome, "The Secret Circus: The Cruelty the Kids Never See," The Beast, No. 4, Dec.-Jan. 1980, pp. 28-29.

1954. Burr, Stephen I., "Movie Cruelty,"

Animals, Massachusetts Society
for the Prevention of Cruelty
to Animals, April, 1978.

1955. Christenson, F.M., and Christenson,
H.M., Wild Animal Actors, Albert
Whitman, Chicago, 1935. (Juvenile.)

1956. Cooper, Courtney R., With the Circus,
Little, Brown, Boston, 1930.

1957. Court, Alfred, Wild Circus Animals,
Burke, London, 1954.

1958. Curtis, Patricia, "Ride 'Em Cowboy!
The Use of Animals for Entertainment," in Curtis' Animal Rights
(1313), pp. 109-28.

1959. Dawson, Giles E., "London's Bull-
Baiting and Bear-Baiting Arena
in 1562," Shakespeare Quarterly,
Vol. 15, Winter, 1964, pp. 97-
101.

1960. Derby, Pat, The Lady and Her Tiger,
E.P. Dutton & Co., New York, 1976.
(About animal training for circuses
and other entertainment.)

1961. Duffy, Maureen, "Beasts for Pleasure,"
(hunting, fishing, and circuses) in
Animals, Men and Morals, ed. by
Godlovitch and Harris (1172).

1962. Fitz-Barnard, Lawrence, Fighting
Sports, Odhams Press, London,
1921.

1963. Fox, Charles P., A Pictorial History
of Performing Horses, Superior Publishing, Seattle, 1960.

1964. Galsworthy, John, "On Performing
Animals," in Galsworthy's A
Sheaf (1322).

1965. Gillespie, T.H., Is It Cruel? A
Study of the Condition of Cap-
tive and Performing Animals,
Herbert Jenkins, London, 1934.

1966. Hartwig, Hermann, Willingly to
School: How Animals Are Taught,
trans. by Charles Johnson,
Taplinger, New York, 1970.

1967. Helfer, Ralph D., President and
Founder, Gentle Jungle Wild
Animal Affection Training
School, School Catalog, Jan-
uary 1, 1980, P.O. Box 38797,
Hollywood, CA 90038. Gentle
Jungle trains and rents animals
for motion pictures and television.
The training school emphasizes
exotic animal care and handling
and training.

1968. Jarvis, C.S., "Bloodsports and
Hypocrisy," Cornhill Magazine,
March, 1939, pp. 368-78.

1969. Jennison, George, Animals for Show
and Pleasure in Ancient Rome,
Manchester University Press, Manchester, U.K., 1937.

1970. Lewis, George W., Elephant Tramp,
An Autobiography As Told to
Byron Fish, Peter Davis, Chicago,
1955.

1971. Nicolson, Harold, "Visit to the
Circus," Spectator, Vol. 180,

January 2, 1948, p. 11.

1972. Norwood, Edwin P., The Circus Menagerie, Doubleday, Garden City, New York, 1929.

1973. Nugent, William H., "Cock Fighting Today," American Mercury Magazine, May, 1929.

1974. Palmer, William, "Butchery in the Bull Ring," Saturday Review, Vol. 159, February 2, 1935, pp. 137-8.

1975. Pridgen, Tim, Courage: The Story of Modern Cockfighting, Little, Brown and Co., Boston, 1938.

1976. Proske, Roman, Lions, Tigers, and Me, Henry Holt, New York, 1956.

1977. Sasser, Charles W., "Dealth Fight: An Inside Look at the Brutal Sport of Cockfighting," Animals, Massachusetts Society for the Prevention of Cruelty to Animals, Vol. 113, August, 1980, pp. 7-10.

1978. Scott, George R., The History of Cockfighting, C. Skilton, London, 1957.

1979. Stoutenberg, Adrien (Lace Kendall), Tigers, Trainers and Dancing Whales, Wild Animals of the Circus, Zoo, and Screen, Macrae Smith, Philadelphia, 1968.

1980. Trevelyan, Helen, Laugh, Clown, Laugh, C.W. Daniel, London, 1936.

1981.   Westacott, Evalyn A., comp., Spot-
        light on Performing Animals,
        extracts from evidence given be-
        fore the Select Committee of
        Enquiry on Performing Animals of
        1921 and 1922, C.W. Daniel,
        Rochford, Essex, U.K., 1962.

1982.   Yeats-Brown, F., "Horrors of the
        Circus," Spectator, Vol. 141,
        December 15, 1928, pp. 913-4.

1983.   Yeats-Brown, F., "Woes of the Cages,"
        Spectator, Vol. 143, December 21,
        1929, pp. 939-40.

1984.   Zora, Lucia, Sawdust and Solitude,
        Little, Brown, Boston, 1928.

20: Trapping, Furs, Seal Hunt

(For additional entries related to this topic
see 3135, 2804, 2809, 2853, 2907, 2916, 2925,
2952, 2980, 2984, 2989, 3016, 3019, 3020,
3021, 3024, 3029, 3036, 3037, 3047, 3063,
3065, 3096, 2691, 2701, 2708, 2709, 2710,
2715, 2716, 2717, 2654, 2687, 2037, 2220,
1889, 1901, 1010, 1329, 1343.)

1985. Adams, Richard, "Warm Blood on White Ice," The Beast, No. 4, Dec.-Jan. 1980, pp. 22-26.

1986. Bateman, James, Animal Traps and Trapping, Stackpole, Harrisburg, Pennsylvania, 1971.

1987. Bogue, Gary L., "A Trapper Remembers," Harold Dobyns was a master coyote killer; nowadays, he calls for an end to cruelty, Defenders, Magazine of Defenders of Wildlife, June, 1980, pp. 152-6.

1988. Cherfas, Jeremy, "Rationality and the Slaughter of Seals," New Scientist, March 16, 1978, p. 724.

1989. Curtis, Patricia, "Whose Wildlife? Hunting and Trapping," in Curtis' Animal Rights (1313), pp. 51-71.

1990. Davies, Brian, Savage Luxury: the Slaughter of the Baby Seals, Taplinger, New York, 1971.

1991. Davies, Brian, and Porter, Eliot, Seal Song, Viking Press, New York, 1978.

1992. Dowding, Muriel the Lady, "Furs and Cosmetics: Too High a Price?" in Animals, Men and Morals, ed. Godlovitch and Harris (1172).

1993. Gilsvik, Bob, The Complete Book of
       Trapping, Chilton, Radnor,
       Pennsylvania, 1976.

1994. Howard, Ronald A., and Kelly, John
       W., Trapping Furbearers, New York
       State College of Agriculture and
       Life Sciences, (4-H Members' Guide
       M-5-11), Ithaca, New York, 1976.

1995. Kaplan, David G., World of Furs,
       Fairchild Publications, New York,
       1974.

1996. Lust, Peter, The Last Seal Pup,
       Harvest House, Montreal, Quebec,
       1967.

1997. Nilsson, Greta, et al., Facts about
       Furs, Animal Welfare Institute,
       Washington, D.C., 1980.

1998. Powys, Llewelyn, "Christian Fingers,"
       The Nation and The Athenaeum, Vol.
       39, May 22, 1926, pp. 174-5.

1999. Thornton, Allan, "The Canadian Seal
       Hunt: A Reply," New Scientist,
       Vol. 78, April 13, 1978, pp. 82-3.

2000. Vinter, F.J., "Hunting, Trapping and
       Rearing for Furs," Animal Regula-
       tion Studies, Vol. I, No. 2,
       November, 1977.

2001. Watson, E.L. Grant, "The Price of
       Fur," New Statesman and Nation,
       Vol. 14, August 28, 1937,
       pp. 304-5.

20: War

2002. Chapple, Steve, "The Pentagon: Killer Dolphins and the Organic Arsenal," Penthouse, June, 1977.

2003. Fox, Frank, "The War and the Animals," Spectator, Vol. 122, March 29, 1919, pp. 389-90.

2004. Hooper, Frederick, The Military Horse, The Equestrian Warrior Through the Ages, Barnes, New York, 1976.

2005. Lubow, Robert E., The War Animals, Garden City, New York, Doubleday & Co., 1977.

20: Whaling and Treatment of Dolphins and Other Cetaceans

(For additional entries related to this topic see 2769, 2795, 2853, 2863, 2875, 2877, 2888, 2907, 2915, 2933, 2977, 3016, 3019, 3022, 3024, 3128, 2696, 2623, 2648, 2649, 2660, 2668, 2672, 2599, 2396, 2494, 2248, 2249, 2253, 2268, 2281, 2285, 2294, 2301, 2040, 870, 2061, 2002, 1531.)

2006. Hunter, Robert, and Weyler, Rex, To Save a Whale, Heinemann, London, 1978.

2007. Regan, Tom, "On the Ethics of Whaling," A submission to the Conference on Cetacean Behavior and Intelligence and the Ethics of Killing Cetaceans, Washington, D.C., April, 1980.

2008. Singer, Peter, "Why the Whale Should Live," Habitat, Vol. 6, No. 3, June, 1978, pp. 8-9.

20: Whaling and Treatment of Dolphins and Other Cetaceans

2009. Spence, Bill, Harpooned: The Story of Whaling, Conway Maritime Press, London, 1980.

2010. The Whaling Question, The Inquiry by Sir Sydney Frost of Australia, Friends of the Earth (San Francisco), and The Whale Coalition, 1979.

20: Work

2011. Fox, Freddy, "Commonsense and the Work-Worn Horse," Saturday Review, Vol. 157, June 30, 1934, p. 760.

20: Zoos

(For additional entries related to this topic see 3019, 3033, 3131, 2702, 2597, 2298, 1326.)

2012. Batten, Peter, and Stancil, Deborah, Living Trophies; a Shocking Look at America's Zoos, Crowell, New York, 1976.

2013. Burton, Maurice, "Something in Favor of Zoos," Illustrated London News, Vol. 216, March 18, 1950, p. 426.

2014. Curtis, Patricia, "Prisons or Havens? A Look at the Zoos," in Curtis' Animal Rights (1313), pp. 91-107.

2015. Durrell, Gerald, The Stationary Ark, Fontana/Collins, Glasgow, 1977.

2016. Fisher, James, Zoos of the World: The Story of Animals in Captivity, Doubleday, Garden City, New York, 1975. (Juvenile.)

2017. Hediger, Heini, Man and Animal in

the Zoo, Zoo Biology, trans. by
Gwynne Vevers and Winwood Reade,
Delacourte Press, New York, 1969.

2018. Hediger, Heini, The Psychology and
Behavior of Animals in Zoos and
Circuses, Peter Smith, Gloucester,
Mass., 1969.

2019. Hediger, Heini, Wild Animals in
Captivity, trans. G. Sircom,
Dover, New York, 1964.

2020. Jordan, Bill, and Ormrod, Stephan,
The Last Great Wild Beast Show,
Constable, London, 1978.

2021. Karsten, P., Safety Manual for Zoo
Keepers, Calgary Zoo, Alberta,
Canada, 1974.

2022. McCoy, Joseph J., Our Captive
Animals, Seabury Press, New
York, 1972.

2023. Maroldo, Georgette K., "Zoos World-
wide as Settings for Psychological
Research," American Psychologist,
November, 1978, pp. 1000-4.

2024. Morris, Desmond, Animal Days, Morrow,
New York, 1980.

2025. Wemmer, Chris, "Can Wildlife Be
Saved in Zoos?" New Scientist,
September 8, 1977, pp. 585-7.

20: Conservation (Including Extinct and
Endangered Species, Wildlife Management)
(For additional entries related to this topic
see 3005, 3009, 3029, 3031, 3052, 3060,
3061, 3065, 3071, 3073, 3105, 3131, 2707,
2664, 2666, 2670, 2675, 2677, 2678, 2684,
2597, 2257, 2203, 2309, 2310, 2225, 1342.)

2026. Allen, D.L., "The Need for a New
       North American Wildlife Policy,"
       Transactions of the 37th North
       American Wildlife and Natural
       Resources Conference, Wildlife
       Management Institute, Washington,
       D.C., 1972, pp. 46-54.

2027. Allen, Robert, "Coming to Terms
       with Our Fellow Species," in
       Allen's How to Save the World,
       Prentice-Hall of Canada,
       Scarborough, Ontario, 1980.

2028. Burton, J.A., "The Ivory Connection,"
       New Scientist, April 15, 1976,
       pp. 138-9.

2029. Burton, J.A., "The Ivory Connection,
       Part 2," New Scientist, October
       20, 1977, pp. 168-9.

2030. Burton, Maurice, and Burton, Robert,
       The World's Disappearing Wildlife,
       Arco, New York, 1978.

2031. Caras, Roger, Last Chance on Earth;
       a Requiem for Wildlife, Schocken,
       New York, 1972.

2032. Christian, Garth, A Place for
       Animals, A Plea for the Preserva-
       tion of Wild Life and the Estab-
       lishment of Nature Sanctuaries,
       Lutterworth, London, 1958.

20: Conservation (Including Extinct and Endangered Species, Wildlife Management)

2033. Clement, R.C., "Preliminary Views on Nongame Wildlife Policy," Transactions of the 39th North American Wildlife and Natural Resources Conference, Wildlife Management Institute, Washington, D.C., 1974, pp. 110-15.

2034. Crittendon, A., "Tourism's Terrible Toll," International Wildlife, Vol. 5, 1975, pp. 4-12.

2035. Curry-Lindahl, Kai, Let Them Live: A Worldwide Survey of Animals Threatened with Extinction, Morrow, New York, 1972. (See especially Chap. 1, "From Harmony to Violence-- Human Relations with the Environment Past and Present.")

2036. Engelhardt, Wolfgang, ed., Survival of the Free, The Last Strongholds of Wild Animal Life, trans. from the German by John Coombs, Hamish Hamilton, London, 1962.

2037. "Environmental Outrages III: Animals," Discussion of animals nearing extinction and trapping abuses. Discussants: Alice Herrington, Valerie Maxwell, Dick DeBartola, and Grace Jessen. Archive number BB 3955, Pacific Tape Library, 5316 Venice Boulevard, Los Angeles, California, 90019.

2038. Fisher, James, Simon, Noel, and Vincent, Jack, Wildlife in Danger, Viking, New York, 1969.

2039. Frame, George W., and Frame, Lory
       Herbison, "Cheetahs: In a Race for
       Survival," National Geographic, Vol.
       157, May, 1980, pp. 712-28.

2040. Graham, Alistair D., The Gardeners
       of Eden, George Allen and Unwin,
       London, 1973.

2041. Grainger, David, Animals in Peril, A
       Guide to the Endangered Animals of
       Canada and the United States, Pa-
       gurian Press, Dutton, New York, 1978.

2042. Graves, W., "The Imperiled Giants,"
       National Geographic, Vol. 150, 1976,
       pp. 722-51. (Whales)

2043. Greenway, James C., Jr., Extinct and
       Vanishing Birds of the World,
       Dover, New York, 1967.

2044. Gunn, Alastair S., "Why Should We
       Care about Rare Species?" Environ-
       mental Ethics, Vol. 2, Spring 1980,
       pp. 17-37.

2045. Halliday, Tim, "Birds in Danger: Man
       in Danger," New Scientist, Vol. 78,
       May 25, 1978, pp. 517-19.

2046. Halliday, Tim, Vanishing Birds, Their
       Natural History and Conservation,
       Sidgwick and Jackson, London, 1978.

2047. Hargrove, Eugene C., "Anglo-American
       Land Use Attitudes," Environmental
       Ethics, Vol. 2, Summer, 1980, pp.
       121-48.

2048. Harper, Francis, Extinct and Vanish-
       ing Mammals of the Old World,

American Committee for International Wild Life Protection, New York Zoological Park, New York, 1945.

2049. Harris, Michael, "The War Against the Eastern Coyote," The Progressive, September, 1979, pp. 41-44.

2050. Harrisson, Barbara, Conservation of Nonhuman Primates in 1970, S. Karger, Basel, 1971.

2051. Hill, Lenn, and Wood, Emma, Birdland, The Story of a World Famous Sanctuary, Taplinger, New York, 1976.

2052. Holt, S.J., and Talbot, L.M., "New Principles for the Conservation of Wild Living Resources," Wildlife Monographs, Vol. 59, 1978, pp. 1-33.

2053. Hudnall, J., "A Report on the General Behavior of Humpback Whales Near Hawaii, and the Need for the Creation of a Whale Park," Oceans, Vol. 11, 1978, pp. 8-15.

2054. Jahn, L.R. and Trefethen, J.B., "Funding Wildlife Conservation Programs," in Wildlife and America, H.P. Brokaw, ed., Council on Environmental Quality, Washington, D.C., 1978, pp. 456-70.

2055. Jones, M., "Trampling on Wildlife," New Scientist, Vol. 31, 1966, pp. 13-14.

2056. McClung, Robert, M., Lost Wild Worlds, The Story of Extinct and Vanishing Wildlife of the Eastern Hemisphere,

William Morrow, New York, 1976.

2057. McCoy, J.J., Nature Sleuths: Pro-
tectors of Our Wildlife, Lothrop,
Lee and Shepard, New York, 1969.
(Juvenile)

2058. McCoy, Joseph J., Saving Our Wildlife,
Macmillan, New York, 1970. (Youth
Book)

2059. MacCrimmon, Hugh R., Animals, Man
and Change, Alien and Extinct
Wildlife of Ontario, McClelland
and Stewart, Toronto, 1977.

2060. McNulty, Faith, Must They Die? The
Strange Case of the Prairie Dog
and the Black-footed Ferret, Dutton
New York, 1971.

2061. McVay, Scott, "The Last of the Great
Whales," Scientific American, Vol.
215, August, 1966, pp. 13-21.

2062. Mallinson, J., The Shadow of Extinction, Europe's Threatened Wild
Mammals, Macmillan, London, 1978.

2063. Marnham, Patrick, "Ahmed and the
Gamekeepers," Harpers, January,
1980, pp. 58-67. (On Elephants)

2064. Massingham, H.J., "The Close of the
Age of Mammals," Discovery, Vol.
9, July, 1928, pp. 213-15.

2065. Milne, Lorus J., and Margery, The
Cougar Doesn't Live Here Anymore,
Prentice-Hall, Englewood Cliffs,
N.J., 1971.

2066. Myers, Norman, The Sinking Ark, A
       New Look at the Problems of Disap-
       pearing Species, Pergamon Press,
       New York, 1979.

2067. Olsen, Jack, Slaughter the Animals,
       Poison the Earth, (coyotes, predator
       control), Simon and Schuster, New
       York, 1971.

2068. Pister, Edwin P., "Endangered Species:
       Costs and Benefits," Environmental
       Ethics, Vol. 1, Winter, 1979, pp.
       341-52.

2069. Regenstein, Lewis, The Politics of
       Extinction, Macmillan, New York,
       1975.

2070. Salvadori, F.B. and Florio, P.L.,
       Wildlife in Peril, David and
       Charles, Newton Abbot, Great
       Britain, 1978.

2071. Scheffer, V.B., "The Future of Wild-
       life Management," Wildlife Society
       Bulletin, Vol. 4, 1976, pp. 51-4.

2072. Tinker, J., "Who's Killing Kenya's
       Jumbos?" New Scientist, May 22,
       1975, pp. 452-5.

2073. Train, R.E., "Who Owns American
       Wildlife?" in Wildlife and Amer-
       ica, H.P. Brokaw, ed., Council on
       Environmental Quality, Washington,
       D.C., 1978, pp. 275-8.

2074. Trefethen, James B., Wildlife
       Management and Conservation,
       D.C. Heath, Boston, 1964.

2075. University of Michigan Institute for
      Environmental Quality, _Predator
      Control, 1971; report to the
      Council on Environmental Quality
      and the Department of the Interior
      by the Advisory Committee on
      Predator Control_, University of
      Michigan Institute for Environmental
      Quality, Ann Arbor, 1972.

2076. Verney, Peter, _Animals in Peril: Man's
      War Against Wildlife_, Brigham Young
      University Press, Provo, Utah, 1980.

2077. Wells, S.M. and Burton, J.A., "The
      International Ivory Trade," _Animal
      Regulation Studies_, Vol. 2, Decem-
      ber, 1979, pp. 75-92.

2078. Williams, Jay, _Fall of the Sparrow_,
      Oxford University Press, New York,
      1951.

2079. Wilson, Derek, and Ayerst, Peter,
      _White Gold: The Story of African
      Ivory,_ Heinemann, London, 1976.

2080. Wood, Frances, and Wood, Dorothy,
      Animals in Danger, Dodd Mead, New
      York, 1968.

2081. Ziswiler, Vinzenz, _Extinct and Vanish-
      ing Animals: A Biology of Extinction
      and Survival_, Springer-Verlag, New
      York, 1967.

(For additional entries related to this topic
see 1049, 1056, 1057, 1102, 1222.)

2082. Adams, E.M., "Ecology and Value
Theory," Southern Journal of
Philosophy, Vol. 10, Spring, 1972,
pp. 3-6.

2083. Arenilla, Louis, "Ecology: A Different Perspective," Diogenes, Vol.
104, Winter, 1978, pp. 1-22.

2084. Barr, James, "Man and Nature: The
Ecological Controversy and the Old
Testament," in Spring, David and
Eileen, eds., Ecology and Religion
in History, Harper & Row, New York,
1974.

2085. Bateson, Gregory, Steps to an Ecology
of Mind, Ballantine Books, New York,
1975.

2086. Bennett, John B., "Ecology and Philosophy: Whitehead's Contribution,"
Journal of Thought, Vol. 10, January,
1975, pp. 24-30.

2087. Blackstone, William, ed., Philosophy
and Environmental Crisis, University
of Georgia Press, Athens, Georgia,
1974.

2088. Bryce-Smith, D., "Ecology, Theology,
and Humanism," Zygon, Vol. 12,
September, 1977, pp. 212-31.

2089. Caras, Roger A., Dangerous to Man,
The Definitive Story of Wildlife's
Reputed Dangers, Holt, Rinehart &
Winston, New York, 1975.

2090. Carson, Rachel, Silent Spring, Houghton

Mifflin, Boston, 1962.

2091. Cobb, John B., Jr., "The Population
Explosion and the Rights of the
Subhuman World," IDOC International,
North American ed., New York,
September 12, 1970.

2092. "The Destruction of Nature in the Soviet
Union," M.E. Sharpe, White Plains,
New York, forthcoming. (Manuscript
smuggled out of the U.S.S.R.)

2093. Dewar, James, The Rape of Noah's Ark,
William Kimber, London, 1969.

2094. Diole, Philippe, The Errant Ark:
Man's Relationship with Animals,
Putnam's, New York, 1974.

2095. Dustin, Daniel L., and McAvoy, Leo H.,
"Hardining National Parks," Environmental Ethics, Vol. 2, Spring, 1980,
pp. 39-44.

2096. Ehrenfeld, David W., Conserving Life
on Earth, Oxford University Press,
New York, 1972.

2097. Elton, Charles S., The Ecology of
Invasions by Animals and Plants,
Wiley, New York, 1958.

2098. Goodman, Russell, "Taoism and Ecology,"
Environmental Ethics, Vol. 2, Spring,
1980, pp. 73-80.

2099. Gordon, Douglas, "Nature Opposed to
Artifice," Quarterly Review, Vol.
285, January, 1947, pp. 32-43.

2100. Hay, John, In Defense of Nature, Viking,

New York, 1970.

2101. Hapgood, Fred, "The Urban Jungle," Wildlife Review (Province of British Colombia, Ministry of Environment), Vol. 9, Summer, 1980, pp. 8-9. (Assuming that within our lifetime the world's wildlife is going to be devastated, Hapgood suggests bio-architecture for cities, providing ecological support for flora and fauna and humans.)

2102. Hughes, J. Donald, "Ecology in Ancient Greece," Inquiry, Vol. 18, Summer, 1975, pp. 115-25.

2103. Kainz, Howard P., "Philosophy and Ecology," New Scholasticism, Vol. 47, 1973, pp. 516-19.

2104. Keller, James A., "Types of Motives for Ecological Concern," Zygon, Vol. 6, June, 1971, pp. 197-209.

2105. Laycock, George, The Alien Animals, American Museum of Natural History, Natural History Press, Garden City, New York, 1966.

2106. Leiss, William, "The Imperialism of Human Needs," North American Review, Vol. 259, Winter, 1974, pp. 27-34.

2107. Leopold, Aldo, The Sand County Almanac, Oxford University Press, London, 1968.

2108. Lister-Kaye, John, Seal Cull, Penguin, London, 1979.

2109. Lockington, W.N., "Protection of Animals Useful to Man," Californian,

Vol. 2, 1880, pp. 124-8.(19th Century.)

2110. McCoy, J.J., Wild Enemies, Hawthorn, New York, 1974.

2111. Marietta, Don E., Jr., "The Interrelationship of Ecological Science and Environmental Attitudes," Environmental Ethics, Vol. 1, Fall, 1979, pp. 195-207.

2112. Marietta, Don E., Jr., "Religious Models and Ecological Decision Making," Zygon, Vol. 12, June, 1977, pp. 151-66.

2113. Meyer-Abich, Klaus M., "Toward a Practical Philosophy of Nature," Environmental Ethics, Vol. 1, Winter, 1979, pp. 293-308.

2114. Naess, Arne, "Spinoza and Ecology," Philosophia (Israel), Vol. 7, March, 1977, pp. 45-54.

2115. Odum, E., Fundamentals of Ecology, Saunders, Philadelphia, 1971.

2116. Pedler, Kit, Quest for Gaia. A book of Changes, Souvenir Press, London, 1979.

2117. Rensberger, Boyce, The Cult of the Wild, Anchor Press, Doubleday, Garden City, New York, 1978.

2118. Ricciuti, Edward R., Killer Animals, Walker, New York, 1976.

2119. Robeson, Dave, Louis Roth: Forty Years with Jungle Killers,

Caxton, Caldwell, Idaho, 1941.

2120. Rodman, John, "The Other Side of Ecology in Ancient Greece: Comments on Hughes," Inquiry, Vol. 19, Spring, 1976, pp. 108-12.

2121. Roos, G., Dios, Ecologia y Panteismo, Embat, Barcelona, 1978. Also a privately-printed edition, God, Ecology and Pantheism, sponsored by the Spanish Association for the Defense of Animal Rights, trans. by Robert Latona, 1980.

2122. Roots, Clive, Animal Invaders, Universe Books, New York, 1976.

2123. Scheffer, Victor B., Adventures of a Zoologist, Charles Scribner's, New York, 1980.

2124. Sessions, George, "Spinoza and Jeffers on Man in Nature," Inquiry, Vol. 20, Winter, 1977, pp. 481-528.

2125. Shepard, Paul, "Animal Rights and Human Rites," North American Review, Vol. 259, Winter, 1974, pp. 35-42.

2126. Shepard, Paul, The Tender Carnivore and the Sacred Game, Scribner's, New York, 1973.

2127. Stearns, J. Brenton, "Ecology and the Indefinite Unborn," Monist, Vol. 56, October, 1972, pp. 612-25.

2128. Stoddart, D.M., ed., Ecology of Small Mammals, Chapman and Hall, London, 1979.

2129. Storr, Anthony, "Man's Relationship with the World," North American Review, Vol. 259, Winter, 1974, pp. 18-26.

2130. Thomas, William L., Jr., ed., Man's Role in Changing the Face of the Earth, University of Chicago Press, Chicago, 1956.

2131. White, Lynn, "Continuing the Conversation," in Western Man and Environmental Ethics, ed. by Ian G. Barbour, Addison-Wesley, Reading, MA, 1973.

2132. White, Lynn, "The Historical Roots of Our Ecologic Crisis, Science, Vol. 155, March 10, 1967.

2133. White, Lynn and Watts, Alan, "Ecological Crisis: Religious Cause and Religious Solution," a tape discussion, Eastern and Western views on animals. (Available from Pacific Tape Library, 5316 Venice Blvd., Los Angeles, Ca. 90019.)

2134. Wynne-Edwards, V.C., Animal Dispersion in Relation to Social Behaviour, Oliver and Boyd, Edinburgh, 1962.

20: Environmental Ethics

(For additional entries related to this topic
see 2613, 2290, 1183, 1233, 1297.)

2135. Blackstone, William T., "The Environment and Ethics," Hastings Center Report Supplement, December, 1977, pp. 16-18.

2136. Blackstone, William T., "Ethics and Ecology," Southern Journal of Philosophy, Vol. 11, Spring-Summer, 1973, pp. 55-71.

2137. Blackstone, William T., "The Search for an Environmental Ethic," in Regan, Tom, ed., Matters of Life and Death, Random House, New York, 1980.

2138. Benn, Stanley, "Personal Freedom and Environmental Ethics: The Moral Inequality of Species," World Congress on Philosophy of Law and Social Philosophy, St. Louis, Mo., August, 1975.

2139. Bennett, John B., "A Context for the Land Ethic," Philosophy Today, Vol. 20, Summer, 1976, pp. 124-33.

2140. Callicott, J. Baird, "Elements of an Environmental Ethic: Moral Considerability and the Biotic Community," Environmental Ethics, Vol. 1, Spring, 1979, pp. 71-81.

2141. Darling, F. Fraser, "Man's Responsibility for the Environment," in F.J. Ebling, ed., Biology and Ethics, Academic Press, New York, 1969.

2142. Engel, David E., "Elements in a Theology of Environment," Zygon, Vol. 5,

September, 1970, pp. 216-28.

2143. Fox, Michael W., "What Future for Man and Earth? Toward a Biospiritual Ethic," in On the Fifth Day, ed. by Morris and Fox (1219).

2144. Gray, Elizabeth Dodson, Why the Green Nigger? Re-Mything Genesis, Roundtable Press, Wellesley, MA, 1979.

2145. Hargrove, Eugene C., "The Historical Foundations of American Environmental Attitudes," Environmental Ethics, Vol. 1, Fall, 1979, pp. 209-40.

2146. Heinegg, Peter, "Ecology and Social Justice: Ethical Dilemmas and Revolutionary Hopes," Environmental Ethics, Vol. 1, Winter, 1979, pp. 321-7.

2147. Kantor, Jay E., "The 'Interests' of Natural Objects," Environmental Ethics, Vol. 2, Summer, 1980, pp. 163-71.

2148. Katz, Eric, "Utilitarianism and Preservation," Environmental Ethics, Vol. 1, Winter, 1979, pp. 357-64.

2149. Krieger, Martin, "What's Wrong with Plastic Trees?" Science, Vol. 179, 1973, pp. 451 and 453.

2150. MacDonald, David W., and Boitanti, Luigi, "The Management and Conservation of Carnivores: A Plea for an Ecological Ethic," in Animals' Rights--a Symposium, ed. by David Paterson and Richard D. Ryder,

Centaur Press, Fontwell, Sussex, 1979, pp. 165-77.

2151. McGinn, Thomas, "Ecology and Ethics," _International Philosophical Quarterly_, Vol. 14, June, 1974, pp. 149-60.

2152. Marietta, Don E., Jr., "Humanism and Concern for the Environment," _Religious Humanism_, Vol. 12, Summer, 1978, pp. 114-6.

2153. Martin, John, "The Rehabilitation of Nature: A Course and Its Literature," _Teaching Philosophy_, Vol. 1, Spring, 1976, pp. 253-8.

2154. Nash, Roderick, "Do Rocks Have Rights?" _The Center Magazine_, Vol. 10, No. 6, November/December, 1977.

2155. Nelson, R.J., "Ethics and Decision Making," _Environmental Ethics_, Vol. 1, Fall, 1979, pp. 263-78.

2156. Oelhaf, Robert C., "Environmental Ethics: Atomistic Abstraction or Holistic Affection?" _Environmental Ethics_, Vol. 1, Winter, 1979, pp. 329-39.

2157. Passmore, John, _Man's Responsibility for Nature: Ecological Problems and Western Traditions_, Scribner, New York, 1974.

2158. Rolston, Holmes, "Can and Ought We to Follow Nature?" _Environmental Ethics_, Vol. 1, Spring, 1979, pp. 7-30.

2159. Rolston, Holmes, "Is There an Ecological Ethic?" _Ethics_, Vol. 85, January, 1975, pp. 93-109.

2160. Sagoff, Mark, "On Preserving the Natural Environment," _Yale Law Journal_, Vol. 84, 1974, pp. 205-67.

2161. Selk, Eugene E., "Toward an Environmental Ethic: Royce's Theory of Community and Obligation to Future Generations," _Transactions of the Peirce Society_, Vol. 13, Fall, 1977, pp. 253-76.

2162. Shute, Sara, Review of Elizabeth Dodson Gray's _Why the Green Nigger: Re-Mything Genesis_ (2144), _Environmental Ethics_, Vol. 2, Summer, 1980, pp. 187-91.

2163. Singer, Peter, "Not for Humans Only: The Place of Nonhumans in Environmental Issues," in Goodpaster, Kenneth E. and Sayre, Kenneth M., eds. _Ethics and Problems of the 21st Century_, University of Notre Dame Press, Notre Dame, 1979.

2164. Young, R.V., Jr., "A Conservative View of Environmental Ethics," _Environmental Ethics_, Vol. 1, Fall, 1979, pp. 241-54.

2165. Douglas, William O., _A Wilderness Bill of Rights_, Little & Brown, Boston, 1965.

2166. Godfrey-Smith, William, "The Value of Wilderness," _Environmental Ethics_, Vol. 1, No. 4, Winter, 1979, pp. 309-19.

2167. Gunter, Pete Addison Y., "Wilderness Preservation: Some New Alternatives and an 'Old' Rationale," _National Forum_, Vol. 58, Winter, 1978, pp. 36-40.

2168. Henning, Daniel H., "The Politics of Wilderness: Unique Value Conflicts," _Humanist_, Vol. 39, September-October, 1979, pp. 18-21.

2169. Nash, Roderick, _Wilderness and the American Mind_, Yale University Press, New Haven, 1973.

2170. Shields, Allan, "Wilderness, Its Meaning and Value," _Southern Journal of Philosophy_, Vol. 11, Fall, 1973, pp. 240-53.

2171. Smith, Philip M., and Watson, Richard A., "New Wilderness Boundaries," _Environmental Ethics_, Vol. 1, Spring, 1979, pp. 61-4.

20: Animal Welfare Movement (Humane Movement)

(For additional entries related to this topic see 2849, 2838, 2826, 2821, 2823, 2855, 2881, 2907, 2914, 2956, 2966, 3026, 3029, 3044, 3050, 2597, 2598, 2607, 1508.)

2172. Bellairs, Charles, "Animal Welfare," Politics Today, No. 13, September 17, 1979, Conservative Research Department, Conservative Central Office, Westminster, London.

2173. Brown, Anthony, Who Cares for Animals? 150 Years of the RSPCA, Heinemann, London, 1974.

2174. Carson, Gerald, "The Great Meddler," American Heritage, Vol. 19, No. 1, December, 1967, pp. 28-33, 95-97. (On Henry Bergh.)

2175. Coleman, Sidney H., Humane Society Leaders in America: With a Sketch of the Early History of the Humane Movement in England, The American Humane Association, Albany, 1924.

2176. "The Conservative Manifesto: 1979," Conservative Central Office, London, April, 1979. See page 18 for the provision on "Animal Welfare."

2177. Conservative Party: Conservative Research Department, "Animal Welfare," by Charles Bellairs, Politics Today, No. 13, September 17, 1979.

2178. Fairholme, Edward G., and Pain, Wellesley, A Century of Work for Animals, The History of the R.S.P. C.A., 1824-1924, John Murray, Ltd., London, 1924.

20: Animal Welfare Movement (Humane Movement)

2179. Ford, Lee Ellen, Animal Welfare Encyclopedia, 6 Volumes, Ford Associates, Butler, Indiana, 1973.

2180. Hampson, Judith, "Animal Welfare--A Century of Conflict," New Scientist, October 25, 1979, pp. 280-82.

2181. Harrison, Brian, "Religion and Recreation in Nineteenth-Century England," Past and Present, No. 38, December, 1967, pp. 98-125. (On R.S.P.C.A., and social classes.)

2182. Hollands, Clive, "Animal Welfare Year in Retrospect," in Animals' Rights-- a Symposium, ed. by David Paterson and Richard D. Ryder, Centaur Press, Fontwell, Sussex, 1979, pp. 203-8.

2183. Hollands, Clive, Compassion Is the Bugler, The Struggle for Animal Rights, Macdonald of Edinburgh, Edinburgh, 1980.

2184. Houghton of Sowerby, Lord, "Animals and the Law: Moral and Political Issues," in Animals' Rights--a Symposium, ed. by David Paterson and Richard D. Ryder, Centaur Press, Fontwell, Sussex, 1979, pp. 209-15.

2185. Houghton of Sowerby, Lord, "Putting Animals into Politics," Contemporary Review, Vol. 234, March, 1979, pp. 130-6.

2186. Houghton of Sowerby, Lord, and Platt, Lord, and others, The Houghton/Platt Memorandum: "Experiments on Living Animals, Cruelty to Animals Act 1876," A paper submitted to the Home Secretary by a group of members of the Animal Welfare Parliamentary Group, members of the Animals Experimentation Advisory Committee of the R.S.P.C.A., and the Chairman of Animal Welfare Year 1976. (This memorandum is of great importance in the animal welfare movement in the United Kingdom. Copies can be secured from Clive Hollands, 10 Queensferry Street, Edinburgh, Scotland, EH2 4PG.)

2187. Hubbard, F. Morse, "Prevention of Cruelty to Animals in the States of Illinois, Colorado and California," Academy of Political Science Proceedings, Vol. 6, January, 1916, pp. 209-320.

2188. Hume, E. Douglas, The Mind-Changers, Michael Joseph, London, 1939.

2189. Krause, Flora H., Manual of Moral and Humane Education, Donnelley, Chicago, 1910.

2190. The Labour Party, "Living Without Cruelty: Labour's Charter for Animal Protection," A policy background paper, 1978, The Labour Party, Transport House, Smith Square, London, SWIP 3JA.

2191. "The Labour Party Manifesto: 1979," Labour Party, London, 1979. See page 31 for provision on "Animal Welfare."

2192. "The Liberal Manifesto," Liberal Publication Department, London, April, 1979. See pages 15-16 for provision on animal welfare.

2193. Linzey, Andrew, "The Politics of Animals," Socialist Commentary, December, 1970.

2194. Lynam, S., Humanity Dick: A Biography of Richard Martin, Hamilton, London, 1975.

2195. McCrea, Roswell, The Humane Movement, Columbia University Press, New York, 1910.

2196. Mason, Jim, "The Trouble with Animal Welfare Organizations: Why Are They the Way They Are?" Agenda, Vol. 1, No. 1, Winter 1979/80. P.O. Box 5224, Westport, Ct., 06880.

2197. Morris, Clara, "Riddle of the Nineteenth Century: Mr. Henry Bergh," McClure's Magazine, March, 1902.

2198. Morris, Richard K., "A Philosophy of Humane Education for Our Schools," Teacher Education Quarterly, Vol. 23, No. 3, Spring, 1966.

2199. Moss, Arthur W., Valiant Crusade: The History of the RSPCA, Cassell, London, 1961.

2200. Moss, Arthur W., and Kirby, Elizabeth, Animals Were There, a Record of the Work of the R.S.P.C.A. During the War of 1939-45, Hutchinson, London, not dated.

2201. Niven, Charles D., History of the Humane Movement, Johnson Publications, London, 1967.

2202. Pain Wellesley, Richard Martin, 1754-1834, Leonard Parsons, London, 1925.

2203. Paterson, D.A., "Humane Education," in Animals' Rights--a Symposium, ed. by David Paterson and Richard D. Ryder, Centaur Press, Fontwell, Sussex, 1979, pp. 143-6.

2204. Raymonde-Hawkins, M., Mercy on Us! Animal Welfare and the Story of Raystede Center, Souvenir Press, London, 1967.

2205. Rienow, Leona T., "Defenders of the Defenseless," Defenders of Wildlife, Vol. 51, No. 1, February, 1976, pp. 15-23. (On Henry Bergh and the A.S.P.C.A.)

2206. Rowan, Andrew N., "Animal Experimentation and the Humane Movement in the United States," Journal of Medical Primatology, Vol. 9, 1980, pp. 108-11.

2207. Rowley, Francis H., The Humane Idea, American Humane Education Society, Boston, 1912.

2208. Shultz, William J., The Humane Movement in the United States, 1910-1922, AMS Press, New York, 1968.

2209. Sprigge, T.L.S., "The Animal Welfare Movement and the Foundations of Ethics," in Animals' Rights--a Symposium, ed. by David Paterson and Richard D. Ryder. (1231)

20: Animal Welfare Movement (Humane Movement)

2210. Steele, Zulma, Angel in Top Hat, a
      biography of Henry Bergh, founder
      of American Society for the Preven-
      tion of Cruelty to Animals, Harper
      and Brothers, New York, 1942.

2211. Stillman, William O., "The Prevention
      of Cruelty to Animals," Academy of
      Political Science Proceedings, Vol.
      2, July, 1912, pp. 624-32.

2212. Swallow, William A., Quality of Mercy:
      A History of the Humane Movement in
      the United States, Mary Mitchell
      Humane Fund, Massachusetts SPCA,
      Boston, 1963.

2213. Weichert, H.J., "Animal Protection:
      Ethical Imperative and Economic
      Reality," Animal Regulation Studies,
      Vol. 2, June, 1979, pp. 65-8.

20: Careers Working with Animals
(For additional entries related to this topic
see 2945, 3029, 3032, 3062, 1967.)

2214. Curtis, Patricia, Animal Doctors,
      Delacorte Press, New York, 1972.

2215. Hodge, Guy R., Careers Working with
      Animals, Acropolis Books Ltd.,
      Washington, D.C., 1979.

2216. Mallinson, Jeremy, Earning Your Living
      with Animals, David and Charles,
      London, not dated.

2217. Peterson, Paul, Christensen, Allen C.,
      and Nelson Edward A., Working in
      Animal Science, McGraw-Hill, New
      York, 1978.

2218. Chitty, Susan, The Woman Who Wrote "Black Beauty," Hodder and Stoughton, London, 1971.

2219. Dillard, Annie, Pilgrim at Tinker's Creek, New York, 1974, (Autobiography; perceptions and appreciation of nature in all forms.)

2220. Dowding, Muriel the Lady, Beauty--Not the Beast, An Autobiography, Neville Spearman, Sudbury, Suffolk, U.K., 1980. (Against use of animals for furs and for cosmetics testing and ingredients.)

2221. Eiseley, Loren, Darwin's Century, Evolution and the Men Who Discovered It, Doubleday, New York, 1955.

2222. Hart, Samuel H., "Biography of Anna Kingsford and Edward Maitland," in Addresses and Essays on Vegetarianism, by Anna Kingsford and Edward Maitland, John M. Watkins, London, 1912.

2223. Hendrick, George, Henry Salt: Humanitarian, Reformer and Man of Letters, University of Illinois Press, Urbana, 1977.

2224. Kidd, Beatrice E., and Richards, M. Edith, Hadwen of Gloucester, Man, Medico, Martyr, John Murray, London, 1933.

2225. Muir, Edwin, An Autobiography, Hogarth Press, London, 1964.

2226. Nisbett, Alec, Kønrad Lorenz, Harcourt, Brace, Jovanovich, New York, 1976.

20: Biographies and Autobiographies

2227. Risdon, Wilfrid, Lawson Tait, A Biographical Study, National Anti-
Vivisection Society, London, 1967.

2228. Schweitzer, Albert, Out of My Life and
Thought, Henry Holt, New York, 1949.

2229. Virtanen, Reino, Claude Bernard and
His Place in the History of Ideas,
University of Nebraska Press,
Lincoln, 1960.

2230. Winsten, Stephen, Salt and His
Circle, with a Preface by Bernard
Shaw, Hutchinson & Co., London, 1951.

20: Bibliographies
(For additional entries related to this topic
see 2244, 1266, 1458.)

2231. Hunt, Mary, and Juergensmeyer, Mark,
Animal Ethics: An Annotated Bibli-
ography, Graduate Theological Union,
Berkeley, CA, 1977.

2232. Kelty, Jean M., Once Theirs Alone, A
Bibliographic Study of Animal
Rights, Their Protection and Defense,
Kind, Education Division of the
Humane Society of the United States,
Washington, D.C., 1972.

2233. Magel, Charles R., "An Updated Bibli-
ography," appended to Henry S. Salt's
Animals' Rights, republished by
Society for Animal Rights, Clarks
Summit, Pennsylvania, 1980, pp.
170-218.

2234. Magel, Charles R., and Regan, Tom,
"A Select Bibliography on Animal
Rights and Human Obligations,"

Inquiry, Vol. 22, Summer, 1979, pp. 243-7.

2235. Martin, Rex, and Nickel, James W., "A Bibliography on the Nature and Foundations of Rights," Political Theory, Vol. 6, August, 1978, pp. 395-413.

II. Animals and Law

(For additional entries related to this topic see 2907, 2914, 2925, 2980, 2987, 2988, 3005, 3016, 3029, 3095, 3096, 3107, 2651, 2623-2687, 1063, 1447, 302.)

2236. "The Animal Kingdom in Court," Green Bag, Vol. 10, 1898, pp. 290-1.

2237. Arnold, Earl C., "The Law of Possession Governing the Acquisition of Animals Ferae Naturae," American Law Review, Vol. 55, May, 1921, pp. 393-404.

2238. Bean, M.J., The Evolution of National Wildlife Law, Council on Environmental Quality, Washington, D.C., 1977.

2239. Burr, Stephen I., "Should Animals Have Legal Rights?" Animals, Massachusetts Society for the Prevention of Cruelty to Animals, July/August, 1977.

2240. Burr, Stephen I., "Toward Legal Rights for Animals," Environmental Affairs, Boston College Law School, Vol. 4, No. 2, Spring, 1975.

2241. Burton, Percy M., and Scott, Guy H.G., The Law Relating to the Prevention of Cruelty to Animals, John Murray, London, 1906.

2242. Carson, Hampton, "The Trial of Animals and Insects: A Little Known Chapter of Medieval Jurisprudence," American Philosophical Society Proceedings, Vol. 56, 1917, pp. 410-15.

2243. Chambers, P.G., "Legislating for the Slaughter of Food Animals," Animal Regulation Studies, Vol. 2,

II. Animals and Law

June, 1979, pp. 59-64.

2244. Coggins, George C., and Smith,
Deborah L., "The Emerging Law of
Wildlife: A Narrative Bibliography," Environmental Law, Vol.
6, 1976, pp. 583-618.

2245. Coleridge, Stephen, "The Administration of the Cruelty to Animals Act
of 1876," Fortnightly Review, Vol.
73, March 1, 1900, pp. 392-8.

2246. Cooper, Margaret E., "Animal Welfare
Law: Law for Biologists," Biologist,
Vol 25, 1978, pp. 195-7, and Vol.
26, 1979, pp. 110-13.

2247. Council of Europe, "European Convention for the Protection of Animals
Kept for Farming Purposes," European Treaty Series No. 87, Stras-
bourg, March 10, 1976.

2248. Daws, Gavan, "Dolphin Snatch: The
Untold Story of an Important Legal
Battle," The Beast, Summer, 1980,
pp. 32-5.

2249. Daws, Gavan, "The Hawaii Dolphin
Case: "Animal Liberation" in
Criminal Court," Agenda: A Journal
of Animal Liberation, No. 2, March,
1980. P.O. Box 5234, Westport, CT,
06880.

2250. Deleuran, P., "ECC Legislation and
the Protection of Domestic Animals,"
Animal Regulation Studies, Vol. 1,
No. 2, November, 1977.

2251. de Montmorency, J.E.G., "State Protection of Animals at Home and Abroad," Law Quarterly Review, Vol. 18, 1902, pp. 31-48.

2252. Dichter, Anita, "Legal Definitions of Cruelty and Animal Rights," Boston College Environmental Affairs Law Review, Vol. 7, No. 1, 1978.

2253. Dobra, Peter M., "Cetacians: A Litany of Cain," Boston College Environmental Affairs Law Review, Vol. 7, No. 1, 1978.

2254. Evans, Edward P., The Criminal Prosecution and Capital Punishment of Animals, Heinemann, London, 1906.

2255. Evans, E.P., "Bugs and Beasts Before the Law," Green Bag, Vol. 10, 1898, pp. 540-4.

2256. Evans, E.P., "Bugs and Beasts Before the Law," Green Bag, Vol. 11, 1899, pp. 33-9.

2257. Fawcett, Charles W., "Vanishing Wildlife and Federal Protective Efforts," Ecology Law Quarterly, Vol. 1, Summer, 1971.

2258. Field-Fisher, T.G., Animals and the Law, Universities Federation for Animal Welfare, Herts., England, 1964.

2259. Flint, L.P., and Pearson, Adam, A Legal Handbook for Inspectors of the Royal Society for the Prevention of Cruelty to Animals, R.S.P.C.A., London, 1972.

2260. Frank, Jonny, "Factory Farming: An Imminent Clash between Animal Rights Activists and Agribusiness," Boston College Environmental Affairs Law Review, Vol. 7, No. 3, pp. 423-461.

2261. Friend, Charles E., "Animal Cruelty Laws: The Case for Reform," University of Richmond Law Review, Vol. 8, 1974, pp. 201-31.

2262. Gordon, G.P., "Legal Protection to Animals," Westminster Review, Vol. 166, August, 1906, pp. 218-223.

2263. Greenwood, George, "The Rodeo and the Law," The Nation and the Athenaeum, Vol. 35, August 16, 1924, pp. 618-9.

2264. Hannah, H.W., and Storm, Donald F., Law for the Veterinarian and Livestock Owner, Interstate Printers and Publishers, Danville, Illinois, 1974.

2265. Harris, Stuart, "The Guinea-Pig and the Law," The Listener, Vol. 97, No. 2497, February 24, 1977.

2266. Harrison, Brian, "Animals and the State in Nineteenth-Century England," English Historical Review, Vol. 88, No. 349, October, 1973, pp. 786-820.

2267. Harrison, Ruth, "Steps toward Legislation in Great Britain," in Factory Farming: A Symposium, ed. by J.R. Bellerby, British Association for the Advancement of Science, London, 1970, pp. 3-16.

2268. Herrington, Alice, and Regenstein, Lewis, "The Plight of Ocean Mammals," _Environmental Affairs_, Boston College Law School, Vol. 1, No. 4, March, 1972, pp. 792-825.

2269. Holzer, Henry M., ed., _Animal Rights Law Reporter_, Communicating Current Developments in Animal Rights Law, Published by Society for Animal Rights, Inc., 421 South State Street, Clarks Summit, PA, 18411. Issued four times a year. The purpose of _Animal Rights Law Reporter_ is to provide animal rights activists with information which could aid in legal efforts on behalf of animals. The following headings are typically used:
IN THE COURTS
IN THE LEGISLATURES AND AGENCIES
IN THE LEGAL LITERATURE
BULLETIN BOARD
AVAILABLE RESOURCES
EDITORS COMMENT

2270. Hyde, Walker W., "The Prosecution and Punishment of Animals and Lifeless Things in the Middle Ages and Modern Times," _University of Pennsylvania Law Review_, Vol. 64, pp. 696-730.

2271. Ingham, John, H., _The Law of Animals_, A Treatise of Property in Animals, Wild and Domestic, and the Rights and Responsibilities Arising Therefrom, T. and J.W. Johnson, Philadelphia, 1900.

2272. Jenkins, Hugh, "Why the Cruelty Act Is Really No More Than a Licence to Inflict Pain on Animals," _Times_, January 29, 1977.

2273. Johnson, Howard, "Hunting and the Law," in _Against Hunting_, ed. by Patrick Moore, Victor Gallancz, 1965.

2274. Jones, William, "Legal Prosecution of Animals, _Popular Science Monthly_, Vol. 17, September, 1880, pp. 619-25.

2275. Kerr, M.E.E., "Animals in Court," _Green Bag_, Vol. 14, 1902, pp. 264-5.

2276. LaPage, Geoffrey, "The Legal Control of Experiments on Living Vertebrates," in LaPage's _Achievement_, W. Heffer, Cambridge, 1960, pp. 211-25.

2277. "Lawsuits against Animals," _Green Bag_, Vol. 14, 1902, pp. 471-3.

2278. Leavitt, Emily S., _Animals and Their Legal Rights_, A Survey of American Laws from 1641 to 1978, Animal Welfare Institute, Washington, D.C., 1978.

2279. Loring, Murray, _The Risks and Rights of Animal Ownership_, Arco, New York, 1973.

2280. Lowe, Robert, "The Vivisection Act," _Contemporary Review_, Vol. 28, October, 1876, pp. 713-724.

2281. Lubow, Arthur, "Should This Dolphin Be Set Free? The First Liberation Case Opens in Hawaii," _New Times_, October 14, 1977.

2282. McCoy, J.J., "Our Wildlife Protection Laws," in McCoy's _Nature Sleuths_, Lothrop, Lee and Shepard, New York, pp. 54-64.

2283. Margolin, Steven, "Liability under
the Migratory Bird Treaty Act,"
Ecology Law Quarterly, Vol. 7, 1979,
pp. 989-1010.

2284. "Martin's Act," The Nation and the
Athenaeum, Vol. 31, May 27, 1922,
pp. 303-4.

2285. Mason, Milo, "The Bowhead Whale Controversy: Background and Aftermath
of Adams v. Vance," Harvard Environmental Law Review, Vol. 2, 1977,
pp. 363-88.

2286. Mazor, Debigail, "Veterinarians at
Fault: Rare Breed of Malpracti-
tioners," UCD Law Review, University
of California, Davis, Vol. 7, 1974,
pp. 400-12.

2287. Meth, Theodore Sager, "Animal Rights,"
Animals, Boston, Mass., Vol.110,
No. 6, Nov./Dec., 1977. Published
by the Massachusetts Society for the
Prevention of Cruelty to Animals,
Boston.

2288. Meth, Theodore S., "Legal Implications
in the Alternatives to the Use of
Experimental Animals," Journal of
Clinical Pharmacology, Vol. 16, 1976,
pp. 589-591.

2289. Morris, Clarence, "Rights and Duties
of Beasts and Trees," Journal of Legal
Education, Vol. 17, 1964-5, pp. 185 ff.

2290. Murphy, Earl Finbar, "Has Nature Any
Right to Life?" Hastings Law Journal,
Vol. 22, 1971.

2291. "Of Cruelty to Animals, and Mr. Martin's Act," London Magazine, Vol. 6, December, 1822, pp. 530-6.

2292. Ray, P.M., and Scott, W.N., "UK legislation Relevant to the Keeping of Laboratory Animals," in The UFAW Handbook on the Care and Management of Laboratory Animals, ed. by UFAW, Churchill Livingstone, London, 1976.

2293. Regan, Tom, "Animals and the Law: The Need for Reform," Proceedings of the World Congress on Philosophy of Law and Social Philosophy, Basel, Switzerland, 1979, forthcoming.

2294. Rich, Beckman, "The Tuna-Porpoise Controversy," Harvard Environmental Law Review, Vol. 1, 1976, pp. 142-61.

2295. Rikleen, Lauren S., "The Animal Welfare Act: Still a Cruelty to Animals," Boston College Environmental Affairs Law Review, Vol. 7, No. 1, 1978.

2296. Robertson, John A., "The Scientist's Right to Research: A Constitutional Analysis," Southern California Law Review, Los Angeles, Vol. 51, 1978, pp. 1203-79.

2297. Rodman, John, "Animal Justice: The Counter-revolution in Natural Right and Law," Inquiry, Vol. 22, Spring-Summer, 1979, pp. 3-22.

2298. Rosin, Paula, "Federal Regulation of Zoos," Environmental Affairs, Vol. 5, No. 2, Spring, 1976.

2299. Ryan, A.H., "History of the British
Act of 1876: An Act to Amend the
Law Relating to Cruelty to Animals,"
Journal of Medical Education, Vol.
38, 1963, pp.182-94.

2300. Sandys-Winsch, Godfrey, Animal Law
in England and Wales, Shaw, London,
1978.

2301. Scarff, James E., "The International
Management of Whales, Dolphins, and
Porpoises: An Interdisciplinary
Assessment," Ecology Law Quarterly,
Vol. 6, 1977, pp. 323-427 and 571-
638.

2302. Schwartz, Barbara W., "Estate Planning
for Animals," Trusts and Estates,
Vol. 113, June 1974, pp. 376-9.

2303. Shea, Kevin, "The Endangered Species
Act," Environment, October, 1977.

2304. Slater, J.W., "Laws of Government
among the Lower Animals," Popular
Science Monthly, Vol. 38, March,
1891, pp. 677-85.

2305. Steinhart, P., "The Laws of Nature:
A Case for the Landscape as Plaintiff,"
Harper's, Vol. 253, 1976, pp. 30-2.

2306. Stevens, Christine, "The Legal Rights
of Animals in the United States of
America," Animal Regulation Studies,
Vol. 2, December, 1979, pp. 93-102.

2307. Stone, Christopher D., Should Trees
Have Standing? Toward Legal Rights
for Natural Objects, Kaufmann, Los
Altos, CA, 1974.

2308. Stone C.D., "Toward Legal Rights for Natural Systems," Transactions of the 41st North American Wildlife and Natural Resources Conference, Wildlife Management Institute, Washington, D.C., 1976, pp. 31-8.

2309. Stromberg, David B., "The Endangered Species Act Amendment of 1978: A Step Backwards?" Boston College Environmental Affairs Law Review, Vol. 7, No. 1, 1978.

2310. Stromberg, David B., "The Endangered Species Act of 1973: Is the Statute Itself Endangered?" Boston College Environmental Affairs Law Review, Vol. 6, No. 4, 1978.

2311. Taylor, G.B., "Animal Welfare Legislation in Europe," Animal Regulation Studies, Vol. 1, No. 1, August, 1977.

2312. Teutsch, Gotthard M., "The 'Reasonable Ground' as a Problem of the German Animal Protection Act," International Journal for the Study of Animal Problems, Vol. 1, May/June, 1980, pp. 149-51.

2313. Tischler, Joyce S., "Rights for Non-Human Animals: A Guardianship Model for Cats and Dogs," 14, San Diego Law Review, 484, March, 1977.

2314. Trotter, William F., "Property in Wild Animals," Juridical Review, Edinburgh, Vol. 15, 1903, pp. 138-54.

2315. "Twelve Years' Trial of the Vivisection Act," The Spectator, Vol. 62, March 9, 1889, pp. 339-40.

2316. Visscher, Maurice B., "The Animal Welfare Act of 1970," Science, Vol. 172, No. 3986, May 28, 1971, pp. 916-917.

2317. Visscher, M.B., "Commentary on Laws Relating to the Scientific Use of Unclaimed Impounded Dogs," Journal of American Veterinarian Medical Association, Vol. 163, 1973, pp. 78-9.

2318. Weatherill, John, Horse and the Law, Pelham Books, London, 1979.

2319. White, Henry, "A Curious Page of Animal Life," Student and Intellectual Observer, Vol. 3, 1869, pp. 210-17. (Excommunication and punishment of animals)

2320. Withington, E.T., "Legal Proceedings Against Animals," Cornhill Magazine, Vol. 76, N.S. 3, 1897, pp. 68-75.

2321. Zurvalec, Lori A., "Use of Animals in Medical Research: The Need for Governmental Regulation," Wayne Law Review, Vol. 24, Spring 1978, pp. 1733-51.

III.   Animals and Literature and Art and Music
(For additional entry related to this topic
see 2596.)

2322.   Adams, Richard, The Plague Dogs,
        Knopf, New York, 1978. (A novel
        about two dogs who escape from an
        experimental laboratory; inspired,
        in part, by Peter Singer's Animal
        Liberation.)

2323.   Adams, Richard, Shardik, Penguin,
        New York, 1976. (Novel. Shardik,
        the giant bear, brings truth to
        the land of the Ortelgans.)

2324.   Adams, Richard, Watership Down,
        Macmillan, New York, 1972. (A
        novel. The reader enters the rabbit
        world, seeing things through rabbit's
        eyes, smelling the scents as only
        an animal living in the wild can,
        living their terrors and triumphs.)

2325.   Aesopus, The Fables of Aesop, With
        Designs on Wood by Thomas Bewick,
        Two Continents Publishing Group,
        New York, 1975.

2326.   Aikin, Anna Laetitia (Mrs. Barbauld),
        The Mouse's Petition, Found in the
        Trap Where He Had Been Confined All
        Night, to Dr. Priestly, Demi-Griffin
        Press, Oxford, 1976. (A poem,
        originally written in 1773.)

2327.   Anderson, M.D., Animal Carvings in
        British Churches, The University
        Press, Cambridge, England, 1938.

2328.   Angel, Marie, An Animated Alphabet,
        Harvard College Library, Cambridge,
        1971.

2329. Angel, Marie, A New Bestiary, Harvard College Library, Cambridge, 1964.

2330. "Animal Aesthetics," The Spectator, Vol. 66, May 2, 1891, pp. 621-2.

2331. "Animal Aesthetics: Scents and Sounds," The Spectator, Vol. 66, May 30, 1891, pp. 753-4.

2332. "Animals in Literature," Blackwood's Magazine, Vol. 262, August, 1947, pp. 137-43.

2333. "Animals in Novels," Living Age, Vol. 212, 1897, pp. 411-4.

2334. "Animals in Novels," The Spectator, Vol. 77, December 5, 1896, pp. 816-17.

2335. Anonymous, The Dialogues of Creatures Moralysed, London, about 1535.

2336. Anonymous, The Hare, or Hunting Incompatible with Humanity, Written as a Stimulus to Youth Towards a Proper Treatment of Animals, John Gough, Dublin, 1800. (Written from the perspective of the hare.)

2337. Anonymous, Tuppy, The Autobiography of a Donkey, George Bell, London, 1903. (Juvenile fiction.)

2338. Argus, Arabella, The Adventures of a Donkey, William Darton, London, 1815. (Famous juvenile fiction.)

2339. Argus, Arabella, Further Adventures of Jemmy Donkey, Interspersed with Biographical Sketches of the Horse,

William Darton, London, 1821. (Juvenile Fiction.)

2340. Armstrong, Edward A., "Aspect of the Evolution of Man's Appreciation of Bird Song," in Bird Vocalizations, ed. by R.A. Hinde, Cambridge University Press, Cambridge, 1969.

2341. Arnold, S.T., "Twain Bestiary: Mark Twain's Critters and the Tradition of Animal Portraiture in Humor of the Old Southwest," Southern Folklore Quarterly, Vol. 41, 1977, pp. 195-211.

2342. "Artistic Feeling of the Lower Animals," Eclectic Magazine, Vol. 76, May, 1871, pp. 630-2.

2343. Atkins, Elizabeth, "Man and Animals in Recent Poetry," Modern Language Association of American Publications, Vol. 51, March, 1936, pp. 263-83.

2344. Barber, Richard, and Riches, Anne, A Dictionary of Fabulous Beasts, Macmillan, London, 1971.

2345. Baufle, Jean-Marie, and Varin, Jean-Philippe, Photographing Wildlife, trans. by Carel Amerongen, Oxford University Press, New York, 1972.

2346. Bell, Ernest, ed., Speak Up for the Animals, A Collection of Pieces for Recitation about Animals and Their Welfare, G. Bell, London, 1923.

2347. Belves, Peter, and Mathey, Francis, Animals in Art, A Practical Introduction to Seventy of the Principal

Techniques of Art, Odhams Books, Hamlyn Publishing Group, Feltham, Middlesex, U.K., 1968.

2348. Bender, L., and Rappaport, J., "Animal Drawings of Children," _American Journal of Orthopsychiatry_, Vol. 14, July, 1944, pp. 521-7.

2349. Bennett, John, _Echoes from the Peaceable Kingdom,_ Eerdman's, Grand Rapids, Michigan, 1978.

2350. Berry, Ana M., _Animals in Art_, Tower Books, Detroit, 1971.

2351. Bettelheim, Bruno, "The Animal-Groom Cycle of Fairy Tales," in Bettelheim's _The Uses of Enchantment_, Random House, New York, 1977, pp. 277-310.

2352. Bicknell, Ethel E., comp., _Praise of the Dog_, An Anthology, Grant Richards, London, 1902. (Selections from literature and poetry, from Cicero to the Twentieth Century.)

2353. Blount, Margaret, _Animal Land_, The Creatures of Children's Fiction, Hutchinson, London, 1974.

2354. Blount, Margaret, "Fallen and Redeemed: Animals in the Stories of C.S. Lewis," in Blount's _Animal Land_, Hutchinson, London, 1974.

2355. Bly, Robert, _The Morning Glory_, Harper and Row, New York, 1975. See: "The Dead Seal near McClure's Beach," pp. 52-4; "The Large Starfish," pp. 55-6; "The Hunter," p. 9; "Looking at a Dead Wren in My Hand," p. 5;

"A Turtle," p. 19; "Lobsters Waiting to Be Eaten in a Restaurant Window," p. 27; "Bored Elephants in the Circus Stable," p. 28.

2356. Boas, George, The Happy Beast in French Thought of the Seventeenth Century (the views of Montaigne, Descartes and other French writers on animals), Octagon Books, New York, 1966.

2357. Bodenheimer, F.S., Animal and Man in Bible Lands, E.J. Brill, Leiden, 1972.

2358. Borges, Jorge L., The Book of Imaginary Beings, trans. by Norman T. diGiovanni, Clarke, Irwin, Toronto, 1969.

2359. Bowring, John, "Humanity to Animals," in Bowring's Minor Morals for Young People, Illustrated in Tales and Travels, Whittaker, London, 1843.

2360. Braunstein, Mark M., "Vegetarianism in Art," Vegetarian Times, Issue No. 40, 1980, pp. 20-4.

2361. Brewton, John E., ed., Under the Tent of the Sky, A Collection of Poems about Animals Large and Small, Macmillan, New York, 1937.

2362. Brion, Marcel, Animals in Art, Harrap and Co., London, 1959.

2363. Brodrick, A. Houghton, ed., Animals in Archaeology, Praeger, New York, 1972.

2364. Brophy, Brigid, Hackenfeller's Ape,
Penguin Books, London, 1968. (A
novel about a scientist who saves
an ape from being sent up in a
rocket.)

2365. Brosman, C.S., "Sartre's Nature:
Animal Images in La Nausee,"
Symposium, Vol. 31, Summer, 1977,
pp. 107-25.

2366. Buerschaper, P., Animals in Art,
Bryant Press, Ontario, Canada,
1975.

2367. Bunker, Emma, C., Chatwin, C. Bruce,
and Farkas, Ann R., "Animal Style,"
in Art from East to West, Asia Society,
Weatherhill, Rutland, Vermont, 1970.

2368. Burton, Richard, "Our Elder Brother,"
in Burton's Little Essays in Literature and Life, Century Co.,
New York, 1914.

2369. Butler, Samuel, "The View of an
Erewhonian Prophet Concerning the
Rights of Animals" and "The Views
of an Erewhonian Philosopher Concerning the Rights of Vegetables,"
in Butler's Erewhon and Erewhon Revisited, Modern Library, New York,
1955, Chaps. 26 and 27.

2370. Capek, Karel, The Insect Play; in R.U.R.
and The Insect Play, trans. by P.
Selver, Oxford University Press,
London, 1961.

2371. Carlill, James, and Stallybrass, W.H.S.,
eds., The Epic of the Beast, London,
1924.

2372. Carroll, Lewis, Alice in Wonderland,
       and Through the Looking Glass,
       Children's Press, Chicago, 1969.

2373. Carroll, William M., Animal Conven-
       tions in English Renaissance
       Non-Religious Prose (1550-1600),
       Bookman Associates, New York, 1954.

2374. Carter, Dagney, The Symbol of the Beast:
       The Animal-Style Art of Eurasia,
       Ronald Press, New York, 1957.

2375. Cawte, E.C. Ritual Animal Disguise,
       A Historical and Geographical
       Study of Animal Disguise in the
       British Isles, Rowman and Little-
       field, Totowa, N.J., 1978.

2376. Caxton, William, trans., The History
       of Reynard the Fox, ed. by N.F.
       Blake, Oxford University Press,
       London, 1970.

2377. Cetto, A.M., ed., Animal Drawings
       from the Twelfth to the Ninteenth
       Century, Faber and Faber, London,
       1936.

2378. Cetto, Anna M., comp., Animal Drawings
       of Eight Centuries, Harper, New York,
       1950.

2379. Chase, Mary, Harvey, in Twelve American
       Plays (1920-60), ed. by Richard
       Corbin and Miriam Balf, Scribner's
       New York, 1969. (Comic fantasy in-
       volving a white rabbit.)

2380. Church, F.S. "An American among Animals,"
       Scribner's Magazine, Vol. 14,
       December, 1893, pp. 749-759.

2381. Clark, Anne, Beasts and Bawdy,
Taplinger, New York, 1975. (See
excellent bibliography on early
natural history of animals, animal
lore, Physiologus, bestiaries, and
imaginary animals, pp. 147-54.)

2382. Clark, Joseph D., Beastly Folklore,
Scarecrow Press, Metuchen, New
Jersey, 1968.

2383. Clark, Kenneth, Animals and Men,
Their Relationship as Reflected in
Western Art from Prehistory to the
Present Day, William Morrow, New
York, 1977.

2384. Clarke, Frances E., ed., Poetry's
Plea for Animals: An Anthology of
Justice and Mercy for our Kindred
in Fur and Feathers, Lothrop, Lee
and Shepard Co., Boston, 1927.

2385. Cobbe, Frances P., "Animals in Fable
and Art," Living Age, Vol. 121,
1874, pp. 451-67.

2386. Cobbe, Frances P., "Animals in Fable
and Art," in Cobbe's False Beasts
and True, Ward, Lock and Tyler,
London, 1875.

2387. Cobbe, Frances P., The Friend of Man;
and His Friends,--the Poets, British
Union for the Abolition of Vivisection, London, not dated. (Dogs
portrayed in poetry of Egypt, Persia,
India, Judea, Greece, Rome, Islam,
Scandanavia, Italy, England, Germany.)

2388. Cohen, Noah J., The Concept of Tsa'ar
Ba'ale Hayyim (Kindness and the Prevention of Cruelty to Animals):

Its Bases and Development in Biblical, Midrashic and Talmudic Literature, Catholic University of America, Washington, 1953.

2389. Cohn, Norman, "Monsters of Chaos," Horizon, Vol. 14, No. 2, 1972.

2389. Colette, Sidonie G., Creatures Great
a   and Small, Creature Conversations, Other Creatures, Creature Comfort, Secker and Warburg, London, 1951.

2390. Collins, Arthur H., Symbolism of Animals and Birds, Represented in English Church Architecture, McBride, Nast, New York, 1913.

2391. Crawford, Nelson A., ed., Cats in Prose and Verse, Coward-McCann Co., New York, 1947.

2392. Cushion, John P., Animals in Pottery and Porcelain, October House, New York, 1966. Also Studio Vista, London, 1974.

2393. Dailley, Richard, The Doctor's Dog, A Poem against Vivisection, George Allen, London, 1912.

2394. Damroth, William G., Passport to Nature, Viking Press, New York, 1972. (Photographs of Animals.)

2395. Da Vinci, Leonardo, "Selections from the Bestiary of Leonardo Da Vinci," trans, by Oliver Evans, Journal of American Folklore, Vol. 65, October, 1952, pp. 353-9.

2396. Davis, John Gordon, Leviathan, Michael

Joseph, London, 1977. (Novel
about whales, whaling, and sab-
otaging of whaling ships.)

2397. Davis, R., "Animals and Music,"
Discovery, Vol. 3, March 1940,
pp. 149-50.

2398. De La Ramee, Louise (Ouida), A Dog
of Flanders, Nims and Knight, Troy,
N.Y., 1892. (A novel.)

2399. DeLevie, Dagobert, The Modern Idea
of the Prevention of Cruelty to
Animals and Its Reflection in English
Poetry, S.F. Vanni, New York, 1947.

2400. Dent, Anthony, "Shakespeare's Horse-
borne England," History Today, Vol.
23, July, 1973, pp. 455-61.

2401. Donovan, John, Family, Harper & Row,
New York, 1976. (Fiction; the
story of apes who escape from a
laboratory.)

2402. Douglas, Norman, Birds and Beasts of
the Greek Anthology, Jonathan Cape,
New York, 1929.

2403. Duffy, Maureen, I Want to Go to Moscow,
Hodder, London, 1973. (A novel about
a band of radicals who blow up
things to save animals.)

2404. Dugmore, A. Radclyffe, "Art and Animals,"
Natural History, Vol. 32, May-June,
1932, pp. 228-43.

2405. The Duty of Kindness to Animals, A
Selection of Interesting Anecdotes
with Religious and Moral Precepts

in Prose and Verse, For the Use
of Schools and Young Persons of
Both Sexes, Hatchard, London, 1853.

2406. Edwards, M.S., "The Play of 'Down-
ward Comparisons': Animal Anthro-
pomorphism in the Poems of Robert
Frost," in Frost: Centennial Essays
II, ed. by Jac Tharpe, University
Press of Mississippi, 1976.

2407. Elliott, Harley, Animals That Stand
in Dreams, (poems), Hanging Loose
Press, Brooklyn, 1976.

2408. The Epic of the Beast, Consisting of
English Translations of The History
of Reynard the Fox (Caxton's text
modernized by William S. Stallybrass; with Kaulbach's famous illustrations), and Physiologus (trans.
by James Carlill), George Routledge,
London, 1924 (?).

2409. The Escapes, Wanderings, and Preser-
vation of a Hare, Related by Herself,
J. and C. Evans, London, 1820 (?).
(Juvenile fiction.)

2410. Evans, E.P., Animal Symbolism in
Ecclesiastical Architecture, Heine-
mann, London, 1896. Also Gale
Research, Detroit, Mich., 1969.

2411. Farnham, Willard E., "The Beast Theme
in Shakespeare's 'Timon,'" in California University, Department of
English, Essays and Studies, Vol.
14, University of California Press,
Berkeley, CA, 1943, pp. 49-56.

2412. "Feeling of Beauty in Animals," Chamber's Journal, Vol. 71, December 29,

1894, pp. 821-23.

2413. Fernandez, James, "Persuasions and Performances: The Beast in Every Body and the Metaphors of Everyman," Daedalus, Vol. 101, No. 1, 1972.

2414. Fitzgibbon, Constantine, The Rat Report, Constable, London, 1980. (Fiction: Human history and intellectual development from the rats' viewpoint.)

2415. Fougasse (Kenneth Bird), comp., An Animal Anthology, Universities Federation for Animal Welfare, London, 1954. (Poetry.)

2416. Frucht, K., "Animal Slaughter and Transport in the Mirror of Art," Animal Regulation Studies, Vol. 2, June 1979, pp. 37-58.

2417. Frucht, K., "Art and Animal Welfare," Animal Regulation Studies, Vol. 1, No. 1, August, 1977.

2418. Fuller, Catherine R., comp., Beasts, An Alphabet of Fine Prints, Little, Brown, Boston, 1968.

2419. Fussell, G.E., James Ward: Animal Painter 1769-1859 and His England, Michael Joseph, London, 1974.

2420. Gelli, Giovanni Battista, Circe, consisting of Ten Dialogues between Ulysses and several men transformed into beasts, satirically representing the various passions of mankind and the many infelicities of human life. Translated by Thomas Brown and Robert Adam, Cornell University Press,

Ithaca, New York, 1963.

2421. Giehl, Dudley, "Vegetarianism and Literature," in Giehl's Vegetarianism: A Way of Life, Harper and Row, New York, 1979.

2422. Gill, James E., "Beast over Man: Theriophilic Paradox in Gulliver's 'Voyage to the Country of the Houyhnhnms'," Studies in Philology, Vol. 67, October, 1970, pp. 532-49.

2423. Gittings, Robert, "Keats and Cats," Essays and Studies, 1962, The English Association, John Murray, London, pp. 52-8.

2424. Goldsmid, Edward, ed. and trans., Un-Natural History, or Myths of Ancient Science, Being a Collection of Curious Tracts on the Basilisk, Unicorn, Phoenix, Behemoth or Leviathan, Dragon, Giant Spider, Tarantula, Chameleons, Satyrs, Homines, Candat, etc., Privately Printed, Edinburgh, 1886. (Copy in University of Wisconsin Library.)

2425. Goldsmith, Oliver, "Against Cruelty to Animals. A Story from the Zendevest of Zoroaster," in Goldsmith's The Citizen of the World, Folio Society, London, 1969.

2426. Graves, Robert, "What Is a Monster?" Horizon, Vol 10, No. 3, 1968.

2427. Graves, T.S., "The Ass as Actor," South Atlantic Quarterly, Vol. 15, 1916, pp. 175-82.

2428. Graves, T.S., "The Elizabethen Trained
Ape," Modern Language Notes, Vol.
35, 1920, pp. 248-9.

2429. Graves, Thornton, S., "Human Traits
in Quadruped Actors," South Atlantic
Quarterly, Vol. 25, October, 1926,
pp. 383-95.

2430. Green, Maureen, "In Praise of Beasts:
Round-the-World Museum Observance,"
Smithsonian, November, 1977.

2431. Griffin, Robert J., and Freedman,
William A., "Machines and Animals:
Pervasive Motifs in The Grapes of
Wrath," Journal of English and
Germanic Philology, Vol. 62, July
1963, pp. 569-80.

2432. Grover, Edwin O., ed., The Animal
Lover's Knapsack, An Anthology of
Poems for Lovers of Our Animal
Friends, Thomas Y. Crowell, New
York, 1929.

2433. Hadwen, Walter R., The Difficulties
of Dr. Deguerre, C.W. Daniel,
London, 1918. (Facts about vivsection,
and arguments against vivsection,
put in fictional form.)

2434. Haines, Francis, Appaloosa, the
Spotted Horse in Art and History,
Horsebreeder, Austin, Texas, 1972.

2435. Hall, S.C., ed., Animal Sagacity,
S.W. Partridge, London, 1870 (?).
(Juvenile fiction.)

2436. Hall-Craggs, Joan, "The Aesthetic
Content of Bird Song," in Bird

Vocalizations, ed. by R.A. Hinde,
Cambridge University Press, Cambridge,
1969.

2437. Hamilton, Innes, The Beagle Brigade,
Exposition Press, Hicksville, N.Y.,
1980. (A novel about a national ·
humane · society rescue of beagles
bred for experimentation, action
against export of cattle by ship,
etc.)

2438. Hancocks, David, Animals and Architecture, Praeger, New York, 1971.

2439. Harris, Joel Chandler, The Complete
Tales of Uncle Remus, Compiled by
Richard Chase, Houghton Mifflin,
Boston, 1955. (Juvenile fiction.)

2440. Harris, Joel C., Uncle Remus, D.
Appleton, New York, 1889. (Juvenile.)

2441. Harthan, John P., "Mediaeval Bestiaries,"
Geographical Magazine (London),
Vol. 22, 1919, pp. 182-90.

2442. Hartshorne, Charles, "Animal Music
in General," and "Bird Song Compared
to Human Music," in Hartshorne's
Born to Sing: An Interpretation
and World Survey of Bird Song,
Indiana University Press, Bloomington,
1973.

2443. Harwood, Dix, "The Discovery of a New
Literary World," in Harwood's Love
for Animals, and How It Developed in
Great Britain, Ph. D. Dissertation,
Philosophy, Columbia University,
1928, pp. 172-259, 318-70.

2444. Hastings, Hester, Man and Beast in
       French Thought of the Eighteenth
       Century, The Johns Hopkins Studies
       in Romance Literatures and Languages,
       Vol. XXVII, Johns Hopkins Press,
       Baltimore, 1936.

2445. Hastings, Hester, "Man and Beast:
       Lamartine's Contribution to French
       Animal Literature," Modern Language
       Association of America Publications,
       Vol. 61, December, 1946, pp. 1109-25.

2446. Hellman, George S., "Animals in
       Literature," The Atlantic Monthly,
       Vol. 87, March, 1901, pp. 391-397.

2447. Helme, Elizabeth, James Manners, Little
       John, and Their Dog Bluff, Darton
       and Harvey, London, 1807. (Juvenile
       fiction.)

2448. Highsmith, Patricia, The Animal-
       Lover's Book of Beastly Murder,
       Penguin, London, 1980.

2449. Hirshhorn Museum and Sculpture Garden,
       The Animal in Art, selections from
       the Hirshhorn Museum Collection,
       Smithsonian Institution Press,
       Washington, D.C., 1977, 16 pp.

2450. Hogarth, William, "The Four Stages of
       Cruelty," in Engravings by Hogarth,
       ed. by Sean Shesgreen, Dover, New
       York, 1973, prints 77-80

2451. Hosley, Richard, "The Origins of the
       Shakespearian Playhouse," Shakespeare
       Quarterly, Vol. 15, Spring 1964,
       pp. 29-39. (Originated from animal
       baiting arenas?)

2452. Hurwitz, Johanna, Much Ado About
Aldo, Morrow, New York, 1978.
(Children's book. Story of a boy
who becomes a vegetarian, having
been exposed to the issues of
vegetarianism in the course of
doing a school research project.)

2453. Inniss, Kenneth, D.H. Lawrence's
Bestiary, A Study of His Use
of Animal Trope and Symbol, Moutan,
The Hague, 1971.

2454. Iyer, K. Bharatha, Animals in Indian
Sculpture, Taraporevala, Bombay,
1977.

2455. Jackson, Christine E., Bird Illustra-
tors, Some Artists in Early Lithog-
raphy, Witherby, London, 1975.

2456. Jacobs, Joseph, ed., The Most Delect-
able History of Reynard the Fox,
Schocken Books, New York, 1967.
(Juvenile.)

2457. Jelliffe, S.E., and Brink, L.,
"The Role of Animals in the Un-
conscious with Some Remarks on
Theriomorphic Symbolism as Seen
in Ovid," Psychoanalytic Review,
Vol. 4, 1917, pp. 253-71.

2458. Jennings, Elizabeth, After the Ark,
Oxford University Press, Oxford,
1978.

2459. Johns, Charles R., Aberdeen Mac,
Jarrolds, London, 1971 (?). (A
story about a lost dog, taken to
the circus, put in a scientific
laboratory, finally escapes.)

2460. Kastner, Erich, The Animals' Con-
ference, trans, by Zita de Schauensee,
David McKay, New York, 1949.
(Juvenile fiction.)

2461. Kemp-Welch, Alice, "Beast Imagery and
the Bestiary," Nineteenth Century,
Vol. 54, September, 1903, pp. 501-
509.

2462. Kendall, Frederick A., The Sparrow,
E. Newbery, London, 1798. (A rare
children's book, with an interesting
preface on how children should
treat birds and animals.)

2463. Kilner, Dorothy, The Life and Peram-
bulations of a Mouse, G.S. Appleton,
Philadelphia, 1846. (Juvenile
fiction.)

2464. Kinsley, James, "Dryden's Bestiary,"
Review of English Studies, Vol. 4,
n.s., October, 1953, pp. 331-6.

2465. Kipling, Rudyard, Animal Stories from
Rudyard Kipling, Macmillan, London,
1932.

2466. Kipling, Rudyard, The Jungle Book,
Doubleday, Doran, 1933. (Juvenile
fiction.)

2467. Klingender, Francis D., (Antal, E.
and Harthan, J., eds.), Animals in
Art and Thought to the End of the
Middle Ages, MIT Press, Cambridge,
MA, 1971.

2468. Kotzwinkle, William, Doctor Rat,
Alfred A. Knopf, New York, 1976.
(A novel about a rat in a laboratory.)

2469. Krutch, Joseph Wood, comp., The
World of Animals, A Treasury of
Lore, Legend and Literature by
Great Writers and Naturalists from
the 5th Century B.C. to the Present,
Simon and Schuster, New York, 1961.

2470. Kuchta, Ronald A., organizer, Animals
in African Art, Antelopes and Elephants, Hornbills and Hyenas,
Santa Barbara Museum of Art, October
4-December 2, 1973, Santa Barbara,
California, 1973.

2471. Kyber, Manfred, Among Animals, The
Collected Animal Stories of Manfred Kyber, 1880-1933, trans. from
the German by Olive Fishwick,
Centaur Press, Fontwell, Sussex,
1967.

2472. Landseer, Edwin, The Works of Sir
Edwin Landseer, Illustrated by
Forty-four Steel Engravings and
about Two Hundred Woodcuts, Virtue
and Co., London, 1879-80. (Copy
at University of Wisconsin Art
Library.)

2473. Leach, Maria, God Had a Dog, Folklore of the Dog, Rutgers University
Press, New Brunswick, NJ, 1961.

2474. Leonard, R. Maynard, The Dog in
British Poetry, David Nutt, London,
1893.

2475. Lewis, C.S., Chronicles of Narnia,
7 Books, Macmillan, New York, 1970.
(Juvenile fiction.)

2476. Lewis, N.D.C., "Some Theriomorphic

Symbolisms and Mechanisms in Ancient Literature and Dreams,"
Psychoanalytic Review, Vol. 50,
1963, pp. 5-26.

2477. Lloyd, Bertram, The Great Kinship,
An Anthology of Humanitarian
Poetry, George Allen & Unwin,
London, 1921.

2478. Lloyd, Joan B., African Animals in
Renaissance Literature and Art,
Clarendon Press, Oxford, 1971.

2479. Lofting, Hugh, Story of Dr. Dolittle,
Lippincott, Philadelphia, 1948.
(One of the first children's books
to consider animal rights.)

2480. London, Jack, Call of the Wild,
Macmillan, New York, 1956.

2481. London, Jack, White Fang, Macmillan,
New York, 1963.

2482. Lovejoy, Arthur O., "The Self-Appraisal
of Man," in Lovejoy's Reflections
on Human Nature, John Hopkins Press,
Baltimore, 1961. pp. 1-21. (Seventeenth and Eighteenth Centuries
satires on humans as being irrational
and not superior to animals.)

2483. Lull, Ramon, The Book of the Beasts,
Burns Oates and Washbourne, London,
1927. Reprinted by Hyperion Press,
Westport, Conn., 1978.

2484. Lum, Peter, Fabulous Beasts, Thames
and Hudson, London, 1952.

2485. Mackay, James, The Animaliers, The
Animal Sculptors of the 19th and

20th Centuries, Ward Lock, London,
1973.

2486. McSpadden, Joseph W., ed., Famous Dogs
in Fiction, Books for Libraries
Press, Freeport, N.Y., 1972.

2487. Maniates, Belle, "A Vegetarian Adven-
ture," New England Magazine, Vol.
35, 1906, pp. 60-5.

2488. Marovitz, Sanford E., "Aldous Huxley's
Intellectual Zoo," Philological
Quarterly, Vol. 48, October, 1969,
pp. 495-507.

2489. Marvin, Frederick R., "Romance and
Symbolism of Animal Life," in
Marvin, Frederick R., Fireside
Papers, Books for Libraries Press,
Essay Index Reprint Series, Freeport,
N.Y., 1968.

2490. Masefield, John, Dauber and Reynard
the Fox, Macmillan, New York, 1962.

2491. Maxwell, Gavin, "The Child and the
Animal," New Statesman, Vol. 58,
November 14, 1959, pp. 667-8.
(About children's books on animals.)

2492. Maxwell, J.C., "Animal Imagery in
'Coriolanus'," Modern Language
Review, Vol. 42, October, 1947,
pp. 417-21.

2493. Meckier, Jerome, "Quarles Among the
Monkeys: Huxley's Zoological Novels,"
Modern Language Review, Vol. 68,
April, 1973, pp. 268-82.

2494. Melville, Herman, Moby-Dick; or, The

Whale, Holt, Rinehart and Winston, New York, 1964.

2495. Memoirs of Dick, the Little Pony, Supposed to Be Written by Himself, and Published for the Instruction and Amusement of Pretty Masters and Misses, J. Harris, London, 1804. (Juvenile fiction: probably the first horse "autobiography" ever written.)

2496. Merrill, Boynton, Jr., A Bestiary, University Press of Kentucky, Lexington, 1976.

2497. Merrill, James, "Laboratory Poem," in X.J. Kennedy, An Introduction to Poetry, 4th edition, Little Brown, Boston, 1978, p. 372.

2498. Mery, Fernand, "The Cat in Art and Literature," in Mery's The Life, History, and Magic of the Cat, trans. by Emma Street, Madison Square Press, New York, 1968.

2499. Messum, David, The Life and Work of Lucy Kemp-Welch, Baron Publishing, Suffolk, U.K., 1976.

2500. Morris, Desmond, The Biology of Art, A Study of the Picture-making Behaviour of the Great Apes and Its Relationship to Human Art, Methuen, London, 1962.

2501. Murdoch, Florence, "Trailing the Bestiaries," American Magazine of Art, Vol. 24, January, 1932, pp. 4-12.

2502. Musical selections about or inspired
by or in imitation of or "by"
animals are numerous. See "Birds
and Animals in Music", in The International Cyclopedia of Music and
Musicians, ed. by Oscar Thompson,
Dodd, Mead, New York, 1975, pp.
1727-29. A few selections are:

A. Mainly Instrumental:

1) Saint-Saens, Camille, Carnival
   of the Animals
   "Royal March of the Lion"
   "Hens and Cocks"
   "Fleet-Footed Animals"
   "Turtles"
   "The Elephants"
   "Kangaroos"
   "Aquarium"
   "Long-Eared Personages"
   "Cuckoo in the Deep Woods"
   "Aviary"
   "Fossils"
   "The Swan"

2) Rimsky-Korsakov, Nikolai,
   "Flight of the Bumble Bee"

3) Mussorgsky, Modest P., Pic-
   tures at an Exhibition,
   "Ballet of the Chicks in
   Their Shells"

4) Debussy, Claude, Prelude to
   the Afternoon of a Faun

5) Menotti, Gian C., The Unicorn,
   the Gorgon and the Manticore,
   (mostly dance, with small
   orchestra, spoken narration)

6) Couperin, Francois,
   "The Nightingale in Love"
                  (harpsichord)

353

> "The Nightingale's Song of
> Triumph"
> (harpsichord)
> "The Warbler's Complaint"
> (harpsichord)
> "Bees"
> (harpsichord)
> "The Little Fly"
> (harpsichord)

7) Rameau, Jean-Philippe,
"The Convocation of the Birds"
(harpsichord)
"The Hen"
(harpsichord)

8) Lasso, Orlando di,
"The Nightingale"
(harpsichord)

9) Kerll, Johann Kaspar,
"The Cuckoo (Capriccio Cucu)"
(harpsichord)

10) Poglietti, Alessandro,
"Canzona and Capriccio on
the Cries of Cocks and Hens"
(harpsichord)

11) Dandrieu, Jean Francois,
"Bird Songs in the Forest"
(harpsichord)

12) Messiaen, Olivier,
"The Catalogue of the Birds"
(orchestra)
"The Conversation of the Birds"
(orchestra)
"Exotic Birds"
(piano)
"Bird Sounds"
(orchestra)

13) Dagincourt, Jacques Andre,
"Doves"
(harpsichord)

14) Daquin, Louis Claude,
"The Swallow"
(harpsichord)

15) Cosyn, Benjamin,
"The Goldfinch"
(harpsichord)

16) Crumb, George,
"Voice of the Whale"
(flute, piano,
cello)

17) Prokofieff, Sergei,
"Peter and the Wolf"
(orchestra and
narration)

18) Sibelius, Jean,
"Swan of Tuolela"
(orchestra)

19) Griffes, Charles,
"The White Peacock"
(orchestra)

20) Stravinsky, Igor,
"Circus Polka" (Ballet for
an Elephant)
(orchestra)

21) Poulenc, Francis,
"The Story of Babar, The
Little Elephant"
(instrumen-
tal solo)

22) Koechlin, Charles,
"Les Bandar-Log," about monkeys, one of several selections
based on Kipling's Jungle
Book.
(orchestra)

23) Reif, Paul,
"The Monsieur Pelican" (inspired by Albert Schweitzer's

pelican)
(woodwinds)

B. Mainly Vocal:

1) Rameau, Jean-Philippe,
"The Cricket"
(art song)

2) Brahms, Johannes,
"The Bird in the Pine Tree"
(art song)
"The Lost Hen"
(art song)

3) Devienne, Francois,
"The Return of the Swallows"
(art song)

4) Schumann, Robert,
"The Little Owl"
(art song)

5) Mahler, Gustav, <u>Knaben Wunder-</u>
<u>horn</u>,
"St. Anthony's Sermon to the
Fishes"
(art song)

6) Janequin, Clement,
"The Song of the Birds"
(vocal ensemble)

7) Rossini, Gioacchino,
"Duet for Two Cats"
(two sopranos
& piano)

8) Bennett, Richard Rodney,
"The Insect World"
(voice & piano)
"The Aviary"
(voice & piano)

9) Poulenc, Francis, <u>Le Bestiaire</u>
(song cycle)
"The Dromedary"

356

> "The Tibetan Goat"
> "The Grasshopper"
> "The Dolphin"
> "The Crab"
> "The Carp"

10) Banchieri, Adriano, "Counter Point of the Animals"

11) Janacek, Leos, The Cunning Little Vixen (all characters are animals)
(opera)

C. Recordings Using Animal Sounds

1) "And God Created Great Whales", Alan Hovhaness. Featuring the actual songs of humpback whales. Columbia M30390, Andre Kostelanetz.

2) "Common Ground", Paul Winter. Featuring sounds of whales, eagles and wolves. A and M Records, 1978.

3) "Songs of the Humpback Whale", Capitol Record ST-620, recorded by Roger S. Payne, produced by Communications/Research/ Machines, Inc., 1970.

4) Respighi, Ottorino, "The Pines of Rome," Minneapolis Symphony Orchestra, Antal Dorati, Mercury MG 50011. Use of actual nightingale songs.

2503. Muybridge, Eadweard, Animals in Motion, ed. by Lewis S. Brown, Dover Publications, New York, 1957. (Photographic analysis of motions of animals.)

2504. Muybridge, Eadweard, "The Attitudes

of Animals in Motion," _Journal of the Society of Arts_, Vol. 30, June 23, 1882, pp. 838-43.

2505. Newbolt, Henry, _A Letter from the Front, With Other Animal Poems and Stories_, Collected by M.L. Nott, In Aid of the Fund for Wounded Horses at the Front (World War I), not dated.

2506. Nolan, Frank R., _The Doctor's Nightmare_, William Brown, Belfast, 1929. (Anti-vivisection novel.)

2507. Norelli, Martina R., comp., _American Wildlife Painting_, Watson-Guptill Publications, New York, 1975.

2508. "Orpheus at the Zoo," _The Spectator_, Vol, 67, October 3, 1891, pp. 445-6. Also _The Spectator_ Vol. 67, pp. 491-2.

2509. Orwell, George, _Animal Farm_, Harcourt, Brace and World, New York, 1954.

2510. Ovid, "The Teachings of Pythagoras" in Ovid's _Metamorphoses_, Book 15, Lines 60-476, Indiana University Press, Bloomington, 1957. pp. 367-379.

2511. Owens, Henry J., _The Scandalous Adventures of Reynard the Fox_, A Modern American Version, Knopf, New York, 1945. (Juvenile.)

2512. Peet, Bill, _The Knats of Knotty Pine_, Houghton Mifflin Co., Boston, 1975. (Juvenile: anti-hunting.)

2513. Perry, R. Hinton, "Animals in Art,"
      Outing Magazine, Vol. 43, 1901-4,
      pp. 515-21.

2514. Petti, Anthony G., "Beasts and Politics
      in Elizabethan Literature," _Essays
      and Studies_, 1963, The English
      Association, John Murray, London,
      pp. 68-90.

2515. Pope, Alexander, _An Essay on Man_,
      Bobbs-Merrill, Indianapolis, 1965.

2516. Porter, J.R., and Russell, W.M.S.,
      eds., _Animals in Folklore_, Rowan
      and Littlefield, Totowa, N.J., 1978.

2517. Powys, John Cowper, _Morwyn or the
      Vengeance of God_, Cassell, London,
      1937. (Anti-vivisection novel.)

2518. Pratt, Mr., _Pity's Gift_: A Collection
      of Interesting Tales to Excite the
      Compassion of Youth for the Animal
      Creation, from the Writings of Mr.
      Pratt, Selected by a Lady, Longman,
      Hurst, Rees, and Orme, London, 1810.

2519. Ransome, Hilda M., _The Sacred Bee in
      Ancient Times and Folklore_,
      Houghton Mifflin, New York, 1937.

2520. Rawson, Jessica, _Animals in Art_,
      British Museum Publications, London,
      1977.

2521. Reed, R., "The Animal World in Robert
      Frost's Poetry," in _Frost: Centen-
      nial Essays II_, ed. by Jac Tharpe,
      University Press of Mississippi,
      1976.

Animals and Literature and Art and Music

2522. Rensch, Bernard, "Basic Aesthetic
Principles in Man and Animals,"
in The Human Creature, ed. by
Gunter Altner, Anchor Press, Garden
City, N.Y., 1969.

2523. Repplier, Agnes, "Cruelty and Humour,"
in Repplier, Agnes, Points of Friction
Books for Libraries Press, Essay
Index Reprint Series, Freeport, N.Y.,
1971.

2524. Robin, P. Ansell, Animal Lore in English
Literature, John Murray, London,
1932.

2525. Robinson, Emily, Crowleigh Hall, The
Animals' Guardian, London, 1906.
(Anti-vivisection novel.)

2526. Robinson, Phil, "Beasts of Chase,"
Gentleman's Magazine, Vol. 34, May,
1885, pp. 442-456.

2527. Robinson, Phil, "Some Harmless Beasts:
A Sketch from the Poets," Belgravia,
London, Vol. 51, 1883, pp. 309-26.

2528. Rombauts, E., and Welkenhuysen, A.,
eds., Aspects of the Medieval
Animal Epic, Leuven University Press,
Louvain, Belgium, 1975.

2529. Rook, David, Ballad of the Belstone
Fox, Corgi, London, 1972. (Fiction:
Hunting.)

2530. Rose, William, Ed., The Epic of the
Beast, Dutton, New York, 1924.

2531. Rosenfield, Leonora, From Beast-
Machine to Man-Machine: The Theme

of Animal Soul in French Letters
from Descartes to La Mettrie, Octagon Books Inc., New York, 1968.

2532. Rowland, Beryl, Animals with Human
Faces: A Guide to Animal Symbolism,
University of Tennessee, Knoxville,
1973.

2533. Rowland, Beryl, Blind Beasts,
Chaucer's Animal World, Kent State
University Press, Kent, Ohio, 1971.

2534. Rubin, Louis D., Jr., "Uncle Remus
and the Ubiquitous Rabbit," Southern
Review, Vol. 10, No. 4, October,
1974, pp. 787-804.

2535. Salt, Henry S., "A Lover of Animals,"
An Original Play in One Act, in
George Hendrick's Henry Salt,
University of Illinois Press,
Urbana, 1977, pp. 174-95.

2536. Salzle, Karl, Tier und Mensch;
Gottheit und Damon, Das Tier in der
Geistesgeschichte der Menschheit,
BLV Bayerischer Landwirtschaftverlag,
Munchen, 1965.

2537. Sanborn, Kate, My Literary Zoo,
Appleton, New York, 1896.

2538. Sebeok, Thomas A., "Animals as
Artists," Animals, Massachussetts
Society for the Prevention of
Cruelty to Animals, August, 1979.

2539. Sebeok, Thomas A., "Prefigurements
of Art," Semiotica, Vol. 26, No.
3-4, 1979. (Artistic activities of
animals.)

2540. Sells, A. Lytton, Animal Poetry in
French and English Literature and
the Greek Tradition, Indiana
University Publications, Human-
itites Series No. 35, Bloomington,
Indiana, 1955, pp. 1-329. Also
Thames and Hudson, London, 1958.

2541. Seton, Ernest T., Wild Animals I
Have Known, Grosset, New York,
1966. (Juvenile stories.)

2542. Sewell, Anna, Black Beauty, The
Autobiography of a Horse, World
Publishing New York, 1946.

2543. Shaffer, Peter, Equus, A Play,
Atheneum, New York, 1975.
(Plot centers on the blinding of
horses by a young man.)

2544. Shakespeare, William, Cymbeline, in
The Works of William Shakespeare,
Vol. 5, The International Shake-
spearean Society, London, 1901.
In Act I, Scene V, there is a
discussion of the use of cats and
dogs for testing poisonous compounds,
and the suggestion that such practice
will harden the experimenter's
heart.

2545. Shaw, Bernard, Androcles and the Lion,
Brentano's, New York, 1916. (A two-
act play.)

2546. Shephard, Odell, The Lore of the Unicorn, Houghton Mifflin, London, 1930.

2547. Shugg, Wallace, "The Cartesian Beast-
Machine in English Literature (1663-
1750)," Journal of the History of Ideas,

Vol. 29, April-June, 1968, pp. 279-292.

2548. Sifakis, G.M., Parabasis and Animal Choruses, A Contribution to the History of Attic Comedy, Athalone, London, 1971.

2549. Sinclair, Upton, The Jungle, Penguin, London, 1976. (Fiction: Conditions in Chicago stockyards and slaughter-houses in early Twentieth Century.)

2550. Singer, Isaac Bashevis.
A vegetarian, Singer occasionally introduces the topics of vegetarianism, slaughtering of animals, flesh eating and man's treatment of animals into his novels and stories. For example (in Enemies, A Love Story, Farrar, Straus and Giroux, New York, 1972, p. 157): "As often as Herman had witnessed the slaughter of animals and fish, he always had the same thought: in their behaviour toward creatures, all men were Nazis. The smugness with which man could do with other species as he pleased exemplified the most extreme racist theories, the principle that "might is right."
Another example (in "The Letter Writer" in Singer's The Seance and Other Stories, Farrar, Straus and Giroux, New York, 1968, p. 270.): "In his thoughts, Herman spoke a eulogy for the mouse who had shared a portion of her life with him and who, because of him, had left this earth. 'What do they know--all these scholars, all these philosophers, all the leaders of the world--about

such as you? They have convinced
themselves that man, the worst
transgressor of all the species, is
the crown of creation. All
other creatures were created merely
to provide him with food, pelts, to
be tormented, exterminated. In
relation to them, all people are
Nazis; for the animals it is an
eternal Treblinka.'"
　　Also the short story "The Slaughtere
in An Isaac Bashevis Singer Reader,
Farrar, Straus, and Giroux, New
York, 1977, pp. 219-234.
For a discussion of Singer's views
on vegetarianism, see Dudley
Giehl's Vegetarianism: A Way of
Life, Harper and Row, New York,
1979, pp. 141-145. Also see Singer's
Foreward to this book.

2551. Sivaramamurti, C., Birds and Animals
in Indian Sculpture, National
Museum, New Delhi, 1974.

2552. Skyrme, Raymond, "The Pythagorean
Vision of Ruben Dario in 'La
Tortuga de Oro'," Comparative
Literature Studies, Vol. 11,
No. 3, September, 1974, pp. 233-248.

2553. Smith, Bertha H., "The Wild Animal
in Art," Outlook, Vol. 81, September 23, 1905, pp. 203-214.

2554. Snyder, Gary, "The Incredible Survival of Coyote," based on a talk
given at the Western Writers Conference, Utah State University,
1974, in Snyder's The Old Ways,
City Light Books, San Francisco,
1977, pp. 67-93.

2555. Snyder, Gary, Turtle Island, New
      Directions Books, New York, 1974.
      See: "Steak," p. 10; "The Call
      of the Wild," p. 21; "Mother Earth:
      Her Whales," pp. 47-9; "Two Fawn
      That Didn't See the Light This
      Spring," p. 58; "The Wilderness,"
      pp. 106-10.

2556. Stebbins, Eunice B., The Dolphin
      in the Literature and Art of
      Greece and Rome, George Banta,
      Menasha, Wisconsin, 1929.

2557. Stewart, Desmond, "The Limits of
      Trooghaft," Encounter, London,
      February, 1972. Reproduced in
      Animal Rights and Human Obligations,
      ed. by Tom Regan and Peter Singer.
      (Short Story about the Troogs who
      conquer the earth and factory-
      farm humans for food.)

2558. Strunk, W., Jr., "The Elizabethan
      Showman's Ape," Modern Language
      Notes, Vol. 32, 1917, pp. 215-
      21.

2559. Stuart, Dorothy M., A Book of Birds
      and Beasts: Legendary and Histor-
      ical, Methuen, London, 1957.

2560. Sully, James, "Animal Music," Corn-
      hill Magazine, Vol. 40, July, 1879,
      pp. 605-621.

2561. Swaim, Kathleen M., "Lycidas and the
      Dolphins of Apollo," Journal of
      English and Germanic Philology,
      Vol. 72, July, 1973, pp. 340-9.

2562. Swift, Jonathan, "A Voyage to the

Houyhnhnms," in Swift's _Gulliver's Travels_, ed. by Louis A. Landa, Houghton Mifflin, Boston, 1960. (The Houyhnhnms are horse-like creatures more virtuous than humans, and governed by reason.

2563. Szoke, Peter, "Three Spheres of Music: On the Physical, the Animal, and the Human Level of Existence," (in Hungarian), _Magyar Filozof Szemle_, 1978, pp. 809-49.

2564. Taylor, Basil, _Animal Painting in England_, from Barlow to Landseer, Penguin, Middlesex, 1955.

2565. Taylor, George C., "Shakespeare's Use of the Idea of Beast in Man," _Studies in Philology_, Vol. 42, July, 1945, pp. 530-43.

2566. Taylor, Joseph, ed., _The General Character of the Dog_, In Prose and Verse, Darton and Harvey, London, 1804.

2567. Thompson, Francis, _A Scottish Bestiary_, The Lore and Literature of Scottish Beasts, Molendinar Press, Glasgow, 1978.

2568. Tiptree, James, Jr. (Alice B. Sheldon), "The Psychologist Who Wouldn't Do Awful Things to Rats," _The Best Science Fiction of the Year #6_, ed. by Terry Carr, Holt, Rinehart and Winston, New York, 1977, pp. 115-44.

2569. Tolstoy, Leo, "Strider: The Story of a Horse," in Tolstoy's _The Snow Storm and Other Stories_, trans. by

Louise and Aylmer Maude, Oxford
University Press, London, 1974,
pp. 389-439. (The play <u>Strider</u>
was performed at the Helen Hayes
Theater, New York City, during the
1979-80 season. Not yet published.)

2570. Tomson, Graham R., ed., <u>Concerning</u>
<u>Cats</u>, A Book of Poems by Many
Authors, T. Fisher Unwin, London,
1892.

2571. Trimmer, Mrs., <u>Fabulous Histories De-</u>
<u>signed for the Instruction of</u>
<u>Children Respecting their Treatment</u>
<u>of Animals</u>, J. Johnson, London,
<u>1811</u>.

2572. Trippett, Frank, <u>The First Horse-</u>
<u>men</u>, Time-Life Books, New York, 1974.

2573. Tuttle, Margaret W., <u>Crimson Cage,</u>
Tashmoo Press, Vineyard Haven,
Massachusetts, 1978. (Fictional
in form; based on facts of experimentation on dogs.)

2574. Twain, Mark, <u>A Dog's Tale</u>, Harper and
Brothers, New York, 1904. (Story
of a dog who saves the life of a
child in a fire, and whose puppy is
blinded and killed in the course
of an experiment.)

2575. Van Buren, E. Douglas, "The Fauna of
Ancient Mesopotamia as Represented
in Art," <u>Analecta Orientalia</u> 18,
Pontificum Institutum Biblicum, Rome,
1939.

2576. Varty, Kenneth, <u>Reynard the Fox</u>, A
Study of the Fox in Medieval English

Art, Humanities Press, New York, 1967. (Heavily illustrated.)

2577. Viardot, Louis, "On the Aesthetic Sense in Animals," Popular Science Monthly, Vol. 4, April, 1874, pp. 729-35.

2578. Vinycomb, John, Fictitious and Symbolic Creatures in Art, with Special Reference to Their Use in British Heraldry, Chapman and Hall, London, 1906.

2579. Virch, Claus, The Artist and the Animal, Knoedler and Co., Inc., New York, 1968.

2580. Volker, T., "The Animal in Far Eastern Art," Mededelingen Van Het Rijksmuseum Voor Volkenkunde, Leiden, Nos. 6 and 7, E.J. Brill, Leiden, 1950, pp. 1-190.

2581. Von Frisch, Karl, Animal Architecture, trans. by Lisbeth Gombrich, Harcourt, Brace, Jovanovich, New York, 1974.

2582. Wagoner, David, "Buck Fever," "Duck-Blind," "Setting a Snare," "Trap-line," and "Posing with a Trophy," in Wagoner's In Broken Country, Little, Brown, Boston, 1979, pp. 71-9. (Poetry.)

2583. Wasserman, George R., "Animal Imagery in Hudibras," in Wasserman's Samuel "Hudibras" Butler, Twayne, Boston, 1976, pp. 90-5.

2584. Weimann, Klaus, ed., Middle English Animal Literature, University of Exeter, U.K., 1975.

2585. Wells, H.G., The Island of Dr. Moreau, in Seven Science Fiction Novels of

H.G. Wells, Dover Publications, New York, 1934. (About an experimental physiologist who experiments on animals on a secluded island.)

2586. Whaler, James, "Animal Simile in 'Paradise Lost'," Modern Language Association of America Publications, Vol. 47, June, 1932, pp. 534-53.

2587. White, Andrew D., "Animal Symbolism in Ecclesiastical Architecture," Popular Science Monthly, Vol. 50, 1896-7, pp. 187-96.

2588. White, Beatrice, "Medieval Beasts," Essays and Studies, 1965, The English Association, John Murray, London, pp. 34-44.

2589. White, Terence H., trans. and ed., The Book of Beasts, a translation from a Latin Bestiary of the Twelfth Century, Cape, London, 1956. (See especially pp. 230-270; also the Bibliography.)

2590. Whitlow, R., "Animal and Human Perspectives in Dickens' Novels," CLA Journal, Vol. 19, September, 1975, pp. 65-74.

2591. Wilbur, Richard, comp., A Bestiary, Pantheon Books, New York, 1955.

2592. Wright, Louis B., "Animal Actors on the English Stage Before 1642," Modern Language Association of America Publications, Vol. 42, September, 1927, pp. 656-69.

2593. Yoder, Audrey, Animal Analogy in

Shakespeare's Character Portrayal,
King's Crown Press at Columbia
University, New York, 1947.

2594. Zuelke, Ruth, The Horse in Art,
Lerner Publications, Minneapolis,
1965.

2595. CANADIAN PSYCHOLOGICAL ASSOCIATION,
41ST ANNUAL CONVENTION, Calgary,
1980. "Ethical Issues in Animal
Experimentation," by Alan D. Bowd,
University of Victoria.

2596. ANIMAL RIGHTS AND WELFARE, AND HUMAN
ETHICS, IN TWENTIETH-CENTURY LITER-
ATURE. A session at the annual
convention of the Modern Language
Association of America, Houston,
Texas, December 27-30, 1980.
Chair: Richard Morgan, English
Department, East Tennessee State
University, Johnson City, Tenn.

2597. HUMANE EDUCATION, AN INTERNATIONAL
SYMPOSIUM, Sussex University,
United Kingdom, August 11-14,
1980. Sponsored by the Humane
Education Council, 143 Charing
Cross Road, London WC2H OEE.
Proceedings Program includes:
Ryder, R.D., "Animal/Man
Relationships--Psychological
and Moral Aspects"
Paterson, D.A., "Children's Ideas
on Animals: Preliminary Studies"
Langley, Gill and Chris, "Animals
in British Universities"
McKibben and Heather, "Pet Facili-
tated Psychotherapy"
Heim, Alice, "The Desensitization
of Teachers"
Jordan, W.J. and Ormrod, S.,
"Zoos, Circuses, Safari & Wild-
life Parks"
Scott-Ordish, Lesley, "Dogs in
Society"
Harrison, Ruth, "Food Animals"
Hollands, Clive, "The Animal Wel-
fare Societies"
And under the topic ANIMALS AND

ETHICS:
Sprigg, T.L.S., "The Foundations"
Wynne, Alan, "The Basis of Social and Moral Responsibility"
Linzey, Andrew, "Animal Rights"

2598. CONFERENCE ON MEDICINE, ANIMALS AND MAN, University of Illinois at the Medical Center, Chicago Illini Union, May 21, 1980. (For additional information contact:
Marianna R. Burt, Humanistic Studies Program, Room 314, 715 So. Wood St., Chicago, IL, 60612.)
Papers presented include:
Beck, Alan M., "Political and Public Health Implications of Companion Animals"
Brown, Robert, "History of the Humane Movement and Prospects for the 1980's"
Burt, Marianna R., "Images of Cruelty in Dostoievsky's Novels"
Fern, Richard, "Animal Rights"
McCulloch, Michael J., "Using the Pet as a Prosthesis"
Orlans, R. Barbara, "Ethics of Animal Experimentation"

2599. CETACEAN BEHAVIOUR, INTELLIGENCE AND THE ETHICS OF KILLING CETACEANS, The Freer Gallery of Art, Smithsonian Institution, Washington, D.C., April 28-May 1, 1980. Sponsored by The International Whaling Commission, The Threshold Foundation, The Institute for Dolphinid Research and The Animal Welfare Institute. It is probable that proceedings will eventually be published.

Conferences and Symposia and Meetings

Program includes:

Bossley, Michael I. "Ethical
Implications of Recent Advances
in the Study of Animal Behaviour"

Fortum-Gouin, Jean Paul, "The
Ethics of Hunting Cachalots"

Fox, Michael W., "Animal Rights
and Ecologically Sound Humane
Ethics"

Herman, Louis, "Cognitive Characteristics of Dolphins and the
Communication Systems of Cetaceans"

Jacobs, M.S., "Studies on Cetacean Brain"

Jamieson, Dale, "Experimenting
on Cetaceans: Some Ethical
Considerations"

Kamiya, Toshiro, "Scientific
Observations on the Structure
of Cetacean Brain"

Kelly, John, "The Human Voice of
the Whale: History of the Whale
Conservation Movement"

Kiyomiya, Ryu, and Yamato, Yuzo,
"Why Whaling Is Not Unethical"

Lilly, John, Linden, Eugene, and
Nollman, James, "Non-Scientific
Influences Effecting the Study
and Interpretation of Ape Capacities for Language"

McMillan, R.E., "The Killing of
Whales and the Ethics Involved"

Macnow, Alan, "Whaling: A Food
Production Ethic"

Morgane, P.J., "Neocortical Forma-
tions in Whales and their Meaning"

Payne, Roger, "The Intelligence
of Whaling and the Ethics of
Whales"

Regan, Thomas, "On the Ethics of
Whaling"

373

Ross, Michael, "Intelligence in Cetaceans--Measurement in Theory and Practice"

Saayman, G.S., "The Ethics of Man's Exploitation of Cetacea"

Sabata, Toyouki, "Dangers in Excessive Animal Protection Activities"

Saito, Ninzu, "Ethics Are to Govern Human Beings Only"

Webb, N.G., "Developmental Psychology: Boat Towing and Object Manipulation by a Sociable Wild Bottle-Nose Dolphin--The Social Behaviour of a Wild Dolphin Interacting with Man--Codes of Practice for Dolphinarium Management"

2600. THE QUESTION OF ANIMAL CONSCIOUSNESS: PHILOSOPHICAL AND BIOLOGICAL PERSPECTIVES. A Symposium. April 5, 1980. Michigan State University. It is not known whether proceedings will be published. For information contact: Richard W. Hill, Department of Zoology, Michigan State University, East Lansing, MI 48824.

Papers presented include:

Benjamin, Martin, "The Ethical Significance of Animal Awareness"

Bennett, Jonathan F., "Language and Mind"

Griffin, Donald R., "Awareness and Responsiveness in Animals"

Levy, Jerre, "The Human Right Hemisphere, the Animal Brain, and Consciousness without Language"

Margolis, Joseph, "Animal and Human Minds"

Premack, David, "Language and
Intelligence in Chimpanzee and
Child"

2601. THE ETHICS OF THE USE OF ANIMALS IN
RESEARCH, Bates College, Lewiston,
Maine, March 21-22, 1980.
Program:
Speaker: Tom Regan, "Animal
Rights, Human Wrongs"
Respondents: David Kolb, Mark
Okrent
Speaker: Tom Wolfle, "The Moral
and Scientific Definition of
Adequate Animal Care"
Respondent: Deborah Mayo
Speaker: Emmanuel Bernstein,
"Animal Research in the Name
of Science: At What Cost?"
Respondent: John Cowgell
Moderator and Organizer: Ken
Shapiro
The proceedings of this conference
will not be published.

2602. THE ETHICS OF EXPERIMENTS ON ANIMALS,
University of Durham, United King-
dom, March 19-20, 1980. Sponsored
by The Association for the Study
of Animal Behaviour, c/o R.F. Dre-
wett, Department of Psychology,
University of Durham, Durham, DH1
3LE.
Program includes:
Bateson, P., "How Do We Decide
Whether or Not to Experiment
with Animals?"
Benson, J., "The Fall of a Sparrow:
How Much Should Animals Count
For?"
Bostock, S., "The Ethics of Keep-
ing Animals in Captivity"

375

Ewbank, R., "The Role of Ethical
Committees"
Midgley, M., "The Price to Be
Paid for Knowledge"
Morgan, M., "Animals as Individ-
uals"
Vine, I., "In Defence of Species-
ism"

2603. COLLOQUIUM ON ANIMALS, American Philo-
sophical Association Easter Division
Meeting, December 29, 1979, New York
City.
Chair: Daniel M. Farrell
"Act Utilitarianism and Animal
Liberation," Peter S. Wenz
Commentator: Rolf E. Sartorius
"In Defense of Speciesism," Roger
Wertheimer
Commentator: Tom Regan.

2604. SOCIETY FOR THE STUDY OF ETHICS AND
ANIMALS, meeting in New York City,
December 28, 1979.
Program:
Chair: Harlan B. Miller
"Orangutans and Language: The
Ethics of Ugliness," H. Lyn Miles
"Ethical Implications of Human,
Machine and Animal Communication,"
Thomas W. Simon.

2605. ETHICAL ISSUES CONCERNING THE USE OF
ANIMALS IN AGRICULTURE AND SCIENTIFIC
RESEARCH, University of Guelph,
Guelph, Canada, June 12-13, 1979.
Proceedings will probably be published
in Animal Regulation Studies. For
further information contact:
Hugh Lehman
Department of Philosophy
University of Guelph
Guelph, Ontario, Canada

Papers presented include:
Fox, Michael A., "On Justifying
the Use of Animals for Human Ends"
Fox, Michael W., "From Animal
Science to Animal Rights"
Fraser, Andrew, "Ethics in Livestock
Behavior"
Harrison, Ruth, "Practical Con-
siderations"
Hurnik, Frank, "Animal Welfare
and Modern Agriculture"
Lehman, Hugh, "Concluding Summary"
Loew, Frank, "Animals in Bio-
medical Research"
Martin, Michael, "Vegetarianism,
The Right to Life and Fellow
Creaturehood"
Narveson, Jan, "Animal Rights
Revisited"
Rowsell, Harry, "The Animal in
Research: Domination or Stew-
ardship"
Singer, Peter, "Animals and
Humans as Equals"

2606. THE MORAL FOUNDATIONS OF PUBLIC
POLICY: ETHICS AND ANIMALS, Vir-
ginia Polytechnic Institute and
State University, Blacksburg, Vir-
ginia, May 24-27, 1979.
It is not known whether proceedings
will be published. For further
information contact:
Harlan B. Miller
Department of Philosophy and Religion
Virginia Polytechnic Institute and
State University
Blacksburg, VA, 24061
Papers presented include:
Baier, Annette, "Knowing Our Place
in the Animal World"
Becker, Lawrence C., "The Priority

of Human Interests"
Buchanan, James M., "Moral Community and Moral Order: The Intensive and Extensive Limits of Interaction"
Clark, Stephen R.L., "Men, Animals, and 'Animal Behaviour'"
Fox, Michael W., "Animal Rights and the Law of Ecology: Toward a Human Stewardship"
Franchina, J.J., "Animal Models of Human Behavior"
Frey, R.G., "On Why We Would Be Better to Jettison Moral Rights"
Gross, W.B., "Chicken-Environment Interactions"
Johnson, Edward, "Life, Death and Animals: Prolegomena"
Narveson, Jan, "Animal Rights Revisited"
Rachels, James, "Could Animals have Rights?"
Rollin, Bernard E., "Morality, Law, and the Rights of Animals"
Rumbaugh, Duane M. and Savage-Rumbaugh, E. Sue, "Cognitive Capacities and Moral Standing"
Scanlon, Patrick, "Man as a Hunting Animal"

2607.   ELEVENTH ANNUAL LABORATORY ANIMAL MEDICINE CONFERENCE: ETHICAL ISSUES RELATED TO THE USE OF RESEARCH ANIMALS, Friday, April 27, 1979, and Saturday, April 28, 1979, Kresge Auditorium, Medical Sciences Building, Cincinnati, Ohio.
Sponsored by: Department of Laboratory Animal Medicine, University of Cincinnati Medical Center and CONMED. Papers will probably be published. For further information contact:

Conferences and Symposia and Meetings

Steele F. Mattingly
Professor and Director
Dept. of Laboratory Animal
   Medicine
University of Cincinnati
Cincinnati, Ohio 45267

Papers presented include:

Briggs, G. Bruce, "Government
   Regulation of Industrial Animal
   Utilization"

Brumbaugh, Robert S., "Traditional
   Philosophical Views of Animal
   Rights"

Jagger, Alison, "Morality and
   Society"

Kitchen, Hyram, "Improvement
   through Education"

Leash, Aaron M., "Educational
   Institutions' Use of Research
   Animals"

Loew, Franklin M., "Re-evaluating
   the Humane Objectives of Animal
   Welfare Societies and the
   Scientific Objectives of Biomedical Research Organizations"

Meth, Theodore, "The Limits of
   Legislation in Achieving Social
   Change"

Nielsen, Kai, "Reconciling Conflicting
   Emotional and Ethical Views"

Padgett, George A., "Selection of
   Research Models"

Regan, Tom, "Evolving Ethical Views
   Concerning Animal Rights"

Rowan, Andrew N., "Improving
   Alternative Research Models"

Wolfe, Thomas L., "Psychobiology
   and Animal Rights"

V. University and College Courses

(Most of the information listed below was provided by the Scientists'Center for Animal Welfare (3090) in Newsletter #3, Summer/Fall, 1979 and Newsletter, Vol. 2, No.1, February, 1980.)

The following incomplete list is suggestive of the growing number of courses, partly or completely on animals and ethics, offered at the university level. Ethics courses in philosophy departments often include sections on animals and ethics.

2608. VM 712. Moral and Conceptual Issues in Veterinary Medicine. College of Veterinary Medicine, Colorado State University, Fort Collins, CO. Instructors: Bernard E. Rollin, Ph. D., Professor of Philosophy, and Harry Gorman, D.V.M., Associate Dean, College of Veterinary Medicine.

2609. BY 102. Attributes of Living Systems (Introductory Biology Course.) Honors Biology, Colorado State University, Fort Collins, CO. Instructors: Murray Nabors, Ph. D., Department of Botany and Plant Pathology, and Bernard E. Rollin, Ph.D., Department of Philosophy.

2610. LS 1001. Introductory Life Science. Department of Life Sciences, Worcester Polytechnic Institute, Worcester, MA. Instructor: Betty B. Hoskins, Ph.D.

2611. Philosophy 307. Morality and Human Happiness. Department of Philosophy and Religion, North Carolina State University, Raleigh, NC. Instructor: Tom Regan, Ph.D.

2612. Philosophy 200. Introduction to
      Philosophy (Social ethics). Depart-
      ment of Philosophy, Eastern Michigan.
      University, Ypsilanti, MI. Instructor:
      Sidney Gendin, Ph.D.

2613. Philosophy 0255. Philosophy and Envi-
      ronmental Ethics. Department of
      Philosophy, University of Maryland,
      Baltimore County, MD. Instructor:
      Thomas L. Benson, Ph.D.

2614. Philosophy 4000. Special Topics--
      "Animal Liberation." Department of
      Philosophy, College of Liberal Arts,
      University of Tennessee, Knoxville,
      TN. Instructor: Rem. B. Edwards, Ph.D.

2615. LAS 110. The Use and Abuse of Animals
      in Contemporary Society. Department
      of Philosophy, University of Illinois,
      Urbana, IL. Instructor: Richard
      Fern, Ph.D.

2616. Philosophy 210. Animal Liberation.
      Department of Philosophy, Moorhead
      State University, Moorhead, MN.
      Instructor: Charles Magel, Ph.D.

2617. PHL 494. Ethics and Animals. Veter-
      inary Clinic, School of Veterinary
      Medicine, Michigan State University,
      East Lansing, MI. Instructor: Martin
      Benjamin, Ph.D., Department of Philo-
      sophy.

2618. PHIL 280. Ethics and Animals. Depart-
      ment of Philosophy, Purdue University,
      West Lafayette, Indiana. Instructor:
      Lilly-Marlene Russow, Ph.D., Assistant
      Professor, of Philosophy.

University and College Courses

2619. Philosophy DGS 1941. Animal Rights and Human Obligations. Philosophy Department, California State University, Hayward, CA. Instructor: Steve F. Sapontzis, Ph.D., Associate Professor of Philosophy, School of Arts, Letters, and Social Sciences.

2620. HUE 0502, HUM 4540-30-3 (Humanities). Mankind? We and Other Animals. Elmira College, Elmira, New York. Instructor: Christine Rosner, Ph.D.

2621. PubH 5-303, LACS 5-657. Perspectives: Animal-Human Relationships and Community Health, School of Public Health and the College of Veterinary Medicine, University of Minnesota, Minneapolis, MN. Instructors: R.K. Anderson, D.V.M., and Joseph S. Quigley, D.V.M.

2622. Rachel Carson College 140. Animals, Ethics, and the Environment. The Rachel Carson College of Environmental Studies is chartered by the State University of New York at Buffalo. RCC 140 is given in alternate semesters by James Moran, Professor of Philosophy at Daeman College in Buffalo and Professor Stephen Knaster, Philosophy, State University at Buffalo. An introduction to the ethics of human-animal interactions.

VI. Government Documents

2623. Australia
Frost, the Hon. Sydney, Whales and
Whaling:
Vol. 1: Report of the Independent
Inquiry conducted by the Hon. Sir
Sydney Frost
Vol. 2: Papers commissioned by the
Inquiry conducted by the Hon. Sir
Sydney Frost
Australian Government Publishing
Service, Canberra, 1978.
(Vol. 1 has been published in paper-
back form by Friends of the Earth
(San Francisco) and The Whale Coali-
tion, 1979.)
(See 2010.)

2624. CALIFORNIA LEGISLATION PASSES ANIMAL
RIGHTS RESOLUTION
A leader in protection of animals,
Senator David Roberti steered his
animal rights resolution through the
California legislature to final adoption September 18th, 1979, in amended
form.
Full text of Senate Concurrent Resolution Number 8 is as follows:
"WHEREAS, The State of California
has in the past led the country in
passing legislation which recognizes
the priciple of animal rights; and
"WHEREAS, From childhood man should
be taught to observe, understand, and
respect animal life which is linked
to respect for mankind; and
"WHEREAS, To advance our civilization we must become aware of the
rights of all animals; now, therefore, be it
"Resolved by the Senate of the
State of California, the Assembly
thereof concurring, That the Legislature of the State of California should

> take effective measures to protect
> and defend the rights of animals,
> by enacting humane and environmentally
> sound legislation."

2625. Canada. Animals for Research Act,
revised statutes of Ontario, 1970,
Chapter 22, Queen's Printer and Publisher, Toronto.

2626. Great Britain. House of Lords.
Report of the Select Committee on
the Laboratory Animals Protection
Bill (H.L.) Vols. 1 and 2, Her
Majesty's Stationery Office, April,
1980.

2627. Great Britain. Statistics of Experiments on Living Animals. Her
Majesty's Stationery Office, Command
7628, 1978.

2628. Great Britain. Report of the Technical
Committee to Enquire into the Welfare
of Animals Kept under Intensive
Livestock Husbandry Systems ("The
Brambell Report"), Command Paper
2836, Her Majesty's Stationery Office,
London, 1965.

2629. Great Britain. Report of the Depart-
mental Committee on Experimental
Animals, Sir Sydney Littlewood,
Chairman. Home Office, Her Majesty's
Stationery Office, London, 1965.
("The Littlewood Report"), Cmnd.2641.

2630. Great Britain. Royal Commission on
Vivisection: Final Report.
Parliamentary Papers, 1912-13,
London.

2631. Great Britain. Report of the Royal

Commission on the Practice of
Subjecting Live Animals to Experi-
ments for Scientific Purposes.
Parliamentary Papers, 1876, London.

2632. Great Britain. The Cruelty to Animals Act, 1876. Her Majesty's
Stationery Office, London.

2633. Michigan. Pomerantz, Gerri, Ann.
Young People's Attitudes toward
Wildlife. Lansing: Michigan
Department of Natural Resources,
1977. (Wildlife Division Report
no. 2781.)

2634. Michigan. Shaw, William W., Attitude toward Hunting; a Study of
some Social and Psychological
Determinants. Lansing: Michigan
Department of Natural Resources,
1977. (Wildlife Division Report
No. 2740.)

2635. The Netherlands. Report of the Inquiry into Animal Experiments in
1978 in the Netherlands, Netherlands
Ministry of Public Health. (Dutch
text with summary in English,
available from the Editor.)

2636. United States. House of Representatives. Four bills which have been
introduced, 1979 and 1980.
H.R. 282 (Drinan-D., Mass.) A bill
to "promote the development of
methods of research, experimentation, and testing that minimize the use of, and pain and
suffering to, live animals."
H.R. 4479 (Weiss-D., N.Y.) A bill
to "establish a commission to

study alternative methods to
the use of live animals in
laboratory research and testing."
H.R. 4805 (Richmond-D., N.Y.)
A bill to "establish a National
Center for Alternative Research
to develop and coordinate alternative methods of research
and testing which do not involve
the use of live animals, to develop
training programs in the use of
alternative methods of research
and testing which do not involve
the use of live animals, and to
disseminate information on such
methods, and for other purposes."
H.R. 6847 (Schroeder-D., Colo.)
A bill to "amend the Animal Welfare Act to insure the humane
treatment of laboratory animals."
Copies of above bills available from:
House Document Room, H-226, U.S.
Capitol, Washington, D.C. 20515.

2637. United States. National Toxicology
Program, Public Health Service, De-
partment of Health, Education, and
Welfare, P.O. Box 12233, Research
Triangle Park, North Carolina, 27709.
Publications include:
NTP Technical Bulletin, monthly
NTP Review of Current DHEW Research
Related to Toxicology, Fiscal
Year 1980
NTP Fiscal Year 1980 Annual Plan.

2638. United States. Fish and Wildlife
Service. "Public Attitudes toward
Critical Wildlife and Natural Habitat Issues," first phase of a study
by Stephen Kellert, Yale University

School of Forestry, 1980. Single
copies available free from Publishing Unit, U.S. Fish and Wildlife
Service, Department of the Interior,
Washington, D.C., 20240.

2639. United States. "National Survey of
Laboratory Animal Facilities and
Resources," Office of Science and
Health Reports, Division of Research
Resources, National Institutes of
Health, Bethesda, MD 20205, 1980.

2640. United States. Code of Federal Regulations. Title 16. Commercial
Practices. 1500.40-1500.42, "Method
of Testing Toxic Substances. Method
of Testing Primary Irritant Substances.
Test for Eye Irritants."

2641. United States. "Illustrated Guide
for Grading Eye Irritation by
Hazardous Substances," U.S. Government Printing Office, Washington,
D.C., 1980 (?) (Color Plates showing varying degrees of damage to
rabbits' eyes in tests for eye
irritants.)

2642. United States. Office of the Federal
Register. Code of Federal Regulations.
(Title) 9. Animals and Animal
Products, 1979, Superintendent of
Documents, Washington, D.C.

2643. United States. Congress. Senate.
Committee on Agriculture, Nutrition
and Forestry. Subcommittee on
Agricultural Research and General
Legislation. Humane Methods of
Livestock Slaughter. Hearing on
S. 3092, June 15, 1978. U.S.

Government Printing Office,
Washington, D.C., 1978.

2644. United States. Congress. House.
Committee on Agriculture. Subcommittee on Livestock and Grains.
Humane Methods of Slaughter Act of
1977. Hearing on H.R. 1464, April
25, 1978. U.S. Government Printing
Office, Washington, 1978.

2645. United States. Department of Health,
Education and Welfare, National
Institutes of Health, "Guide for
the Care and Use of Laboratory
Animals," DHEW Publication No.
(NIH) 78-23, Revised in 1978.

2646. United States. Department of Health,
Education and Welfare, Public
Health Service, National Institutes
of Health, Division of Research
Resources, Bethesda, Maryland 20014,
"Animal Resources: A Research Resources Directory," October, 1978.
This directory lists and describes
major projects involving experimentation on animals funded by the
United States Government through
the National Institutes of Health.
The projects are classified as
follows:
    Primate Research Centers
    Animal Diagnostic Laboratories
    Information Projects
    Animal Reference Centers
    Special Animal Colony and Model
        Studies
For each project, names and addresses
and telephone numbers of principal
investigators, directors and contact
persons are given to serve as sources

of additional information.

2647. United States. Animal and Plant Health Inspection Service. Veterinary Services. Licensing and Registration under the Animal Welfare Act: Dealers, Exhibitors, Researchers, Transporters. Dept. of Agriculture, Animal and Plant Health Inspection Service, Veterinary Services, 1977, Washington, D.C., 1977.

2648. United States. "Marine Mammals." Hearings before the Subcommittee on Fisheries and Wildlife Conservation and the Environment of the Committee on Merchant Marine and Fisheries, House of Representatives, Ninety-fifth Congress, Marine Mammal Oversight, February 17, 1977; Tuna-Porpoise Regulations, March 2, 1977; Marine Mammal Authorization-H.R. 4740, March 15, 1977. (Hearings conducted by Congressman Robert Leggett). U.S. Gov't. Printing Office.

2649. United States. "Marine Mammal Protection Act." Hearings before the Committee on Commerce, Science and Transportation, United States Senate, Ninety-fifth Congress, Oversight into the Marine Mammal Protection Act, February 9 and 11, 1977. (Hearings conducted by Senator Daniel K. Inouye). U.S. Gov't. Printing Office.

2650. United States. "Treaties and Other International Agreements on Fisheries, Oceanographic Resources, and Wildlife Involving the United States." Prepared at the request of

Hon. Warren Magnuson, Chairman,
for the use of the Committee on
Commerce, Science, and Transportation, U.S. Senate, by the Congres-
sional Research Service, The Library
of Congress, October 31, 1977.
(U.S. Government Printing Office).

2651. United States. "The Evolution of
National Wildlife Law." Report to
the Council on Environmental
Quality, written by Michael J.
Bean of the Environmental Law
Institute, 1977. (Superintendent
of Documents, U.S. Government
Printing Office, Washington, D.C.
20402).

2652. United States. "Toxic Substances Control Act," Printing Management
Office, PM-215, Environmental Protection Agency, Washington, D.C.,
1976.

2653. United States. Congress. House.
Committee on Agriculture. Busi-
ness Meeting on Animal Welfare
Act Amendments of 1976: S. 1491...
Public Law 940279. U.S. Government
Printing Office, Washington, 1976.

2654. United States. Congress. House.
Committee on Merchant Marine and
Fisheries. Subcommittee on Fish-
eries and Wildlife Conservation and
the Environment. "Painful Trapping
Devices." Hearings, November 17,
18, 1975. U.S. Government Printing
Office, Washington, D.C., 1976.

2655. United States. Public Law 940279,
S. 1941, April 22, 1976. An act

to amend the act of August 24,
1966, as amended, to increase the
protection afforded animals in
transit and to assure humane treatment of certain animals and for
other purposes. U.S. Government
Printing Office, Washington, D.C.,
1976.

2656. United States. "Commission on Humane
Treatment of Animals." Hearing before the Subcommittee on Livestock
and Grains of the Committee on Agriculture, House of Representatives,
Ninety-fifth Congress, on H.R. 11112,
September 30, 1976. (Hearings
conducted by Congressman W.R. Poage.)
U.S. Gov't. Printing Office.

2657. United States. House of Representatives.
Hearings on Toxic Substances Control
Act, June 16, July 9, 10, 11, 1975.
Subcommittee on Consumer Protection and
Finance of the Committee on In-
terstate and Foreign Commerce. Ser-
ial No. 94-41. U.S. Government
Printing Office, Washington, D.C.,
1975. (Especially see pp. 296-309,
"Toxicity Testing at Haskell Labo-
ratory: A Guide to Current Practices".)

2658. United States. Congress. Senate.
Committee on Commerce. Subcommittee
on the Environment. Animal Welfare Improvement Act of 1975.
Hearing on S. 1941, S. 2070, S.
2430, on November 20, 1975. U.S.
Government Printing Office, Washington, D.C., 1975. Serial No. 94055.

2659. United States. Congress. House.
Committee on Agriculture. Sub-

committee on Livestock and Grains.
Animal Welfare Act Amendments of
1975, Hearings on H.R. 5808, September 9 and 10, 1975. U.S. Government
Printing Office, Washington, D.C.,
1975.

2660. United States. "Marine Mammal Protection Oversight." Hearings before the Subcommittee on Fisheries and Wildlife Conservation and the Environment of the Committee on Merchant Marine and Fisheries, House of Representatives, Ninety-fourth Congress, October 21, 29, 30, December 9, 1975. (Hearings conducted by Congressman Robert Leggett.) U.S. Government Printing Office.

2661. United States. Congress. House. Committee on Agriculture. Subcommittee on Livestock and Grains. Animal Welfare Act Amendments of 1974. Hearing on H.R. 15843 and H.R. 16738, August 6-October 2, 1974, U.S. Government Printing Office, Washington, 1974.

2662. United States. "Fish and Wildlife Miscellaneous," Hearings before the Subcommittee on Fisheries and Wildlife Conservation and the Environment of the Committee on Merchant Marine and Fisheries, House of Representatives, Ninety-third Congress on Import Restrictions, H.R. 15508, H.R. 15039, H.R. 15289, H.R. 15290, H.R. 15626, H.R. 15802, H.R. 16179, H.R. 16245, H.R. 16393, June 19, 1974; Endangered Species Act Amendment, H.R. 15893 and H.R. 16079, July 29, 1974; Incidental

Taking of Marine Mammals, H.R.
15273, H.R. 15459, H.R. 15549,
H.R. 15810, H.R. 16043, H.R. 16777,
H.R. 15967, August 8, 9, 1974.
(Hearings conducted by Congressman
John Dingell.) U.S. Government
Printing Office.

2663. United States. National Conference
on Research Animals in Medicine,
Washington D.C., 1972. Research
Animals in Medicine, edited by Lowell
T. Harmison. Sponsored by National
Institutes of Health, U.S. Govern-
ment Printing Office, Washington,
D.C., 1973. (DHEW Publication No.
(NIH) 72-333.)

2664. United States. "Endangered Species
Act of 1973." Hearings before the
Subcommittee on Environment of the
Committee on Commerce, United States
Senate, Ninety-third Congress, on
S. 1591 and S. 1983, to provide for
the conservation, protection, and
propagation of species or subspecies of fish and wildlife that
are presently threatened with
extinction or likely within the
foreseeable future to become threatened with extinction; and for other
purposes, June 18 and 21, 1973.
(Hearings conducted by Senator Ted
Stevens and Senator Frank E. Moss.)
U.S. Government Printing Office.

2665. United States. "Problems in Air Shipment of Domestic Animals." Hearings
before a Subcommittee of the Committee
on Government Operations, House of
Representatives, Ninety-third Congress. September 25, 26, 27, and 28,

1973. (Hearings conducted by Congressman Floyd V. Hicks.) U.S. Gov't. Printing Office.

2666. United States. "Endangered Species." Hearings before the Subcommittee on Fisheries and Wildlife Conservation and the Environment of the Committee on Merchant Marine and Fisheries, House of Representatives, Ninety-third Congress, on H.R. 37, H.R. 470, H.R. 471, H.R. 1461, H.R. 1511, H.R. 2669, H.R. 2735, H.R. 3310, H.R. 3696, H.R. 3795, H.R. 4755, H.R. 4785, Bills to provide for the conservation, protection, and propagation of species or subspecies of fish and wildlife that are threatened with extinction or likely within the foreseeable future to become threatened with extinction, and for other purposes; H.R. 2169, a bill to implement the convention on nature protection and wildlife preservation in the Western Hemisphere, and for other purposes, March 15, 26, 27, 1973. (Hearings conducted by Congressman John Dingell.) U.S. Gov't. Printing Office.

2667. United States. "Horse Protection Act of 1970." Hearing before the Committee on Commerce, United States Senate, Ninety-third Congress, on Horse Protection Act of 1970, May 2, 1973. (Hearing conducted by Senator John Tunney.) U.S. Gov't. Printing Office.

2668. United States. "Ocean Mammal Protection." Hearings before the Subcommittee on Oceans and Atmosphere of the Committee on Commerce, United States Senate, Ninety-Second Congress, on S. 685, 1315, 2579, 2639, 2871, 3112, 3161, and amendment 1048, ocean mammal legislation, February 12, 15, 16, March 7, and May 11, 12, and 13, 1972. (Hearings conducted by Senator Ernest F. Hollings.) U.S. Gov't. Printing Office.

2669. United States. House of Representatives. Committee on Merchant Marine and Fisheries. A Compilation of Federal Laws Relating to Conservation and Development of Our Nation's Fish and Wildlife Resources, Environmental Quality, and Oceanography, Washington, D.C., 1972.

2670. United States. "Predatory Mammals and Endangered Species." Hearings before the Subcommittee on Fisheries and Wildlife Conservation of the Committee on Merchant Marine and Fisheries, House of Representatives, Ninety-second Congress, on Predatory Mammals. H.R. 689, H.R. 1081, H.R. 3561, H.R. 7260, H.R. 8256, H.R. 8673, H.R. 9668, H.R. 10214, H.R. 10231, H.R. 10418, H.R. 11785, H.R. 13152, H.R. 13153, H.R. 13261; Endangered Species, H.R. 3616, H.R. 3844, H.R. 7154, H.R. 7240, H.R. 8099, H.R. 8258, H.R. 8505, H.R. 8507, H.R. 12986, H.R. 13081, H.R. 13111, H.R. 13489, H.J. Res. 873, March 20, 21, April 10 and 11, 1972. (Hearings conducted by Congressman John Dingell.) U.S. Government Printing Office.

2671. United States. Department of Health, Education and Welfare, Public Health Service, National Institutes of Health, "A Comprehensive Animal Program for a College of Medicine," March. 1971.

2672. United States. "Marine Mammals." Hearings before the Subcommittee on Fisheries and Wildlife Conservation of the Committee on Merchant Marine and Fisheries, House of Representatives, Ninety-second Congress on H.R. 690, H.R. 4370, H.R. 4733, H.R. 6554, H.R. 6558, H.R. 6801, H.R. 6804, H.R. 7217, H.R. 7229, H.R. 7431, H.R. 7463, H.R. 7477, H.R. 7530, H.R. 7555, H.R. 7556, H.R. 7638, H.R. 7706, H.R. 7794, H.R. 7861, H.R. 7891, H.R. 7952, H.R. 8105, H.R. 8183, H.R. 8255, H.R. 8391, H.R. 8526, H.R. 8804, H.R. 9041, H.R. 9356, H.R. 9409, H.R. 9557, H.R. 9917, H.R. 10420, H.R. 10569, H.R. 10803, H.R. 10814, H. Con. Res. 77. and H. Con. Res. 173, Legislation for the Preservation and Protection of Marine Mammals, September 9, 13, 17, 23, 1971. (Hearings conducted by Congressman John Dingell.) U.S. Gov't. Printing Office.

2673. United States. House of Representatives. Committee on Agriculture. Subcommittee on Livestock and Grains. Care of Animals Used for Research, Experimentation, Exhibition, or Held for Sale as Pets. Hearing on H.R. 13957, June 8 and 9, 1970. U.S. Gov't. Printing Office, Washington, D.C., 1970.

2647. United States. "Horse Protection
       Act of 1970." Hearing before
       the Subcommittee on Public Health
       and Welfare of the Committee on
       Interstate and Foreign Commerce,
       House of Representatives, Ninety-
       first Congress, on H.R. 14151 and
       H.R. 15261, Bills to protect
       interatate and foreign commerce
       by prohibiting the movement in such
       commerce of horses which are "sored"
       and for other purposes (and iden-
       tical bills) and S. 2543, an Act
       to prohibit the movement in inter-
       state or foreign commerce of horses
       which are "sored," and for other
       purposes (and identical bills),
       September 21, 1970. (Hearings con-
       ducted by Congressman John Jarman).
       U.S. Gov't. Printing Office.

2675. United States. "Endangered Species."
       Hearings before the Subcommittee
       on Fisheries and Wildlife Con-
       servation of the Committee on
       Merchant Marine and Fisheries,
       House of Representatives, Ninety-
       first Congress, First Session on
       H.R. 248, H.R. 992, H.R. 3790,
       H.R.4812, H.R. 5252, H.R. 6634,
       bills to prevent the importation
       of endangered species of fish or
       wildlife into the United States;
       to prevent the interstate shipment
       of reptiles, amphibians, and other
       wildlife taken contrary to state
       law; and for other purposes, Feb-
       ruary 19, 20, 1969. (Hearings
       conducted by Congressman John
       Dingell.) U.S. Gov't. Printing
       Office.

2676.   United States. "Horse Protection Act
        of 1969." Hearing before the
        Subcommittee on Energy, Natural
        Resources, and the Environment
        of the Committee on Commerce,
        United States Senate, Ninety-first
        Congress, First Session on S. 2543,
        to protect interstate and foreign
        commerce by prohibiting the movement
        in such commerce of horses which
        are "sored," and for other purposes,
        September 17, 1969. (Hearing con-
        ducted by Senator Joseph D. Tydings.)
        U.S. Gov't. Printing Office.

2677.   United States. "Endangered Species."
        Hearings before the Subcommittee
        on Energy, Natural Resources, and
        the Environment of the Committee on
        Commerce, United States Senate,
        Ninety-first Congress, First Session
        on S. 335, S. 671, and S. 1280, to
        prevent the interstate shipment of
        reptiles, amphibians and other wild-
        life taken contrary to state law,
        and for other purposes, May 14, and
        15, 1969. (Hearings conducted by
        Philip A. Hart.) U.S. Gov't. Print-
        ing Office.

2678.   United States. "Endangered Species."
        Hearing before the Subcommittee on
        Merchant Marine and Fisheries of
        the Committee on Commerce, United
        States Senate, Ninetieth Congress,
        Second Session on S. 2948, and H.R.
        11618, to prevent the importation
        of endangered species of fish or
        wildlife into the United States; to
        prevent the interstate shipment of
        reptiles, amphibians, and other
        wildlife contrary to state law; and

for other purposes, July 24, 1968.
(Hearing conducted by Senator
Daniel B. Brewster.) U.S. Gov't.
Printing Office.

2679. United States. "Wild Birds and Wild
Animals." Hearings before the Committee on Finance, United States
Senate, Eighty-eighth Congress,
First Session on H.R. 1839, an act
to amend the tariff act of 1930 to
provide for the free importation of
wild animals and wild birds which
are intended for exhibition in the
United States, July 23, 1963.
(Hearings conducted by Senator Harry
F. Byrd.) U.S. Gov't. Printing Office.

2680. United States. House of Representa-
tives. Committee on Interstate and
Foreign Commerce. Humane Treatment
of Animals Used in Research. Hear-
ing on H.R. 1937 and H.R. 3556,
September 28 and 29, 1962. U.S.
Gov't. Printing Office, Washington,
D.C., 1962.

2681. United States. "Humane Slaughter."
Hearings before the Subcommittee
on Livestock and Feed Grains of the
Committee on Agriculture, House of
Representatives, Eighty-fifth Con-
gress, First Session on H.R. 176,
H.R. 2880, H.R. 3029, H.R. 3049,
H.R. 5671, H.R. 5820, H.R. 6422,
and H.R. 6509, April 2 and 12,
1957. U.S. Gov't. Printing Office.

2682. United States. Senate. Committee on
Agriculture and Forestry. Humane
Slaughtering of Livestock and Poultry.

Hearing on S. 1636, May 9 and 10, 1956. U.S. Government Printing Office, Washington, D.C., 1956.

2683. United States. Vivisection. Hearing before the Senate Committee on the District of Columbia, February 21, 1900, on the Bill (S-34) for the Further Prevention of Cruelty to Animals in the District of Columbia, Government Printing Office, Washington, 1900.

2684. United States. "Endangered Species." Hearings before the Subcommittee on Fisheries and Wildlife Conservation of the Committee on Merchant Marine and Fisheries. House of Representatives, Ninetieth Congress, First Session, on H.R. 6138, H.R. 8693, and H.R. 11618, bills to prevent the importation of endangered species of fish or wildlife into the United States; to prevent the interstate shipment of reptiles, amphibians, and other wildlife taken contrary to state law; and for other purposes, October 4, 1967. (Hearings conducted by Congressman John Dingell.) U.S. Gov't. Printing Office.

2685. United States. House of Representatives. Committee on Agriculture. Subcommittee on Livestock and Grains. Regulate the Transportation, Sale, and Handling of Dogs and Cats Used for Research and Experimentation. Hearing, March 7 and 8, 1966. U.S. Government Printing Office, Washington, D.C., 1965, and 1966.

2686. United States. "Animal Dealer Regulation." Hearings before the Committee on Commerce, United States Senate, Eighty-ninth Congress, Second Session, on S. 2322, a bill to authorize the Secretary of Agriculture to regulate the transportation, sale, and handling of dogs and cats intended to be used for purposes of research or experimentation and for other purposes, S. 3059, a bill to authorize the Secretary of Agriculture to regulate the transportation, sale and handling of dogs, cats, and other animals intended to be used for purposes of research or experimentation and for other purposes, S. 3138, a bill to authorize the Secretary of Agriculture to regulate the transporation, purchase, sale, and handling of dogs and cats in commerce, March 25, 28, and May 25, 1966. (Hearings conducted by Senator Warren Magnuson and Senator A.S. Mike Monroney.) U.S. Gov't. Printing Office.

2687. United States. Bureau of Sport Fisheries and Wildlife. Trapping Tips for Young Trappers. Washington, D.C., U.S. Government Printing Office, 1965. (Conservation Note 16).

(For additional entry related to this topic
see 2907.)

2688. Scott, Ronald, and Stewart, Jean, eds.,
Films for Humane Education, Argus
Archives (See 2984), New York, 1979.
Covers over 100 films, providing
titles, release and availability
information, descriptions, Argus
audience reactions, Argus' opinions,
and possible discussion materials.
Subject classifications include:
Euthanasia
Exhibitions (Zoo, etc.)
Food and Commercial Uses
Branding
Cosmetics
Intensive Farming
Seals
Slaughter of Livestock
Humane Education
Hunting
Performing Animals
Pets and Shelters
Wildlife
Research and Testing
Riding (Horses)
Service and Companion Animals
Trapping
Veterinary Medicine

2689. "The Animals Are Crying," 16 mm, 28
minute, color, on pet population
explosion.
Available through:
Humane Society of United States
(3029)
Animal Protection Institute of
America (2977)
Society for Animal Rights (3096)

2690. "Blinded by Science," makes a reasoned
case against animal experimentation

as practised today, presented by
well-known scientists and by of-
ficials of the National Anti-
Vivisection Society (London.)
Produced by British Films for the
National Anti-Vivisection Society,
16 mm., 28 minute, color.

2691. "The Coat," 14 minute, color, on furs,
and trapping. Available through:
Society for Animal Rights (3096)

2692. "The Curiosity that Kills the Cat,"
on animal experimentation. Avail-
able through:
British Films
Carlyle House
235 Vauxhall Bridge Road
London, England, SWIV 1EJ
West Glen Films
565 Fifth Avenue
New York, N.Y., 10017
The Scottish Society for the
Prevention of Vivisection
(2914)

2693. "Do Animals Reason?" 16 mm., color,
14 minutes. National Geographic
Society, 1975. Analysis of behavior of triggerfish, starlings and
dolphins.

2694. "Don't Look Now...Here Comes Your
Dinner," on factory farming. Avail-
able through:
Animal Protection Institute of
America (2977)

2695. "First Signs of Washoe," on teaching
language to chimpanzees. Available
through:
Time-Life Multimedia

Time-Life Building
Rockefeller Center
New York, N.Y. 10020

2696. "Greenpeace: Voyages to Save the
Whales," winner of five film fes-
tival awards including the American
Film Festival and the Canadian Film
Awards. The film offers a brief
history of modern whaling and the
International Whaling Commission,
and tells the story of two historic
Greenpeace expeditions.

The original 53 minute version of
this film is available for rental
from either:
Canadian Filmmakers Distribution
Center, 406 Jarvis Street,
Toronto, Ontario, M4Y 2PG,
Telephone (416) 921-4121, or
Pacific Cinamatheque Pacifique,
1616 West 3rd Avenue, Vancouver,
B.C. V6J 1K2, Telephone (604)
732-5322.

A shortened 27 minute version of
this film is also available for
rental from:
Pyramid Films, Box 1048, Santa
Monica, CA 90406, Telephone
(213) 828-7577, for use in the
U.S. only.

2697. "The Guns of August," 77 minute docu-
mentary on hunting. Available through:
University of Michigan
Audio-Visual Educational Center
416 Fourth Street
Ann Arbor, Mich. 48103

Films

2698. "Meat," produced by Fred Wiseman, 16mm. film, 2 hours, available through television station WNET, 356 West 58th Street, New York, N.Y. 10019. Powerful portrayal of meat-packing operation.

2699. "Meditations on Hunting," the Spanish philosopher Jose Ortega y Gasset's views on hunting. 29 minutes, color. Available free from:
National Rifle Association (3060)

2700. "Miss Goodall and the Baboons of Gombe," 16mm. color, 52 minutes. Films, Inc., Wilmette, IL, 1974. Focuses on the inter-group relationships, including mating habits, child care and leadership.

2701. "Northern Lights: Rites of Spring, 58 minutes, documentary televised in the United States on the PBS network. The film is about the Newfoundland seal hunt, and contains footage of Greenpeace campaigns during three successive years. Purchase price $600.00 The film can be rented from:
Canadian Filmmakers Distribution Center, 406 Jarvis Street, Toronto, Ontario, M4Y 2PG, Telephone (416) 921-4121, or
Pacific Cinamatheque Pacifique, 1616 West 3rd Avenue, Vancouver, B.C. V6J 1K2, Telephone (604) 732-5322.

2702. "The Other, Barred," 10 minute, color, on New York City Central Park Zoo. Available through:
Society for Animal Rights (3096)

408

2703. "The PAWS film," 10 minute, color, on
      animal birth control, animal shelters,
      euthanasia.
         Available through:
            Society for Animal Rights (3096)

2704. "Primate," produced by Fred Wiseman,
      16 mm film, 105 minutes, available
      from Zipporah Films, 54 Lewis Wharf,
      Boston, Mass., 02110. Controversial
      film on the Yerkes Primate Research
      Center, Atlanta, GA. See 1456 for
      a discussion of this film.

2705. "A Question of Hunting," 30 minutes,
      produced by Remington Arms Co.,
      on hunting and anti-hunting.
         Available through:
            Film Department
            Ducks Unlimited, Inc.
            P.O. Box 66300
            Chicago, IL 60666

2706. "A Right to Hunt," 28 minutes, history
      and role of hunting.
         Available through:
            Ducks Unlimited Inc. (See
            above entry for address)

2707. "Say Goodbye," 52 minute, color, on
      animals threatened with extinction.
         -- Available through:
            Films, Inc.
            1144 Wilmette Avenue
            Wilmette, Ill. 60091

2708. "Seal Song," 24 minute, color, on
      seals and seal hunting.
         Available through:
            Society for Animal Rights (3096)

Films

2709. "Seals," 12 minute, color.
      Available through:
          Friends of Animals (3016)

2710. "Skins," 12 minute, color, on furs,
      trapping, mink farming.
          Available through:
              Society for Animal Rights (3096)
              Friends of Animals (3016)

2711. "Teaching Sign Language to the Chimpan-
      zee Washoe," 16 mm. sound film,
      Psychological Cinema Register, State
      College, PA, 1973.

2712. "They Have No Say,"
          Available through:
              The Scottish Society for the
              Prevention of Vivisection
              (2914)

2713. "The Tool Users," 16 mm, color, 15
      minutes. National Geographic
      Society, Washington, D.C., 1975.
      Shows tool-using activities of ants,
      finches and chimpanzees.

2714. "Trapped"
          Available through:
              The Scottish Society for the
              Prevention of Vivisection
              (2914)

2715. "Trapping: A Modern Day Necessity,"
      27 minutes.
          Available through:
              Woodstream Corp.
              Lititz, PA 17543

2716. "Warm Blood on White Ice," film on
      Canadian seal slaughter, produced
      by International Fund for Animal

Welfare, P.O. Box 193, Yarmouth
Port, MA 02675.

2717. "What Price Beauty?" 28 minute, color,
cosmetic testing on animals, trapping and fur and perfume production.
Available through:
Society for Animal Rights (3096)

2718. "Women Can Hunt, Too," 16½ minutes,
color.
Available free from:
National Rifle Association (3060)

2719. Animal Liberation, c/o Total Environment Centre, 18 Argyle Street, Sydney 2000, Australia.

2720. The Animal Welfare League of South Australia, Inc., 11 Cormack Road, Wingfield, 5013, South Australia, Australia.

2721. Australian Association Against Painful Experiments on Animals, 13a Rose Street, Armadale 3143, Australia.

2722. Australian Association for Humane Research, P.O. Box 356, Broadway, New South Wales, 2007, Australia. Issues **Newsletter** periodically.

2723. Laboratory Animal Centre of Australia, Institute of Medical and Veterinary Science, P.O. Box 14, Rundle Street, Adelaide, South Australia.

2724. Rosa Tingey Memorial Research Trust, Box 140 Post Office, Christies Beach, South Australia 5165.

2725. The Working Group Against Animal Experiments, G.P.O. 3719, Sydney 2001, Australia.

VIII. Organizations Interested in Animals
Canada

2726. Action Volunteers, 412 Jarvis Street, Apt. 17, Toronto, Canada.

2727. Alternative Research, Box 1294, Kitchener, Ontario, Canada. A clearing-house for information on the alternative movement.

2728. The Animal Defence and Anti-Vivisection Society of British Columbia, P.O. Box 391, Station A, Vancouver, B.C.

2729. Animal Defense League of Canada, Inc., Box 713, Ottawa, Ontario, KIP 5P8, Canada. Issues News Bulletin quarterly.

2730. Animal Liberation Collective, Attn., Harriet Schleifer, P.O. Box C.P. 148, South Durham, Quebec JOH 2CO, Canada.

2731. Animal Rights Coalition, Ontario, 1316 Oak Lane, Mississauga, Ontario L5H 2X7, Canada. Union of several small activist groups in and around Toronto.

2732. Animal Welfare Foundation of Canada, 8064 Yonge Street, Thornhill, Ontario, Canada.

2733. Association for the Protection of Fur-Bearing Animals, 1316 East 12th Avenue, Vancouver, B.C., V5N 1Z9, Canada. Educates through films and newsletters; seeks ban on leg-hold traps.

2734. B.C. Foundation for Non-Animal Research, 92 East 37th Ave., Vancouver, B.C. V5W 1E2, Canada.

2735. Bide-A-While Shelter Society Inc.,
12 Eaton Ave., Dartmouth, N.S.
B2Y 2X5, Canada. Operates shelter
for stray animals.

2736. Calgary Vegetarians, c/o Pamela Gill,
2604, 17th Street, S.W., Calgary T2T
4N1, Alberta, Canada.

2737. Canadian Council on Animal Care, 151
Slater St., Ottawa, Ontario, Canada,
KIP 5H3. The Canadian Council on
Animal Care (CCAC), an autonomous
advisory and supervisory body, is
responsible for surveillance of
experimental animal care and use in
universities, pharmaceutical houses
and government laboratories, nation-
wide.
Issues <u>Resource</u> semi-annually.
Literature includes:
"Surveillance Over the Care and
Use of Experimental Animals in
Canada"
"Ethics of Animal Experimentation"
"Humane Air Transportation of Live
Animals" (Audio-visual training
package)
"Summary of CCAC Activities"
"The Right Animal for the Right
Reason," by H.C. Rowsell and
A.A. McWilliam
"The Animal in Research: Dominion
or Stewardship," by H.C. Rowsell
and A.A. McWilliam
"The Ethics of Biomedical Experi-
mentation," by H.C. Rowsell.
"Guide to the Care and Use of Ex-
perimental Animals"

2738. Canadian Federation of Humane Societies,
101 Champagne Avenue, Ottawa KIS 4P3,

Ontario, Canada. Federation of 35
SPCA's and humane societies across
Canada; publishes newspaper, Ani-
mals Canada, Literature Includes:
"Pets and Society: An Emerging
Municipal Issue"

2739. Canadian League for Animal Rights,
P.O. Box 5201, Station "B", Victoria,
B.C., Canada, V8R 6N4.
Literature includes:
"Rights for Animals?" by Joyce
Lambert

2740. Canadian Society for the Prevention
of Cruelty to Animals, 5215 Jean
Talon Street, W., Montreal, P.Q.
H4P 1X4, Canada. First-established
SPCA in Canada. Inspection force
and publishes quarterly magazine
Courier.
Literature includes:
"Report of a Workshop on Alter-
natives to the Use of Laboratory
Animals in Biomedical Research
and Testing"

2741. Canadian Wild Horse Society, R.R. #3,
3660 40th Street, S.E., Salmon Arm,
B.C. VOE 2TO, Canada. Seeks protection of wild horses and publishes
regular magazine, "Cayuse Conserver.

2742. Citizens' Association for Predator Conservation, 23293-34A Avenue, Langley,
B.C. V3A 7B9, Canada. Opposes
indiscriminate killing of wildlife.

2743. Council for Laboratory Animals, 616-198
West Hastings Street, Vancouver, B.C.
V6B 1H2, Canada. Studies animal ex-
perimentation, publishes a newsletter.

2744. Foundation for Non-Animal Research,
92 East 37th Street, Vancouver,
B.C. V5W 1E2, Canada. Finances
scholarships in non-animal research.

2745. Friends of Animals, 2713 Seaview Road,
Victoria, B.C., Canada, V8N 1K7.
(There is no connection with Friends
of Animals, Inc., New York City.)
Literature includes:
   "Science, Health & Fair Play, The
   Problem of Animals in Research,"
   by Joyce Lambert

2746. Fund for Animals, P.O. Box 48466,
Vancouver, B.C. V7X 1A2, Canada,
or 140 West 57th St., New York,
N.Y. 10019.

2747. Good Shepherd Shelter Foundation,
Trans-Canada Highway, R.R.#1, Mill
Bay, Vancouver Island, B.C. V0R
2P0, Canada. Refuge for all stray
and unwanted animals. Publishes
Shepherd's Crook magazine.

2748. Greenpeace Foundation, 2108 W. 4th
Avenue, Vancouver, B.C. V6K 1N7,
Canada. Conducts world operations
with vessel. Publishes Greenpeace
Chronicles.

2749. Humane Educators of British Columbia,
4631 Cedarcrest Avenue, North Vancouver, B.C., Canada. Affiliated with
Kindness Club.

2750. International Wildlife Protection
Association, P.O. Box 728, Kamloops,
B.C., Canada V2C 5M4.
Issues IWPA Report periodically.

2751. The Kindness Club, 252 Waterloo Row, Fredericton, New Brunswick, Canada E3B 1Z3. An organization of children's kindness clubs throughout Canada, United States and England, started in 1959 with Albert Schweitzer serving as Honorary President. The purpose is to encourage children to be kind to both animals and people. Issues Fur and Feathers: Kindness Club Quarterly. Literature includes Joyce Lambert's How to Be Kind, the book of the Kindness Club, Brunswick Press, Fredericton, N.B., Canada. (In the U.S. this book is available through the North American Vegetarian Society, 501 Old Harding Highway, Malaga, NJ 08328)

2752. Ocean Contact Ltd., P.O. Box 10, Trinity, Trinity Bay, Newfoundland, A0C 250, Canada.

2753. Ontario Wolf League, P.O. Box 177, Stn. "S", Toronto, Ontario, Canada.

2754. Peoples' Animal Welfare Society, Box 127, Stn. "B", Scarborough, Ont., Canada. Promotes low-cost spaying and neutering.

2755. Quebec Society for the Defense of Animals, 1509 Quest, Rue Sherbrooke, Suite 5, Montreal, Que., H3M 1M1, Canada. Education and legislation.

2756. Society for Animals in Distress, 1721 Eglington Ave. W., Toronto, Ont. M6E 2H4, Canada. Runs low-cost clinic for animals; publishes regular Newsletter.

Organizations: Canada

2757. The Toronto Humane Society, 11 Wellesley Street West, Toronto, Canada.
Issues *Humane Viewpoint* periodically.

2758. Toronto Vegetarian Association, 28
Walker Avenue, Toronto M4V IG2,
Ontario, Canada.

2759. Vegetarians of Windsor (VOW), 3280
Everts Avenue, Windsor N9E 2V8,
Ontario, Canada.

VIII. Organizations Interested in Animals
France

2760. Collectif Parisien Anti-Vivisection,
65 Boulevard Arago, 75013, Paris,
France.

2761. Roc Saboteurs de la Chasse, 173
Faubourg St. Antoine, 75011,
Paris, France.

VIII. Organizations Interested in Animals
India

2762. Beauty Without Cruelty, An International
Educational Charitable Trust, India
Branch, 4 Prince of Wales' Drive,
Wa Nowrie, Poona 411001.

2763. Laboratory Animals Information Service,
Cancer Research Institute, Parel,
Bombay--12, India.

VIII. Organizations Interested in Animals
International

2764. Committee of Experts on the Protection
of Animals, Council of Europe, Stras-
bourg.
Literature includes:

420

"Explanatory Report on the European
Convention on the Protection of Animals Kept for Farming Purposes."
1976. Includes the text of the
"European Convention for the Protection of Animals Kept for Farming
Purposes."

2765. International Association against
Painful Experiments on Animals,
51 Harley Street, London WIN 1DD,
England. The International Association Against Painful Experiments
on Animals, founded April 1969,
seeks to prohibit the use of
animals for experimental purposes,
including all processes carried
out for scientific, medical,
cosmetic, industrial or other purposes. With headquarters in London, the Association has at present
44 member societies in 23 countries.
The IAAPEA has no individual members,
only affiliated organizations, but
welcomes the help and support of
all who sympathize with its objectives.
Issues <u>International Animal Action</u>
periodically.
Literature includes:
  "Survey of Legislation Relating
    to Experiments on Animals"
Member societies include:
  <u>Australia</u>
    The Animal Welfare League of
      South Australia Inc.
    Australian Association Against
      Painful Experiments on Animals
    The Working Group Against Animal
      Experiments
    Rosa Tingey Memorial Research
      Trust

421

Australian Association for
Humane Research
Canada
The Animal Defence and Anti-
Vivisection Society of British
Columbia
Denmark
Landsforeningen Forsogsdyrenes
Vaern
Western Europe
Europaische Union gegen den
Missbrauch der Tiere
Finland
Forsoksdjurens Varn
France
Notre Dame de Toute Pitie
(Association Catholique pour
le Respect de la Creation
Animale)
Western Germany
Berliner Tierschutzverein
(Tierheim Lankwitz)
Hungary
Association Hongroise pour la
Protection des Animaux
India
Bombay Humanitarian League
Ireland
The Irish Anti-Vivisection
Society
Italy
Unione Antivivisezionista
Italiana
Lega Antivivisezionista Lombarda
Japan
Japan Animal Welfare Society
Netherlands
Nederlandse Bond tot Bestrijding
van de Vivisectie
Stichting ter Bestrijding van
Wreedheden jegens Dieren in de
Benelux-Landen
Anti-Vivisectie-Stichting

New Zealand
  Save Animals from Experimenta-
    tion
Norway
  Nordisk Samfunn mot smertvoldende
    dyreforsok
  Norsk Liga for Dyrs Rettigheter
Poland
  Towarzystwo Opieki Nad Zwierzetami
  Towarzystwo Opieki Nad Zwierzetami
    (Katowice Branch)
  Towarzystwo Opieki Nad Zwierzetami
    (Poznan Branch)
Switzerland
  Bund zum Schutze der Tiere und
    Verein gegen die Vivisektion
Sweden
  Nordiska Samfundet Mot Plagsamma
    Djurforsok
  Foreningarna Djurens Vanners
    Riksorganisation
South Africa
  Animal Anti-Cruelty League
  South African Association Against
    Painful Experiments on Animals
United Kingdom
  Animals' Vigilantes
  Catholic Study Circle for Animal
    Welfare
  Japan Animal Welfare Society Ltd.
  National Anti-Vivisection So-
    ciety Ltd.
  Scottish Anti-Vivisection Society
United States of America
  New England Anti-Vivisection
    Society
  Cat and Cat Owners Aid Inc.
  American Fund for Alternatives
    to Animal Research
Yugoslavia
  Drustvo Za Varstvo Zivali Sr.
    Slovenije

2766. International Committee on Laboratory
Animals (ICLA), National Institute
of Public Health, Postuttak, Oslo 1,
Norway.
The aims of ICLA are:
1. To assist the development of
laboratory animal sciences
throughout the world.
2. To promote international
collaboration in laboratory
animal science.
3. To promote standardization
in laboratory animal science.
4. To collect and disseminate
information on laboratory
animal science.
Issues ICLA Bulletin periodically.
Literature Includes:
"Guidelines for the Regulation
of Animal Experimentation"

2767. International League for Animal Rights,
Peter J. Hyde, Secretary-General,
P.O. Box 3574, Station C, Ottawa,
Canada. This organization adopted
a "Universal Declaration of the
Rights of Animals," and a "Declaration By Young Friends of Animals,"
which, on October 15, 1978, were
presented to the Director General
of UNESCO, in Paris:
DECLARATION BY YOUNG FRIENDS OF ANIMALS

1. All animals have the right to live
and be happy, like me.
2. I will not abandon any animal who
lives with me because I would not like
my parents to abandon me.
3. I will not harm animals; they
suffer like men.
4. I will not kill animals; killing
for fun or for money is a crime.

5. Animals, like me, have the right to be free; circuses and zoos are prisons for animals.
6. I will learn to observe, understand and love animals; animals will teach me to respect nature and all forms of life.

UNIVERSAL DECLARATION OF THE RIGHTS OF ANIMALS

Preamble

Whereas all animals have rights,
Whereas disregard and comtempt for the rights of animals have resulted and continue to result in crimes against nature and against animals,
Whereas recognition by the human species of the right to existence of other animal species is the foundation of the co-existence of species throughout the animal world,
Whereas genocide has been perpetrated by man on animals and the threat of genocide continues,
Whereas respect for animals is linked to the respect of man for men,
Whereas from childhood man should be taught to observe, understand, respect and love animals.

IT IS HEREBY PROCLAIMED:

Article 1

All animals are born with an equal claim on life and the same rights to existence.

Article 2

1. All animals are entitled to respect.
2. Man as an animal species shall not arrogate to himself the right to exterminate or inhumanely exploit other animals.

It is his duty to use his knowledge
for the welfare of animals.
3. All animals have the right to
the attention, care and protection
of man.

Article 3

1. No animal shall be illtreated or
be subject to cruel acts.
2. If an animal has to be killed,
this must be instantaneous and without distress.

Article 4

1. All wild animals have the right
to liberty in their natural environment, whether land, air or water, and
should be allowed to procreate.
2. Deprivation of freedom, even for
educational purposes, is an infringement of this right.

Article 5

1. Animals of species living tra-
ditionally in a human environment have
the right to live and grow at the
rhythm and under the conditions of
life and freedom peculiar to their
species.
2. Any interference by man with this
rhythm or those conditions for purposes of gain is an infringement of this
right.

Article 6

1. All companion animals have the
right to complete their natural life
span.

2. Abandonment of an animal is a cruel and degrading act.

Article 7

All working animals are entitled to a reasonable limitation of the duration and intensity of their work, to the necessary nourishment and to rest.

Article 8

1. Animal experimentation involving physical or psychological suffering is incompatible with the rights of animals, whether it be for scientific, medical, commercial or any other form of research.
2. Replacement methods must be used and developed.

Article 9

Where animals are used in the food industry they shall be reared, transported, lairaged and killed without the infliction of suffering.

Article 10

1. No animal shall be exploited for the amusement of man.

2. Exhibitions and spectacles involving animals are incompatible with their dignity.

Article 11

Any act involving the wanton killing of an animal is biocide, that is, a crime against life.

427

Article 12

1.   Any act involving mass killing
of wild animals is genocide, that
is, a crime against the species.
2.   Pollution or destruction of the
natural environment leads to genocide.

Article 13

1.   Dead animals shall be treated
with respect.

2.   Scenes of violence involving
animals shall be banned from cinema
and television, except for humane
education.

Article 14

1.   Representatives of movements
that defend animal rights should
have an effective voice at all levels
of government.
2.   The rights of animals, like human
rights, should enjoy the protection
of law.

2768.   International Society for the
Protection of Animals, 106
Jermyn Street, London, England,
SW1Y 6EE. Registered Charity
established in 1959 to promote
effective means for the protection and
conservation of animals in any part
of the world. Maintains fully
trained field-staff; more than 50
countries represented by member
societies in the organization.
ISPA has consultative status with the
UN, the Council of Europe and other
inter-governmental bodies.

Organizations: International

2769. International Whaling Commission,
The Red House, Station Rd. Histon,
Cambridge CB4 4NP, U.K.

2770. United Animal Nations Foundation,
c/o Franz Weber, CH-1820, Montreux,
Switzerland. New international
organization aiming to establish
a kind of UN for animals.

2771. World Federation for the Protection
of Animals, Dreikoningstrasse
37, CH-8002, Zurich, Switzerland.
Issues Animalia quarterly.
Issues Spotlight quarterly (a
bibliographic record, listing
references to selected articles
in the animal welfare press and
in other periodicals.)
Sponsors Animal Regulation Studies
(began 1977) published by Elsevier
North-Holland, Inc., 52 Vanderbilt
Avenue, New York, N.Y. 10017.
A world movement for a more con-
siderate attitude to animals of all
kinds so that their suffering and
distress can be reduced and prevented.

VIII. Organizations Interested in Animals
Ireland

2772. Irish Anti-Vivisection Society, c/o
Mr. Charles Slatter, "Shamrock",
Weavers Point, Crosshaven, Co.
Cork, Ireland.

2773. Irish Council Against Blood Sports,
16 The Grove, Wood Park, Ballinteer,
Dublin 14, Ireland.

2774. Irish Society for the Prevention of
Cruelty to Animals, 1 Grand Canal
Quay, Dublin 2, Republic of Ireland.

The ISPCA is a federation of
26 Member Societies which cover
most of the Counties in Ireland.

VIII. Organizations Interested in Animals
Japan

2775. Japan Animal Welfare Society Ltd.,
73 George Street, London W1N 1DD,
England.

2776. Japan Experimental Animal Research
Association, Institute of Medical
Science, University of Tokyo,
P.O. Takanama, Tokyo 108.
Issues Experimental Animals
periodically.

VIII. Organizations Interested in Animals
New Zealand

2777. The Anti-Cruelty Society, Inc.,
447 Albert Street, Palmerston
North, New Zealand

2778. SAFE (Save Animals From Experiments),
P.O. Box 647, Auckland 1, New
Zealand.

VIII. Organizations Interested in Animals
Norway

2779. Norwegian League for Animal Rights,
Maridalsvie 9, B, Oslo 1, Norway.

VIII. Organizations Interested in Animals
South Africa

2780. Animal Anti-Cruelty League, P.O.
Box 49007, Rosettenville,
Transvaal, South Africa.

Organizations: South Africa

2781. Karakul Farmers' Association, P.O.
Box 52, Upington 8800, South Africa.

2782. National Committee on Laboratory
Animals, c/o South African Medical
Research Council Scientia, Pretoria
(Private Bag 380.)

2783. South African Association against
Painful Experiments on Animals,
P.O. Box 85228, Enmarentia 2029,
Johannesburg, South Africa.
Issues SAAAPEA News periodically.

VIII. Organizations Interested in Animals
Sweden

2784. Djurfront, Drottninggatan 12A
37100 Karlskrona, Sweden. Contact
Birgitta Carlsson. Anti-vivisection
magazine with 15,000 subscribers,
funded by the largest AV society in
Sweden.

2785. Nordic Antivivisection Society,
Swedish Section, Cederflychtsvagen 5
44300 Lerum, Sweden.

VIII. Organizations Interested in Animals
U.S.S.R.

2786. Laboratory of Experimental Animals,
c/o Academy of Medical Sciences,
Solyanka Street, 14, Moscow, U.S.S.R.

VIII. Organizations Interested in Animals
United Kingdom

2787. Air Chief Marshall the Lord Dowding
Fund for Humane Research, 51
Harley Street, London, England,
W1N 100. Issues Bulletin period-
ically. Literature includes:
"Summary of Alternative Techniques".

2788. Anatomical Society of Great Britain
and Ireland, c/o Programme Secretary,
Prof. J.W.S. Harris, Department of
Anatomy, Royal Free Hospital
School of Medicine, 8 Hunter Street,
London WC1N 1 BP, England.

2789. The Angelican Society for the Welfare
of Animals, c/u Rt. Rev. Dr.
Edward Carpenter, Dean of Westminster, The Deanery, Westminster,
London, SW 1 3 PP.

2790. Animal Activists, P.O. Box 1,
Biggin Hill, Westerham, Kent,
U.K. Tackle all fields of animal
abuse. Restrict membership to vegans
and vegetarians.

2791. Animal Aid, 111 High Street, Tonbridge,
Kent, U.K. Campaigning for the total
abolition of vivisection and factory
farming. Publishes Outrage! monthly.
Literature includes;
"Guidelines for Action"
"Dialogue: Between Animal Aid and
Scientist"
"The Great 'Scientific' Con': Vivi-
section"
"You Can Help Laboratory Animals"
"In Sickness or in Wealth", Clementina
Narborough.

2792. Animal Aid Action Group (S.E. Kent),
Flat 3,8 Shorncliffe Road, Folkestone,
Kent, U.K.

433

2793. Animal Aid Emergency Unit, 48
Boothmeadow Court, Thorplands,
Northampton, U.K.

2794. Animal Liberation Front, Box 190,
8 Elm Avenue, Nottingham, England.
Our Long term aim is simply to end
the exploitation of animals by
human beings. In the short term
we hope to save as many animals
as possible from suffering. Our
methods are direct action.

2795. Animal Protection Association, 21
Warwick Court, Burley Lane, Horsforth,
Leeds LS18 4TB, U.K. Their Ocean
Crusader appeal fund needs 1 million
pounds to buy anti-whaling/sealing
campaign ship.

2796. Animal Protectors Defence Group,
91 Home Close, Hockwell Ring,
Luton, Beds LU4 9NS, U.K. The
group exists to help those who find
themselves in trouble with the law
through helping persecuted animals.

2797. Animal Rights Association, 18 Annadale
Rd., London, S.E. 10, ODA. Formed
a few years ago to demonstrate and
picket at key locations which are
involved in the cruel exploitation
of animals, A.R.A. now publishes a
quarterly news sheet, Clarion, covering animal rights in general, and
hopes to arrange further mass rallies
to promote the cause of Animal
Liberation.

2798. Animal Rights Group, 1 Eagle Street,
Penn Fields, Wolverhampton WV2 2AQ,
U.K.

2799. Animal Saviours, 9 Westfield Street,
Edinburgh EH11 2RB, Scotland.
One-man activist outfit run by Jorn
Cowen. He also publishes an inform-
ative magazine.

2800. Animal Welfare Trust, Hendon and
Aldenham Kennels, Watford By-Pass,
Bushey Heath, Herts., U.K. Registered
Charity set up to care for animals
which are neglected, abused or unwanted.
Literature includes: "Pet Concern".

2801. Animals' Vigilantes, James Mason
House, 24 Salisbury Street, Ford-
ingbridge, Hampshire, SP6 1AF,
U.K. Trust formed to educate and
encourage young people in the care
and welfare of animals, and to teach
the young to reverence and respect
all life. Issues UACTA Magazine
periodically.

2802. Association for the Study of Animal
Behaviour, Dr. R.F. Drewett,
Secretary, Department of Psy-
chology, University of Durham, South
Road, Durham DH1 3LE, U.K.

2803. Association of the British Pharmaceutical Industry, 162 Regent
Street, London W1R 6DD, England.

2804. Beauty Without Cruelty, 1 Calverley
Park, Tunbridge Wells, Kent TN1
2SG, England. Beauty Without
Cruelty came into being to provide
alternatives to furs, leathers and
cosmetics that are tested on animals
and contain animal ingredients. In
fact, we have our own limited
company which manufactures these

cruelty-free cosmetics. BWC
has 37 branches in Britain and
abroad, lectures and puts on
fashion shows showing the
alternatives to furs.
Issues Compassion semi-annually,
Issues Newsletter periodically.
Literature includes: "Why Beauty
Without Cruelty?" Beauty Without
Cruelty cosmetics and toiletries
are available through Beauty Without
Cruelty, Ltd., Avebury Avenue, Tonbridge, Kent, TN9 1TL, England.

2805.   Beecham Group Limited, Beecham House,
Great West Road, Brentford,
Middlesex, TW89BD, U.K.

2806.   Brain Research Association, Secretary:
John O'Keefe, Department of Anatomy
and Embryology, University College,
Gower Street, London WC1E 6BT, England.

2807.   British Federation of Poultry
Industries, High Holborn House,
52/4 High Holborn, London, WC1,
England.

2808.   British Field Sports Society, 26
Caxton Street, London, SW1H
ORG, England.

2809.   British Fur Trade Association, 68,
Upper Thames St., London, England.
EC4V 3AN. Literature includes:
"The Fascination of Fur".

2810. British Institute of Radiology, 32
Welbeck Street, London W1N
7PG, England.

2811. British Pharmacological Society,
c/o Department of Pharmacology,
Royal College of Surgeons,
35-43 Lincolns Inn Fields,
London WC2A 3PN, England.

2812. British Pharmacology Society, c/o
Department of Pharmacology, Medical and Dental Building,
University of Leeds, Leeds LS2
9JT, U.K.

2813. The British Psychological Society,
St. Andrews House, 48 Princess
Road East. Leicester LE1 7DR,
U.K.   Literature includes:
"Report of Working Party on Animal
Experimentation", 1979.

2814. British Toxicology Society (Attn:
Dr. Rose), I.C.I. Ltd., Central
Toxicology Lab., Alderley Park,
Macclesfield, Cheshire, U.K.

2815. British Union for the Abolition
of Vivisection (BUAV), 143
Charing Cross Road, London W1,
England, BUAV publishes Animal
Welfare, a bi-monthly journal.
Organization formed in 1898 to
oppose vivisection in any form.
Its approach to the issues raised
is modern, ethical and scientific.
Literature includes:
"Experimental Animals--Have We
The Right?".

"The Use of Animals in British
Laboratories"
"Does Science Need Animals?"
"Animals and Cosmetics--What Is
the Connection?"
"Putting the Cat Out at Night--
Could Be the Last You Ever See
of Your Pet"
"The Dr. Hadwen Trust for Humane
Research, 1970-1980"
Hadwen, Walter R. "Vivisection:
Its Follies and Cruelties,
and the Way to Fight It", British
Union for the Abolition of Vivi-
section, London, 1905. 12p.

2816. British Veterinary Association, 7
Mansfield Street, London W1M
OAT, England.

2817. Captive Animal Protection Society,
17 Raphael Road, Hove, Sussex,
BN3 5QP, U.K.

2818. Catholic Study Circle for Animal
Welfare, Ealing Abbey, London
W5 2DY, England.
Issues the Ark periodically.
Literature includes:
"The Relationship Between Men
and the Animals" (Victor
Hugo, August 1969, Ark)
"Speeches Against Vivisection"
(Cardinal Manning)
By Dom Ambrose Agius:
"Widening Horizons
"God's Animals"
By Rev. Basil Wrighton:
"Animals in Other Religions"
"Away with Dogmatic Slumber"
"Cruelty and Sport"

"The Golden Age Must Return--
a Catholic's Views On
Vegetarianism"
"Humanism, Vivisection and
Devil-Worship"
"Unity in a Good Cause"
"Morals in the Melting Pot"
"A Matter of Philosophy"
"The Moral and Religious
Aspects of Vivisection"
"The Ethical Heresy"
By Rev. Kevin Daley:
"The Catholic Study Circle
as an Authentic Form of
the Lay Apostolate"
"On the Christian Responsibil-
ity for the Whole of
Creation"
"Speech at the Annual General
Meeting, Dublin, 1969"
By Sir George Trevelyan:
"Man and the Animal World"
By Liam Brophy:
"Ernest Hemingway, the man who
glorified Cruelty"
"The Courage and Kindness of
Mahatma Ghandi"
By K.H. Gray:
"Poem: The Prayer of the Tor-
toise and the Manger"
By Y.W. Zielinska:
"The Revival of Scotism: a
New Hope"
"To Bethlehem", Poems by
Father Ambrose Agius
"Return to Eden" Charlotte Baker
"Few Eggs and No Oranges" Vere
Hodgson
"Musings in Verse", James A.
Smith

2819.   Cats Protection League, 20 North St.,
Horsham, West Sussex RH12 1BN, U.K.

2820.   Chicken's Lib, 6 Pilling Lane,
Skelmanthorpe, Huddersfield, U.K.

2821.   The Christian Consultative Council
for the Welfare of Animals,
Secretary: The Rev. Alan Wynne,
Archbishop Tenison's Grammar
School, Kennington, London, S.E. 11,
England.
The Council was formed in 1978
to co-ordinate the endeavours
of Christians involved in animal
protection.
Participating societies and
organizations include:
The Anglican Society for the
Welfare of Animals.
British Union for the Abo-
lition of Vivisection.
The Catholic Study Circle for
Animal Welfare.
The International Council Against
Bullfighting.
Quaker Concern for Animal Welfare.
The Royal Society for the Preven-
tion of Cruelty to Animals.
Society of United Prayer for
Animals.
St. Andrew Animal Fund.
The Willowtree Sanctuary for the
Welfare of Animals.
Worcester Association for the
Protection of Animals.
Literature includes:
"Vivisection: A Christian
Approach," January, 1980.

2822.   Committee for Information on Animal
Research (CIAR), 9D Stanhope Road
London N6 5NE, England.

Issues Information Sheets:
"The LD 50 Test"
"Where Do Laboratory Animals
Come From?"
"Protection of Animals (Scientific
Purposes) Bill"
"Statistics of Experiments on Living
Animals for 1978"
"Laboratory Animals Protection
Bill"
"Safety Testing and the Cruelty
to Animals Act 1876"
"Experiments Performed Without
Anaesthesia"

2823. Committee for the Reform of Animal
Experimentation (CRAE), 10
Queensferry St., Edinburgh EH 2
4 PG, Scotland. This committee,
formed in 1977, is drawn from
both Houses of Parliament and from
the fields of animal welfare, science
and medicine. It is devoted to
the reform of the law and admin-
istration of the Cruelty to
Animals Act, 1876, relating to
the care and use of living
animals in research, experiments
and other laboratory purposes.
Literature includes:
Annual Reports
"Proposals for Change in the
Legislation Governing the
Use of Live Animals in
Research, Experiments and
Other Laboratory Purposes,"
November, 1979
"The LD 50 Test," August, 1977

"Comments on the LD 50 Test
Report (The Report sub-
mitted to the Secretary
of State by the Advisory
Committee on the Admin-
istration of the Cruelty
to Animals Act, 1876), "
October 1979.

2824. Compassion in World Farming, Lyndum
House, High Street, Petersfield,
Hampshire, U.K. This public
Trust opposes violence in farm-
ing whether to farm animals, wildlife, the amenities of the country-
side, or the soil itself.
Issues Ag newsletter periodically.
Literature includes:
"One Man's Meat"
"Factory Farm '80--What You
Can Do"
"Battery Egg Production"
"Veal Production"
"The 10 Mandates--an eclectic
summary of requirements for
intensive animal farming
applicable to creatures
kept for food or clothing"
"All Animals Have Rights," a
factual educational kit
that raises question on the
well-being of animals on
factory farms, (15 projector
slides, teacher notes, 5
study prints, 3 work cards,
wall chart.)
"The Thinking Behind Direct
Foods"
"Unicar Cow"
"Cage Pigs"

2825. Conquest, 16 Pembroke Road, Winkle-
       bury, Basingstoke, Hampshire, U.K.
       Action group for the Protection of
       wildlife and animal welfare. Rad-
       ical approach, quarterly infor-
       mation newssheet.

2826. Co-ordinating Animal Welfare (CAW),
       P.O. Box 61, Camberley, Surrey,
       GU15 4EN, U.K. CAW consists of
       a loose structure of people who
       feel disillusioned with the present
       methods of campaigning adopted by
       the animal welfare movement and
       was formed to provide a link between
       those actively seeking to bring
       about reforms in all areas of animal
       abuse.
          Issues a bulletin.
          Literature includes:
             "Animal Liberation Booklist"

2827. Crusade Against All Cruelty to Animals,
       Avenue Lodge, Bounds Green Road,
       London M22, England.

2828. Dartmoor Badgers Protection League,
       Spitchwick Manor, Poundsgate,
       Devon TQ13 7PB, U.K. Founded on
       July 27, 1979, the League already
       has 3000 members opposed to the
       unjustified slaughter of badgers.

2829. Dartmoor Livestock Protection Society,
       c/o Mrs. J. Vinson, Crooked Meadow,
       Stidston Lane, South Brent, Devon, U.K.

2830. Department of Health and Social Security,
       Finsbury Square House, 33-37A Finsbury
       Square, London EC2A 1PP, England.

2831. Dr. Hadwen Trust for Humane Research, 143 Charing Cross Road, London WC2H 0EE, England. A Registered Charity founded to give support to scientists using research techniques which will reduce or replace the use of living animals in experiments.

2832. East London Protection of Animals, Mr. L. Marks, Chairman, 414 A Roman Road, Bow, London E3, England. ELPA was formed as a pressure group concerned mainly with the fight for the abolition of vivisection except in strictly medical fields, and the research of tactics calculated to lend weight to Animal Welfare Dialogue with the Establishment.

2833. East Midland Hunt Saboteurs, 4 The Maltings, Shardlow, Derby, U.K.

2834. Ecology Party, 121 Selly Park Road, Birmingham 29, U.K.

2835. Ecology Party (Glasgow Branch), 30 Edgement Street, Shawlands, Glasgow G41 3EL, Scotland.

2836. ECOS Conservation, 218 Ravenhill Road, Belfast BT6 8EF, U.K. Trying to raise 50,000 pounds to purchase and convert a 150 ft. trawler for campaigns.

2837. Farm and Food Society, 4 Willifield Way, London NW11 7XT, England. Works constructively for agriculture based on respect for the

natural world, especially livestock,
which should form a part of any
mixed farming system.
Issues Newsletter periodically.
Literature includes:
"Environmental Pollution by
Modern Methods of Livestock
Production"
"Annual Report of Farm and Food
Society"
"Intensive Livestock Production"
"Food: A Consensus of Opinion"
"Knowledge and Practice of
Responsible Husbandry as a
Basic Educational Principle"

2838. Farm Animal Welfare Co-ordinating
Executive (FAWCE), Secretary: Miss
D. Hayman, Dolphin House, Charl-
ton Park Gate, Cheltenham, Glos.,
U.K. This Joint Consultative Body
was formed in July 1977 to:
discuss, investigate, review
and make recommendations upon
matters relating to the improve-
ment of conditions and/or protec-
tion of animals, birds and fish
used for the production of food
or farmed for other purposes.
Societies represented include:
Anglican Society for Animal
Welfare.
Animal Welfare Trust.
Catholic Study Circle for Animal
Welfare.
Chickens Lib.
Compassion in World Farming.
Dartmoor Livestock Protection
Society.
Farm and Food Society.

FREGG
International Society for the Pro-
tection of Animals.
National Society Against Factory
Farming Ltd.
Pennine Group Against Live Animal
Exports.
Quaker Concern for Animal Welfare.
Royal Society for the Prevention
of Cruelty to Animals.
St. Andrew Animal Fund.
World Federation for the Protec-
tion of Animals.

Literature includes:
"Pre-Slaughter Stunning Methods
and Slaughter house Operation
in British Abattoirs,"
September, 1979.

2839. Fauna Preservation Society, c/o
Zoological Society of London,
Regent's Park, London N4 RY.
Publishes a journal, *Oryx*, three
times a year.

2840. Feminists for Animal Liberation, 75
Agar Grove, London, England.

2841. FOE Wolverhampton, 263 Cannock Road,
Park Village, Wolverhampton, U.K.

2842. Food and Drug Manufacturers Federation Inc., 6 Catherine Street,
London, WC2B 5JJ, England.

2843. Food Manufacturers Federation, Inc.
4 Lygon Place, London SW1, England.

2844. Free Range Egg Association, c/o
Mrs. M. Battcock, Maresfield
Gardens, Hampstead, London NW3,
England.

2845. Friends of the Earth, 9 Poland Street,
London W1V 3DG, England. Prime
information source on environmental matters, FOE Ltd. tends
to work through established systems
but also has 250 local groups active
in U.K.

2846. Friends of the Earth (Scotland),
2a Ainslie Place, Edinburgh 3,
Scotland, U.K.

2847. Fund for the Replacement of Animals
in Medical Experimentation (FRAME),
312A Worple Road, Wimbleton, London,
SW 20 8QU. "FRAME provides up-to
the- minute information to scientists
and the public on new research
techniques that reduce the need for
laboratory animals. We are a
scientific organization and approach
the whole issue practically and
unemotionally."
Issues ATLA Abstracts periodically,
a journal on alternatives.
Issues Technical News twice yearly.
Literature includes:
"Alternatives to Laboratory
Animals"
Information sheets, covering
toxicity tests, numbers of
animals used, computers and
related topics.
Reprinted FRAME articles
Progress Reports.
"What FRAME Does"
"What Price Vanity"

Technical Reports
"Alternatives and the LD/50
Toxicity Test"
"Tissue Culture: A Trend of
The Future"
"Cosmetic Production, Animal
Testing and the Potential
for Developing Alternatives"
"A Programme for Diminishing
the Use of Animals in Teach-
ing and Research"
"Alternatives to Living Animals
in Medical Experiments"
"The Application of Tissue
Culture to Drug and Toxicity
Testing"
"Computer Simulation as an Aid
to the Replacement of Exper-
imentation on Animals and
Humans"
"Alternatives to the Use of
Animals in Toxicity Testing"
"Alternatives to Laboratory
Animals in Biomedical pro-
grammes"
"Bibliography of Alternatives
to Laboratory Animals"
"The Use of Alternatives in
Drug Research"

2848.   Gay Vegetarians, B/M Sequel, London,
WCIV 6XX, England.

2849.   The General Election Co-ordinating
Committee for Animal Protection,
10 Queensferry Street, Edinburgh,
EH2 4PG, Scotland. A unique
committee representing a large
number of animal welfare and
protection societies with the goal
of putting animals into politics.

Literature includes:
"Putting Animals into Politics"
Six areas of concern are:
Factory farming
Experiments on living animals
Treatment of horses
Export of live farm animals
Dogs in the community
Blood sports

2850. Genetical Society, c/o Department
of Genetics, University of
Glasgow G11 5JS, U.K.

2851. Glasgow & West of Scotland Society
for the Prevention of Cruelty to
Animals, 15 Royal Terrace, Glasgow, Scotland G3 7NY. Formed over
120 years ago, the society is a
public instrument to combat
cruelty and ignorance in the
treatment of animals. Twelve
uniformed SPCA Inspectors available throughout the Strathclyde
and Central Regions of Scotland.

2852. Gravesham Animal Rights Group, Top
Flat, 21 Harmer Street, Gravesend,
Kent, U.K.

2853. Greenpeace, Columbo Street,
London, SE1, England. Direct-
action group concerned with a
wide range of environmental
issues from seal culling to
saving the whale, from nuclear
power to oil spills.

2854. Group for the Study of the Human
Companion Animal Bond, Animal
Studies Centre, Freeby Lane,

Waltham-on-the-Wolds, Melton
Mowbray, Leicestershire LE 14
4RT, U.K.
Issues Newsletter periodically.

2855. Humane Education Council, Brook
House, 29 Bramhall Lane South,
Bramhall, Cheshire SK7 2DN, U.K.
A coordinating and advisory
body which aims to establish the
teaching and practice of Humane
Education at all levels in the
community. Produces a quarterly
journal, plus a Schools Project
Pack.

2856. Humane Research Trust, Brook House,
29 Bramhall Lane South, Bramhall,
Stockport, Cheshire SK7 2DN,
U.K. A registered charity for
the promotion of medical and
scientific research. They support scientists who don't use
animals in their experiments.

2857. Hunt Saboteurs Association (HSA),
P.O. Box 19, Tonbridge, Kent.
An activist group. Publish
Howl four times a year.

2858. Imperial Chemical Industries, Ltd.,
Millbank, London SW1P 3JF,
England.

2859. Individual Books (Diana Daniels),
Blyth House, 9 Hammers Lane,
Mill Hill, London NW7 4BY,
Speciality: Animals in Art,
Literature and Life.

2860. Institute of Animal Technicians,
      16 Beaumont Street, Oxford,
      Oxfordshire, U.K.

2861. Institute of Biology, 41 Queens
      Gate, London, SW7 5HU, England.

2862. International Council Against Bull-
      fighting, 13 Graystone Road,
      Tankerton, Nr. Whitstable, Kent
      CT5 2JY, U.K.

2863. International Dolphin Watch,
      'Dolphin',Parklands, North
      Ferriby, Humberside HU14 3ET,
      U.K.

2864. International League for the
      Protection of Horses, P.O.
      Box 166, 67a Camden High
      Street, London NW1 7JL.

2865. International Primate Protection
      League (UK), Regent House,
      19-25 Argyll Street, London W1V
      2DU, England. A registered
      charity concerned with the
      welfare and conservation of
      monkeys and apes throughout the
      world. Publish monthly
      Newsletter.

2866. International Vegetarian Union,
      10 King's Drive, Marple,
      Stockport, Cheshire, SK6
      6NQ, U.K.

2867. Isle of Wight Animal Preservation
      & Action Group, Amsden's Kennels,
      Atherson, PO 38 2LG, I.O.W., U.K.

2868. The Jewish Vegetarian Society,
"Bet Teva," 855 Finchley Road,
London, NW 11, England.

2869. Joint Advisory Committee on Pets
in Society, c/o Walter House,
418-422 Strand, London WC 2
England. An independent study
group formed in 1947 to consider
the position of the dog in contemporary life.

2870. Laboratory Animal Breeders Asso-
ciation of Great Britain Ltd.,
Secretary Alan R. Smith, Charles
River UK Ltd. Manston Road.
Margate, Kent, U.K.

2871. Laboratory Animals Centre, Medical
Research Council Laboratories
Woodmansterne Road, Carshalton,
Surrey, SM5 4EF, U.K.
Issues:
LAC News Letter periodically
Guinea-Pig Newsletter periodically
Mouse Newsletter periodically
Rat Newsletter periodically
Literature includes:
"Laboratory Animal Houses"
"Genetic Monitoring (GM) Scheme"
"The Accreditation and Rec-
ognition Schemes for
Supplies of Laboratory
Animals"
"Register of Accredited Breed-
ers and Recognized Suppliers"
"Standardized Laboratory Animals"
"Laboratory Non-human Primates
for Biomedical Research in
the United Kingdom"

"International Index of Laboratory Animals"

2872. Laboratory Animals Science Association, 38 Mill Road, Buckden, Huntingdon, PE 18 9SS, U.K.
Literature includes:
"Laboratory Animals Buyers Guide"

2873. LAIR, 49 Pratt St., London, NW1, England. LAIR, League for Animals' Irreducible Rights, is a group of women deeply concerned about the oppression and exploitation of non-humans.

2874. League Against Cruel Sports, 1 Reform Row, London, England N17 9TW.
Issues Cruel Sports Bulletin periodically.
Literature includes:
"Blood Sports"
"Report on Live Hare Coursing"
"Otters in Danger"
"Stag Hunting... And Some Call This Sport!"
"Fox Hunting Is Cruel"
"The History of Hunting" (L.G. Pine)

2875. Leviathan, 41 Chelmsford Road, North End, Portsmouth PO2 0JY, U.K. Levianthan is a national cordination scheme for anti-whaling groups in the UK.

2876. The Lockwood Home of Rest for
Old and Sick Donkeys, Sandhills,
Wormley, Nr. Godalming, Surrey,
U.K.

2877. Marine Action Centre, 60 Metcalfe
Road, Cambridge, U.K. Liaison/
information center on whales,
krill and marine conservation.
Publish international newsletter
10 times a year.

2878. Medical Research Council, 20 Park
Crescent, London W1N 4AL, England.

2879. Ministry of Agriculture, Fisheries
and Food, Great Westminster House,
Horseferry Road, London SW1P
2AE, England.

2880. National Anti-Vivisection Society,
51 Harley Street, London W1N
1DD, England.
Issues <u>Animals' Defender</u> bi-
monthly.
Issues periodically:
<u>Bulletin</u> of the Air Chief
Marshall the Lord Dowding
Fund for Humane Research.
Literature includes:
"Do You Know? Facts about
Animal Experiments"
"Animal Experiments--Steps
towards Reform"
Booklets:
"Monkeys and Men"
"The Zeigler Monkey Chair"
"10,000 Shakes of a Rat's
Leg"

"Experiments on the Brain in
Conscious Living Rabbits"
"Two-Headed Dogs: Wrong
Headed Scientists"
"The Shocking Truth about
Cosmetic Tests on Animals"
"Beauty and the Poor Little
Beasts"
"Are Your Cosmetics Tested
on Living Animals?"
"Abolition of Certificates
Bill"
"The 'Pain Conditions' "
"Vivisection--What It Means"
(A leaflet for children)
"The Ethics of Vivisection"
"Vivisection" by C.S. Lewis
"Animal Report"
"A Summary of Some Alternative
Techniques that Replace
Living Animals in Research"
(Lord Dowding Fund)
"The Concept of a Government
Sponsored Humane Research
Institute"

Books:
The Dark Face of Science by
John Vyvyan
Progress Without Pain
The Moral, Scientific and
Economic Aspects of Research
Techniques Not Involving the
Use of Living Animals
Books published by N.A.V.S. include:
Bayly, M. Beddow, The Futility
of Experiments on Animals, 1962
Bayly, M. Beddow, Spotlight on
Vivisection, 1948

Bayly, M. Beddow, More Spot-
lights on Vivisection, 1960
Bayly, M. Beddow, Clinical
Medical Discoveries, 1961

2881. The National Consultative Committee
for Animal Protection, 143
Charing Cross Road, London
WC2H OBP, England. A National
'umbrella' group which helps
to ensure cooperation between
the various interest-groups in
animal welfare, establishing a
forum for discussion and the
formulation of common approaches,
so ensuring a concentration of
united and useful effort to
advance this common cause.

2882. National Equine (and Smaller Animals)
Defense League, 138 Blackwell
Road, Carlisle CA2, 4DL, Great
Britain.

2883. National Institute for Medical
Research, Mill Hill, London,
NW 7 1 AN, England.

2884. National Institute of Biological
Standards and Control, Holly Hill,
London NW3 6RB, England.

2885. National Society Against Factory
Farming, 42 Mount Pleasant Road,
London SE13, England.

2886. National Society for the Abolition
of Cruel Sports, 33 Forest Rise,
Jarvis Brook, Crowborough, East
Sussex, U.K.

2887. National Society for the Abolition of Factory Farming, c/o Lucy Newman, 42 Mt. Pleasant Rd. Lewisham, London SE 13, England.

2888. Orca, 5 Suncroft Place, London SE26, England. Established whale conservation group.

2889. Pharmaceutical Society of Great Britain, 1 Lambeth High Street, Longon, SE1 7JN, England.

2890. Physiological Society, Physiology Laboratory, Downing Street, Cambridge CB2 3EG, U.K.

2891. Physiological Society, c/o Prof. Whitneridge, Laboratory of Physiology, Oxford University, Oxford , U.K.

2892. The Pennine Group Against Live Animal Exports, c/o Mrs. J. Miles, Helsby Ridge, Green End Lane, Radnage, Nr. Stokenchurch, Bucks., U.K.

2893. People's Trust for Endangered Species, 19 Quarry Street, Guildford, Surrey GU1 3EH, U.K.

2894. Performing Animals Defense League, 62a Chiswick High Road, London W4 15Y, England.

2895. Political Ecology Research Group (PERG), 34 Cowley Road, Oxford, U.K.

2896. Protect Our Livestock Group, The Court House, Newcourt Road, Charlton Kings, Cheltenham, Glos.

GL53 9AY, U.K. (Attempting
to stop export of live food
animals from the United Kingdom.

2897. Quaker Concern for Animal Welfare,
c/o Mrs. Angela Howard, Webb's
Cottage, Saling, Nr. Braintree,
Essex, CM7 5DZ, U.K.
QCAW exists to encourage Quakers
to witness against all forms of
ill-treatment and cruel exploitation of animals in accordance
with the advice to "let the law
of kindness know no limits. Show
a loving consideration for all
God's creatures."
Literature includes:
"Vivisection--Right or Wrong?" by
Frieda Le Pla.

2898. Radley College Animal Liberation
Society, Abingdon, Exon., U.K.

2899. Research Defense Society, 11
Chandor Street, Cavendish Square,
London W1M 9DE, England.
Issues Conquest periodically.
Literature includes:
"Why We Need Animal Research"
"Guidance Notes on the Law
Relating to Experiments
on Animals in Great Britain."

2900. Rock Against Bloodsports, 26 Denzil
Avenue, Newtown, Southampton, U.K.
By expressing our disapproval
of bloodsports through the medium
of rock music, we hope to share
the success that Rock Against
Racism had, in creating a greater
awareness of "the cause."

2901. Royal College of Physicians, 11
       St. Andrews Place, London NW 1
       4LE, England.

2902. Royal College of Physicians and
       Surgeons of Glasgow, 242 St.
       Vincent Street, Glasgow G2 5RJ,
       U.K.

2903. Royal College of Surgeons of Edin-
       burgh, 18 Nicholson Street,
       Edinburgh, U.K.

2904. Royal College of Surgeons of England,
       35-43 Lincoln's Inns Fields,
       London WC2A 3PN, England.

2905. Royal College of Veterinary Surgeons,
       32 Belgrave Square, London SW1X
       8QP, England.

2906. Royal Society, 6 Carlton House
       Terrace, London SW1, England.

2907. Royal Society for the Prevention
       of Cruelty to Animals, Causeway,
       Horsham, Sussex, RH12 1 HG,
       England.
       Issues:
           Humane Education Journal 3
           times a year.
           Animal Ways 5 times per year
           (for children 7-11)
           Animal World 5 times per year
           (for youth, 12-17)
           RSPCA Today 3 times per year.
       Annual Reports
       Literature includes:
           "RSPCA Policies on Animal Welfare,"
           which includes this Declaration
           of Animal Rights:

459

Inasmuch as there is ample
evidence that many animal
species are capable of
feeling, we condemn totally
the infliction of suffering
upon our fellow creatures
and the curtailment of their
behavioural and other needs
save where this is necessary
for their own individual
benefit.

We do not accept that a
difference in species alone
(any more than a difference
in race) can justify wanton
exploitation or oppression
in the name of science or
sport, or for use as food,
for commercial profit or
for other human gain.

We believe in the evolution-
ary and moral kinship of all
animals and declare our belief
that all sentient creatures
have rights to life, liberty
and natural enjoyments. We
therefore call for the protection of these rights.

Animal Welfare Pamphlets:
"Cats and Kittens"
"Dogs and Puppies"
"Horses and Ponies"
"Animal Travel"
"Donkeys"
"Goats"
"Aquaria"
"Tortoises and Terrapins"

460

"Hamsters"
"Gerbils"
"Guinea Pigs"
"Parrots and Tropical Birds"
"Rabbits"
"British Amphibia and Reptiles"
"Order of Service for Animal
    Welfare"
"Exotic Pets"
"Cruelty to Animals and the
    Law"
"Animal Experimentation"
"The Testing of Cosmetic
    and Toiletry Preparations"
"List of Firms Which Do Not
    Use Animals to Test Cosmetic
    Products"
"The LD/50 Test"
"Speciesism: The Ethics of
    Animal Abuse," by Richard
    D. Ryder
"The Tortoise Trade"
"The Slaughter of the Whale"
"Charter for Animals"
"The RSPCA Today"
"Price List and Catalogue"
"Report of the Panel of Enquiry
    into Shooting and Angling--
    1976-1979"
"100,000 Animals Used in Research
    Each Week"
"RSPCA Junior Membership"
"Who Cares for Animals"
"How Should You Cope with
    an Unfriendly Dog?"
"Films on Animal Welfare"
"Stop the Export of Live
    Food Animals"
"Prevent Unwanted Litters"
"Pets at Holiday Time"

461

"The Pet Owners' Code of Conduct"
"You and Your Puppy"
"Your Pet Budgie"
"First Aid for Your Dog"
"First Aid for Your Cat"
"First Aid for Animals Involved
in Road Accidents"
"RSPCA Policies on Animals
Welfare"
"The Case Against Killing Harp
Seal Pups in Canada"
"Performing Animals"
"On With the Circus--But not
Using Live Animals"
"Educational Materials and
Visual Aids"
In 1977, sponsored a symposium on
"Animal Rights" at Cambridge.
In 1978, sponsored a symposium on
"Animal Experimentation" in
London.
The Proceedings of these symposia
have been published and are
available from RSPCA.

2908.   Royal Society for the Protection of
Birds (RSPB), The Lodge, Sandy,
Bedfordshire SG19 2DL, U.K.

2909.   St. Andrew Animal Fund, 10 Queensferry Street, Edinburgh, Scotland
EH2 4PG. An organization to
promote humane attitudes towards
animal life and the development
of a proper understanding and
appreciation of all living things.

2910.   Save Our Stags, 1 Guernsey Avenue,
Broomhill, Bristol BS4 4SH, U.K.

West Country based group concerned
exclusively with stag hunting and
deer poaching. Sanctions the use
of direct action against deer
hunts.

2911. Science Association, Laboratory Animals,
Ltd., 7 Warwick Court, London, WC1
Issues Laboratory Animals journal
semi-annually.

2912. Scottish Anti-Vivisection Society,
121 West Regent Street, Glasgow,
Scotland, U.K.
The Objectives of the SAVS are:
the total suppression of vivisection on animals and uncon-
senting human adults, and the
promotion of kindness to and
protection of animals.

2913. Scottish Society for the Prevention
of Cruelty to Animals, 19 Melville
Street, Edinburgh, Scotland EH3
7PL. The Scottish SPCA Provides an
Inspectorate and full SPCA
services for the whole of Scotland including the Western Isles
but excluding Strathclyde.

2914. The Scottish Society for the Prevention of Vivisection, 10
Queensferry Street, Edinburgh EH2
4PG, Scotland.

Literature includes:
"Annual Pictorial Review"
"Animal Welfare Year in
Retrospect"

"Near Human Model for Research"
(Monkeys)
"Horror in Her Vanity Case" by
William Hamilton (Cosmetic
Tests)
"Experiments on Humans"
"Speciesism: The Ethics of
Vivisection" by Richard D.
Ryder
"Scientific Cruelty for Commer-
cial Profit" by Richard D.
Ryder
"A Scientist Speaks on the
Extensive Use of Animals in
Non-Medical Research" by
Richard D. Ryder
"Medical Opinions against Vivi-
section"
"Lord Dowding Speaks About
Animals"
"Experiments on Living Animals"
Cruelty to Animals Act 1876
"Two-Headed Dogs: Wrong-Headed
Scientists" by M. Beddow
Bayly
"Monkeys and Men" by M. Beddow
Bayly
"The Ziegler Monkey-Chair"
Address by Clive Hollands, World
Day of Prayer for Animals,
October 7, 1973
Address by the Right Reverend
Hugh Montefiore, World Day of
Prayer for Animals, October
3, 1976
"Is Mass Vaccination with B.C.G.
Always Warranted in the
Scandanavian Countries?"

2915. Sea Shepherd Fund, 16 Newton Terrace, Glasgow G3, Scotland, U.K. Trying to raise money to refloat the Sea Shepherd. Anti-Whaling.

2916. Seal Preservation Action Group, The Green Scarton, Longhope, By Stromness, Orkney KW16 3PQ, Scotland, U.K.

2917. Soap and Detergent Industry Association, P.O. Box 9, Hayes Gate House, Hayes, Middlesex, UB4 OJD, U.K.

2918. Society for the Abolition of Blood Sports, 109 Oxford Road, Manchester 1, U.K.

2919. Society for Drug Research, Chelsea College, Manresa Road, London SW3 6LX, England.

2920. Society for Experimental Biology, Harvest House, 62 London Road, Reading RG1 5AS, U.K.

2921. The Society for the Protection of Animals in North Africa (SPANA), 15 Buckingham Gate, London SW1E 6LB, England.

2922. Society of United Prayer for Animals, c/o Mrs. Chrisine Phillips, 145 Barry Rd., East Dulwich, London, SE22 OJP, England.

2923. Toxicol Laboratories Ltd., Bromyard Road, Ledbury, Herts, HR8 1LG, U.K.

2924. Traffic, 1 Marshall Street, London
W1, England. Information source
on the trade in endangered species.

2925. Universities Federation for Animal
Welfare, 8 Hamilton Close, South
Mimms, Potters Bar, Herts.,
EN6 3QD, U.K.
Issues Annual Report
Literature includes:
HANDBOOKS AND TECHNICAL PUBLICA-
TIONS
"Handbook on the Care and Manage-
ment of Laboratory Animals"
"Handbook on the Care and Manage-
ment of Farm Animals"
"Humane Killing of Crabs and
Lobsters"
"Predatory Mammals Britain
3rd Edition 1977"
"The Otter Report"
"Diseases of Animals Communi-
cable to Man," by W.N. Scott
"Live Animals in School Teaching,"
W.N. Scott
"Physiological Effects of Elec-
trical Stunning and Venesection
in the Fowl," by S.A. Richards
and A.H. Sykes
"The Status of Animals in the
Christian Religion," by C.W.
Hume
"The Neighbors," an animal
anthology compiled and illus-
trated by Fougasse
"An Introduction to the Anaes-
thesia of Laboratory Animals"
"Kind Killing"
"Humane Killing of Animals"

PROCEEDINGS OF UFAW SYMPOSIA-
1979 "The Humane Treatment of Food Animals in Transit"
1978 "The Welfare of Food Animals"
1977 "The Pharmaceutical Applications of Cell Culture Techniques"
1976 "The Welfare of Laboratory Animals: Legal, Scientific and Humane Requirements"
1975 "The Humane Destruction of Unwanted Animals"
1974 "Animals and the Law"
1974 "Transport of Farm Animals"
1972 "The Welfare and Management of Wild Animals in Captivity"
1971 "Humane Killing and Slaughterhouse Techniques"
1971 "The Rational Use of Living Systems in Bio-Medical Research"
1969 "The Humane Control of Animals Living in the Wild"
1969 "The Use of Animals in Toxicological Studies"
1968 "Sealing in U.K. and Canadian Waters"

INFORMATION LEAFLETS ON THE CARE OF ANIMALS-
(Particularly suitable for schools and pet owners)
"The Cat"
"The Dog"
"The Rabbit"
"Guinea Pigs"
"Hamsters and Gerbils"
"The Tortoise"
"Cage Birds"
" A Few Bird Friends of Ours"
"Poultry"

"Goats and Sheep"
"Cattle and Pigs"
"Horses and Donkeys"
"Mammals in Britain"
"The Goldfish"
"Cold Water Aquaria"
"The Rat and the Mouse"
"Reptiles and Amphibia"
REPRINTS OF PUBLISHED PAPERS
"Humane Considerations in the
Use of Experimental Animals,"
by W.N. Scott
"Control of Feral Cat Popu-
lations by Long Term Admin-
istration of Megestrol
Acetate," by J. Remfry
"The Slaughter of Poultry for
Human Consumption" by W.N.
Scott
"A Comparison of the Behavior
and Production of Laying Hens
in Experimental and Controlled
Battery Cages," J.E. Bareham
"The Control of Animal Exper-
imentation," by J. Remfry
"The Behavior of Lambs on the
First Day after Birth," J.R.
Bareham
"Observations on the Use of
Grottos by Mediterranean
Monk Seals," by J.U. Bareham
and A. Furreddu, S.J.
"Research in Farm Animal Behavior,"
J.R. Bareham
"Training in Laboratory Animal
Science," (Summary), by P.M.Ray
"Animal Health in the EEC," by
P.M. Ray and W.N. Scott
"Effects of Cages and Semi-Inten-
sive Deep Litter Pens on the
Behavior, Adrenal Response
and Production in Two Strains

of Laying Hens," by J.R.
Bareham

2926. Vegan Views, 1 Gincroft Lane,
Edenfield, Ramsbottom, Bury,
Lancashire BLO OJW, U.K.

2927. The Vegan Society, 47 Highlands
Road, Leatherhead, Surrey,
U.K.
Issues The Vegan quarterly.
Literature includes:
"The Power of Kindness"
"Two Population Explosions:
Humans and Domestic Animals"
"What Happens to the Calf?"
"Is Cow Milk Good Food?"
"Blueprint for a Humane World"
"Pioneers of the New Age:
Twelve Vegans"
"Vegan Mothers and Children"
"The Reasons for Veganism"
"What's Cooking?", by Eva Batt
"Introduction to Practical
Veganism"
"Vegan Nutrition" by T.A.B.
Sanders and Frey R. Ellis
"Plant Foods for Human Health,"
Prof. Dickerson
"In Lighter Vein," Eva Batt
(Poetry)
"Saladings from the Garden"
Mabel Cluer
"Practical Veganism"
"First Hand--First Rate"

2928. Vegetarian and Animal Liberation
Society, c/o Gillian Whibley,
12 Antigua Street, Edinburgh 1,
Scotland, U.K.

Recently established as an Edinburgh University society. Non-
students are welcome.

2929. Vegetarian Centre and Bookshop,
53 Marloes Road, Kensington,
London, W8 6LA, England.

2930. The Vegetarian Society, Parkdale,
Dunham Road, Altrincham, Cheshire,
WA 14 4QG, U.K. Vegetarian Centre
and Bookshop at 53 Marloes Road,
Kensington, London, W86LA, England.
Issues Alive journal bi-monthly.
Literature includes:
"World Food Production in Balance"
"Three Myths: The Vegetarian
    Answer"
"Vegetarianism"
"The Bible and Vegetarianism"
"Was the Master a Vegetarian?"
"Vegetarianism for You"
"Vegetarianism: Diets for Cats
    and Dogs"
"The Rights of Animals," by
    Brigid Brophy
"Vegetarianism: The Ethics"
"Vegetarianism: Infant Feeding"
"Vegetarianism: Slimplan"
"Vegetarianism: Well-Being of the
    Elderly"
"Vegetarianism: The World Food
    Problem"
"Outline of Vegetarian Nutrition"
"International Vegetarian Health-
    food Handbook"
"Vegetarian Cookbook," by Doreen
    Keighley
"Vegetarian Cuisine," by Isabel
    James
"On Behalf of the Creatures,"
    by Jack W. Lucas

470

"First Steps in Vegetarian
Cookery," by Kathy Silk
"Books and Things"
"Vegetarianism: Basic Recipes"
"Vegetarianism: Wholemeal
Recipes"
"Vegetarianism: Just for One"
"Vegetarianism and Health"
"CAMREB: The Campaign for Real
Bread and Flour"
"The Price of Meat These Days
Is Sheer Murder"
"Easy Meatless Recipes"
"Recipes Based on Pulses"
"Cheap and Cheerful: Alterna-
tive Eating on a Budget,"
by Joanna Lawton
"Meals in a Moment:Quick Cook-
ing Without Meat," by Joanna
Lawton
"London Vegetarian Restaurant
List"
"Other London Restaurants Serv-
ing Vegetarian Dishes"
"Information Sheet for Teachers
and Students"

2931.   Vegetarians Against the Nazis,
13 Upper Addison Gardens,
London, W 14, England.

2932.   Vegfam, The Santuary, Lyford, Oke-
hampton, Devon, U.K. (The vegetarian counterpart of Oxfam,
the British hunger relief organization.)

2933.   Whale People, 171 Peckham Rye East,
London SE15, England, London-
based non-violent activists for
whales.

2934.   Willowtree Sanctuary for the Welfare
of Animals, c/o Miss P. Townsend,
Gainsford End, Nr. Topplesfield,
Halstead, Essex, U.K.

2935.   World League Against Vivisection,
3A North View, Wimbledon Common,
London, S.W. 19, England.
Issues Animals' Champion and the
Way to Health periodically.

2936.   World Wildlife Fund, Panda House,
29 Greville Street, London
ED1N, 8AX, England.

2937.   Young Indian Vegetarians, 25 Lynd-
hurst Road, Thornton Heath,
Surrey, U.K.

2938.   Zoological Society of London, Zoological Gardens, Regents Park,
London NW1 4RY, England.

VIII. Organizations Interested in Animals
United States

2939. Academy of Pharmaceutical Sciences, 2215 Constitution Ave., N.W., Washington, D.C. 20037

2940. African-American Vegetarian Network, 163-38 145th Road, Jamaica, N.Y. 11434

2941. African Wildlife Leadership Foundation, 1717 Massachusetts Ave., N.W., Washington, D.C. 20036 AWLF works for wildlife conservation in Africa. It is cooperating with the International Primate Protection League to put an end to the poaching of mountain gorillas in Rwanda.

2942. Afro-American Vegetarian Society c/o Ron Davis, Pres., Apt 9-B 159-14 Harlem River Drive, New York, NY 10039

2943. American Anti-Vivisection Society, Suite #204 Noble Plaza, 801 Old York Road, Jenkintown, Pa., 19046 Monthly journal: The AV Magazine Literature includes:
"Stop--Why We Oppose Vivisection"
"Cruel, Brutal, Futile"
"People and Principles Make A-V History"
"Moment of Truth"
"Human Diploid Cells in Making Vaccines"
"Man's Animal Helpers"
"The Humane Movement as a Movement of Thought"
"Death of a Vivisectionist"
"Diabetes Mellitus"

"The Rabies Racket"
"One Doctor's Views on Vivi-
section"
"Useless Vaccines Stay on the
Market"
"The Young Vivisectors"
"Pavlov's Techniques of Terror"
"Vivisection: Subject Matter
of Nightmares"
"Mad Dogs and Medicine Men"

2944. American Association for Accreditation of Laboratory Animal Care,
2317 W. Jefferson St., Suite 135,
Joliet, IL 60435.

2945. American Association for Laboratory
Animal Science, 2317 West Jefferson
St., Suite 208, Joliet, IL 60435.
Issues AALAS Bulletin periodically
Issues Laboratory Animal/Science
Bi-monthly
Literature includes:
"Careers in Laboratory Animal
Technology".

2946. American College of Radiology, 20
North Wacker Drive, Chicago, IL
60606.

2947. American College of Surgeons, 55
East Erie Street, Chicago, IL
60611.

2948. American Dairy Association, 6300
North River Rd., Rosemont, IL
60018.

2949. American Dairy Science Association,
309 West Clark St., Champaign,
IL 61820.

2950. American Egg Board, 1460 Renaissance,
Park Ridge, IL 60068.

2951.   American Fund for Alternatives to
Animal Research, c/o Thurston,
175 West 12th Street, New York,
N.Y.   10011
The American Fund for Alternatives to Animal Research (AFAAR)
stimulates and encourages the
development of research and testing methods without the use of
live animals in fields where
animals are presently used.   It
does this mainly by funding
research grants.   The projects
must be likely to lead to the
prevention or alleviation
of human or animal suffering.
Furthermore, the project shall
not at any stage involve the use
of live animals for experimental
purposes.
Issues AFAAR News periodically
Literature includes:
   "Animal Experiments and
      Tissue Culture: Comparative
      Costs"
   "The Role of the American Fund
      for Alternatives to Animal
      Research"
   "Laboratory Animals and Politics"
      by Richard D. Ryder
   "The Use of Animals in Experi-
      mental Psychology," by Alice
      Heim
   "The Shocking Truth About Cos-
      metic Tests on Animals," by
      Jon Evans
   "The Use of Protozoa for Screen-
      ing of Drugs and Metabolites,"
      by Oscar Frank

475

"Animal Experiments, the
Law and the Public," by
The Rt. Hon. Lord Houghton
of Sowerby
"An Alternative to Animals
for Assessing Tumorigen-
icity," by John Petricciani
"Progress Without Pain,"
Alex Szogyi
"News Abstracts"

2952.   American Fur Industry, 855 Avenue
of the Americas, New York, N.Y.
10001
Literature includes:
"Fur--Now More Than Ever"
"Naturally"

2953.   American Genetic Association,
1028 Connecticut Ave., N.W.
Washington, D.C. 20036

2954.   American Hereford Association,
715 Hereford Drive, Kansas City,
Missouri, 64105
Literature includes:
"The Future Cattleman"

2955.   American Horse Protection Association, 1312 18th St. NW,
Washington, D.C. 20036
The American Horse Protection
Association, Inc., is a
national non-profit, tax-
exempt organization dedicated
entirely to the welfare of
horses both wild and domestic.
It works for the enforcement
of all humane legislation for
both wild and domestic horses.

2956.   American Humane Association,
        5351 South Roslyn Street,
        Englewood, Co.
        Issues <u>American Humane Magazine</u>
        monthly.
        Literature includes:
          Pamphlets:
          "Dogs"
          "Cats"
          "Birds"
          "Fish"
          "Horses"
          "Small Mammals"
          "Riding Horses"
          "Outdoor Dog"
          "Animal Epidemic"
          "Stop! Protect Pets!
            Protect Yourself!"
          "You--Cruel to Your
            Pet?"
          "Sit Heel Down Stay Come"
          Teacher's Aids
          "Teacher's Guide on Pet
            Owner Responsibility"
          "Care and Management of
            Animal Visitors at School"
          "'Animals in Art' Kindness
            Contest Guidelines"
          "Pets-n-Care Kit"
          "Guidelines: School Science
            Projects"
          Flyers
          "Overpopulation"
          "Rescue Me From This Hot
            Car"
          Special Publications
          "The Hearing Dog"
          "The Caring Society"
          "Command-and Final-Performance:
            Animals in the Film Industry"

"Memo of Understanding"
"Red Cross Agreement"
Agency Materials
"Operational Guide" (includes
all updated supplements)
"Developing A Junior Humane
Organization"
Studies and Reports:
"Proceedings of the National
Conference on the Ecology
of the Surplus Dog and
Cat Problem"
"Proceedings of the National
Conference on Cat and Dog
Control" (1976)
"Agency Directory"
"Clearinghouse Directory for
Humane Education Materials"

2957.   The American Humane Education
Society, 450 Salem End Road,
Framingham, MA 01701.
Issues The Course of Humane
Events newsletter periodically
(jointly with Massachusetts
Society for the Prevention of
Cruelty to Animals)
Literature includes:
"The Animal Connection:
A Teacher's Guide to
Humane Education"
"Living with Animals"

2958.   American Institute of Biological
Sciences, 1401 Wilson Blvd.,
Arlington, VA   22209.

2959.   American Meat Institute, P.O. Box
3556, Washington, D.C. 20007.

Literature includes:
"Meatfacts; A Statistical
Summary about America's
Largest Food Industry"
"Nitrite"
"Keeping Meat Fresh"
"The Other Half of the Animal:
A Commentary on Meat Animal
Byproducts"

2960.   American Medical Association,
535 N. Dearborn St., Chicago,
IL 60610

2961.   American Pharmaceutical Association,
2215 Constitution Ave., N.W.,
Washington, D.C. 20037

2962.   American Physiological Society,
9650 Rockville Pike, Bethesda,
Md. 20014

2963.   American Psychological Association,
1200 Seventeenth Street, N.W.,
Washington, D.C. 20036
Literature includes:
"Ethical Principles in the
Conduct of Research with
Human Participants"
"Ethical Standards of Psychol-
ogists"
"Graduate Study in Psychology"
"Career Opportunities for
Psychologists"
"Casebook on Ethical Standards
of Psychologists"
"Principles for the Care and
Use of Animals"
Issues the APA Monitor periodically.

2964.   American Registry of Certified
        Animal Scientists, 113 N. Neil
        St., Champaign, IL   61820.
        Issues Animal Industry Today
        periodically.

2965.   American Sheep Producer Council,
        200 Clayton St., Denver, CO
        80206.

2966.   American Society for the Prevention
        of Cruelty to Animals, 441 East
        92nd Street, New York, N.Y.   10028.
        Issues ASPCA Bulletin period-
        ically.
        Daggett, Herman, "The Rights
        of Animals," an oration
        delivered at Providence
        College, September 7, 1791.
        Reprinted by the American
        Society for the Prevention of
        Cruelty to Animals, 1926.
        13 p. (Is catalogued in Univer-
        sity of Minnesota Library,
        179.3 D132.)
        Literature includes:
           "Battle of the Puddle"
           (Hints on Housebreaking)
           "First Aid Hints"
           "The Horse" (Anatomy and Tack)
           "The Horse's Prayer"
           "External Regions of the
           Horse"
           "Henry Bergh" (The Man Who
           Started the ASPCA)
           "Choose Your Pet--Pethood or
           Parenthood"
           "What You Should Know About
           Canine Distemper"
           "What You Should Know About
           Rabies"

"What You Should Know About
   Canine Heartworm Disease"
"Your Pet's Health" (Distemper
   Discussion)
"Dear Mr. ASPCA" (Letters from
   school children)
"Small Animal Care"
"Horses, Ponies, Burros"
"How to Build a Doghouse"
"ASPCA Guide to Pet Care"
"Traveling with Your Pet"

2967. American Society of Laboratory
       Animal Practitioners (ASLAP)
       c/o Dr. Ronald L. Bell, Secre-
       tary-Treasurer, The Ohio State
       University, College of Medicine,
       333 West 10th Avenue, Columbus,
       Ohio 43210.

2968. American Society of Primatologists,
       c/o O.A. Smith, Regional
       Primate Research Center SJ-50
       University of Washington,
       Seattle, WA 98195.

2969. American Society of Zoologists,
       Bos 2739, California Lutheran
       College, Thousand Oaks, CA 91360.

2970. American Vegan Society, 501 Old
       Harding Highway, Malaga, N.J. 08328.
       Issues _Ahimsa_ magazine semi-
       annually.
       Literature includes:
         "Here's Harmlessness"
         "Health Can Be Harmless"
         "Out of the Jungle: Special
            Schweitzer Centennial
            Edition"

"What Happens to the
Calf?"
"Why Veganism?"
"How to Be a Total
Vegetarian"
"The Protein Problem"
"Second-Hand Foods:
Carnivorism and Food
From Animals"
"Two Population Explosions:
Human and Domestic
Animals"
"The Vegan Cookbook," by
Freya Dinshah
"The Vegan Kitchen" by
Freya Dinshah

2971. American Vegetarians, Box 32323,
Washington, D.C. 20007.

2972. American Veterinary Medical
Association, 930 North Meacham
Road, Schaumberg, Il., 60196.
Literature includes:
"Programs in Animal Tech-
nology"
"Animal Technology"

2973. Animal Behavior Society, National
Zoological Park, Washington,
D.C. 20008.

2974. Animal Health Institute, 1717
K St., N.W., Suite 1009,
Washington, D.C. 20006.

2975. Animal-Kind, 1627 Main St., Kansas
City, Mo. 64108.

2976. Animal Liberation, Inc., 319
       West 74th Street, New York,
       N.Y. 10023
       Literature includes:
       "Vegetarianism: A Selected
          Reading List," compiled
          by Dudley Giehl.

2977. Animal Protection Institute of
       America, 5894 South Land Park
       Drive, P.O. Box 22505, Sac-
       ramento, Ca. 95822.
       Issues Mainstream quarterly.
       Literature includes:
          "How to Care for Your Pet"
          "First Aid for Dogs and Cats"
          "The Pet Population Tragedy"
          "Help Save the Great Whales"
          "14 Ways You Can Help Save
             Wildlife"
          "Horse Care"
          "Finding Good Homes for Pets"
          "How to Become Actively
             Involved in Your Community
             for the Animals"
          "Proposed Course Outline for
             Ethics and Experimentation"

2978. Animal Rights Club, United Nations
       Staff Recreation Council,
       United Nations, P.O. Box 20,
       Grand Central Station, New York
       N.Y. 10017
       The ARC was established in
       1977 by a group of United
       Nations employees to promote
       animal rights through lectures,
       discussions, distribution of
       literature, participation in
       demonstrations, letter-writing,

exchange of information with
other AR organizations and
individuals and common action
with them (when feasible),
etc. The ARC is not an
official organ of the UN.
Issues The Animal Rights
Journal bi-monthly.

2979. Animal Rights Network, Inc.,
P.O. Box 5234, Westport, CT
06880. Animal Rights Network
(ARN) pursues the animal liberation philosophy as set forth
in Peter Singer's 1974 book of
the same name. It is a movement-building organization
whose primary aim is to act as
coordinating body within the
movement for fair treatment of
animals. Through the use of
publications it aims to: (1)
promote unity within an otherwise fragmented archipelago of
animal rights/welfare groups;
(2) establish a communications
network among existing national
and international pro-animal
concerns; (3)work to establish
mutual respect for and cooperation with other progressive
organizations to include women's
and minority rights groups,
anti-nuclear and other related
organizations struggling for
political, social and economic
justice.
Issues Animal Rights Network
News bimonthly.

Literature includes:
Love and Anger: An Organizing Manual for Animal Rights Activists, by Richard Morgan.

2980. Animal Welfare Institute, P.O. Box 3650, Washington, D.C. 20007.
Issues Information Report quarterly.
Literature includes:
"Animal Expressions: A Photographic Footnote to Charles Darwin's Expressions of the Emotions in Man and Animals"
"Animals and Their Legal Rights"
"The Neighbors: An Anthology of Animal Poems"
"The Status of Animals in the Christian Religion"
"Let Us Live" (on trapping)
"Facts About Furs"
"Predator Control"
"Federal Measures Against the Abuse of Wild Animals"
"Dognapping"
"Comfortable Quarters for Laboratory Animals"
"Modular Kennels for Laboratory Animals"
"The Principles of Humane Experimental Technique"
"Towards the Ideal in an Animal Shelter"
"Humane Slaughter"
"The Rational Use of Living Systems in Bio-Medical Research"

"More About Alternatives"
"Human Considerations for
   Animal Models"
"Human Perspectives"
"The Bird Business. A Study of
   the Importation of Birds into
   the United States," by Greta
   Nilsson
"Beyond Adequate Veterinary
   Care"
"Basic Care of Experimental
   Animals"
"Humane Biology Projects"
"First Aid and Care of Small
   Animals"
"Canada's Experience with
   Student Use of Living
   Animals"
"Regulations for Animal
   Experimentation in Science
   Fairs"
"Live Organisms in High School
   Biology"
"Attitudes toward Animals"
"Sanctified Torture"
"Administrative Control Over
   Science Fair Projects"
"Biology Students as Exper-
   imental Subjects"
"Statement on Animals in
   Secondary Schools"
" Physical and Mental Suffer-
   ing of Experimental Animals:
   A Review of Scientific
   Literature, 1975-1978."

2981. Animals Need You, Inc., P.O.
   Box 65, West New York, NJ
   07093. Animals Needs You is a
   non-profit animal welfare organization. It is a humane

education group, not a
shelter or pound. Issues a
bimonthly newsletter.

2982. Anti-Cruelty Society, 157 W.
Grand Ave., Chicago, Illinois
60610.

2983. Anti-Vivisection Society of New
York, 40 West 59th Street, New
York, NY 10019. The Society
protests cruel laboratory experiments on animals and deplores
the abuse of beagles in painful
experiments with poison gas and
forced inhalation of ciga-
rette smoke. It also objects
to experiments on any human
being without that individual's
informed consent.

2984. Argus Archives, 228 East 49th St.,
New York, N.Y. 10017.
In its archives Argus maintains
active files on over five hundred
organizations in the US and abroad.
The files contain publications of
these organizations dealing with
animal suffering or conditions
which affect the well-being of
animals. There is a related
collection of books, magazines,
newspaper clippings and film
reviews. Writers, researchers and members of organizations engaged in humane work
or conservation are welcome
to consult the archives by
appointment.

Literature includes:
"Films for Humane Education"
"Traps and Trapping--Fur and
Fashion"
"Painful Experiments on Animals
and the Alternatives"
"Unwanted Pets and the Animal
Shelter--The Pet Population
Problem in New York State"

2985. Associated Human Societies,
124 Evergreen Avenue, Newark,
NJ   07114.

2986. Association for Pet Facilitated
Therapy, 1230 Grant Avenue,
Box 203, San Francisco, Ca.,
94133.

2987. Attorneys for Animal Rights,
c/o Laurence W. Kessenick,
One Kearney St., San Francisco,
Ca.   94108.

2988. Attorneys for Animal Rights
(Los Angeles), c/o Marcelle
Philpott-Bryant, 234 E.
Colorado Blvd., Suite 620
Pasadena, CA   91101.

2989. Beauty Without Cruelty, 175
West 12th Street, New York,
N.Y.   10011.
Issues News Abstracts period-
ically.
Literature includes:
"The Compassionate Shopper"
(Lists stores in the United
States where Beauty Without
Cruelty cosmetics are sold.)
"Information on Soaps, Shampoos,

Cosmetics, Perfumes and
Household Products"
"Beauty Without Cruelty
Cosmetics and Toilet-
ries" (Price list and
retail order form avail-
able from Mrs. Lynn
Zimmerman, 2577 South
Superior Street, Milwau-
kee, Wisconsin, 53207)
"Don't Let Them Pull the
Wool Over Your Eyes,"
by Freya Dinshah
"Wool Factories," by Eva
Batt
"Letter from an Ex-trapper"
"Boycott Meat to Save the
Animals"
"Please Excuse Me for Ap-
proaching You" (Furs
and Trapping)
Distributes Compassion, the
official journal of Beauty
Without Cruelty (publish-
ed in England.)

2990. The Beaver Defenders, Unexpected
Wildlife Refuge, Inc., Newfield, N.J. 08344.

2991. Berks County Vegetarian Society,
R.D. 1--Box 53-A, Barto, PA
19504.

2992. Better Health and Nutrition So-
ciety of Palm Beach, 707
Chillingworth Drive, West
Palm Beach, FLA 33409.

2993.   The Bide-A-Wee Home Association,
        410 East 38th Street, New
        York, NY 10016.   The Bide-A-
        Wee Home Association, a refuge
        for friendless animals, was
        founded in 1903 on the prin-
        ciple: "We never destroy an
        animal unless incurably ill."

2994.   The Breach Foundation, P.O. Box
        855, Sausalito, CA 94965.
        The Breach Foundation is a non-
        profit, member supported organ-
        ization.   The purpose of the
        foundation is to safe-guard
        marine mammals, especially
        whales and dolphins.

2995.   Bucks County Vegetarians, Box 909,
        Southampton, PA 18966.

2996.   The Buffalo Animal Rights Commit-
        tee, State University of New
        York at Buffalo, Buffalo, NY
        14214.
        Literature includes:
          "In Defense of the Earth's
            Creatures"
          "The Animal Connection"
            Extending Moral Treat-
            ment to Members of Other
            Species," by Walter
            Simpson

2997.   Cats and Cat Owners Aid Inc.,
        26 Aubrey Road, Upper Mont-
        clair, NJ 07043.

2998.   Catskill Vegetarian Society,
        Attn: Muriel G. Collura, Box
        657, South Fallsburg, NY 12779.

2999. Central Florida Vegetarian
Society, P.O. Box 31, Uma-
tilla, Florida 32784.

3000. The Charles River Breeding
Laboratories, Inc., Corpo-
rate Headquarters, 251 Ballard-
vale St., Wilmington, MA 01887.
(See entries under the name
Henry L. Foster: 1459, 1472,
1650)
Issues Charles River Digest
quarterly.
Charles River Portage, Shaver
Road, P.O. Box 176, Portage,
Michigan 49081.
Charles River Kingston, Route
209, Box 241, Stoneridge,
NY 12484.
Charles River Lakeview, Wey-
mouth Road, P.O. Box 85,
Newfield, NJ 08344.
Primate Imports Corporation,
34 Munson Street, Port
Washington, NY 11050.
Key Lots Inc., U.S. Highway
1, Summerland Key, Florida
33042.
Charles River France, S.A.,
B.P. 29, 76410 St. Augin-
les-Elbeut, France.
Canadian Breeding Farm & Lab-
oratories Ltd., 188 La
Salle, St. Constant, Quebec,
Canada.
Charles River Italia, S.p.A.,
Via Indipendenza 11, 22050
Calco, Italy.
Charles River Japan, Atsugi,
Japan.

Charles River U.K. Ltd.
Margate, Kent, U.K.

3001. Chemical Industry Institute of
Toxicology, P.O. Box 12137,
Research Triangle Park, NC
27709.

3002. Chicago Vegetarian Society, P.O.
Box 1068, Chicago, Illinois
60690.

3003. Citizens for Animals, 421 S.
State St., Clarks Summit,
PA 18411.
The national political/lobby
arm of Society for Animal
Rights, Inc.

3004. Coalition to End Animal Suffering
in Experiments (CEASE), P.O. Box
2711, Woburn, MA 01888.
Coalition to End Animal Suffering in Experiments (CEASE) is a
non-profit, all-volunteer
activist organization whose
members possess common ded-
ication to the liberation of
animals from suffering caused
by the gross abuse inherent in
current laboratory experimentation and testing methods. The
group feels that experimentation
is the most abhorrent form of
human tyranny over nonhumans.

3005. Committee for Humand Legislation,
Inc., 2101 L Street, N.W.
Washington, D.C. 20037.

The Committee for Humane Legislation is the lobbying arm
of Friends of Animals, a non-
profit, national animal rights
and welfare organization head-
quartered in New York City.
Literature includes:
"Model State Animal Protection Statutes"
"Extinct Is Forever"
"The Pittman-Robertson Act--
Fifty-five Questions and
Answers"
"A Time To Choose: Beauty
or Brutality"

3006. The Committee to Abolish Sport
Hunting, Inc., P.O. Box 65,
West New York, N.J. The
Committee is an activist
organization designed to in-
form the public of the ecological impact and damages to
our wildlife heritage caused
by "sport hunting" and the
concomitant wildlife management policies. It also takes
special interest in the philosophic implications and
consequences of these activities, and advocates available
ecologically positive alternatives.

3007. Cosmetic, Toiletry and Fragrance
Association, 1133 15th St.,
N.W., Washington, D.C. 20005.

3008.   Defenders of Animal Rights, Inc.
P.O. Box 4786, Baltimore,
Maryland, 21211.
Issues Newsletter periodically.
Literature includes:
"Why We Are Vegetarians"
"The Case Against Hunting"

3009.   Defenders of Wildlife, 1244
Nineteenth Street, N.W.,
Washington, D.C. 20036.
Literature includes:
"Predator Control: A
National Disaster"
Issues Defenders Magazine
Bimonthly.

3010.   Environmental Defense Fund,
475 Park Avenue South, New
York, New York 10016.

3011.   Fairfield County Vegetarian
Society, c/o Bradley Smith,
93 Westport Road, Wilton,
Connecticut   06897.

3012.   The Farm, Summertown, Tennessee
38483.
Literature includes:
"Yay Soybeans: How You Can
Eat Better for Less and
Help Feed the World"
"The Farm Vegetarian Cook-
book"

3013.   Federation of American Scientists,
307 Massachusetts Avenue, NE.
Washington, D.C. 20002.

Issues F.A.S. Newsletter
periodically.   Vol. 30,
No. 8, October 1977 was
a special issue:
Animal Rights.

3014.   Federation of American Societies
for Experimental Biology,
9650 Rockville Pike, Bethesda,
MD 20014.

3015.   Foundation for Nutritional Re-
search, c/o Anna Massy, 722
East 102nd Street, Brooklyn,
New York 12236.

3016.   Friends of Animals, Inc.,
11 West 60th Street, New York,
N.Y. 10023.
Friends of Animals, Inc., (FOA)
is a national non-profit organ-
ization founded in 1957.
Literature includes:
"The Case Against Leghold
Traps"
"Some Things You're Not Suppos-
ed to Know About Hunting"
"Boycott Tuna"
"Animal Protective Legislation,
Model Laws for States" (James
Mason)
"Have Your Pet Spayed"
"Save the Animals"
"Factory Farming"
"Is This The Trap That Caught
Your Coat?"
"Rodeo"
"Animal Liberation" by Peter
Singer (reprint)

"Animal Experimentation"
"A Time to Choose...
    Beauty or Brutality"
"U.S. Seal Slaughter--
    The Facts"
In 1977-78, Friends of Animals,
Inc. granted three Regina
Bauer Frankenberg Scholarship
Awards for essays written on
"Why Should Congress, on Behalf
of the People, the Animals and
the Environment, Ban the Leg-
Hold Trap?"
Winners were:
  (1) Anne E. Reiner, Dallas,
      Texas, essay entitled
      "The Trap."
  (2) Robert Dingman, Moor-
      head State University,
      Moorhead, Minn., essay
      entitled, "The Question
      of Trapping."
  (3) Valerie L. Egar, Titus-
      ville, N.J., essay
      entitled "Ban the Leg-
      Hold Trap Now: Testimony
      to the Congress of the
      United States."
The 1978-1979 Essay Contest
was on the topic: "Why Should
the Congress End Funding of
Research and Education Programs
that Involve the Use of Animals
and Divert These Funds to Alternative Methods?"
Under the Freedom of Information Act, Friends of Animals,
Inc. has secured detailed
reports of federally funded

research grants involving experiments on animals. These
reports are being analyzed
by over 500 physicians and
scientists, the analysis .
to be submitted to interested members of Congress and
also publicized elsewhere.

3017. Friends of the Earth, 124
Spear St., San Francisco,
CA 94105.
Issues Not Man Apart period-
ically.
Literature includes:
"Whale Manual: 1978"

3018. Fruitarian Network, Box 4333,
Washington, D.C. 20012.

3019. The Fund for Animals, Inc.,
140 West 57th Street,
New York, N.Y. 10019
Issues The Fund for Animals
bulletin periodically.
Has practiced direct confron-
tation, especially in seal
hunt and whaling.
Literature includes:
"So You Want to Do Something
About Cruelty"
"So You Want to Help the
Animals and You're Only
Nine Years Old"
"So You Want to Do Something
about Over-Population of
Animals"
"So You Want to Start a
Shelter"
"So You Want to Help Strays"

"So You Want to Help the
Tennessee Walking Horse"
"So You Want to Help Wild
Animals"
"So You Want to Do Some-
thing About Zoos"
"So You Want to Do Some-
thing About Trapping"
"Save the Whales"
"A Hunter Tells the Truth
about Trapping"
"Zoo Animals Have Rights
Too"
" I Could Have Been a Dog-
Napper"
"Do Not Adopt for the
Summer Only"
"Must We Use Torture to
Get Fur Coats?"
"How Man Gets His Best
Friend to Run Like
Crazy" (Greyhound
racing)
"Saving the Dolphins"
"A Last Chance for America's
Wolves"
"Fund Zeroes in on Zoos"
"Amory's Book, A Call to
All: End the War on Wild-
life Now! "
"Confrontation with the
Russians-A Fund Eye Wit-
ness Report"

3020.   Fur and Trapping Ethics (FATE),
P.O. Box 7283, Minnneapolis,
Minn., 55407.
Issues FATE: Fur and Trapping
Ethics bulletin period-
ically.

Literature includes:
"Who Speaks for Them?"
"The Leghold Trap:
  Questions and Answers"

3021. Fur Takers of America, 3057
Nettie Drive, St. Louis,
Mo. 63129.
Issues monthly F.T.A. Journal.
Literature includes:
"Is Mother Nature Humane?"
"Educational Brochure of
  Primer Trapping"

3022. General Whale, P.O. Box Save
the Whale, Alameda, California
94501.
Produce whale awareness advertisements, education packs for
schools, exhibits, public
service announcements for
radio, press and tv, jewelry
and life-size whale sculp-
tures.

302 3. The Gorilla Foundation, 700
Middle Avenue, Menlo Park,
Ca. 94025.
Issues Gorilla periodical
  journal.

3024. Greenpeace Foundation, 860
Second Street, San Francisco,
CA 94107. Has used non-
violent confrontation tactics,
especially in seal hunt and
whaling.

3025. Harvard/Radcliffe Vegetarian
Association, Attn: John

Stern, Winthrop E-32, Harvard
University, Cambridge, MA
02138.

3026. Henry Spira, 1 West 85th Street,
New York, N.Y. 10024. Mr.
Spira might well be classified
as a one-person organization.
He organized demonstrations
at the American Museum of
Natural History, with the
result that the experiments
on the sex life of cats (funded by the National Institutes
of Health) were stopped. He
organized a coalition which
played a leading role in
repealing New York's Metcalf
Hatch Act, an act which au-
thorized medical research laboratories to requisition dogs
and cats from pounds. He is
also active in the Coalition
to Stop the Draize Rabbit
Blinding Tests, 507 Fifth Avenue, N.Y., N.Y. 10017, focusing
on Revlon, Inc.
Articles by Henry Spira
include:
"Killing Cats Isn't the Way
to Spend Our Tax $$,"
Health Street Journal,
Vol. 1, No. 1, October, 1978.
"Metcalf-Hatch Act: Profit,
Politics and Pain," Our
Town, Manhattan's Weekly
Newspaper, March 18, 1979.
"Born To Be Killed" (Mr.
Spira criticizes many

animal welfare and humane
societies as really being
slaughterhouses, killing
factories).
"Animals Have Feelings Too",
The Liberator, Haaren
High School, New York
City, Vol. 8, No. 6,
January 20, 1975.
"Metcalf-Hatch Repeal Means
Lab Accountability,"
Our Town, April 29, 1979.
"Amnesty for Animals,"
Our Town, October 22, 1978.
"Congress Pays for Sex Sadism
at Museum," Our Town Supp-
lement, August 20, 1976.
"Animals Suffer for Science:
Two Billion Government
Dollars Spent Annually for
Experimentation," Our Town
July 23, 1976.
"Animal Feelings and Animal
Rights,"
"Amnesty International
Scandal," Our Town, Oc-
tober 28, 1977.
"The Meek Don't Make It:
Notes of an Animal Activ-
ist," The Beast, No. 3,
October-November, 1977.
"Is Another Revlon Shampoo
Worth Blinding Rabbits?"
Part I, Our Town, March 23,
1980.
"Is Another Revlon Shampoo
Worth Blinding Rabbits?"
Part II, Our Town, March 30,
1980.

3027. The Humane Crusade, P.O. Box
       31, Maryland Line, MD 21105.
       The Crusade believes that
       only through an ever-growing
       awareness of shockingly true
       facts can and <u>will</u> the pub-
       lic bring an end to such
       atrocities.

3028. Humane Information Services, Inc.,
       4495 Ninth Avenue North, St.
       Petersburg, Florida 33713.
       Issues <u>Report to Humanitarians</u>
       quarterly.
       Literature includes:
         "The Poultry and Egg Indus-
           try: Mechanized Cruelty"
         "How to Increase Shelter
           Adoptions"
         "Good News about Humane
           Slaughter"
         "Can Anything Be Done to
           Stop Rodeos?"
         "Veal Calves and Factory
           Farming"
         "Rapid Decompression in
           High Altitude Chambers--
           Humane or Cruel?"

3029. Humane Society of the United
       States, 2100 L Street,
       N.W. Washington, D.C. 20037.
       The Society (HSUS) is a
       national, non-profit organ-
       ization for the prevention of
       cruelty to animals. It is
       active in virtually every
       area of animal protection,
       including cruelty investi-
       gations, shelter inspec-
       tions, legislation affecting

animals, humane education,
attacking the major national
cruelties, marine mammal pro-
tection and domestic, compan-
ion animal, and wildlife
protection.
Issues:
  The Humane Society News
    quarterly.
  Kind, 6 times per year
    (children).
  Close-Up Reports, 4 times
    a year
  Humane Education, quarter-
    ly, published by HSUS's
    National Association for
    the Advancement of Humane
    Education Center.
  Shelter Sense, bi-monthly,
    published by HSUS's Nat-
    ional Association for
    the Advancement of Hum-
    ane Education Center.
ANIMAL RIGHTS AND HUMAN OBLI-
  GATIONS
  Members and constituents of
  The Humane Society of the
  United States, assembled
  in the Annual Conference
  in Dearborn, Michigan, on
  this 14th day of October,
  1978, do hereby proclaim,
  by resolution, with reference to animal rights and
  human obligations, that
  animals possess certain inalienable and legally pro-
  tectable rights, and mankind
  and his governments possess
  certain inalienable and
  enforceable obligations

and duties with respect
thereto, as follows:
1. Animals have the right
   to live and grow under
   conditions that are
   comfortable and reason-
   ably natural;
2. Animals that are used by
   man in any way have the
   right to be free from
   abuse, pain and torment
   caused or permitted by
   man, other than pain
   necessarily resulting
   from treatment for the
   welfare of the animal;
3. Animals that are domesticated or whose natural
   environment is altered
   by man have the right
   to receive from man adequate food, shelter and
   care;
4. Animals that are or should
   be under the control
   and protection of man
   have the right to receive
   such control and medical
   treatment as will pre-
   vent propagation to an
   extent that causes over-
   population and suffering;
   and
THE HUMAN SOCIETY OF THE UNITED
STATES RECOGNIZES FURTHER that
it is a duty common to all mankind of whatever religion or
philosophical conceptions, of
whatever people or culture, to
protect animals against cruelty
and avoidable pain and to treat

them well, to cultivate an
attitude of compassion and
of kindness towards them, and
to respect their dignity,
their life, their liberty and
their own sphere of existence.
Literature includes:
HUMANE EDUCATION MATERIALS
For the Teacher:
"Guidelines for Study of
Live Animals in Ele-
mentary and Secondary
Education"
"Code of Practice for
Animal Related Projects
in Science Fairs"
"Meeting Animal Friends"
"My Kindness Coloring
Book"
"Teaching Aids for Living
and Learning"
"Sharing Sam," Flannel-
board-patterns-for-
teaching kit that stress-
es pet ownership respon-
sibility. For preschool and
early years.
For the Student:
P=Primary Level I=Interme-
diate Level J=Junior High
Level H=High School Level
"You and your Pet," PI
"Caring for your Cat," PI
"Caring for your Dog," IJH
"Good Kind Lion," PI
"The Bluebird," IJH
"You and the Birds," IJH
"Animals, the Vanishing
Americans," IJH

505

"Golden Rules of Con-
servation," IJH
"Careers Brochure"
"Careers: Working with
Animals"
PROMOTIONAL MATERIALS:
"Handout on Rodeo Cruelty"
Awareness kit on cruel-
ties of trapping
"Death Trap," your car may
be a death trap for your
pets.
"Why Do We Euthanize?"
"A Checklist for Potential
Pet Owners"
"Let's Put an End to Rodeo
Cruelties"
"There Are Too Many Cats
and Dogs in Our Community"
"Questions and Answers about
Greyhound Racing"
"Help Seals"
ANIMAL CONTROL AND SHELTER OPER-
ATIONS
"Recommended Standards and
Procedures for the Oper-
ation of an Animal Shelter"
"Suggested Adoption Policies
for Animal Shelters"
"Architectural Plans, De-
scription, and Recommenda-
tions for Prototype Animal
Shelters"
"How to Administer Sodium
Pentobarbital for Small
Animal Euthanasia"
"Carbon Monoxide Euthanasia"
"Why HSUS is Opposed to the
Use of High Altitude De-
compression Chamber for
Animal Euthanasia"

"Responsible Animal
Regulation"
"How to Establish Spay
and Neuter Programs
and Clinics"
"Recommendations for Humane
Pigeon Control"
"HSUS Guidelines on the
Sale and Rental of
Equines"
"The Pet Population
Explosion"
"What's Your Excuse?"
Describes the need for
sterilizing pets.
Cartoon format.
"If You Love Them," for
the pet owner who needs
information about sur-
plus breeding.
"Controlling America's
Pet Population"
LEGISLATION:
"Model State Anti-Cruel-
ty Laws"
"Model Bill on Easter Pets/
Animals as Prizes"
"Model State Trapping Bills"
"Suggested State Law for
Licensing of Pet Shops
and Kennels"
"Report on Animal Welfare
Laws"
"Model Bill on the Study of
Animals in Elementary
and Secondary Schools
and Science Fairs"
GENERAL READING:
Magazine Reprints
"How to Travel With Your Pet"
"The Hidden Cost of Factory
Farming"

507

"Why Must We Euthanize?"
"Setting the Pace for
Humane Education"
"Partial List of Cosmetic
and Toiletry Companies
Which Claim to Avoid
Animal Exploitation"
Animal Rights and Human
Ethics:
On The Fifth Day
Trapping:
"Trapping: Facts and
Fallacies"
Special Reports:
"Rodeos"
"Controlling America's
Pet Population"
"HSUS Role in Washington
as Voice for Animals"
Close-Up Reports:
"Cock fighting"
"Circus Cruelty"
"Puppy Mills"
"Oil Spill Disasters &
Waterfowl"
"Food Animals Are Suffering"
"Seal Clubbing"
"Homeless Pets"
"Cruelty in Pounds"
"Dogfight/Cockfighting"
"Trapping"
"Animals Are Suffering"
"Major Dogfight Raided"
"Drugs and Horse Racing"
"Factory Farming," by
Michael W. Fox
AUDIO-VISUAL:
"Humane Concerns of Factory
Farming," 80 35mm color
slides, and an audio
cassette of Dr. Michael

Fox's commentary on modern
farming methods. Also available on 3/4 inch video-
cassette. 20 minutes. For
rent or purchase. Humane
Society of the United States.

3030. Imperial Valley Vegetarian Society,
c/o Ken Patterson, 543 Brighton,
El Centro, CA 92243.

3031. Institute for the Study of Animal
Problems, 2111 L Street, N.W.
Washington, D.C. 20037. A di-
vision of the Humane Society of
the United States.
Issues:
International Journal for the
Study of Animal Problems, bi-
monthly.
Literature includes:
"Legal Steps for the Procure-
ment of Sodium Pentobarbi-
tal for Euthanasia of Cats
and Dogs"
"Nicotine Sulfate and Nico-
tine Alkaloids"
"Succinylcholine Chloride
(Sucostrin, U-Tha-Sol)
Not for Euthanasia"
"Euthanasia with T-61: An
Update"
"Euthanasia of Cats and Dogs"
"Evaluation of Awarded Grant
Applications Involving
Animal Experimentation (1979)"
by M.W. Fox, M.A. Ward, and
A.N. Rowan
"Alternatives to Laboratory
Animals: Definition and
Discussion," by Andrew N.
Rowan

"Edging Toward Extinction:
The Status of Wildlife
in Latin America" by
Douglas R. Shane
"Use of Animals in High
School Biology Classes
and Science Fairs"
"Animals in Education"
Proceedings of the Con-
ference on Use of Animals
in High School Biology
Classes and Science
Fairs ed. by H. Mc-
Griffin and N. Brownley.

3032. Institute for Wild and Exotic
Animal Studies, Moorpark
College, Ventura County
Community College District,
Moorpark, CA 93021. (Two
year program training for
recreational animal parks,
zoos, circuses, animal entertainment centers, animal
research facilities, etc.)

3033. Institute of Laboratory Animal
Resources, National Academy of
Sciences, National Re-
search Council, 2101 Constitution Avenue, N.W. Washington,
D.C. 20418
The ILAR Serves as a coordinating agency to disseminate
information, survey existing
and required resources, establish guidelines, promote
education, hold conferences,
and, generally, to upgrade
laboratory animal resources.

The ILAR is a working body
of the Division of Biolog-
ical Sciences within the
Assembly of Life Sciences
of the National Research
Council, the principal op-
erating agency of the
National Academy of Sciences.
Issues ILAR News quarterly.
Literature includes:
"Animals for Research" (A
source directory for lab-
oratory animals)
"Research in Zoos and Aquar-
iums: A Symposium"
"The Future of Animals,
Cells, Models and Systems
in Research, Development,
Education and Testing:
Proceedings of a Sympos-
ium"
"Standards and Guidelines for
the Breeding, Care, and
Management of Laboratory
Animals"
"Defining the Laboratory
Animal"
"Laboratory Animal Housing"
"Laboratory Animal Management:
Wild Birds"

3034.   Institute of Medicine, 2101 Constitution Ave., Washington,
D.C. 20418.

3035.   International Ecology Society
(IES) , 1471 Barclay Street,
St. Paul, Minnesota 55106.

3036.   International Fund for Animal
Welfare, P.O. Box 193,

Yarmouth Port, Ma., 02675.
Has emphasized rescue of
polar bears, seal hunt and
iguana hunt.

3037.   International Primate Pro-
tection League, P.O. Box 9086,
Berkeley, Ca., 94709.
Issues <u>Newsletter</u> periodically.
Literature includes:
"His Name Was Digit"
"Chimpanzee Rehabilitation"
"Zoo Primate Babies of
1977"
"Yerkes Primate Center's
Planned Pygmy Chimpanzee
Project"
"The Colobus Monkey Fur
Trade"
"India's Ban on Primate
Exports"
"U.S. Military's Radiation
Experiments on Monkeys"
"Chimpanzee Heart Trans-
plant Controversy"
"The Smuggling of 100 Pri-
mates from Laos to Bel-
gium"
" Bangladesh Monkey Export
Ban"

3038.   International Primatological
Society, c/o Allan M. Schrier,
Psychology Department, Brown
University, Providence, RI
02912.

3039.   International Society for Animal-
Assisted Therapy, c/o Dr.
Bruce M. Feldmann, 1042
Oxford St., Berkeley, CA 94707.

3040. Jewish Vegetarian Society,
       c/o Judah Grosberg, 68-38
       Yellowstone Boulevard,
       Forest Hills, NY 11375.

3041. Jewish Vegetarian Society of
       Maryland, Att., J. Izak
       Luchinsky, 10 Valdivia
       Ct. Apt. B--Twin Lakes,
       Rockdale, Baltimore City,
       Md., 21207.

3042. Lazarian Society for Animals,
       R.D. #1, Buzzy Hollow,
       Andes, New York 13731.

3043. Maine Vegetarian Society, Attn.
       Skip Howard, c/o WLBZ-TV
       Channel 2, Mt. Hope Avenue
       Bangor, ME 04106.

3044. Massachusetts Society for the
       Prevention of Cruelty to
       Animals, 350 South Hun-
       tington Avenue, Boston, Mass.,
       02130.
       Issues _Animals_ magazine six
          times per year.
       Issues _The Course of Humane_
          Events newsletter period-
          ically (jointly with
          American Humane Education
          Society).

3045. Michigan Animal Rights Society,
       90 Oakwood, Ypsilanti, MI 48197.
       MARS is concerned with abuses
       of animals in the bio-medical
       industry, the cosmetics industry,in

hunting and trapping, in
trade in and transport of
animals, in factory farm-
ing, in rodeos, zoos, and
circuses, and with the
neglect of endangered species.

3046.   Michigan Vegetarian Society,
Robert Zuraw, President,
6563 Devereaux, Detroit,
Michigan 48210.

3047.   Millennium Guild (Concern for
Animals: Vegetarian), 40
Central Park South, New York,
NY 10019.   The Guild was
founded in 1912 by ethical
vegetarians who believe that
"when the Millennium comes,
it will arrive--not by force
of divine fiat--but because
believing and repenting men
have, for generations, been
cooperating with God in the
working out of His plan for
millennial bliss.
Believing...
All sentient creatures have a
right to life, and except
in cases of self-defense, to
protection in that life by
human beings;
Consistent humaneness cannot
be practiced by persons who
feed upon the products of the
slaughter house, who kill other
creatures for food, or whose
habits necessitate the doing

of this degrading work by
others;
Man is not intended by nature
for an even partly carnivo-
rous diet, and that those
desiring of becoming informed
on this subject can do so by
consulting recognized au-
thorities;
That vivisection whether for
so-called medical research,
or as practiced on animals
used for food, or for the
procuring of fur by the steel-
trap (or by various other cruel
methods used for seal, ermine,
etc.) is unjustifiable on any
grounds either scientific,
moral, or utilitarian;
Killing for sport is prompted
by and can satisfy only the
lowest instinct of men and
women;
The use of furs, feathers from
slain birds, kid, leather,
tortoise shell and ivory in-
volves cruelty;
That when possible the use of
substitutes for these and other
articles of vanity's charnel
house, is obligatory upon the
thoughtful;
Universal peace is possible
only when man evolves a true
sense of right of all races,
human and sub-human."
The Millennium Guild placed
a full-page advertisement in
the New York Times, April 15,

1980, with the headline:
"How Many Rabbits Does
Revlon Blind for Beauty's
Sake?"

3048.   Monitor Consortium, 1506 19th
St., N.W., Washington, D.C.
20036.   Conservation, environmental and animal welfare
groups.

3049.   National Anti-Vivisection Society,
100 East Ohio Street, Chicago,
Illinois 60611.
Issues *Bulletin* periodically.
Literature includes:
"Christian Science Monitor
Examines Vivisection
Issue", by Clarence E.
Richard.
"Humane Experimentation on
Humans and Animals...or
Muddling Through," by
Charles R. Magel (copies
are available, without
cost, from NAVS).

3050.   The National Association for the
Advancement of Humane Educa-
tion, Norma Terris Humane
Education Center, P.O. Box
98, East Haddam, CT 06423.
The National Association for
the Advancement of Humane
Education (NAAHE) is designed
to promote humane education,
that which teaches consideration for the value of all
living things, as a viable and
necessary part of the American

education system.
Issues: Humane Education
magazine quarterly
Newsletter quarterly.

3051. National Association of Biology
Teachers, 11250 Roger Bacon
Dr., Reston, VA 22090.

3052. National Audubon Society, 950
Third Avenue, New York, N.Y.
10022.
Issues Audubon magazine
bi-monthly.

3053. National Broiler Council, The
Madison Building, 1155
15th St., N.W., Washington,
D.C. 20005.

3054. National Cat Protection Society,
340 W. Willow Street, P.O.
Box 6065, Long Beach, CA
90806.

3055. National Cattlemen's Association,
1001 Lincoln Street, Denver,
Colorado 80201.
Issues Factsheet periodically.
Literature includes:
   "Cattle: A Vital Link in the
   Global Food Chain"
   "Cattle Production and World
   Hunger"

3056. National Coalition for Alternatives to Animal Experimentation, P.O. Box 224, Springfield Gardens, New York 11413.

Intent:
To create the means by which:
1. Unnecessary experimen-
   tation on animals can be
   stopped and
2. Alternatives to the use
   of animals can be developed for that experimentation
   which remains to be done.

Sponsored a "Symposium on Animal
Experimentation" at Newark, N.J.
February 3 and 4, 1979, attended
by about 60 persons. The main
topics of concern were law and
ethics. Participants included
lawyers, scientists, philosophers, writers, and representatives of animal welfare organizations and humane associations.
There was representation from
Canada and Great Britain.

The Following philosophical
statement was accepted as con-
veying the general view of the
group:

People should not be treated
as mere things. We are not
tools to be used merely for
another's pleasure, profit,
or curiosity. People have
a life that is valuable regardless of whether they are
of use to others. To treat
people in ways that deny
them value in themselves is
to violate their rights.

3058. National Live Stock and Meat
Board, 444 N. Michigan Avenue,
Chicago, Illinois, 60611.
Literature includes:
"The Meat Board Meat Book"
"Meat and your Heart"
"The Good Things We Get
From Cattle Besides Beef"
"A Steer's Not All Steak"
"Meat and the Vegetarian
Concept"
"Beef's Role in Feeding a
Hungry World"
"Educational Publications
and Audio-Visual Aids"
"Hog Is Man's Best Friend"
"A Hog's Not All Chops"
"The Case for Meat"
"The Nutritive Value of
Meat"

3059. National Research Council, 2101
Constitution Ave., Washington,
D.C. 20418.

3060. National Rifle Association of
America, 1600 Rhode Island
Avenue, N.W., Washington, D.C.
20036.
Literature includes:
"The NRA Guidebook for
Hunters"
"Wildlife Management:
Principles-Practice"
"NRA Conservation Yearbook"
NRC Free Loan Films Include:
"Meditations on Hunting"
(Jose Ortega y Gasset)
"Women Can Hunt Too"

3061. National Shooting Sports
    Foundation, 1075 Post Road,
    Riverside, Connecticut
    06878.
    Literature includes:
        "The Hunter and Conservation"
        "What They Say about Hunting"
        Filmstrip: "Man the Hunter"
        "Hunting and Shooting Sports-
            manship"
        "Handguns for Sport"
        "Speaker's Kit" (For use
            by hunters. Contains two
            sample speeches and a list
            of questions most commonly
            asked by non-hunters).
        "The Anti-Hunting Menace"
        "Sport Hunting in North
            America"
        "Questions and Answers on
            Hunting and Conservation"

3062. National Society for Medical
    Research, 1029 Vermont Avenue,
    N.W., Suite 1100, Washington,
    D.C. 20005.
    The National Society for Med-
    ical Research (NSMR) was organ-
    ized in 1946 as a non-profit
    scientific and educational
    organization to generate public
    understanding of the benefits
    derived through responsible
    animal experimentation in bio-
    medical research and teaching.
    NSMR strives to: insure the
    freedom of investigators and
    teachers to use laboratory
    animals without unduly restric-
    tive rules and regulations;
    engender public and government

support for medical research;
encourage optimal care of laboratory animals; and conserve
animal resources essential for
biomedical research. (See 1550.)
Issues <u>NSMR Bulletin</u> monthly.
News service: A series of bi-
monthly articles concerning biomedical research with animals
sent to over 600 newspapers
and free-lance writers, magazines,
house organs, radio and TV
stations.
Gives annual $1,000 Claude Ber-
    nard Science Journalism Awards.
Literature includes:
    "Guiding Principles in the
        Use of Animals by Sec-
        ondary School Students
        and Science Club Members"
    "Principles of Laboratory
        Animal Care"
    "A Career in Laboratory
        Animal Science and Tech-
        nology"
    "A Guide for the Care and
        Use of Laboratory Animals"
    "A Student's Guide--Animals
        in Biology"
    "Laboratory Animals: Are
        They Treated Humanely?"
    "A Short Essay on the Im-
        portance of Dogs in
        Medical Research"
    "How to Work with Labora-
        tory Animals"
    "Medical Miracles of the
        1970's"

"A Humanist View of Rev-
erence for All Life"
"Vivisection--Vivistudy:
The Facts and the Bene-
fits to Animal and Human
Health"
"Threats to Medical Research"
Assorted articles concern-
ing historical and edu-
cational aspects of animal
experimentation.
"Pain Is Cruel, But Disease
Is Cruel, Too"
"History of Antivivisection"
"A Critical Issue in Science
Animal Experimentation--
How Humane?"
"Ethics" Various articles
concerning the ethics of
animal experimentation.
"The Decline in Emphasis
on Basic Medical Sciences
in Medical School Cur-
ricula"
"History and Education"
Various articles concern-
ing historical and edu-
cational aspects of animal
experimentation.

3063. National Trappers Association,
Inc., 15412 Tau Road, Marshall,
Michigan 49068.
Literature includes:
"A Trapper Tells the Truth"

3064. National Turkey Federation,
Reston International Center,
11800 Sunrise Valley Dr.,
Suite 302, Reston, VA 22091.

3065.   National Wildlife Federation,
        1412 16th St., N.W., Washing-
        ton, D.C. 20036.
        Literature includes:
          "Trapping and Conservation"

3066.   Nermin's Dry Goods, Box 53A,
        R.D. 1, Hillcrest Route,
        Barto, PA 19504. This mail
        order and shopping-by-appoint-
        ment business sells only animal-
        free products that have not been
        tested on animals. Products
        sold include belts and wallets,
        cosmetics and toiletries,
        calendars, notecards, and
        stationery.

3067.   New England Anti-Vivisection So-
        ciety, 9 Park Street, Boston,
        MA.

3068.   New Hampshire Animal Rights League,
        c/o Winona Richardson, 24
        Center St., Concord, N.H. 03301.

3069.   New Jersey Congress for Animals,
        R.D. 3, Elmer, N.J. 08318.
        New Jersey Congress for Animals
        is a coalition of animal-wel-
        fare and conservation groups
        and individuals who work for
        humane laws within the state.
        They are concerned with prob-
        lems of both domestic and wild
        animals. They will lobby for
        better laws, and also will
        develop and implement state-
        wide educational programs
        to enlighten and enlist the
        public.

3070. North American Vegetarian Society,
501 Old Harding Highway,
Malaga, N.J. 08328.
Issues Vegetarian Voice four
times per year.
Literature includes:
"Facts on Vegetarianism"
"What's Wrong with Eating
Meat?"
"World Vegetarian Congress
Cookbook" (by Freya Dinshah)
"Vegetarian Cooking for 100"
(Freya Dinshah)
"The Happy Truth about
Protein"
"The Vegetarian Way"
"Feeding Vegan Babies"
"Your Vegetarian Baby"
"Vegetarian Traveling:
International Vegetarian
Health Food Handbook"
(Lists groups, restau-
rants, etc. by nation.)

3071. North American Wildlife Park
Foundation, Battle Ground,
Indiana 47920. This group
exists to help wolves, their
prey, and the wilderness,
and to preserve these assets
for future generations.
Publishes The Predator.

3072. Northwestern Coordinator for
NAVS Affiliate Groups,
Marcia Pearson, 4111 77th
Place, N.W., Marysville,
Washington 98270.

526

3073. The Oceanic Society, 315 Fort
Mason, San Francisco, CA
94123. The Oceanic Society,
seeking equilibrium between
preservation and consumption,
promotes a sensitive awareness and wise management of
the marine environment.

3074. Olin Corporation, Winchester
Group, Conservationist
Department, East Alton, Ill.
62024.
Literature includes:
"Anti-Hunting: A Wasteful
Issue"
"Tomorrow's Hunters-
Gadgeteers or Sportsmen?"
"For the Young Hunter"
"Pheasant Hunting"

3075. Outdoor Writers Association of
America, 4141 West Bradley
Road, Milwaukee, WI 53209.

3076. Pennsylvania Society for the
Prevention of Cruelty to
Animals, 350 East Erie St.,
Philadelphia, Pa. 19134.
Issues _Animaldom_ monthly.

3077. Pets Against Laboratories
(P.A.L.), Joy Donovan, President, 4514 Washburn North,
Minneapolis, Minn. 55412.
Active in efforts to repeal
the Pound Seizure Law in
Minnesota, and in the
passage of a Minnesota law
allowing pets in homes for
the retarded, the handicapped
and the elderly.

3078. Pharmaceutical Manufacturers
　　　　Association (PMA), 1155,
　　　　15th Street, N.W., Washington,
　　　　D.C. 20005.
　　　　Issues:
　　　　Newsletter, weekly
　　　　State Capitol Reports, weekly
　　　　Trademark Bulletin, weekly
　　　　Bulletin, monthly
　　　　Administrative Officers
　　　　　(directory), annual
　　　　Also publishes Trademarks
　　　　listed with PMA.

3079. Philadelphia Vegetarians, Box
　　　　175, Philadelphia, PA　19105.

3080. Poultry and Egg Institute of
　　　　America, 1815 N. Lynn St.,
　　　　Suite 801, Arlington, VA　22209.

3081. Poultry Science Association,
　　　　309 W. Clark St.,
　　　　Champaign, IL 61820.

3082. Professional Rodeo Cowboys
　　　　Association, 101 Prorodeo
　　　　Dr., Colorado Springs,
　　　　Co. 80901
　　　　Literature includes:
　　　　　"Facts: Professional Rodeo
　　　　　　Is Humane to Its Animals"

3083. Protect Animal Life, Inc.,
　　　　Evelyn Hughes, President,
　　　　1413 Wyoming Way, Madison,
　　　　Wisconsin, 53704.
　　　　Sponsored the Harlan Klint-
　　　　wood Memorial Symposium on
　　　　Animal Experimentation in
　　　　Laboratories, Madison, Wis-
　　　　consin, May 12, 1979.

3084.   Research Animal Alliance, P.O.
Box 23, Newton, MA 02160.
Research Animal Alliance is
a non-profit organization
set up to address the needs
of laboratory animal community in the legislative and
regulatory areas.

3085.   Rockland County Vegetarian So-
ciety, c/o Fred Schiller, 10
Strathmore Drive, Spring
Valley, N.Y. 10977.

3086.   Salem Children's Trust, Lower
New Germany Road, Star
Route, Box 60c, Frostburg,
MD 21532.   The Salem Children's Trust, Inc. is a
Christian, charitable, non-
profit organization.   It
was incorporated in July, 1976 to
provide care, housing, therapy,
occupational training, and if
necessary, a permanent home for
socially and/or mentally handicapped
children in the United States.
The Salem Children's Trust
is the parent umbrella organization for the regional Salem
organizations now operating
in Maryland, Michigan and
New Hampshire.   It is phil-
osophically tied to other
Salem organizations in West
Germany, Switzerland, Israel
and England.   Salem is a
world-wide fellowship for
the care of all living things,

both human and non-human
animals. Organic gardening
is emphasized and the diet
is lacto-vegetarian.
Issues The Salem News period-
ically.
Literature includes:
"The Salem Children's Trust"
"In the Burning Orient"
by Gottfried Mueller
"Information about the Salem
Research Institute in
Munich and Its Work in
Documenting Alternatives
to the Use of Laboratory
Animals in Scientific
Research."

3087. San Francisco Vegetarian Society,
c/o Billy Leonard, 52864
Ellis, San Francisco, CA 94109.

3088. SAVE--Society for the Advancement
of Vegetarian Ethics, Jona-
than Rosenthal, Coordinator,
Box 1285, Colby College,
Waterville, ME 04901.

3089. Save the Animals Fund, P.O.
Box 57216, Los Angeles,
CA 90057.
Issues Animal Talk period-
ically.

3090. Scientists' Center for Animal
Welfare, P.O. Box 3755,
Washington, D.C. 20007.
A new organization, the Scien-
tists' Center for Animal

Welfare is a non-profit organization for natural and social
scientists, animal care specialists, lawyers, philosophers,
educators and other scholars,
who use, study, or are concerned about animals, as well as
for all citizens concerned
about ethics as related to
our behaviour towards animals.
The major areas of interest
of the Center are wildlife
animals, agricultural animals
and laboratory animals.
Issues Newsletter periodically.
Literature includes:
  "Scientists' Center for
     Animal Welfare"
  "Bibliography"

3091. Seattle Vegetarian Society,
       P.O. Box 5431, Seattle, Wash-
       ington   98105.

3092. Seventh-Day Adventist Church
       in North America.
       Literature includes:
         "Unmeat: The Case for
            Vegetarianism," by Stoy
            Proctor, Southern Pub-
            lishing Association,
            Nashville, Tennessee, 1973.
         "Diseases of Food Animals,"
            by Owen S. Parrett, M.D.
            Review and Herald Pub-
            lishing Association, Wash-
            ington, D.C., 1974.
         "The Joy of Being a Vegetar-
            ian," by Philip S. Chen,
            Pacific Press Publishing

Association, Mountain View,
Ca., 1977.
There are over 50 Adventist
Book Centers in the United
States and Canada where these
books can be purchased.

3093. Soap and Detergent Association,
475 Park Ave., S., New York,
N.Y. 10016.

3094. Society Against Vivisection,
c/o Judy Striker, P.O. Box
206, Costa Mesa, CA 92626.

3095. Society for Animal Protective
Legislation, P.O. Box 3719,
Georgetown Station, Washington, D.C. 20007. Devoting
its efforts to enactment of
needed legislation to protect
animals, this society is
registered under the Federal
Lobbying Act.

3096. Society for Animal Rights, Inc.
421 South State Street,
Clarks Summit, PA 18411.
The Society for Animal Rights,
Inc., is a national organization, founded in 1959,
engaged in calling attention
to and seeking to prevent the
main forms of exploi-
tation and abuse which cause
suffering in animals. SAR's
ultimate goal is to achieve
for animals the rights now
denied them both in law and
in practice.

Issues: <u>Society for Animal
Rights Report</u> period-
ically.
<u>Animal Rights Law Reporter</u>,
ed.by Henry M. Holzer,
quarterly.
Literature includes:
  "Cosmetic Tests on Animals"
  "A Message to Dog and Cat
    Owners"
  "A Rodeo Isn't Sport or
    Entertainment"
  "If You Love Your Cat,
    Don't De-Claw!"
  "Planned Parenthood for
    Pets?"
  "The Moral Basis of Vege-
    tarianism" by Tom
    Regan
  "Human Rights and Animal
    Rights" by Charles
    Magel
  "Animal Liberation," by
    Peter Singer (Reprint
    of Singer's essay-
    review of <u>Animals</u>,
    <u>Men and Morals</u>, ed.
    by Godlovitch and
    Harris)
  "A Message to Those Con-
    cerned about Animal
    Suffering"
  "Vivisection and the True
    Aims of Education in
    Biology," by George
    K. Russell
  "Low Cost Spay/Neuter
    Clinics"
  "How to Use the Freedom
    of Information Act"

"10 Easy Ways to Be Kind"
"This Coat Is Too Expensive
at Any Price"
"Help Stop the Slaughter of
the Seals"
"Animal Rights" by Jeanie Blake
(Reprint of a three-part
series appearing in the
New Orleans, L.A. Times-
Picayune)
This Society published a new
edition of Henry S. Salt's
book, Animals' Rights, in 1980.

3097. Society for the Protection of Animal
Young, Martha's Vineyard, Massachusetts 02568.
S.P.A.Y. raises funds to help people
on The Island with spaying and/or
neutering costs. It has published
a book, The Crimson Cage by Margaret
Wheaton Tuttle, the royalties of
which are contributed by the author to the fund.

3098. Society for the Study of Ethics and
Animals, Harlan B. Miller, Executive Secretary, Department of
Philosophy and Religion, Virginia
Polytechnic Institute and State
University, Blacksburg, Virginia
24061. The Society for the Study
of Ethics and Animals has been
established to provide for the exchange of information and to provide
arenas for discussion and debate
between those interested in ethical
questions concerning human treatment of non-human animals. The
Society will not take sides, and
is committed only to open discussion. The Society will have

534

at least one meeting each year,
in conjunction with the annual
convention of the Eastern Division of the American Philosophical Association in late December.
Issues Bulletin of the Society for the
Study of Ethics and Animals
quarterly.

3099. Society of Vegetarian Biologists, P.O.
Box 2961, Washington, D.C. 20013.

3100. South Suburban Vegetarian Community,
c/o Betty and Linda Sapinsky, 3658
Lake Street, Lansing, Illinois
60438.

3101. Soycrafters Association of North
America, 305 Wells Street, Green-
field, Ma. 01301. Trade and craft
association of people producing
soyfoods (tofu, soymilk, tempeh,
miso, shoyu, etc.)
Issues Soycraft magazine quarterly.

3102. S.P.A.R.E. (Sympathetic People for
Animal rights on Earth, Inc.) 579
Broadway, Hastings-on-Hudson,
NY 10706.

3103. Theosophical Order of Service, Department of Ecological Research, Animal
Welfare Committee, c/o Candi Phillips,
6341 Switzer Lane, Shawnee, Kansas
66203.
Issues All Creation Newsletter
periodically.

3104. Thunderbolt Federation, 616 6th Street,

Brooklyn, New York, N.Y. 11215.
The Federation sees a near future
of unusual anarchist activity,
theatrical, dramatic, and even
civil disobedience as the expressive mode to gain worldwide attentic
to the oppression of animals on a
cultural, economic, ethical and
sociological level.

3105. Traffic (USA), 1601 Connecticut
Avenue, N.W., Washington, D.C.
20009. Recently established group
aimed at monitoring the trade in
endangered species.

3106. Tucson Vegetarian Society, Attn.,
Carmine Cardamone, 1415 North
Third Avenue, Tucson, Arizona
85707.

3107. United Action for Animals, Inc.,
205 East 42nd Street, New York,
N.Y. 10017.
United Action for Animals, Inc.,
(UAA) was organized in 1967 to
work for the use of modern,
sophisticated research and test-
ing methods instead of live
animals. Following liberaliza-
tion of the tax laws in 1967,
the Society became a registered
lobby to speak in opposition in
Washington, D.C.
Literature includes:
"Higher Education U.S.A., or
Animal Models of Terror and
Pain"
"Congress: The World's Biggest
Promoter of Animal Fighting
and Killing"

"The Death Sciences in Veterinary
Research and Education"
"Animal Models of Agony and
Death: The Veterinary Killings"
"Congress Rockets Animal Agony
into Orbit, Creates New Vivi-
section Industry"
"What You Always Wanted to Know
about Sex but Didn't Dare Ask
Congress"
"The Other Face of Animal Welfare"
"Congress Betrays Man, the Ultimate
Experimental Animal"
"Man's Predation upon Animals:
Wildlife Deserves a Better Fate"
"The Environment: Government Pro-
motes New 'Safety' Tests"
"Political 'Dirty Tricks' perpet-
uate Laboratory Animal Agony"
"No More Lies about 'Humane Treat-
ment' Needed"
"It's Time for a Change in Lab-
oratory Animal Welfare Work"
"The Neutron Bomb and the Military
Torture-Killing of Animals"
"Animal Models of Agony and Death:
The Radiation Killings"
"Congress and the N.I.H.:   How to
Torture, Torment and Terrorize
Animals"
"Cancer 'Safety' Testing and Po-
litical Crimes against Labo-
ratory Animals"
"Laboratory Animals: Replace Them
Now"
"Alternatives in Car Crash Research"
"Congress and Animal Agony: Hind-
limb Beatings"
"Abstracts Regarding Testing of
Environmental Chemicals"

"Mathematical Modelling in Biomedical Research"

"How Isolated Organs Can Be Used
in Research, Testing and
Teaching"

"The NSF, Psychobiology and the
Real Meaning of 'Animal
Behavior' "

"New Laboratory Animal Bill Introduced" U.A.A. has been active
in securing the introduction
of this bill.

On July 16, 1979, a bill, H.R. 4805,
the Research Modernization Act,
was introduced in the House of
Representatives by Congressmen
Frederick W. Richmond (D-NY),
Robert A. Roe (D-NJ), Harold C.
Hollenbeck (R-NJ), and Lester L.
Wolff (D-NY).

Under H.R. 4805, a National Center
for Alternative Research would be
established within the National
Institutes of Health to promote
the use of alternatives instead
of live animals in research and
testing. The bill provides that
no less than 30% and no more than
50% of the animal research money
of all Federal animal-using
agencies be directed to the National Center to promote the use
of alternatives and the development of more.

3108. United Dairy Industry Association,
6300 North River Rd., Rosemont, IL
60018.

3109. United International Vegetarian Society, 333 Edgewood Ave., Atlanta, Georgia 30312.

3110. Vegetarian Action, 835 Carroll Street, Brooklyn, N.Y. 11215

3111. Vegetarian Activist Collective, Attn. Connie Salamone, 616 6th Street, Apt. #2, Brooklyn, N.Y. 11215.

3112. Vegetarian Association of America, P.O. Box 86, Livingston, N.J. 07039.

3113. Vegetarian Educational Growth Society, P.O. Box 10110, Cleveland, Ohio 44110.

3114. Vegetarian Friends of Rochester, P.O. Box 6, Rochester, Minnesota 55901.

3115. Vegetarian Inclined People (VIP), Attn., Dorothy Gardner, Pres., 383 Walnut Street, Arroyo Grande, California 93420.

3116. Vegetarian Information Service, Box 5888, Washington, D.C. 20014. A non-profit educational organization dedicated to the dissemination of knowledge on the vegetarian way of life.

3117. Vegetarian Society, P.O. Box 4303, Palm Springs, California 92262.

3118. Vegetarian Society, Inc., P.O. Box 5688, Santa Monica, California 90405. Also Chapters throughout Southern California.

3119. Vegetarian Society of Colorado,
      1764 Gilpin Street, Denver, Colo-
      rado 80218.

3120. Vegetarian Society of D.C., Box 4328,
      Washington, D.C.

3121. Vegetarian Society of Milwaukee, Attn.
      Dr. Bernard Sharp, 7201 West Bur-
      leigh Street, Milwaukee WI 53210.

3122. Vegetarian Society of New York, Attn.,
      Murray Mickenberg, Secy., 277 Broad-
      way, New York, N.Y. 10007.

3123. Vegetarian Society of Portland, Box
      1434, Portland, Oregon 97207.

3124. Vegetarian Society of S. Florida, 130
      Lake Shore Drive, Hallandale, Flor-
      ida 32784.

3125. Vegetarians in New Energy Sources
      (V.I.N.E.S.), Maynard S. Clark,
      155 Westminster Avenue, Arlington,
      MA 02174.

3126. Vegetarians of Delaware Valley, Attn.,
      Anella Izquierdo, 613 Convent Road,
      Ashton, PA 19014

3127. Waimea Vegetarian Information Service
      c/o Alisha Kashaya, 154 Puako Beach
      Drive, Kawai Lae, Hawaii 96743.

3128. The Whale Protection Fund/CEE, 1925
      K Street, N.W., Washington, D.C.
      20006. The Whale Protection Fund
      is a project of the Center for En-
      vironmental Education, Inc., a non-
      profit corporation founded in 1972.

Issues The Whale Report newsletter
four times per year.

3129. Wild Canid Survival and Research Center
(Wolf Sanctuary), P.O. Box 16204,
St. Louis, MO   63105.

3130. Wild Horse Organized Assistance (WHOA!),
P.O. Box 555, Reno, Nevada   89504.
A foundation for the welfare of wild
free-roaming horses and burros.
Issues a News Bulletin periodically.

3131. Wildlife Preservation Trust International, Inc., 34th St. and Girard Ave.,
Philadelphia, Pennsylvania   19104.
(Objectives: Zoos for conservation
and scientific research.)

3132. Writers for Animal Rights, c/o Richard
Morgan, English Department, Box
19120A, East Tennessee State University, Johnson City, TN   37601.
Writers for Animal Rights is an organization of concerned writers
working to end institutionalized
forms of cruelty inflicted upon
animals, such as vivisection, intensive farming (and flesh-eating
generally), trapping and fur-
farming, sport-cruelties, irre-
sponsible attitudes toward domestic
pet overpopulation.

IX. Magazines and Journals
(Unless indicated otherwise, published in the United States)

3133. Trade Magazines Related to Factory Farming:

Aberdeen-Angus Journal
Alberta Hog Journal (Canada)
American Agriculturalist
American Hampshire Herdsman
American Hereford Journal
Animal Production (United Kingdom)
Beef
British Poultry Science (United Kingdom)
Broiler Business
Broiler Industry
Cattlemen: The Beef Magazine (Canada)
Cattleman
Canada Poultryman (Canada)
Confinement
Dairy Herd Management
Egg and Poultry Producer (Australia)
Egg Industry
Farm Journal
Farmer and Stockbreeder (United Kingdom)
Farmers Weekly (Australia)
Feedlot Management
Hoard's Dairyman
Hog Farm Management
Hog Marketplace Quarterly (Canada)
Journal of Dairy Science
Livestock Farming (United Kingdom)
Livestock International (United Kingdom)
Livestock Market Digest
National Livestock Producer
National Hog Farmer
Pig Farmer (Australia)
Pig Farmer (United Kingdom)
Progressive Farmer
Pig International

Poultry Digest
Poultry Science
Poultry Tribune
Poultry World (Australia)
Poultry World (United Kingdom)
Stall Street Journal, by Provimi, Inc.
  Watertown, Wisconsin. A private
  journal published by a manufac-
  turer of equipment for efficient
  production of calves for veal.
Successful Farming
Turkey World
Western Livestock Journal

3134. A Few of the Many Technical and
      Scientific Journals Reporting
      Experiments on Animals:

Aerospace Medicine
American Journal of Physiology
American Journal of Veterinary
  Research
British Medical Journal (United
  Kingdom)
Canadian Medical Association
  Journal (Canada)
Canadian Veterinary Journal
  (Canada)
Journal of Animal Science
Journal of Applied Physiology
Journal of Comparative and Physio-
  logical Psychology
Journal of Medical Primatology
  (Switzerland)
Journal of Pharmacy and Pharmacol-
  ogy (United Kingdom)
Journal of the American Veter-
  inary Medical Association

> Journal of the Experimental Analy-
> sis of Behavior
> Journal of the Institute of Animal
> Technicians
> Journal of Trauma
> Laboratory Animal Care
> Laboratory Animal Science
> Laboratory Animals: Journal of the
> Laboratory Animal Science
> Association (United Kingdom)
> Laboratory Practice (United Kingdom)
> Pharmaceutical Journal (United
> Kingdom)
> Physiology and Behavior
> Quarterly Journal of the Animal
> Technicians Association (United
> Kingdom)

3135. Hunting, Fishing, Trapping and Fur
Magazines:

> American Hunter
> Bowhunter
> Field and Stream
> Fishing World
> Fur Age Weekly
> Fur-Fish-Game
> Fur Parade
> Fur Review (United Kingdom)
> Fur Taker
> Fur Trade Journal (Canada)
> Hides and Skins Quarterly (United
> Kingdom)
> Outdoor Life
> U.S. Fur Rancher

3136. Trade Magazines Having to Do with Meat
Production and Processing:

Magazines and Journals

> Meat (United Kingdom)
> Meat Industry
> Meat Plant Magazine
> Meat Processing
> Meat Science
> Meat Trades Journal (Australia)

3137. Pet Magazines:

> Pet Dealer
> Pet News

3138. Vegetarian Magazine:

> Vegetarian Times, 41 East 42nd Street,
> Suite 921, New York, N.Y. 10017

3139. Animal Liberation Magazines:

> (a) The Beast, 2 Blenheim Crescent,
> London, England, W11 1NN.
> The Beast is a magazine designed
> to serve and represent the Animal
> Liberation movement. Concern about
> cruelty to animals, species extinc-
> tion, and environmental issues in
> general is at an all-time peak.
> The aim of The Beast is to voice
> that concern as clearly and loudly
> as possible.
>
> The Beast will provide a much-
> needed overview by covering the
> activities of all animal liberation
> and allied groups. The magazine
> will serve as an information ex-
> change and as a forum for people
> who are curious about animal
> activism but are still uncommitted.

Produced by a combination of professional journalists and experts from outside the movement, The _____ Beast will contain a mixture of investigative reporting, exclusive interviews and the latest news from our correspondents in Britain, Europe, and the U.S.A. There will also be a letters page, an opinion column, book and film reviews, and the most complete listing, to date, of Animal Liberation organizations in the U.K. and abroad.

(b) Agenda: A Journal of Animal Liberation, edited and published by Jim Mason, P.O. Box 5224, Westport, Ct., 06880.

Agenda, a journal of animal liberation, is devoted to fostering greater cooperation and unity within the animal liberation/rights/welfare movement. It tries to provide a forum in which the movement can exchange ideas and discuss the problems and issues before it. It tries to activate and facilitate two processes vital to the building of a more effective, progressive movement: (1) the refinement and filling out of our theoretical base, and (2) the evolution of strategies and tactics for political change.
Agenda is currently funded by the Animal Rights Network, Inc., but is editorially separate from any animal welfare or animal rights organization.

(c) <u>Co-ordinating Animal Welfare
Bulletin</u>, P.O. Box 61, Camberly
Surrey, England.

CAW "is intended to provide a link
between those who actively and real-
istically seek to minimize animal
suffering, and thereby increase
their effectiveness. The link is
provided by regular informal meetings in London and the circulation
of a bulletin....CAW was not set up
to criticize and discredit Animal
Welfare Societies but lend weight,
as members of these societies, to
constructive criticism and the re-
buttal of outmoded tactics which
have been seen over the years to do
little to help the plight of defenseless creatures."
CAW is a movement-building association of animal rights activists
in England.

3140.   Other Journals Concerned with Animal
Welfare:

(a)   <u>Animal Regulation Studies</u>,
Elsevier Scientific Publishing
Co., P.O. Box 330, Amsterdam,
The Netherlands. The journal
publishes original studies, reviews and exchanges of views
designed to increase the knowledge necessary for improving
man-animal relationships and for
moderating abuses caused by
man's exploitation of animals.
Exploitation of domesticated and
wild animals, whether for purposes of agriculture, science,

companionship, amusement or
commerce, is covered.

(b) International Journal for
the Study of Animal Problems,
Institute for the Study of
Animal Problems, 2100 L Street,
N.W. Washington, D.C. 20037.
The Journal is aimed at an academic and professional audience
and will explore issues in the
animal welfare field in a schol-
arly and technical manner. The
Journal will carry major review
and original articles on a wide
variety of topics, including
philosophical and legal aspects,
as well as news items, editorials,
comment pieces and book reviews.
The Journal will provide a much
needed focus for a multi-
disciplinary field and establish
animal welfare science as a
professional and credible academic
pursuit.

X. Easy-on-Animals Cookbooks

3141. Baker, Ivan, Complete Vegetarian
Recipe Book, Bell and Hyman,
London, 1978.

3142. Batt, Eva, What's Cooking?, The Vegan
Society, Surrey, U.K., 1980.

3143. Bauer, Cathy, and Andersen, Juel,
The Tofu Cookbook, Rodale Press,
Emmaus, Pennsylvania, 1979.

3144. Berg, Sally and Lucien, Vegetarian
Gourmet, McGraw-Hill, New York,
1971.

3145. Brooks, Karen, The Forget-About-Meat
Cookbook, Rodale Press, Emmaus, Pa.,
1974.

3146. Brown, Edith and Sam, Cooking Crea-
tively with Natural Foods, Ballantine, New York, 1973.

3147. Brown, Edward E., Tassajara Cooking:
A Vegetarian Cooking Book, Sham-
bhala Publications, Boulder, Colorado, 1973.

3148. Bryant, Clare, Everyday Vegetarian and
Food Reform Cooking, Keith Reid,
Shaldon, Devon, U.K. 1974.

3149. Buchner, Greet, Alternative Cooking,
New Ways With Nature's Abundance,
trans. from the Dutch by Helena
Brandt, Thorsons, Wellingborough,
Northamptonshire, 1979.

3150. Chen, Philip S., and Chung, Helen
D., Soybeans for Health and a
Longer Life, Keats Publishing, New
Canaan, Connecticut, 1973.

551

3151. Corlett, Jim, Super Natural Cookery,
Receipes for Vegetarian Gourmets,
David and Charles, London, 1974.

3152. D'Silva, Joyce, Healthy Eating for
the New Age, A Vegan Cookbook,
Wildwood House, London, 1980.

3153. Elliot, Rose, Simply Delicious, The
White Eagle Publishing Trust, New
Lands, Liss, Harts., U.K.

3154. Eno, David, The Little Brown Books:
"The Little Brown Soup Book," 1979
"The Little Brown Bread Book," 1976
"The Little Brown Nut Book," 1979
"The Little Brown Book of Greens,"
1975
"The Little Brown Salad Book," 1979
"The Little Brown Egg Book," 1973
"The Little Brown Bean Book," 1978
"The Little Brown Rice Book," 1973
The Juniper Press, Winchester,
Hampshire, U.K.

3155. Ewald, Ellen B., Recipes for a Small
Planet, Ballantine Books, New York
1973.

3156. Fisher, Patty, 500 Recipes for Vegetarian Cookery, Hamlyn, London, 1969.

3157. Fliess, Walter and Jenny, Modern
Vegetarian Cookery, Penguin, New
York, 1979.

3158. Ford, M.W., Hillyard, Susan, and
Koock, M.F., The Deaf Smith Country
Cook Book, Collier Macmillan, New
York, 1973.

3159. Gaulke, Judith A., ed., <u>Sunset Ideas</u>
<u>for Cooking Vegetables</u>, Lane Books,
Menlo Park, Ca., 1973.

3160. Gregory, Dick, <u>Dick Gregory's Natural</u>
<u>Diet for People Who Eat</u>, Harper-Row,
New York, 1974.

3161. Grossinger, Jennie, <u>The Art of Jewish</u>
<u>Cooking</u>, Bantam, New York, 1972.
(Not vegetarian, but some vegetarian
recipes.)

3162. Haedrich, Ken, <u>Good Food-Good Folks</u>:
<u>A Collection of Vegetarian Recipes</u>
<u>from Across America</u>, American Impres-
sions, 410 Cleveland Avenue, Plain-
field, N.J. 1978.

3163. Hagler, Louise, ed., <u>The Farm Vegetar-</u>
<u>ian Cookbook</u>, Revised Edition, The
Book Publishing Co., Summertown,
Tenn., 1978.

3164. <u>The Hare Krishna Cookbook</u>, Chilton Book
Co., Radnor, Pa. 1974.

3165. Highton, N.B. and R.B., <u>The Home Book</u>
<u>of Vegetarian Cookery</u>, Faber and Faber,
London, 1979.

3166. Hooker, Alan, <u>Vegetarian Gourmet Cookery</u>,
101 Productions, San Francisco, Ca.
1970.

3167. Hunt, Janet, <u>A Vegetarian in the Family</u>,
Meatless Recipes for the Odd One Out,
Thorsons, Wellingborough, Northampton-
shire, 1977.

3168. Hurd, Frank J. and Rosalie, A Good Cook:
Ten Talents, published by Dr. and
Mrs. Frank J. Hurd, Chisholm,
Minn., 1968.

3169. James, Isabel, Vegetarian Cuisine, The
Vegetarian Society (UK) Limited, Parkdale, Dunham Road, Altrincham, Cheshire, 1976.

3170. Jones, Dorothy V., The Soybean Cookbook, Arco, New York, 1980.

3171. Katzen, Mollie, Moosewood Cookbook, Ten
Speed Press, Berkeley, Ca., 1977.

3172. King, Marilyn, and Scott, William, Food
for Thought, Prism Press, Dorchester,
Dorset, U.K., 1973.

3173. Kloss, Jethro, Back to Eden Cookbook,
Woodbridge Press, Santa Barbara, Ca.,
1974.

3174. Laden, Alice, The George Bernard Shaw
Cookbook, Garnstone Press, London,
1972; and Harcourt-Brace-Jovanovich,
New York, 1977.

3175. Lager, Mildred and Van Gundy Jones,
Dorothea, The Soybean Cookbook,
Arco, New York, 1968.

3176. Lappe, Frances M., and Ewald, Ellen
B., Great Meatless Meals, Ballantine,
New York, 1974.

3177. Lass, Jaime, The Happy Herbivore, A
Vegetarian Cookery Book, Canongate,
Edinburg, 1979.

3178. Lee, Gary, The Chinese Vegetarian Cook Book, Nitty Gritty Productions, Concord, California, 1972.

3179. Leneman, Leah, Slimming the Vegetarian Way, Thorsons, Wellingborough, Northamptonshire, 1980.

3180. Lo, Kenneth H.C., Chinese Vegetable and Vegetarian Cooking, Faber and Faber, London, 1977.

3181. Lovejoy, Marie, International Vegetarian Cuisine, Theosophical Publishing House, Wheaton, Ill., 1978.

3182. Lucas, Jack, Vegetarian Nutrition, The Vegetarian Society, Altrincham, Cheshire, U.K., 1979.

3183. Mahadevan, Shyamala, Vegetarian Delicacies, Based on the South Indian Style of Cooking, Shri Bharat Bharati Private Ltd., Delhi, India, 1973.

3184. Santa Maria, Jack, Indian Vegetarian Cookery, Samuel Wise, New York, 1977.

3185. Miller, Lindsay, The Apartment Vegetarian Cookbook, Peace Press, Culver City, California, 1978.

3186. Moore, Shirley T., and Byers, Mary P. A Vegetarian Diet, What It Is, How To Make It Healthful and Enjoyable, Woodbridge Press, Santa Barbara, California, 1978.

3187. Null, Gary, The New Vegetarian, Delta Books, Delta Publishing, New York, 1979.

3188. Phillips, Ann and David, Soil to Psyche Recipe Book, Woodbridge Press, Santa Barbara, Ca., 1977.

3189. Robertson, Laurel, Flinders, Carol, and Godfrey, Bronwen, Laurel's Kitchen: A Handbook for Vegetarian Cookery and Nutrition, Nilgiri Press, Berkeley, Ca., 1976.

3190. Roden, Claudia, A Book of Middle Eastern Food, Alfred A. Knopf, New York, 1972. (Not vegetarian, but many recipes adaptable to vegetarian.)

3191. Rosicrucian Fellowship, New Age Vegetarian Cookbook, The Rosicrucian Fellowship, P.O. Box 713, Oceanside, California, 1975.

3192. Sacharoff, Shanta Nimbark, Flavors of India, Recipes from the Vegetarian Hindu Cuisine, 101 Productions, San Francisco, 1972.

3193. Sams, Craig and Ann, The Brown Rice Cookbook, Delicious Wholesome Macrobiotic Recipes, Thorsons, Wellingborough, Northamptonshire, 1980.

3194. Scott, Dave, and Roberts, Alan, Recipes for Living, A Book of Western and Eastern Vegetarian Recipes and Ideas on Food, Nutrition, Diet, and Exercise, Wildwood House, London, 1979.

3195. Shulman, Martha R., The Vegetarian Feast, Harper and Row, New York, 1979.

3196. Shurtleff, William, and Aoyagi, Akiko, The Book of Miso, Autumn Press, Brookline, Ma., 1977.

3197. Shurtleff, William, and Aoyagi, Akiko, The Book of Miso II, Miso Productions, New-Age Foods Study Center, Lafayette, Ca.

3198. Shurtleff, William, and Aoyagi, Akiko, The Book of Tempeh, A super soyfood from Indonesia, Harper and Row, New York, 1979.

3199. Shurtleff, William, and Aoyagi, Akiko, The Book of Tempeh II, Tempeh Productions, New-Age Foods Study Center, Lafayette, Ca.

3200. Shurtleff, William, and Aoyagi, Akiko, The Book of Tofu, Ballantine Books, New York, 1975.

3201. Shurtleff, William, and Aoyagi, Akiko, The Book of Tofu II, Tofu and Soy-milk Production, New-Age Foods Study Center, Lafayette, Ca.

3202. Richmond, Sonya, International Vegetarian Cookery, Arco, New York, 1965.

3203. Thomas, Anna, The Vegetarian Epicure, Random House, New York, 1972.

3204. Thomas, Anna, Vegetarian Epicure Book II, Knopf, New York, 1978.

3205. Thurman, Jimmie J., Adventures of Vegetarian Cooking, Southern Publishing Association, Nashville, Tenn., 1969.

Easy-on-Animals Cookbooks

3206. Walker, Janet, Vegetarian Cookery,
       Granada, London, 1978.

3207. Wason, Betty, The Art of Vegetarian
       Cookery, Ace Books, Charter Commu-
       nications, New York, 1965.

3208. White, Beverly, Bean Cuisine, A Culi-
       nary Guide for the Ecogourmet,
       Routledge and Kegan Paul, London,
       1977.

3209. Wigmore, Ann, Recipes for Life,
       Recipes for Vegetarian Meals, Omango,
       Wethersfield, Conn.

3210. Wilson, Frank, Successful Sprouting,
       Thorsons, Wellingborough, Northampton-
       shire, 1978.

NAME INDEX

Either the person named is the author or producer of a work listed in the bibliography or the instructor of a course or a participant in a conference; or the numbered entry is about the person or the person's views.

Abbott, Rosa G., 271
Abhendenada, Swami, 404
Abreu, Madam, 966
Adams, Carol, 1720
Adams, Charles, 272
Adams, Donald K., 453
Adams, E.M., 2082
Adams, Richard, 989 1423, 1456, 1985, 2322-24
Adamson, Joy, 787-89
Addis, William E., 1054
Addison, Joseph, 2547
Aelian, 13
Aesopus, 2325
Aflalo, F.G., 441
Agius, Dom Ambrose, 1043, 2818
Aiken, William, 1121
Aikin, Anna Laetitia (Mrs. Barbauld), 2326
Akmajian, A., 519
Alcott, Bronson, 1747, 1777
Alcott, William A., 405, 1735, 1747, 1764, 1777
Aldrich, Thomas B., 273

Alexander, Samuel, 758
Allaway, Gertrude E., 1721
Allee, Warder C., 520, 749
Allen, Durward L., 759, 2026
Allen, Robert D., 1902, 2027
Alpers, Antony, 838
Alrawi, B., 1651
Altman, Nathaniel, 1722-23
Altman, Norman H., 1560
Altman, Stuart, 874
Altmann, A., 1044
Alverdes, F., 454-55
Amaral, Anthony A., 1947
Ambrose, Saint, 16
Amory, Cleveland, 1304, 3019
Andersen, Juel, 3143
Anderson, Allen C., 1424
Anderson, G.J., 1510
Anderson, M.D., 2327
Anderson, Marilyn, 1652
Anderson, R.K., 2621
Anderson, R.S., 1903
Angel, Marie, 2328-29

Angell, George T.,
243, 2175
Angress, Shimon,
1815
Anthony, Edward,
1949
Aoyagi, Akiko, 3196-
3201
Appleton, Tim, 522
Archer, John, 523
Archibald, J., 1471
Ardrey, Robert, 627,
808
Arenilla, Louis,
2083
Argus, Arabella,
2338-39
Aristotle, 1-6, 89,
158, 1022
Armitt, A., 274
Armstrong, David M.,
524
Armstrong, Edward A.,
735-36, 1046,
2340
Armstrong, Susan B.,
1122
Arnold, Earl C.,
2237
Arnold, Edwin, 69
Arnold, F.S., 275
Arnold, S.T., 2341
Arnold, Thomas,
1054
Aronson, Lester R.,
1426
Arrington, Lewis R.,
1427
Atherton, Margaret,
525
Atkins, Elizabeth,
2343
Austen, C.R., 1428
Austin, Jack, 1047

Austin, P., 205
Auxter, Thomas, 1725
Avery, B.P., 244
Axon, William E.A.,
406, 1726
Aygun, S.T., 1643
Azrin, N.H., 1429

Baasch, M.L., 1430
Bachrach, Arthur J.,
1431
Back, K.C., 1526
Bacon, Francis, 1567
Baier, Annette, 2606
Baillairs, Charles,
2172
Baillie-Weaver, Mr.,
1354
Bain, Read, 760
Baker, Charlotte,
2818
Baker, Ivan, 3141
Baker, J.A., 1048
Baker, M.A., 1566
Balfour-Murphy, K.,
456
Ballou, William H.,
70
Balls, M., 1432
Baltimore, David,
1457
Balz, Albert G.A.,
526
Banchieri, Adriano,
2502
Banks, Edwin M.,
527
Barber, Bernard,
1433
Barber, Carolyn, 528
Barber, Richard,
2344
Barbour, Ian G.,
1049

560

Bareham, J.E., 2925
Bargen, Richard, 1727
Barkas, Janet, 1728
Barnes, Donald, 1434, 1438
Barnett, R.J., 618
Barnett, Samuel A., 1435
Barr, James, 2084
Barrow, P., 1810
Barry, Alfred, 276
Barter, Gwendolen, 1854
Basil, Saint, 2201
Bateman, James, 1986
Bates, Angela, 1132
Bates, H.E., 1731, 1782
Bateson, Gregory, 2085
Bateson, P., 2602
Bateson, P.P.G., 529
Batt, Eva, 2927, 2989, 3142
Batten, Peter, 2012
Bauer, Cathy, 3143
Baufle, Jean-Marie, 2345
Baumann, Charly, 1948
Bayle, Pierre, 23
Bayless, Raymond, 530
Bayly, M. Beddow, 2880, 2914
Beaglehood, Ernest, 1855
Bean, M.J., 2238
Beary, E.G., 1436
Beatty, Clyde, 1949-50

Beatty, William, 1302
Beck, Alan M., 1904-06, 2598
Beck, Benjamin B., 531
Beck, C.C., 1801
Becker, Earnest, 532
Becker, Laurence C., 2606
Beeson, Trevor, 1132
Begley, Sharon, 1507
Beljan, J.R., 1802
Bell, Charles, 272, 361, 370, 383, 1466
Bell, Clive, 1856
Bell, Ernest, 277, 1305, 2346
Bell, Luther V., 1764
Bell, Robert, 1767
Bell-Taylor, Charles, 278-79
Bellerby, John R., 1653
Belves, Peter, 2347
Bender, L., 2348
Benedict, Saint, 1747
Benjamin, Martin, 2600, 2617
Benn, Stanley, 1123, 2138
Bennett, Jonathan F., 533, 2600
Bennett, John, 2349
Bennett, John B., 2086, 2139
Bennett, Richard R., 2502
Benning, Lee E., 1907
Benson, J., 2602
Benson, John, 1124-25
Benson, Thomas L., 2613
Benson, V.W., 1654

Bourne, Geoffrey H.,
876-78, 1440-
41
Bowd, Alan D., 1442-
44, 2595
Bowen, Francis, 72
Bowman, John C.,
1306
Bowman, R.E., 1519,
1808
Bowring, John, 2359
Boysen, Sarah, 950-
53
Bradford, Nettie,
1107
Bradley, F.H., 1108
Brahms, Johannes,
2502
Brambell, Michael,
1132
Brander, Michael,
1857-59
Braunstein, Mark M.,
1732, 2360
Breck, Edward, 2201
Brewton, John E.,
2361
Bridges, J.H., 283,
305
Briggs, G. Bruce,
2607
Brink, L., 2457
Brinton, Howard H.,
1052
Brion, Marcel, 2362
Britt, Kent, 873
Britten, S., 1446
Broad, William J.,
1447
Broadhurst, Peter,
1448
Broadie, Alexander,
1126, 1235,
1241

Brockhaus, Wilhelm,
1733
Brodrick, A. Houghton,
2363
Bromfield, Louis, 540
Brook, Maurice, 1449
Brooks, Karen, 3145
Brophy, Brigid, 541,
1127-28, 1450-51,
1729, 1734, 2364,
2930
Brophy, Liam, 2818
Brosman, C.S., 2365
Brower, Kenneth, 839
Brown, Abbie F., 206
Brown, Anthony, 2173
Brown, C.E., 790
Brown, Edith, 3146
Brown, Edward E.,
3147
Brown, Larry T., 991
Brown, Robert, 2598
Brown, Robin, 840
Brown, Sam, 3146
Brown, W. Norman,
1053
Brown Dog, The,
1373, 1643
Browne, Alister, 1452
Browning, Robert,
1357
Brownley, N., 3031
Bruemmer, F., 841
Brumbaugh, Robert S.,
1129, 2607
Brunton, T. Lander,
284
Bryan, Benjamin, 285
Bryant, Arthur, 1656
Bryant, Clare, 3148
Bryant, Clifton D.,
809
Bryant, J.M., 1860
Bryant, Nelson, 1861

Carr, Harvey, 470
Carr, Raymond, 1864
Carrier, L.S., 549
Carrighar, Sally,
    550
Carrington, R., 784
Carroll, Lewis, 287,
    2372
Carroll, William M.,
    2373
Carson, Gerald,
    1308, 1735,
    2174
Carson, Hampton, 2242
Carson, Rachel, 2090
Carter, Dagney, 2374
Carter, Sarah N.,
    246
Carter, W.R., 1133
Carus, Paul, 288,
    318, 389, 407
Carver, Mavis, 1326
Cary, George L., 77
Cass, Jules S., 1458
Cawte, E.C., 2375
Caxton, William,
    2376
Cetto, Anna M.,
    2377-78
Chalmers, Dr., 1309
Chalmers, Patrick,
    1865
Chambers, P.G., 2243
Chapple, Steve, 2002
Charles River Breed-
    ing Laboratories,
    Inc. (See en-
    tries for Henry L.
    Foster)
Charron, Pierre, 2201
Chase, Mary, 2379
Chatwin, C. Bruce,
    2367

Chaucer, Geoffrey, 2533
Chauvin, Remy, 551
Chen, Philip S., 3150
Chenevix-Trench, Charles,
    1817
Cherfas, Jeremy, 1460,
    1988
Chesney, W.D., 1461
Chesterman, J., 552
Chesterton, Gilbert K.,
    1736, 1747, 1781
Chimpsky, Neam, 882
Chimpsky, Nim, 960
Chitty, Susan, 2218
Chomsky, Noam, 947
Chowin, W., 890
Christensen, Allen C.,
    2217
Christenson, F.M.,
    1955
Christian, Garth, 2032
Chrysostom, Saint,
    2201
Chung, Helen D., 3150
Church, F.S., 2380
Claparede, Edouard,
    471
Clark, Anne, 2381
Clark, David L., 1737
Clark, Joseph D.,
    2382
Clark, Kenneth, 993,
    2383
Clark, Stephen R.L.,
    1134-38, 1142,
    1191, 1211, 1228,
    1252, 1287, 1290,
    1465, 2606
Clarke, Frances E.,
    2384
Clarke, James F., 79,
    553
Clarke, R.F., 247

565

Clarke, Robert F.,
289
Clarkson, Ewan, 761
Clement, R.C., 2033
Clement of Alexan-
dria, 1747
Clever Hans, 516
614, 691, 806-
07
Clooney, F.X., 1738
Cloudsley-Thompson,
John, 554
Clubb, Henry, 1735
Cluer, Mabel, 2927
Coates, M.E., 1463
Cobb, John B., Jr.,
1055-58, 2091
Cobbe, Frances P.,
191-92, 199, 208,
222-24, 272, 290-
301, 329, 495,
1347, 1357, 1419,
1490, 1644, 2180,
2188, 2201, 2385-
87
Cocchi, Antonio, 33
Cockerill, George,
1701
Cockrill, W. Ross,
1818
Coffey, David, 1132
Coggins, George C.,
2244
Cohen, A., 1059
Cohen, Daniel, 555
Cohen, Maury, 878
Cohen, Noah J., 2388
Cohn, Norman, 2389
Cohn, Ronald H., 937
Colbert, Edwin H.,
762
Cole, William C.,
1648
Coleman, Sidney H.,
2175

Coleman, V., 1464
Coleridge, Gilbert, 472
Coleridge, Lord, 302-03,
1357
Coleridge, Samuel T.,
2399
Coleridge, Stephen, 304,
377, 1310, 1356-64,
1373, 1402-03, 1643,
2245
Colette, Sidonie G.,
2389a
Collias, N.E., 737
Collier, W., 80
Collingwood, Bertram,
1365
Collins, Arthur H.,
2390
Collins, Arthur W.,
819a
Collins, J., 1759
Collins, June M.,
994
Condillac, Etienne
Bonnot de, 2444
Congo, 2500
Congreve, Richard, 305
Conrad, Jack R., 995
Cooper, Courtney R.,
1956
Cooper, Madeline L.,
1426
Cooper, Margaret E.,
2246
Cooper, William
Earnshaw, 209
Corlett, Jim, 3151
Cornish, C.J., 81
Cosyn, Benjamin, 2502
Cottingham, John, 1139
Couch, Jonathan, 111
Couperin, Francois,
2505
Court, Alfred, 1957

Davis, Patrick D.C.,
1819
Davis, R., 2397
Davis, Roger T.,
646
Davis, William H.,
1690
Dawkins, Richard,
561, 652
Daws, Gavan, 2248-
49
Dawson, Giles E.,
1959
Deacon, C.F., 474
DeBartola, Dick,
2037
DeBoer, J., 1471
Debussy, Claude,
2502
de Cyon, E., 308
Deely, John N., 562
De La Ramee, Louise
(Ouida), 253,
310, 2398
Delboeuf, M.J., 86
Deleuran, P., 2250
DeLevie, Dagobert,
2399
Demaree, Allan T.,
1472
Dembeck, Hermann,
563
Demers, R.A., 519
Democritus, 1018
de Montmorency, J.
E.G., 2251
de Neuville, A.,408
Dennehy, Raymond,
1473
Dennis, Clarence,
1474
Dent, Anthony A.,
798, 2400
Derby, Pat, 1960

Descartes, Rene, 24,
86, 89, 103, 109,
158, 471, 526,
593, 679, 706,
1067, 1139, 1347,
1567, 2201, 2229,
2399, 2444, 2531,
2547
Desmond, Adrian J.,
564, 882
Devienne, Francois,
2502
Devine, Philip E.,
1740
DeVogel, C.J., 10
DeVore, Irven, 1878
Dewar, James, 2093
Dewey, John, 1367
Diamond, Cora, 1691
Dichter, Anita, 2252
Dickens, Charles,
2590
Diet, W.H., Jr.,
1742
Dillard, Annie, 2219
Dillon, Wilton S.,
571
Dimbleby, G.W., 1837
Dimmick, F.L., 1368
Diner, Jeff, 1475
Dingman, Robert,
3016
Dinshah, Freya, 2970,
2989, 3070
Diogenes, the Cynic,
1018
Diole, Phillippe, 843-
44, 1314, 2094
Dixon, Bernard, 1476-
79
Djerassi, Carl, 1910
Dobbs, Horace E.,
845
Dobra, Peter M., 2253

Dobyns, Harold, 1987
Domalain, Jean-Yves,
    1803
Domer, Floyd R.,
    1480
Donaghy, Kevin, 1141
Donovan, John, 2401
Dooley-Clarke,
    Dolores, 1142
Dost, F.N., 1481
Dostoevski, Fedor,
    2598
Douglas, Gordon
    476, 1867
Douglas, J.S., 1315
Douglas, J.W.B., 477
Douglas, Norman, 2402
Douglas, William O.,
    2165
Douglas-Hamilton,
    Iain, 785
Douglas-Hamilton,
    Oria, 785
Douglis, Marjorie B.,
    738
Dowding, Lord, 1482,
    1643, 2914
Dowding, Muriel the
    Lady, 1729,
    1992, 2220, 2804
Downie, H.G., 1472
Downs, James F., 1820
Doyle, Rodger, 1741
Drewett, R.F., 1840
Dreyfus, Marie, 1316
Droscher, Vitus B.,
    565-66
Drummond, W.H., 226
Drury, Samuel H., 478
Dryden, John, 45,
    2464
D'Silva, Joyce, 3152
Dubois-Desaulle,
    Gaston, 1944

Dubos, Rene, 810
Duchess of Hamilton
    and Brandon, 1703
Duffy, Maureen, 1143,
    1483, 1961, 2403
Dugmore, A. Radclyffe,
    2404
Duncan, I.J.H., 1689
Duncan, R., 1060
Dunn, P.G.C., 1658
Dunstan, G.R., 1061
Durkheim, Emile, 996
Durrell, Gerald, 567,
    2015
Dustin, Daniel L.,
    2095
Duthiers, M.D., 90
Dworkin, Ronald, 1144
Dwyer, J.T., 1742
Dyson, Robert H., Jr.,
    1821
Eagles, Julie, 1484
Ealand, C.A., 479
Edwards, M.S., 2406
Edwards, Rem B.,
    1485, 2614
Egar, Valerie L., 3016
Ehrenfeld, David W.,
    997, 2096
Eibl-Eibesfelt,
    Irenaus, 568-70
Einon, Dorothy, 977
Eiseley, Loren, 572
    2221
Eisenberg, John F.,
    571
Eisner, Thomas, 573
Ekman, Paul, 574
Elberfeld, 516
Elliot, Robert, 1145
Elliot, Rose, 3153
Elliott, Harley, 2407
Ellis, Frey R., 2927

Flexner, J.T., 1371
Flexner, S., 1371
Fliess, Jenny, 3157
Fliess, Walter,
    3157
Flinders, Carol,
    3189
Flint, L.P., 2259
Florio, P.L., 2070
Flourens, P., 89,
    158
Foley, John P., Jr.,
    884, 1372
Folsch, D.W., 1659
Foot, Philippa, 1150
Ford, Edward K.,
    1373
Ford, Lee Ellen,
    2179
Ford, M.W., 3158
Forel, Auguste, 820
Fortum-Gouin, Jean
    Paul, 2599
Forward, Charles W.,
    410
Fossey, Dian, 885-
    86
Foster, Burnside,
    1374
Foster, E.B., 796
Foster, Henry L.,
    1459, 1472, 1650,
    3000
Foster, Michael, 317
Foster, R.N., 318
Fougasse (Kenneth
    Bird), 2415
Fouts, Roger S., 882,
    887-91, 927
Fowler, C., 1759
Fowler, Corbin, 1151
Fowler, Murray E.,
    1805
Fox, Charles P.,
    1963

Fox, Frank, 2003
Fox, Freddy, 2011
Fox, George, 1052
Fox, Michael A.,
    1152-54, 1247,
    1278, 1318, 2605
Fox, Michael W.,
    579-82, 764-68,
    792, 1155-58,
    1219, 1225, 1660-
    62, 1913, 2143,
    2599, 2605-06,
    3029, 3031
Fox, Robin, 1319
Frame, George W.,
    2039
Frame, Lory Herbison,
    2039
Franchina, J.J., 2606
Francis, Leslie
    Pickering, 1159
Francis, Saint, 19,
    206, 1046, 1075,
    1081, 1087
Frank, Jonny, 2260
Frank, Oscar, 2951
Frankena, William K.,
    1160
Frankenberg, Regina
    Bauer, 3016
Franklin, Benjamin,
    405, 1728, 1764
Fraser, Andrew F.,
    1161, 1663, 2605
Fraser, D., 1689
Fraser-Harris, D.F.,
    480
Frazer, Sir James G.,
    481, 999
Freedman, William A.,
    2431
Freeman, B.M., 1664
Freeman, Dan, 892
Freeman, Edward A.,
    319-20, 438

French, Richard D.,
1489-90
Frenkel, I., 1430
Freshel, M.R.L.,
1491
Freud, Sigmund,
1000
Freund, P.A., 1492
Frey, R.G., 1162-67,
1185, 1248, 1692,
2606
Friedrich, Heinz,
583
Friend, Charles E.,
2261
Frost, Robert, 2521
Frucht, K., 1320,
2416-17
Fuller, B.A.G., 482
Fuller, Catherine R.,
2418
Furreddu, S.J.,
2925
Fussell, G.E., 2419

Gaertner, Frederick,
321
Gagliardi, Gregg, J.,
896
Galdikas, Birute,
893-94
Gallimore, W.W.,
1665
Gallup, Gordon G.,
Jr., 895-96,
1444, 1493
Galsworthy, John,
1321-23, 1375,
1643, 1705,
1868, 1964
Galton, Francis,
437
Galton, Lawrence,
1494

Gandhi, Mohandas, K.,
1001, 1745-47
Ganzfried, Solomon,
1063
Gardner, Beatrice, T.,
584, 882, 897-
900, 927
Gardner, Martin, 901
Gardner, R. Allen,
584, 882, 897-
900, 927
Garrison, W.B., 1104,
1495
Gates, Arthur M.,
1914
Gates, Georgina S.,
793
Gaulke, Judith A.,
3159
Gaunt, Stanley N.,
1666
Gay, John, 45, 2399
Gay, W.I., 1496
Geach, Peter, 1064
Geison, Gerald L.,
1497
Gelli, Giovanni
Battista, 2420
Gendin, Sidney,
2612
Gerber, G.J., 1634
Gesner, Konrad von,
29
Giehl, Dudley, 1747,
2421, 2976
Gilbert, Bil, 586
Gill, James E., 1002,
2422
Gill, Timothy, 905
Gillespie, T.H., 1965
Gilliam, W., 1488
Gilsvik, Bob, 1993
Ginzberg, Louis, 1065
Gittings, Robert, 2423

Glacken, Clarence J.,
1066, 1826,
1869
Godfrey, Bronwen,
3189
Godfrey, Peter, 1168
Godfrey-Smith,
William, 1169,
2166
Godlovitch, Roslind,
1170-72, 1271
Godlovitch, Stanley,
1172, 1271,
1324
Goldfarb, William,
1003
Goldin, Hyman E.,
1063
Goldman, Louis,
1498-1500
Goldsmid, Edmund,
2424
Goldsmith, Oliver,
1747, 2399,
2425
Gompertz, Lewis,
227-28
Gooch, G.B., 483
Goodin, L., 890
Goodman, Lenn E.,
18
Goodman, Russell,
2098
Goodpaster, Kenneth,
1173
Goodrich, T., 1174
Gordon, C.A., 322
Gordon, Douglas,
484, 740, 2099
Gordon, G.P., 2262
Gorman, Harry, 2608
Gould, Donald, 1501-
04
Gould, J.L., 821-22

Gould, Stephen J.,
587-88
Goulding, F.R., 100
Gowans, J.L., 1505
Graham, Alistair D.,
2040
Graham, Michael, 589
Graham, Sylvester,
1735, 1747
Graham-Jones, O.,
1806
Grainger, David,
2041
Grandin, Temple,
1667, 1706-07
Grant, Brewin, 323
Graven, Jacques, 585
Graves, Robert, 2426
Graves, Thornton S.,
2427-29
Graves, W., 2042
Gray, E. Conder, 324
Gray, Elizabeth
Dodson, 2144
Gray, K.H., 2818
Green, Maureen, 2430
Green, Thomas H., 229
Greene, John C., 590
Greenway, James C.,
Jr., 2043
Greenwood, George,
325, 2263
Gregory, Dick, 1729,
3160
Gregory, Michael S.,
811
Grey Owl (Wa-sha-
quon-asin), 733-
34
Griffes, Charles,
2502
Griffin, Donald R.,
591-92, 2600
Griffin, E.I., 848

Harris, Joel
Chandler, 2439-40
Harris, John, 1172,
1271, 1749-50
Harris, Michael,
2049
Harris, Stuart,
2265
Harrison, Brian,
2181, 2266
Harrison, Frank R.,
1178
Harrison, Ruth,
1132, 1669-71,
1708-09, 2267,
2597, 2605
Harrisson, Barbara,
2050
Hart, Ernest, 329
Hart, H.L.A.,
1179-80
Hart, Samuel H.,
2222
Harthan, John P.,
2441
Harthoorn, Antonie,
M., 1807
Hartshorne, Charles,
597-98, 1181,
2442
Hartwig, Hermann,
1966
Harvey, P.N., 1680
Harvey, Paul, 1761
Harvey, William,
272, 283
Harwood, Dix, 1006,
1109, 2443
Hasker, William,
1067
Hass, G., 1742
Hastings, Hester,
2444-45

Haussleiter, Johannes,
1751
Hawkins, T.S., 599
Haworth, Lawrence,
1182
Hay, John, 2100
Hayes, Catherine, 906
Hayes, Harold T.P.,
905
Hayes, Keith J., 906
Hays, H.R., 600
Hazard, Rowland G.,
104
Heather, D., 2597
Hebb, D.O., 485
Hediger, Heini,
2017-19
Hegarty, Terence,
1514-16
Heim, Alice, 601,
1517-18, 2597,
2951
Heimann, Marcel,
769
Heinegg, Peter,
2146
Heinrich, Bernd,
823-24
Helfer, Ralph D.,
1967
Hellman, George S.,
2446
Helme, Elizabeth,
2447
Hendrick, George,
2223
Henerey, M., 822
Heneson, Nancy,
1936
Henig, R.M., 1841
Henney, Peter W.,
980
Henning, Daniel H., 2168

Henry, K.R., 1519,
1808
Henson, Rev. H.,
1378
Herder, B., 1504
Herman, Louis, 2599
Hermanns, Mattias,
1827
Herrington, Alice,
2037, 2268
Hewes, Gordon, 907
Hewitt, W.I., 1872
Hibberd, Shirley,
105
Hieover, Harry, 106
Higginson, A. Henry,
1873
Highsmith, Patricia,
2448
Highton, N.B., 3165
Highton, R.B., 3165
Hildrop, John, 35
Hill, A.V., 1379
Hill, Jane H., 602,
908
Hill, Lenn, 2051
Hill, Peter Waverly,
1177
Hill, Richard W.,
2600
Hillman, H., 1520-
21, 1842
Hillyard, Susan,
3158
Hinde, Robert A.,
603-04, 742,
812
Hirsch, Samson R.,
1747
Hitler, Adolf, 1728
Hobbes, Thomas, 26
Hodge, C.F., 330
Hodge, Guy R., 2215
Hodgson, Vere, 2818

Hoff, Christina,
1522-23
Hogarth, William,
2450
Hoggan, George, 331-
32
Hollands, Clive,
1425, 1524-25,
2182-83, 2597,
2914
Holliday, Laurel,
1874
Hollis, J., 954
Holmes, Samuel J.,
1380
Holmes-Gore, Vincent
A., 1068
Holt, S.J., 2052
Holzer, Hans, 1752
Holzer, Henry M.,
2269
Hooker, Alan, 3166
Hooper, Frederick,
2004
Hooton, Earnest A.,
909
Hopkins, A.F., Jr.,
1915
Hopson, Janet, 605
Hornaday, William T.,
486, 1110
Horsley, Victor, 333
Horton, M.L., 1526
Hoskins, Betty B.,
2610
Hosley, Richard,
2451
Houghton of Sowerby,
Lord, 1527,
2184-86, 2951
Houssay, Frederic,
107
Hovhaness, Alan,
2502

581

Mushet, David, 261
Mussorgsky, Modest
    P., 2502
Musto, David F.,
    1567
Muybridge, Eadweard,
    2503-04
Myers, C.S., 1388,
    1397
Myers, Norman,
    2066

Nabors, Murray,
    2609
Naess, Arne, 1222,
    2114
Napier, C.O. Groom,
    412
Napier, Prue, 935
Narveson, Jan, 1223,
    1250, 2605-06
Nash, Roderick,
    2154, 2169
Nearing, Helen,
    1729, 1766
Nearing, Scott, 1729
    1766
Nelson, Edward A.,
    2217
Nelson, Leonard,
    1224
Nelson, R.J., 2155
Nevin, David, 1225
Newbold, William R.,
    151
Newbolt, Henry,
    2505
Newman, Francis W.,
    262, 413
Newman, Cardinal,
    1357
Newton, Isaac, 405
Newton, John F., 414
Nicholson, Edward B.,
    235

Nicholson, George, 45
Nickel, James W.,
    2235
Nicolson, Harold, 1971,
Nielsen, Kai, 1226,
    2607
Nielson, Lewis T.,
    828
Nietzsche, Friedrich,
    203, 1033
Nilsson, Greta, 1922,
    1997, 2980
Nim, 882, 901, 961-
    62
Nisbett, Alex, 2226
Niven, Charles D.,
    2201
Noble, Ruth R., 502
Nolan, Frank R.,
    1399, 2506
Nollman, James, 2599
Norelli, Martina R.,
    2507
Norman, Richard,
    1159
Northrup, F.S.C.,
    1085
Norwood, Edwin P.,
    1972
Nottebohm, Fernando,
    751
Nowell, Iris, 1923
Nozick, Robert, 1177,
    1227, 1457
Nugent, William H.,
    1973
Null, Gary, 3187
Nutting, C.C., 152
Nyman, J., 1569

O'Connor, John J.,
    1885
Odum, E., 2115

Perry, R. Hinton,
    2513
Peters, Michael, 663
Peterson, Paul,
    2217
Petitto, L.A., 957
Petricciani, John,
    2951
Petti, Anthony G.,
    2514
Pfungst, Oscar, 801,
    806-07
Philemon, 1018
Phillips, Ann, 3188
Phillips, David,
    3188
Phillips, Davis A.,
    1769
Philo Judaeus, 1018
Phineas, Charles,
    1924
Pickering, G., 1404
Pierce, Christine,
    1232
Pimlott, Douglas H.,
    776
Pine, Leslie G.,
    1888, 2874
Pister, Edwin P.,
    2068
Pitt, Frances, 504
Plato, 9, 89, 629,
    1751
Platt, Lord, 2186
Pliny, 11, 1018
Plutarch, 12, 45, 89,
    158, 405, 1002,
    1018, 1747, 1751
Poglietti, Alessandro,
    2502
Pope, Alexander, 46,
    155, 405, 2399,
    2515, 2547
Porphyry, 14-15, 405,
    1747

Porter, Eliot, 1991
Porter, George,
    1579
Porter, J.R., 2516
Portmann, Adolf,
    670
Post, Charles W.,
    1735
Poulenc, Francis,
    2502
Povilitis, Anthony
    J., 1233
Powell, E.P., 236
Power, J.W., 417
Powys, John Cowper,
    1419, 2517
Powys, Llewelyn,
    1998
Pratt, Dallas, 1580
Pratt, Mr., 2518
Premack, Ann J.,
    938-39
Premack, David, 664-
    66, 882, 927,
    939-42, 2600
Prestrude, A.M., 558
Pridgen, Tim, 1975
Primatt, Humphrey,
    47
Prince, Jack H.,
    667-68
Pringle, Allen, 155
Prokofieff, Sergei,
    2502
Proske, Roman, 1976
Puka, Bill, 1234
Pybus, Elizabeth,
    1126, 1235, 1241
Pycraft, W.P., 505
Pye, David, 684
Pythagoras, 10, 405,
    1022, 1728, 1751,
    1764, 1769, 2201,
    2510

Quarelli, Ecena, 1032
Quarles, Philip, 2493
Queen Victoria, 1357, 1474
Quiddam, Roger, 364
Quigley, Joseph S., 2621

Rabbit, Peter, 506
Rachels, James, 1236-37, 1770, 2606
Rameau, Jean-Philippe, 2502
Ramsay, Alexandra, 696
Ransome, Hilda M., 2519
Rappaport, E.A., 1945
Rappaport, J., 2348
Ratner, Stanley C., 671
Rawls, John, 1238, 1294
Rawnsley, H.M., 1562
Rawson, Jessica, 2520
Ray, P.M., 2292, 2925
Raymond, Robert, 546
Raymonde-Hawkins, M., 2204
Reed, Charles A., 1815, 1832
Reed, James, 157
Reed, R., 2521
Reed, T.J., 1033
Rees, R.J.W., 672
Reeve, E. Gavin, 1239

Regan, Tom, 1121, 1145, 1185, 1240-53, 1288, 1582, 1771-72, 1787, 2007, 2234, 2293, 2599, 2601, 2603, 2607, 2611, 3096
Regenstein, Lewis, 2069, 2268
Reid, John, 1386, 1419
Reif, Paul, 2502
Reiger, George, 863, 1889, 1925
Reiner, Anne E., 3016
Remfry, J., 1583, 2925
Rensberger, Boyce, 1034, 2117
Rensch, B., 786, 2522
Repplier, Agnes, 2523
Respighi, Ottorino, 2502
Revesz, Geza, 507, 673
Reynolds, Vernon, 943
Rheingold, Harriet L., 674
Rhine, J.B., 675-76, 802-03
Rhine, Louisa E., 802-03
Rhodes, G.M., 264
Rhodes, Richard, 1773
Ribot, Th., 159
Ricard, Matthieu, 677
Ricciuti, Edward R., 2118
Rich, Beckman, 2294

Richards, M. Edith, 2224
Riches, Anne, 2344
Richet, Charles, 366, 1405
Richmond, Rev. Legh, 215
Richmond, Sonya, 3202
Rickaby, Father Joseph, 216
Riddle, Maxwell, 774
Rienow, Leona T., 2205
Rikleen, Lauren S., 2295
Rimsky-Korsakov, Nikolai, 2502
Riopelle, A.J., 678
Risdon, Wilfred, 1584, 2227
Ritchie, A.M., 679
Ritchie, Carson I.A., 829
Ritchie, D.G., 238-40
Ritson, Joseph, 419-20
Roberts, Alan, 3194
Roberts, Catherine, 680, 1585-86
Roberts, Peter, 1683
Roberts, William A., 646
Robertson, A.M., 1687
Robertson, John A., 2296
Robertson, Laurel, 3189
Robertson, Robert B., 864

Robeson, Dave, 2119
Robin, P. Ansell, 2524
Robinson, Emily, 2525
Robinson, Phil, 2526-27
Robinson, W.W., 1488
Robson, Frank, 865
Rock, M.A., 944
Roden, Claudia, 3190
Rodham, C., 984
Rodman, John, 1035, 1255, 2120, 2297
Rogers, C.M., 881
Rohlfing, A.H., 1890
Rollin, Bernard E., 1256-58, 1587-88, 2606, 2608-09
Rolph, C.H., 1338
Rolston, Holmes, 2158-59
Romanes, George J., 58-59, 74, 118, 121, 148, 153-54, 160-66, 174, 488
Romans, John R., 1695
Rombauts, E., 2528
Rood, Ronald, 1036
Rook, David, 2529
Roos, G., 2121
Roosevelt, Theodore, 461
Roots, Clive, 681, 2122
Rose, William, 2530
Rosenfield, Leonora, 2531
Rosin, Paula, 2298

Scott, W.N., 1717, 2292, 2925
Scott, William, 3172
Scott-Ordish, Lesley, 2597
Scullard, H.H., 1039
Searle, George M., 371
Sebeok, Thomas A., 687-96, 778, 901, 955-56, 2538-39
Sebond, Raymond, 22
Secord, D., 1852
Seidenberg, M.S., 957
Seidler, Michael J., 697
Seligman, Martin E. P., 1617-18
Selk, Eugene E., 2161
Sells, A. Lytton, 2540
Selye, H., 698
Seneca, 1002, 1018, 1747
Serban, George, 1619
Serjeant, Richard 1344
Sessions, George, 2124
Seton, Ernest T., 2541
Sever, Efrat, 1853
Sewell, Anna, 2542
Shaffer, Peter, 2543
Shaftesbury, The Earl of, 372, 1006, 1357, 1490, 1644, 2188, 2547

Shakespeare, William, 1567, 2400, 2411, 2451, 2544, 2565, 2593
Shaler, N.S., 444
Shane, Douglas R., 3031
Shapiro, Ken, 2601
Sharp, John A., 1620
Sharp, W.V., 1510
Shaw, George Bernard, 1407-11, 1419, 1567, 1728, 1731, 1734, 1747, 1782-83, 1896, 2545, 3174
Shaw, Terry G., 991
Shea, Kevin, 2303
Shedd, Graham, 1457
Sheldon, Charles M., 1784
Shelley, Percy B., 405-06, 423-24, 434, 1341, 1726, 1728, 1737, 1747, 1764
Shepard, Paul, 699, 1268, 2125-26
Shephard, Odell, 2546
Sheppard, Vera, 1897
Sherley-Price, Leo, 19, 1087
Shields, Allan, 2170
Short, Douglas J., 1621
Shoshan, A., 1088
Shrubsole, O.A., 425
Shugg, Wallace, 2547
Shulman, Martha R., 3195
Shultz, William J., 2208
Shurtleff, William, 3196-3201

Spira, Henry, 1282, 3026
Spragg, S.D.S., 986, 1413
Sprague, Lynn T., 512
Sprigge, T.L.S., 1283, 2209, 2597
Squadrito, Kathleen, 706, 1090, 1284
Stade, George, 707
Stallybrass, W.H.S., 2371
Stancil, Deborah, 2012
Stanfield, James L., 976
Stearns, J. Brenton, 2127
Stebbins, Eunice B., 2556
Steele, Zulma, 2210
Steinbeck, John, 2431
Steinbock, Bonnie, 1285
Steinhart, P., 2305
Stenuit, Robert, 872
Stephens, Wilson, 1875
Sternbach, Richard A., 1630
Stevens, Christine, 2306
Stevens, V.J., 643
Stevenson, Lloyd G., 1631-32
Stewart, Desmond, 2557
Stewart, Jean, 2688
Stich, Stephen P., 708

Stillman, W.J., 440
Stillman, William O., 2175, 2211
Stoddart, D.M., 2128
Stone, Christopher D., 1255, 2307-08
Stonehouse, B., 1633
Storm, Donald F., 2264
Storr, Anthony, 2129
Stoutenberg, Adrien (Lace Kendall), 1979
Strachey, John, 1718
Stratmann, C.J., 1598
Stravinsky, Igor, 2502
Street, Philip, 709
Stretch, R., 1634
Stromberg, David B., 2309-10
Strunk, W., Jr., 2558
Stuart, Dorothy M., 2559
Styles, J.A., 1941
Styles, John, 225, 237
Suarez, S.D., 1444, 1493
Sully, James, 174, 2560
Sumner, L.W., 1286-88
Susking, R., 1742
Sussman, Vic, 1788
Sutch, Diane, 811
Sutton, W.A., 175
Swaim, Kathleen M., 2561
Swallow, William A., 2212
Swan, Christopher, 1688

Swedenborg, 157,
1045
Swift, Jonathan,
48, 2562
Syme, G.J., 710
Syme, L.A., 710
Szasz, Kathleen,
1929
Szogyi, Alex, 2951
Szoke, Peter, 2563

Tait, Lawson, 282,
376, 1584, 2227
Talbot, L.M., 2052
Tamir, Pinchas, 1853
Taylor, Basil, 2564
Taylor, Edward B.,
1091
Taylor, G.B., 2311
Taylor, George C.,
2565
Taylor, Joseph, 2566
Taylor, Thomas, 49
Teas, Jane, 958
Temerlin, Maurice
K., 959
Tennyson, 1357, 1747
Terrace, Herbert S.,
882, 901, 960-62
Tertullian, 1744,
1747
Teutsch, Gotthard M.,
2312
Thomas, Anna, 3203-04
Thomas Aquinas, Saint,
20-21, 2201
Thomas, Ruth Edith,
1092
Thomas, William L.,
Jr., 2130
Thompson, Francis,
2567
Thompson, Henry,
415, 428-29

Thompson, Ralph, 377
Thomson, James, 1006,
1747, 2399
Thomson, Sir John A.,
513
Thoreau, Henry David,
204, 1747
Thorndike, Edward,
138, 144, 152,
177-79, 488
Thornhill, Mark, 378
Thornton, Allan, 1999
Thorpe, William H.,
711-15, 756, 817,
1132
Thurman, Jimmie J.,
3205
Thurston, Robert H.,
180
Tiger, Lionel, 1319
Tinbergen, Nicholaas,
716-20
Tinker, J., 2072
Tiptree, James, Jr.,
(Alice B. Sheldon),
2568
Tirbutt, Susan, 1942
Tischler, Joyce S.,
2313
Tolman, Edward C.,
514, 984
Tolstoy, Leo, 430,
1728, 1747, 1764,
2569
Tomilin, Michael I.,
974
Tomson, Graham R.,
2570
Tooley, Michael, 1289
Topsell, Edward, 29-
30
Torrey, L., 552
Towne, Charles W.,
1835

Wemmer, Chris, 2025
Wenner, Adrian M.,
    836
Wentworth, Edward
    N., 1835
Wenz, Peter S., 1299,
    2603
Wertheimer, Roger,
    2603
West, Kenyon, 434
Westacott, Evalyn
    A., 1418-19,
    1981
Westbrook, William
    H., 1902
Westermarck, Edvard
    A., 1041, 1097
Weyler, Rex, 2006
Whaler, James, 2586
Whately, Richard,
    111
Wheaton, Margaret,
    3097
Whipple, George H.,
    1420
White, Andrew D.,
    1098, 2587
White, Anna, 435
White, Beatrice,
    2588
White, Beverly,
    3208
White, Caroline E.,
    393
White, Elinor, 1350
White, Ellen B.,
    1728, 1735,
    1747
White, Henry, 2319
White, Lynn, 2131-
    33
White, Robert, 1486,
    1586

White, Terence H.,
    2589
Whitehead, Alfred
    North, 1122,
    2086, 2139
Whiteman, A., 1368
Whitfield, Philip,
    726
Whitlow, R., 2590
Whitney, Leon F.,
    780
Whitney, Robert A.,
    Jr., 1648
Whittaker, Alan,
    1649
Whittingham, R.A.,
    1812
Whitty, C.W.M., 477
Wickler, Wolfgang,
    727-28
Wigmore, Ann, 3209
Wilberforce, Basil,
    394
Wilberforce, Canon,
    329
Wilbur, Richard,
    2591
Wilde, J.R., 403
Wilder, Burt G.,
    395
Wilhoite, Fred H.,
    Jr., 964
Wilkinson, Clennell,
    1796
Wilkinson, Paul F.,
    1838
Wilks, Louis P.,
    1943
Wilks, Samuel, 298,
    396-97
Williams, Howard,
    430, 436
Williams, Jay, 2078

Williams, Meredith,
    1300
Willis, Roy G.,
    1042
Wilson, Derek, 2079
Wilson, Earl, 1950
Wilson, Edward O.,
    573, 729, 819,
    837
Wilson, Frank, 1797-
    98, 3210
Wilson, J. Stitt,
    518
Windeatt, Phil,
    1650, 1900
Winograd, Eugene,
    730
Winsten, Stephen,
    2230
Winter, Paul, 2502
Wiseman, Frederick,
    1457, 2698,
    2704
Wissler, Clark,
    1105
Withington, E.T.,
    2320
Wittgenstein, 731
Witzig, T.J., 1654
Wolf, Hugo, 1747
Wolfe, John B., 986
Wolfe, Thomas L.,
    2607
Wolfe, Tom, 2601
Wong, Yuk, 1099
Wood, David, 1351
Wood, Dorothy, 2080
Wood, Emma, 2051
Wood, G.H., 781
Wood, H.C., 398
Wood, John G.,
    188, 219
Woodcock, N., 1901

Wood-Gush, D.G.M.,
    1689
Woodnott, Dorothy P.,
    1621
Woodruff, Guy, 666
Woolman, John, 1052
Worden, Alastair,
    1456
Wordsworth, 1006,
    2540
Wray, J.D., 1843
Wright, Louis B.,
    2592
Wrighton, Basil,
    2818
Wundt, Wilhelm, 189
Wye, Charles, 1301
Wylder, Joseph, 1930
Wynne, Alan, 2597
Wynne-Edwards, V.C.,
    2134
Wynne-Tyson, Jon,
    1352, 1799-1800

Yamato, Yuzo, 2599
Ydstie, John, 1210,
    1302
Yeats-Brown, F.,
    1982-83
Yeo, Gerald F., 399,
    400
Yerkes, Ada W., 972
Yerkes, Robert M.,
    965-74, 987, 1421-
    22
Yoder, Audrey, 2593
Youatt, William, 193
Young, E.M., 1813
Young, Egerton R.,
    190
Young, R.V., 2164
Young, Robert, 1303
Young, Thomas, 270